THE LION BOOK OF

# Bible
# Quotations

Compiled by Martin H. Manser

A LION PAPERBACK
Oxford · Batavia · Sydney

Copyright © 1982 Lion Publishing

Published by
**Lion Publishing plc**
Sandy Lane West, Oxford, England
ISBN 0 7459 2208 2
**Lion Publishing Corporation**
1705 Hubbard Avenue, Batavia, Illinois 60510, USA
ISBN 0 7459 2208 2
**Albatross Books Pty Ltd**
PO Box 320, Sutherland, NSW 2232, Australia
ISBN 0 7324 0574 2

First published as Lion Concise Book of Bible Quotations,
1982
Reprinted 1983
Second edition 1986
This edition 1992
Reprinted 1992

A catalogue record for this book is available
from the British Library

Printed and bound in Great Britain
by Cox & Wyman Ltd, Reading

**Acknowledgments**

Copyright of quotations, used by kind permission
of the publishers, as follows:

Authorized King James Version of the Bible and the
Prayer Book of 1662, Crown Copyright

Revised Standard Version, copyright 1946 and 1952,
second edition 1971, Division of Christian Educa-
tion, National Council of the Churches of Christ in
the USA

Good News Bible, copyright 1966, 1971 and 1976
American Bible Society, published by the Bible
Societies/Collins

Holy Bible, New International Version,
copyright 1973, 1978, 1984 International Bible
Society

The New English Bible, second edition, copyright
1970 Oxford and Cambridge University Presses

The Jerusalem Bible, copyright 1966, 1967 and 1968
Darton, Longman & Todd Ltd and Doubleday &
Company Inc

The New Testament in Modern English, copyright 1960
J.B.Phillips

The Living Bible, copyright 1971 Tyndale House
Publishers

# CONTENTS

Books of the Bible                                    6

**Part One (by theme)**                               **7**

**Part Two (book by book)**                         **159**

Old Testament                                       160

New Testament                                       196


Appendix (special features)                         233

Five portraits of the church                        233
Christian fellowship: secrets of success            233
Names, titles and descriptions of God               233
Parables of Jesus                                   234
Miracles of Jesus                                   235
Titles and portraits of Jesus                       236
Prayers of the Bible                                237

# HOW TO USE THIS BOOK

## Part One

Verses appear **under nearly 300 themes arranged in alphabetical order.** This part is useful if you want to know what the Bible says about a particular subject. It is also helpful for finding a specific quotation: look up the main idea of the verse to discover its reference. Under each entry, the references are arranged in Bible order, so the verses can be looked up—and the content checked—in the Bible itself. A number of detailed entries may be found especially useful: 'God', 'Jesus Christ', 'Holy Spirit'; also subjects such as 'Faith', 'Comfort', 'Prayer', to find help on living the Christian life or meeting a particular need.

## Part Two

Passages from the Bible are listed **in the order of the books in the Bible itself.** They include both well-known verses and some of those that are most significant for an understanding of each book. If you know roughly where in the Bible a quotation comes from, this part can be used for checking it.

## Abbreviations used for Bible versions

BCP
The Book of Common Prayer

GNB
Good News Bible

JBP
J. B. Phillips, New Testament in Modern English

JB
The Jerusalem Bible

KJV
King James Version
(Authorized)

LB
The Living Bible

NEB
The New English Bible

NIV
Holy Bible, New International Version

RSV
Revised Standard Version

# INTRODUCTION

Quotations from the Bible are among the best-known of all quotations in the English language. This book has been compiled both for reference and for those who like to browse. In Part One, the quotations are listed according to themes; in Part Two in the order in which they appear in the Bible itself.

The quotations have been taken from a number of different translations. Often they are most familiar in the words of the **Authorized** or **King James Version** and so this has been quoted. The words of the **Revised Standard Version** and the more recent **New International Version** echo the older language but are more easily understood today. Others, such as the 'common-language' **Good News Bible** or more formal **New English Bible**, have been quoted where appropriate or where the fresh renderings have been recently taken up and become well-known.

The aim throughout has been to try to be as faithful as possible to the Bible itself. 'All Scripture is God-breathed and is useful for teaching, rebuking, correcting and training in righteousness,' wrote the apostle Paul to Timothy, 'so that the man of God may be thoroughly equipped for every good work.' So it is hoped that the book will help the reader enjoy something of the riches of the Bible, and that the quotations will lead to the discovery of passages which may not have been noticed before.

In addition it is hoped that the first part will serve as a valuable reference tool and source of help, for following up studies of words and themes and simply discovering where to find passages to meet a particular need.

This book has been compiled with the desire that it may lead to a greater reading of the Bible, and response to its message.

Martin H. Manser

# BOOKS OF THE BIBLE

## Old Testament

| | | |
|---|---|---|
| Genesis | 2 Chronicles | Daniel |
| Exodus | Ezra | Hosea |
| Leviticus | Nehemiah | Joel |
| Numbers | Esther | Amos |
| Deuteronomy | Job | Obadiah |
| Joshua | Psalms | Jonah |
| Judges | Proverbs | Micah |
| Ruth | Ecclesiastes | Nahum |
| 1 Samuel | Song of Solomon | Habakkuk |
| 2 Samuel | Isaiah | Zephaniah |
| 1 Kings | Jeremiah | Haggai |
| 2 Kings | Lamentations | Zechariah |
| 1 Chronicles | Ezekiel | Malachi |

## New Testament

| | | |
|---|---|---|
| Matthew | Ephesians | Hebrews |
| Mark | Philippians | James |
| Luke | Colossians | 1 Peter |
| John | 1 Thessalonians | 2 Peter |
| Acts | 2 Thessalonians | 1 John |
| Romans | 1 Timothy | 2 John |
| 1 Corinthians | 2 Timothy | 3 John |
| 2 Corinthians | Titus | Jude |
| Galatians | Philemon | Revelation |

# Part 1

## BY THEME

## Accepting the will of God

Moses said, 'No, Lord, don't send me. I have never been a good speaker, and I haven't become one since you began to speak to me. I am a poor speaker, slow and hesitant.' The Lord said to him, 'Who gives man his mouth? Who makes him deaf or dumb? Who gives him sight or makes him blind? It is I, the Lord. Now, go! I will help you to speak, and I will tell you what to say.'
EXODUS 4:10–12 GNB

Though he slay me, yet will I trust in him: but I will maintain mine own ways before him.
JOB 13:15 KJV

It is good for me that I was afflicted, that I might learn thy statutes.
PSALM 119:71 RSV

My son, do not despise the Lord's discipline or be weary of his reproof, for the Lord reproves him whom he loves, as a father the son in whom he delights.
PROVERBS 3:11–12 RSV

Thy kingdom come. Thy will be done, in earth as it is in heaven.
MATTHEW 6:10 BCP

And going a little farther he fell on his face and prayed, 'My Father, if it be possible, let this cup pass from me; nevertheless, not as I will, but as thou wilt.'
MATTHEW 26:39 RSV

But one of you will say to me, 'If this is so, how can God find fault with anyone? Who can resist God's will?' But who are you, my friend, to answer God back? A clay pot does not ask the man who made it, 'Why did you make me like this?' After all, the man who makes the pots has the right to use the clay as he wishes, and to make two pots from the same lump of clay, one for special occasions and the other for ordinary use.
ROMANS 9:19–21 GNB

He said to me, 'My grace is sufficient for you, for my power is made perfect in weakness.' I will all the more gladly boast of my weaknesses, that the power of Christ may rest upon me.
2 CORINTHIANS 12:9 RSV

Beloved, do not be surprised at the fiery ordeal which comes upon you to prove you, as though something strange were happening to you. But rejoice in so far as you share Christ's sufferings, that you may also rejoice and be glad when his glory is revealed.
1 PETER 4:12–13 RSV

See also *Comfort; Contentment; Submission.*

## Access

Who shall ascend the hill of the Lord? And who shall stand in his holy place? He who has clean hands and a pure heart, who does not lift up his soul to what is false, and does not swear deceitfully.
PSALM 24:3–4 RSV

Jesus saith unto him, I am the way, the truth, and the life: no man cometh unto the Father, but by me.
JOHN 14:6 KJV

'Father, I desire that they also, whom thou hast given me, may be with me where I am, to behold my glory which thou hast given me in thy love for me before the foundation of the world.'
JOHN 17:24 RSV

By whom [Jesus Christ] also we have access by faith into this grace wherein we stand, and rejoice in hope of the glory of God.
ROMANS 5:2 KJV

But now in Christ Jesus you who once were far off have been brought near in the blood of Christ . . . for through him we both have access in one Spirit to the Father.
EPHESIANS 2:13, 18 RSV

In union with Christ and through our faith in him we have the boldness to go into God's presence with all confidence.
EPHESIANS 3:12 GNB

Therefore, brethren, since we have confidence to enter the sanctuary by the blood of Jesus, by the new and living way which he opened for us through the curtain, that is, through his flesh, and since we have a great priest over the house of God, let us draw near with a true heart in full assurance of faith, with our hearts sprinkled clean from an evil conscience and our bodies washed with pure water.
HEBREWS 10:19–22 RSV

Draw near to God and he will draw near to you.
JAMES 4:8 RSV

For Christ also died for sins once for all, the righteous for the unrighteous, that he might bring us to God, being put to death in the flesh but made alive in the spirit.
1 PETER 3:18 RSV

See also *Adoption; Assurance; Prayer.*

## Adam

So God created man in his own image, in the image of God created he him; male and female created he them.
GENESIS 1:27 KJV

And the Lord God formed man of the dust of the ground, and breathed into his nostrils the breath of life; and man became a living soul ... and the Lord God said, It is not good that the man should be alone; I will make him an help meet for him.
GENESIS 2:7, 18 KJV

As by one man sin entered into the world, and death by sin ... so death passed upon all men, for that all have sinned.
ROMANS 5:12 KJV

Then as one man's trespass led to condemnation for all men, so one man's act of righteousness leads to acquittal and life for all men. For as by one man's disobedience many were made sinners, so by one man's obedience many will be made righteous. Law came in, to increase the trespass; but where sin increased, grace abounded all the more, so that, as sin reigned in death, grace also might reign through righteousness to eternal life through Jesus Christ our Lord.
ROMANS 5:18-19 RSV

For as in Adam all die, so also in Christ shall all be made alive.
1 CORINTHIANS 15:22 RSV

Thus it is written, 'The first man Adam became a living being'; the last Adam became a life-giving spirit.
1 CORINTHIANS 15:45 RSV

See also *Eden, garden of; Fall, the; Man.*

## Adoption

'But now I tell you: love your enemies and pray for those who persecute you, so that you may become the sons of your Father in heaven.'
MATTHEW 5:44-45 GNB

Our Father, which art in heaven ...
MATTHEW 6:9 BCP

Therefore take no thought, saying, What shall we eat? or, What shall we drink? or Wherewithal shall we be clothed? (For after all these things do the Gentiles seek:) for your heavenly Father knoweth that ye have need of all these things. But seek ye first the kingdom of God, and his righteousness; and all these things shall be added unto you.
MATTHEW 6:31-33 KJV

But as many as received him, to them gave he power to become the sons of God, even to them that believe on his name.
JOHN 1:12 KJV

For all who are led by the Spirit of God are sons of God. For you did not receive the spirit of slavery to fall back into fear, but you have received the spirit of sonship. When we cry, 'Abba! Father!' it is the Spirit himself bearing witness with our spirit that we are children of God, and if children, then heirs, heirs of God and fellow heirs with Christ, provided we suffer with him in order that we may also be glorified with him.
ROMANS 8:14-17 RSV

'I will be your father, and you shall be my sons and daughters, says the Lord Almighty.'
2 CORINTHIANS 6:18 GNB

[God sent his Son] to redeem those who were under the law, so that we might receive adoption as sons. And because you are sons, God has sent the Spirit of his Son into our hearts, crying, 'Abba! Father!'
GALATIANS 4:5-6 RSV

He destined us in love to be his sons through Jesus Christ, according to the purpose of his will.
EPHESIANS 1:5 RSV

See what love the Father has given us, that we should be called children of God; and so we are. The reason why the world does not know us is that it did not know him. Beloved, we are God's children now; it does not yet appear what we shall be, but we know that when he appears we shall be like him, for we shall see him as he is.
1 JOHN 3:1-2 RSV

See also *Access; Assurance; Confidence.*

## Adultery
See *Marriage.*

# Advice

See *Counsel.*

# Angels

For he will give his angels charge of you to guard you in all your ways.

PSALM 91:11 RSV

Nebuchadnezzar said, 'Blessed be the God of Shadrach, Meshach and Abednego, who has sent his angel and delivered his servants, who trusted in him, and set at naught the king's command, and yielded up their bodies rather than serve and worship any god except their own God.'

DANIEL 3:28 RSV

'At that time shall arise Michael, the great prince who has charge of your people. And there shall be a time of trouble, such as never has been since there was a nation till that time; but at that time your people shall be delivered, every one whose name shall be found written in the book.'

DANIEL 12:1 RSV

'See that you don't despise any of these little ones. Their angels in heaven, I tell you, are always in the presence of my Father in heaven.

MATTHEW 18:10 GNB

When the Son of man shall come in his glory, and all the holy angels with him, then shall he sit upon the throne of his glory.

MATTHEW 25:31 KJV

In the sixth month the angel Gabriel was sent from God to a city of Galilee named Nazareth.

LUKE 1:26 RSV

'Just so, I tell you, there is joy before the angels of God over one sinner who repents.'

LUKE 15:10 RSV

'You who received the law as delivered by angels and did not keep it.'

ACTS 7:53 RSV

Do you not know that we are to judge angels? How much more, matters pertaining to this life!

1 CORINTHIANS 6:3 RSV

To make all men see ... that through the church the manifold wisdom of God might now be made known to the principalities and powers in the heavenly places.

EPHESIANS 3:9–10 RSV

What are the angels, then? They are spirits who serve God and are sent by him to help those who are to receive salvation.

HEBREWS 1:14 GNB

Then I looked, and I heard around the throne and the living creatures and the elders the voice of many angels, numbering myriads of myriads and thousands of thousands, saying with a loud voice, 'Worthy is the Lamb who was slain, to receive power and wealth and wisdom and might and honour and glory and blessing!'

REVELATION 5:11–12 RSV

# Anger

## OF GOD

The Lord is merciful and gracious, slow to anger, and plenteous in mercy. He will not always chide: neither will he keep his anger for ever.

PSALM 103:8–9 KJV

They have rejected the law of the Lord of hosts, and have despised the word of the Holy One of Israel. Therefore the anger of the Lord was kindled against his people, and he stretched out his hand against them and smote them, and the mountains quaked; and their corpses were as refuse in the midst of the streets. For all this his anger is not turned away and his hand is stretched out still.

ISAIAH 5:24–25 RSV

O Lord, revive thy work in the midst of the years, in the midst of the years make known; in wrath remember mercy.

HABAKKUK 3:2 KJV

But when he [John the Baptist] saw many of the Pharisees and Sadducees coming for baptism, he said to them, 'You brood of vipers! Who warned you to flee from the wrath to come?'

MATTHEW 3:7 RSV

And he looked around at them with anger, grieved at their hardness of heart.

MARK 3:5 RSV

He that believeth on the Son hath everlasting life: and he that believeth not the Son shall not see life; but the wrath of God abideth on him.

JOHN 3:36 KJV

For the wrath of God is revealed from heaven against all ungodliness and unrighteousness of men, who hold the truth in unrighteousness.

ROMANS 1:18 KJV

Among these we all once lived in the passions of our flesh, following the desires of body and mind, and so we were by nature children of wrath, like the rest of mankind.

EPHESIANS 2:3 RSV

Jesus, who delivers us from the wrath to come.

1 THESSALONIANS 1:10 RSV

[They] said to the mountains and rocks, Fall on us, and hide us from the face of him that sitteth on the throne, and from the wrath of the Lamb. For the great day of his wrath is come; and who shall be able to stand?

REVELATION 6:16 KJV

See also *Propitiation; Punishment.*

## OF MAN

If you stay calm, you are wise, but if you have a hot temper, you only show how stupid you are.

PROVERBS 14:29 GNB

Hot tempers cause arguments, but patience brings peace.

PROVERBS 15:18 GNB

He who is slow to anger is better than the mighty, and he who rules his spirit than he who takes a city.

PROVERBS 16:32 RSV

'You have heard that people were told in the past, "Do not commit murder; anyone who does will be brought to trial." But now I tell you: whoever is angry with his brother will be brought to trial.'

MATTHEW 5:21–22 GNB

[Love] is not touchy.

1 CORINTHIANS 13:5 JBP

Now the works of the flesh are plain: . . . anger . . .

GALATIANS 5:19–20 RSV

Be angry but do not sin; do not let the sun go down on your anger, and give no opportunity to the devil . . . Let all bitterness and wrath and anger and clamour and slander be put away from you, with all malice.

EPHESIANS 4:26–27, 31 RSV

Know this, my beloved brethren. Let every man be quick to hear, slow to speak, slow to anger, for the anger of man does not work the righteousness of God.

JAMES 1:19–20 RSV

# Antichrist

'While I was thinking about the horns, there before me was another horn, a little one, which came up among them; and three of the first horns were uprooted before it. This horn had eyes like the eyes of a man and a mouth that spoke boastfully.'

DANIEL 7:8 NIV

'He shall speak words against the Most High, and shall wear out the saints of the Most High, and shall think to change the times and the law; and they shall be given into his hand for a time, two times, and half a time.'

DANIEL 7:25 RSV

'For many will come in my name, saying, "I am the Christ," and they will lead many astray . . . For false Christs and false prophets will arise and show great signs and wonders, so as to lead astray, if possible, even the elect.'

MATTHEW 24:5, 24 RSV

Let no one deceive you in any way; for that day [the day of the Lord] will not come, unless the rebellion comes first, and the man of lawlessness is revealed, the son of perdition, who opposes and exalts himself against every so-called god or object of worship, so that he takes his seat in the temple of God, proclaiming himself to be God.

2 THESSALONIANS 2:3–4 RSV

And now you know what is holding him back, so that he may be revealed at the proper time. For the secret power of lawlessness is already at work; but the one who now holds it back will continue to do so till he is taken out of the way. And then the lawless one will be revealed, whom the Lord Jesus will overthrow with the breath of his mouth and destroy by the splendour of his coming. The coming of the lawless one will be in accordance with the work of Satan displayed in all kinds of counterfeit miracles, signs and wonders, and in every sort of evil that deceives those who are perishing. They perish because they refused to love the truth and so be saved.

2 THESSALONIANS 2:6–10 NIV

My children, this is the last hour! You were told that Antichrist was to come, and now many antichrists have appeared; which proves to us that this is indeed the last hour.

1 JOHN 2:18 NEB

Who is the liar? Who but he that denies that Jesus is the Christ? He is Antichrist, for he denies both the Father and the Son.

**1 JOHN 2:22 NEB**

Every spirit which does not confess Jesus is not of God. This is the spirit of antichrist, of which you heard that it was coming, and now it is in the world already.

**1 JOHN 4:3 RSV**

## Apostles

And he called to him his twelve disciples and gave them authority over unclean spirits, to cast them out, and to heal every disease and every infirmity. The names of the twelve apostles are these: first, Simon, who is called Peter, and Andrew his brother; James the son of Zebedee, and John his brother; Philip and Bartholomew; Thomas and Matthew the tax collector; James the son of Alphaeus, and Thaddaeus; Simon the Cananaean, and Judas Iscariot, who betrayed him.

**MATTHEW 10:1–4 RSV**

'So one of the men who have accompanied us during all the time that the Lord Jesus went in and out among us, beginning from the baptism of John until the day when he was taken up from us—one of these men must become with us a witness to his resurrection.'

**ACTS 1:21–22 RSV**

But when the apostles Barnabas and Paul heard of it, they tore their garments and rushed out among the multitude . . .

**ACTS 14:14 RSV**

Am I not free? Am I not an apostle? Have I not seen Jesus our Lord? Are not you my workmanship in the Lord? If to others I am not an apostle, at least I am to you; for you are the seal of my apostleship in the Lord.

**1 CORINTHIANS 9:1–2 RSV**

Now you are the body of Christ and individually members of it. And God has appointed in the church first apostles . . .

**1 CORINTHIANS 12:28 RSV**

So then you are no longer strangers and sojourners, but you are fellow citizens with the saints and members of the household of God, built upon the foundation of the apostles and prophets, Christ Jesus himself being the cornerstone.

**EPHESIANS 2:19–20 RSV**

Therefore, holy brethren, who share in a heavenly call, consider Jesus, the apostle and high priest of our confession.

**HEBREWS 3:1 RSV**

[To the church in Ephesus]' ''I know your works, your toil and your patient endurance, and how you cannot bear evil men but have tested those who call themselves apostles but are not, and found them to be false.'' '

**REVELATION 2:2 RSV**

## Ascension

See *Jesus Christ, Ascension.*

## Assurance

All that the Father giveth me shall come to me; and him that cometh to me I will in no wise cast out.

**JOHN 6:37 KJV**

And I give unto them [my sheep] eternal life; and they shall never perish, neither shall any man pluck them out of my hand.

**JOHN 10:28 KJV**

Therefore being justified by faith, we have peace with God through our Lord Jesus Christ: by whom also we have access by faith into this grace wherein we stand, and rejoice in hope of the glory of God. And not only so, but we glory in tribulations also: knowing that tribulation worketh patience; and patience, experience; and experience, hope: and hope maketh not ashamed; because the love of God is shed abroad in our hearts by the Holy Ghost which is given unto us.

**ROMANS 5:1–5 KJV**

Since, therefore, we are now justified by his blood, much more shall we be saved by him from the wrath of God. For if while we were enemies we were reconciled to God by the death of his Son, much more, now that we are reconciled, shall we be saved by his life.

**ROMANS 5:9–10 RSV**

There is therefore now no condemnation for those who are in Christ Jesus.

**ROMANS 8:1 RSV**

What then shall we say to this? If God is for us, who is against us? He who did not spare his own Son but gave him up for us all, will he not also give us all things with him? Who shall bring any charge against God's elect? It is God who justifies; who is to condemn? Is it Christ Jesus, who died, yes, who was raised from the dead, who is at the right hand of God, who indeed intercedes for us? Who shall separate us from the love of Christ? Shall tribulation, or distress, or persecution, or famine, or nakedness, or peril, or sword? . . . No, in all these things we are more than conquerors through him who loved us. For I am sure that neither death, nor life, nor angels, nor principalities, nor things present, nor things to come, nor powers, nor height, nor depth, nor anything else in all creation, will be able to separate us from the love of God in Christ Jesus our Lord.

**ROMANS 8:31–35, 37–39 RSV**

And so I am sure that God, who began this good work in you, will carry it on until it is finished on the Day of Christ Jesus.

**PHILIPPIANS 1:6 GNB**

But I am not ashamed, for I know whom I have believed, and I am sure that he is able to guard until that Day what has been entrusted to me.

**2 TIMOTHY 1:12 RSV**

Let us draw near with a true heart in full assurance of faith, with our hearts sprinkled clean from an evil conscience and our bodies washed with pure water.

**HEBREWS 10:22 RSV**

If we walk in the light, as he is in the light, we have fellowship with one another, and the blood of Jesus his Son cleanses us from all sin . . . If we confess our sins, he is faithful and just and will forgive our sins and cleanse us from all unrighteousness.

**1 JOHN 1:7, 9 RSV**

By this we know that we abide in him and he in us, because he has given us of his own Spirit.

**1 JOHN 4:13 RSV**

He that hath the Son hath life; and he that hath not the Son of God hath not life.

**1 JOHN 5:12 KJV**

See also *Adoption; Comfort; Victory.*

## Atonement

And he shall put his hand upon the head of the burnt offering; and it shall be accepted for him to make atonement for him.

**LEVITICUS 1:4 KJV**

Surely he hath borne our griefs, and carried our sorrows: yet we did esteem him stricken, smitten of God, and afflicted. But he was wounded for our transgressions, he was bruised for our iniquities: the chastisement of our peace was upon him; and with his stripes we are healed. All we like sheep have gone astray; we have turned every one to his own way; and the Lord hath laid on him the iniquity of us all . . . Yet it pleased the Lord to bruise him; he hath put him to grief: when thou shalt make his soul an offering for sin, he shall see his seed, he shall prolong his days, and the pleasure of the Lord shall prosper in his hand. He shall see of the travail of his soul, and shall be satisfied: by his knowledge shall my righteous servant justify many; for he shall bear their iniquities. Therefore will I divide him a portion with the great, and he shall divide the spoil with the strong; because he hath poured out his soul unto death; and he was numbered with the transgressors; and he bare the sin of many, and made intercession for the transgressors.

**ISAIAH 53:4–6, 10–12 KJV**

'For the Son of man also came not to be served but to serve, and to give his life as a ransom for many.'

**MARK 10:45 RSV**

But God shows his love for us in that while we were yet sinners Christ died for us.

**ROMANS 5:8 RSV**

For the love of Christ constraineth us; because we thus judge, that if one died for all, then were all dead.

**2 CORINTHIANS 5:14 KJV**

For our sake he made him to be sin who knew no sin, so that in him we might become the righteousness of God.

**2 CORINTHIANS 5:21 RSV**

And walk in love, as Christ loved us and gave himself up for us, a fragrant offering and sacrifice to God.

**EPHESIANS 5:2 RSV**

The Son is the radiance of God's glory and the exact representation of his being, sustaining all things by his powerful word. After he had provided purification for sins, he sat down at the right hand of the Majesty in heaven.

**HEBREWS 1:3 NIV**

He himself bore our sins in his body on the tree, that we might die to sin and live to righteousness. By his wounds you have been healed.

**1 PETER 2:24 RSV**

For Christ also died for sins once for all, the righteous for the unrighteous, that he might bring us to God, being put to death in the flesh but made alive in the spirit.

**1 PETER 3:18 RSV**

See also *Blood; Jesus Christ, Death; Redemption.*

# Authority

'For the lips of a priest should guard knowledge, and men should seek instruction from his mouth, for he is the messenger of the Lord of hosts.'

**MALACHI 2:7 RSV**

He [Jesus] taught . . . as one who had authority, and not as their scribes.

**MATTHEW 7:29 RSV**

[A centurion] 'I, too, am a man under the authority of superior officers, and I have soldiers under me.'

**MATTHEW 8:9 GNB**

'But that you may know that the Son of man has authority on earth to forgive sins'—he then said to the paralytic—'Rise, take up your bed and go home.'

**MATTHEW 9:6 RSV**

And he called to him his twelve disciples and gave them authority over unclean spirits, to cast them out, and to heal every disease and every infirmity.

**MATTHEW 10:1 RSV**

And when they saw him they worshipped him; but some doubted. And Jesus came and said to them, 'All authority in heaven and on earth has been given to me . . .'

**MATTHEW 28:18 RSV**

And they were all amazed, so that they questioned among themselves, saying, 'What is this? A new teaching! With authority he commands even the unclean spirits, and they obey him.'

**MARK 1:27 RSV**

'I will warn you whom to fear: fear him who, after he has killed, has authority to cast into hell. Believe me, he is the one to fear.'

**LUKE 12:5 NEB**

But as many as received him, to them gave he power to become the sons of God, even to them that believe on his name.

**JOHN 1:12 KJV**

'For as the Father has life in himself, so he has granted the Son to have life in himself. And he has given him authority to judge because he is the Son of Man.'

**JOHN 5:27 NIV**

'No-one takes it [my life] from me, but I lay it down of my own accord. I have authority to lay it down and authority to take it up again. This command I received from my Father.'

**JOHN 10:18 NIV**

'For you [the Father] gave him [the Son] authority over all mankind, so that he might give eternal life to all those you gave him.'

**JOHN 17:2 GNB**

Everyone must obey the state authorities, because no authority exists without God's permission, and the existing authorities have been put there by God.

**ROMANS 13:1 GNB**

See also *Power.*

# Backsliding
See *Falling away.*

# Baptism

[John the Baptist] 'I baptize you with water for repentance, but he who is coming after me is mightier than I, whose sandals I am not worthy to carry; he will baptize you with the Holy Spirit and with fire.'

**MATTHEW 3:11 RSV**

And when Jesus was baptized, he went up immediately from the water, and behold, the heavens were opened and he saw the Spirit of God descending like a dove, and alighting on him.

**MATTHEW 3:16 RSV**

'Go therefore and make disciples of all nations, baptizing them in the name of the Father and of the Son and of the Holy Spirit . . .'

MATTHEW 28:19 RSV

And Peter said to them, 'Repent, and be baptized every one of you in the name of Jesus Christ for the forgiveness of your sins; and you shall receive the gift of the Holy Spirit' . . . So those who received his word were baptized, and there were added that day about three thousand souls.

ACTS 2:38, 41 RSV

And as they went along the road they came to some water, and the eunuch said, 'See, here is water! What is to prevent my being baptized?' And he commanded the chariot to stop, and they both went down into the water, Philip and the eunuch, and he baptized him.

ACTS 8:36, 38 RSV

And he [the Philippian jailer] took them the same hour of the night, and washed their wounds, and he was baptized at once, with all his family.

ACTS 16:33 RSV

Paul said, 'The baptism of John was for those who turned from their sins; and he told the people of Israel to believe in the one who was coming after him—that is, in Jesus.' When they [disciples in Ephesus] heard this, there were baptized in the name of the Lord Jesus.

ACTS 19:4–5 GNB

Know ye not, that so many of us as were baptized into Jesus Christ were baptized into his death? Therefore we are buried with him by baptism into death: that like as Christ was raised up from the dead by the glory of the Father, even so we also should walk in newness of life.

ROMANS 6:3–4 KJV

For by one Spirit we were all baptized into one body—Jews or Greeks, slaves or free—and all were made to drink of one Spirit.

1 CORINTHIANS 12:13 RSV

## Beatitudes
See Matthew 5:1–12.

## Benedictus
See *Prayer, Prayers of the Bible.*

## Bereavement
See *Comfort, in bereavement and sorrow.*

# Bible

For as the rain cometh down, and the snow from heaven, and returneth not thither, but watereth the earth, and maketh it bring forth and bud, that it may give seed to the sower, and bread to the eater: so shall my word be that goeth forth out of my mouth: it shall not return unto me void, but it shall accomplish that which I please, and it shall prosper in the thing whereto I sent it.

ISAIAH 55:10–11 KJV

'It is written, "Man shall not live by bread alone, but by every word that proceeds from the mouth of God."'

MATTHEW 4:4 RSV

[To the Jews] 'You search the scriptures, because you think that in them you have eternal life; and it is they that bear witness to me; yet you refuse to come to me that you may have life.'

JOHN 5:39–40 RSV

'But the Counsellor, the Holy Spirit, whom the Father will send in my name, he will teach you all things, and bring to your remembrance all that I have said to you.'

JOHN 14:26 RSV

[The Jews at Berea] These were more noble than those in Thessalonica, in that they received the word with all readiness of mind, and searched the scriptures daily, whether those things were so.

ACTS 17:11 KJV

The Jews are entrusted with the oracles of God.

ROMANS 3:2 RSV

And take the helmet of salvation, and the sword of the Spirit, which is the word of God.

EPHESIANS 6:17 KJV

Let the word of Christ dwell in you richly in all wisdom; teaching and admonishing one another in psalms and hymns and spiritual songs, singing with grace in your hearts to the Lord.

COLOSSIANS 3:16 KJV

And we also thank God constantly for this, that when you received the word of God which you heard from us, you accepted it not as the word of men but as what it really is, the word of God, which is at work in you believers.

1 THESSALONIANS 2:13 RSV

Do your best to present yourself to God as one approved, a workman who has no need to be ashamed, rightly handling the word of truth.
2 TIMOTHY 2:15 RSV

How from childhood you have been acquainted with the sacred writings which are able to instruct you for salvation through faith in Christ Jesus. All scripture is inspired by God and profitable for teaching, for reproof, for correction, and for training in righteousness, that the man of God may be complete, equipped for every good work.
2 TIMOTHY 3:15–17 RSV

For the word of God is living and active, sharper than any two-edged sword, piercing to the division of soul and spirit, of joints and marrow, and discerning the thoughts and intentions of the heart.
HEBREWS 4:12 RSV

First of all you must understand this, that no prophecy of scripture is a matter of one's own interpretation, because no prophecy ever came by the impulse of man, but men moved by the Holy Spirit spoke from God.
2 PETER 1:20–21 RSV

## Bishops
See *Elders*.

## Blasphemy

Thou shalt not take the name of the Lord thy God in vain; for the Lord will not hold him guiltless that taketh his name in vain.
EXODUS 20:7 KJV

'For my people have been taken away for nothing, and those who rule them mock,' declares the Lord. 'And all day long my name is constantly blasphemed.'
ISAIAH 52:5 NIV

'Therefore, son of man, speak to the people of Israel and say to them, "This is what the Sovereign Lord says: In this also your fathers blasphemed me by forsaking me."'
EZEKIEL 20:27 NIV

'Therefore I tell you, every sin and blasphemy will be forgiven men, but the blasphemy against the Spirit will not be forgiven.'
MATTHEW 12:31 RSV

And the high priest said to him, 'I adjure you by the living God, tell us if you are the Christ, the Son of God.' Jesus said to him, 'You have said so. But I tell you, hereafter you will see the Son of man seated at the right hand of Power, and coming on the clouds of heaven.' Then the high priest tore his robes, and said, 'He has uttered blasphemy. Why do we still need witnesses? You have now heard his blasphemy.'
MATTHEW 26:63–65 RSV

[In the last days] Men shall be lovers of their own selves, covetous, boasters, proud, blasphemers . . .
2 TIMOTHY 3:2 KJV

Is it not they [the rich] who blaspheme that honourable name which was invoked over you?
JAMES 2:7 RSV

See also *Vow*.

## Blessing

Now the Lord had said unto Abram, Get thee out of thy country, and from thy kindred, and from thy father's house, unto a land that I will shew thee: and I will make of thee a great nation, and I will bless thee, and make thy name great; and thou shalt be a blessing: and I will bless them that bless thee, and curse him that curseth thee: and in thee shall all families of the earth be blessed.
GENESIS 12:1–3 KJV

And he [Jacob] said, Let me go, for the day breaketh. And he said, I will not let thee go, except thou bless me.
GENESIS 32:26 KJV

The Lord bless thee, and keep thee: the Lord make his face shine upon thee, and be gracious unto thee: the Lord lift up his countenance upon thee, and give thee peace.
NUMBERS 6:24–26 KJV

'And all these blessings shall come upon you and overtake you, if you obey the voice of the Lord your God . . .'
DEUTERONOMY 28:2 RSV

'Bring the full tithes into the storehouse, that there may be food in my house; and thereby put me to the test, says the Lord of hosts, if I will not open the windows of heaven for you and pour down for you an overflowing blessing.'
MALACHI 3:10 RSV

[Jesus and young children] And he took them up in his arms, put his hands upon them, and blessed them.
MARK 10:16 KJV

Bless those who persecute you; bless and do not curse.
ROMANS 12:14 NIV

Blessed be the God and Father of our Lord Jesus Christ, who has blessed us in Christ with every spiritual blessing in the heavenly places.
EPHESIANS 1:3 RSV

Do not return evil for evil or reviling for reviling; but on the contrary bless, for to this you have been called, that you may obtain a blessing.
1 PETER 3:9 RSV

See also **Christian life, Character of the Christian.**

# Blood

'For the life of the flesh is in the blood; and I have given it for you upon the altar to make atonement for your souls; for it is the blood that makes atonement, by reason of the life.'
LEVITICUS 17:11 RSV

'This is my blood of the covenant, which is poured out for many for the forgiveness of sins.'
MATTHEW 26:28 RSV

[Christ Jesus] whom God hath set forth to be a propitiation through faith in his blood.
ROMANS 3:25 KJV

Since, therefore, we are now justified by his blood, much more shall we be saved by him from the wrath of God.
ROMANS 5:9 RSV

In him [Christ] we have redemption through his blood, the forgiveness of our trespasses, according to the riches of his grace which he lavished upon us.
EPHESIANS 1:7 RSV

Making peace by the blood of his cross.
COLOSSIANS 1:20 RSV

Indeed, under the law almost everything is purified with blood, and without the shedding of blood there is no forgiveness of sins.
HEBREWS 9:22 RSV

Therefore, brethren, since we have confidence to enter the sanctuary by the blood of Jesus . . .
HEBREWS 10:19 RSV

Now the God of peace, that brought again from the dead our Lord Jesus, that great shepherd of the sheep, through the blood of the everlasting covenant . . .
HEBREWS 13:20 KJV

You know that you were ransomed from the futile ways inherited from your fathers, not with perishable things such as silver or gold, but with the precious blood of Christ, like that of a lamb without blemish or spot.
1 PETER 1:18–19 RSV

If we walk in the light, as he is in the light, we have fellowship with one another, and the blood of Jesus his Son cleanses us from all sin.
1 JOHN 1:7 RSV

To him who loves us and freed us from our sins by his blood and made us a kingdom, priests to his God and Father, to him be glory and dominion for ever and ever. Amen.
REVELATION 1:5–6 RSV

'And they have conquered him by the blood of the Lamb and by the word of their testimony, for they loved not their lives even unto death.'
REVELATION 12:11 RSV

# Body

Now as they were eating, Jesus took bread, and blessed, and broke it, and gave it to the disciples and said, 'Take, eat; this is my body.'
MATTHEW 26:26 RSV

I beseech you therefore, brethren, by the mercies of God, that ye present your bodies a living sacrifice, holy, acceptable unto God, which is your reasonable service.
ROMANS 12:1 KJV

Do you not know that your body is a temple of the Holy Spirit within you, which you have from God? You are not your own; you were bought with a price. So glorify God in your body.
1 CORINTHIANS 6:19–20 RSV

Now you are the body of Christ and individually members of it.
1 CORINTHIANS 12:27 RSV

It is sown a physical body, it is raised a spiritual body. If there is a physical body, there is also a spiritual body.
1 CORINTHIANS 15:44 RSV

[Jesus] He is the head of the body, the church; he is the beginning, the first-born from the dead, that in everything he might be pre-eminent.
COLOSSIANS 1:18 RSV

## Boldness
See *Confidence.*

## Bribe

'Moreover choose able men from all the people, such as fear God, men who are trustworthy and who hate a bribe; and place such men over the people as rulers of thousands, of hundreds, of fifties, and of tens.'
EXODUS 18:21 RSV

'Do not accept a bribe, for a bribe makes people blind to what is right and ruins the cause of those who are innocent.'
EXODUS 23:8 GNB

If you try to make a profit dishonestly, you will get your family into trouble. Don't take bribes and you will live longer.
PROVERBS 15:27 GNB

Corrupt judges accept secret bribes, and then justice is not done.
PROVERBS 17:23 GNB

They are all experts at doing evil. Officials and judges ask for bribes. The influential man tells them what he wants, and so they scheme together.
MICAH 7:3 GNB

## Celibacy

His disciples said to him, 'If this is how it is between a man and his wife, it is better not to marry.' Jesus answered, 'This teaching does not apply to everyone, but only to those to whom God has given it. For there are different reasons why men cannot marry: some, because they were born that way; others, because men made them that way; and others do not marry for the sake of the Kingdom of heaven. Let him who can accept this teaching do so.'
MATTHEW 19:10–12 GNB

I wish that all were as I myself am. But each has his own special gift from God, of one of one kind and one of another.
1 CORINTHIANS 7:7 RSV

I would like you to be free from worry. An unmarried man concerns himself with the Lord's work, because he is trying to please the Lord.
1 CORINTHIANS 7:32 GNB

## Children
See *Family.*

## Christian life

### CALLING OF THE CHRISTIAN

But now thus saith the Lord that created thee, O Jacob, and he that formed thee, O Israel, Fear not: for I have redeemed thee, I have called thee by thy name; thou art mine.
ISAIAH 43:1 KJV

Ye are the salt of the earth: but if the salt have lost his savour, wherewith shall it be salted? It is thenceforth good for nothing, but to be cast out, and to be trodden under foot of men. Ye are the light of the world. A city that is set on a hill cannot be hid. Neither do men light a candle, and put it under a bushel, but on a candlestick; and it giveth light unto all that are in the house. Let your light so shine before men, that they may see your good works, and glorify your father which is in heaven.
MATTHEW 5:13–16 KJV

'But you shall receive power when the Holy Spirit has come upon you; and you shall be my witnesses in Jerusalem and in all Judea and Samaria and to the end of the earth.'
ACTS 1:8 RSV

We know that in everything God works for good with those who love him, who are called according to his purpose . . . And those whom he predestined he also called; and those whom he called he also justified; and those whom he justified he also glorified.
ROMANS 8:28, 30 RSV

God is faithful, by whom you were called into the fellowship of his Son, Jesus Christ our Lord.
1 CORINTHIANS 1:9 RSV

I therefore, a prisoner for the Lord, beg you to lead a life worthy of the calling to which you have been called.
EPHESIANS 4:1 RSV

God, who saved us and called us with a holy calling, not in virtue of our works but in virtue of his own purpose and the grace which he gave us in Christ Jesus ages ago.

2 TIMOTHY 1:8–9 RSV

Be holy in all that you do, just as God who called you is holy.

1 PETER 1:15 GNB

But you are a chosen race, a royal priesthood, a holy nation, God's own people, that you may declare the wonderful deeds of him who called you out of darkness into his marvellous light.

1 PETER 2:9 RSV

For what credit is there if you endure the beatings you deserve for having done wrong? But if you endure suffering even when you have done right, God will bless you for it. It was to this that God called you, for Christ himself suffered for you and left you an example, so that you would follow in his steps.

1 PETER 2:20–21 GNB

See what love the Father has given us, that we should be called children of God; and so we are.

1 JOHN 3:1 RSV

To those who are called, beloved in God the Father and kept for Jesus Christ.

JUDE 1 RSV

See also *Church; Disciples; Election.*

## CHARACTER OF THE CHRISTIAN

Blessed is the man who walks not in the counsel of the wicked, nor stands in the way of sinners, nor sits in the seat of scoffers; but his delight is in the law of the Lord, and on his law he meditates day and night. He is like a tree planted by streams of water, that yields its fruit in its season, and its leaf does not wither. In all that he does, he prospers.

PSALM 1:1–3 RSV

And seeing the multitudes, he went up into a mountain: and when he was set, his disciples came unto him: and he opened his mouth, and taught them, saying, Blessed are the poor in spirit: for theirs is the kingdom of heaven. Blessed are they that mourn: for they shall be comforted. Blessed are the meek: for they shall inherit the earth. Blessed are they which do hunger and thirst after righteousness: for they shall be filled. Blessed are the merciful: for they shall obtain mercy. Blessed are the pure in heart: for they shall see God. Blessed are the

peacemakers: for they shall be called the children of God. Blessed are they which are persecuted for righteousness' sake: for theirs is the kingdom of heaven. Blessed are ye, when men shall revile you, and persecute you, and shall say all manner of evil against you falsely, for my sake.

MATTHEW 5:3–11 KJV

But the fruit of the Spirit is love, joy, peace, patience, kindness, goodness, faithfulness, gentleness, self-control; against such there is no law.

GALATIANS 5:22–23 RSV

His [God] divine power has given us everything we need for life and godliness through our knowledge of him who called us by his own glory and goodness. Through these he has given us his very great and precious promises, so that through them you may participate in the divine nature and escape the corruption in the world caused by evil desires. For this very reason, make every effort to add to your faith goodness; and to goodness, knowledge; and to knowledge, self-control; and to self-control, perseverance; and to perseverance, godliness; and to godliness, brotherly kindness; and to brotherly kindness, love. For if you possess these qualities in increasing measure, they will keep you from being ineffective and unproductive in your knowledge of our Lord Jesus Christ.

2 PETER 1:3–8 NIV

## COMING TO FAITH

Seek ye the Lord while he may be found, call ye upon him while he is near. Let the wicked forsake his way, and the unrighteous man his thoughts: and let him return unto the Lord, and he will have mercy upon him; and to our God, for he will abundantly pardon.

ISAIAH 55:6–7 KJV

'Come to me, all who labour and are heavy-laden, and I will give you rest.'

MATTHEW 11:28 RSV

Now great multitudes accompanied him; and he turned and said to them, 'If any one comes to me and does not hate his own father and mother and wife and children and brothers and sisters, yes, and even his own life, he cannot be my disciple. Whoever does not bear his own cross and come after me, cannot be my disciple.'

LUKE 14:25–27 RSV

But as many as received him, to them gave he power to become the sons of God, even to them that believe on his name.
JOHN 1:12 KJV

For God so loved the world, that he gave his only begotten Son, that whosoever believeth in him should not perish, but have everlasting life.
JOHN 3:16 KJV

All that the Father giveth me shall come to me; and him that cometh to me I will in no wise cast out.
JOHN 6:37 KJV

Jesus saith unto him, I am the way, the truth, and the life: no man cometh unto the Father, but by me.
JOHN 14:6 KJV

Now when they heard this they were cut to the heart, and said to Peter and the rest of the apostles, 'Brethren, what shall we do?' And Peter said to them, 'Repent, and be baptized every one of you in the name of Jesus Christ for the forgiveness of your sins; and you shall receive the gift of the Holy Spirit.'
ACTS 2:37–38 RSV

'Men, what must I do to be saved?' And they said, 'Believe in the Lord Jesus, and you will be saved, you and your household.'
ACTS 16:30–31 RSV

'The times of ignorance God overlooked, but now he commands all men everywhere to repent, because he has fixed a day on which he will judge the world in righteousness by a man whom he has appointed, and of this he has given assurance to all men by raising him from the dead.'
ACTS 17:30–31 RSV

For whosoever shall call upon the name of the Lord shall be saved.
ROMANS 10:13 KJV

So we are ambassadors for Christ, God making his appeal through us. We beseech you on behalf of Christ, be reconciled to God. For our sake he made him to be sin who knew no sin, so that in him we might become the righteousness of God.
2 CORINTHIANS 5:20–21 RSV

For Christ also died for sins once for all, the righteous for the unrighteous, that he might bring us to God, being put to death in the flesh but made alive in the spirit.
1 PETER 3:18 RSV

See also *Conversion*.

## CONTINUING IN THE FAITH

Jesus then said to the Jews who had believed in him, 'If you continue in my word, you are truly my disciples.' . . . 'Truly, truly, I say to you, if any one keeps my word, he will never see death.'
JOHN 8:31, 51 RSV

'I am the vine, you are the branches. He who abides in me, and I in him, he it is that bears much fruit, for apart from me you can do nothing . . . As the Father has loved me, so have I loved you; abide in my love.'
JOHN 15:5, 9 RSV

'And now I am no more in the world, but they are in the world, and I am coming to thee. Holy Father, keep them in thy name which thou hast given me, that they may be one, even as we are one.'
JOHN 17:11 RSV

And they continued stedfastly in the apostles' doctrine and fellowship, and in breaking of bread, and in prayers.
ACTS 2:42 KJV

[Paul and Barnabas] Strengthening the souls of the disciples, exhorting them to continue in the faith, and saying that through many tribulations we must enter the kingdom of God.
ACTS 14:22 RSV

And so I am sure that God, who began this good work in you, will carry it on until it is finished in the Day of Christ Jesus.
PHILIPPIANS 1:6 GNB

Him we proclaim, warning every man and teaching every man in all wisdom, that we may present every man mature in Christ.
COLOSSIANS 1:28 RSV

Let us hold fast the confession of our hope without wavering, for he who promised is faithful.
HEBREWS 10:23 RSV

Therefore, since we are surrounded by so great a cloud of witnesses, let us also lay aside every weight, and sin which clings so closely, and let us run with perseverance the race that is set before us, looking to Jesus the pioneer and perfecter of our faith, who for the joy that was set before him

endured the cross, despising the shame, and is seated at the right hand of the throne of God.
HEBREWS 12:1–2 RSV

[We] who by God's power are guarded through faith for a salvation ready to be revealed in the last time.
1 PETER 1:5 RSV

Therefore, brethren, be the more zealous to confirm your call and election, for if you do this you will never fall.
2 PETER 1:10 RSV

Keep yourselves in the love of God, looking for the mercy of our Lord Jesus Christ unto eternal life . . . Now unto him that is able to keep you from falling, and to present you faultless before the presence of his glory with exceeding joy . . .
JUDE 21, 24 KJV

' ''I am coming soon; hold fast what you have, so that no one may seize your crown.'' '
REVELATION 3:11 RSV

See also **Endurance.**

### LONGING FOR GOD

Moses said, 'I pray thee, show me thy glory.'
EXODUS 33:18 RSV

One thing have I desired of the Lord, that will I seek after; that I may dwell in the house of the Lord all the days of my life, to behold the beauty of the Lord, and to inquire in his temple.
PSALM 27:4 KJV

As the hart panteth after the water brooks, so panteth my soul after thee, O God. My soul thirsteth for God, for the living God: when shall I come and appear before God?
PSALM 42:1–2 KJV

O God, thou art my God, I seek thee early with a heart that thirsts for thee and a body wasted with longing for thee, like a dry and thirsty land that has no water. So longing, I come before thee in the sanctuary to look upon thy power and glory.
PSALM 63:1–2 NEB

Whom have I in heaven but thee? And there is none upon earth that I desire beside thee.
PSALM 73:25 KJV

I pine, I faint with longing for the courts of the Lord's temple; my whole being cries out with joy to the living God.
PSALM 84:2 NEB

[Some Greeks] came therefore to Philip, which was of Bethsaida of Galilee, and desired him, saying, Sir, we would see Jesus.
JOHN 12:21 KJV

For I delight in the law of God, in my inmost self . . .
ROMANS 7:22 RSV

Unto you therefore which believe he is precious.
1 PETER 2:7 KJV

See also **Worship.**

## Church

And I say also unto thee, That thou art Peter, and upon this rock I will build my church; and the gates of hell shall not prevail against it.
MATTHEW 16:18 KJV

'If he [a fellow Christian] refuses to listen to them [witnesses], tell it to the church; and if he refuses to listen even to the church, let him be to you as a Gentile and a tax collector.'
MATTHEW 18:17 RSV

And they continued stedfastly in the apostles' doctrine and fellowship, and in breaking of bread, and in prayers.
ACTS 2:42 KJV

And so it was that the church throughout Judaea, Galilee, and Samaria had a time of peace. Through the help of the Holy Spirit it was strengthened and grew in number, as it lived in reverence for the Lord.
ACTS 9:31 GNB

And when they had appointed elders for them in every church, with prayer and fasting, they committed them to the Lord in whom they believed.
ACTS 14:23 RSV

'Take heed to yourselves and to all the flock, in which the Holy Spirit has made you overseers, to care for the church of God which he obtained with the blood of his own Son.'
ACTS 20:28 RSV

For the husband is the head of the wife as Christ is the head of the church, his body, and is himself its Saviour . . . Husbands, love your wives, as Christ loved the church and gave himself up for her, that he might sanctify her, having cleansed her by the washing of water with the word, that he

might present the church to himself in splendour, without spot or wrinkle or any such thing, that she might be holy and without blemish.
**EPHESIANS 5:23, 25–27 RSV**

Not neglecting to meet together, as is the habit of some, but encouraging one another, and all the more as you see the Day drawing near.
**HEBREWS 10:25 RSV**

# Circumcision

'This is my covenant, which you shall keep, between me and you and your descendants after you: Every male among you shall be circumcised. You shall be circumcised in the flesh of your foreskins, and it shall be a sign of the covenant between me and you. He that is eight days old among you shall be circumcised; every male throughout your generations, whether born in your house, or bought with your money from any foreigner who is not of your offspring . . . shall be circumcised.'
**GENESIS 17:10–13 RSV**

The Lord says, 'The time is coming when I will punish the people of Egypt, Judah, Edom, Ammon, Moab, and the desert people, who have their hair cut short. All these people are circumcised, but have not kept the covenant it symbolizes. None of these people and none of the people of Israel have kept my covenant.'
**JEREMIAH 9:25–26 GNB**

For he is not a real Jew who is one outwardly, nor is true circumcision something external and physical. He is a Jew who is one inwardly, and real circumcision is a matter of the heart, spiritual and not literal. His praise is not from men but from God.
**ROMANS 2:28–29 RSV**

For whether or not a man is circumcised means nothing; what matters is to obey God's commandments.
**1 CORINTHIANS 7:19 GNB**

For when we are in union with Christ Jesus, neither circumcision nor the lack of it makes any difference at all; what matters is faith that works through love.
**GALATIANS 5:6 GNB**

For we are the true circumcision, who worship God in spirit, and glory in Christ Jesus, and put no confidence in the flesh.
**PHILIPPIANS 3:3 RSV**

# Comfort

### WHEN AFRAID

After these things the word of the Lord came unto Abram in a vision, saying, Fear not, Abram: I am thy shield, and thy exceeding great reward.
**GENESIS 15:1 KJV**

The Lord is my light and my salvation; whom shall I fear? The Lord is the strength of my life; of whom shall I be afraid?
**PSALM 27:1 KJV**

I sought the Lord, and he answered me, and delivered me from all my fears.
**PSALM 34:4 RSV**

God is our refuge and strength, a very present help in trouble. Therefore will not we fear, though the earth be removed, and though the mountains be carried into the midst of the sea.
**PSALM 46:1–2 KJV**

The name of the Lord is a strong tower; the righteous man runs into it and is safe.
**PROVERBS 18:10 RSV**

But now thus saith the Lord that created thee, O Jacob, and he that formed thee, O Israel, Fear not: for I have redeemed thee, I have called thee by thy name; thou art mine. When thou passest through the waters, I will be with thee; and through the rivers, they shall not overflow thee: when thou walkest through the fire, thou shalt not be burned; neither shall the flame kindle upon thee.
**ISAIAH 43:1–2 KJV**

But when the disciples saw him walking on the sea, they were terrified, saying, 'It is a ghost!' And they cried out for fear. But immediately he spoke to them, saying, 'Take heart, it is I; have no fear.'
**MATTHEW 14:26–27 RSV**

And the angel said unto them [the shepherds], Fear not: for, behold, I bring you good tidings of great joy, which shall be to all people.
**LUKE 2:10 KJV**

Fear not, little flock; for it is your Father's good pleasure to give you the kingdom.
**LUKE 12:32 KJV**

'Peace I leave with you; my peace I give to you; not as the world gives do I give to you. Let not your hearts be troubled, neither let them be afraid.'

JOHN 14:27 RSV

[Christ] himself . . . partook of the same nature, that through death he might destroy him who has the power of death, that is, the devil, and deliver all those who through fear of death were subject to lifelong bondage.

HEBREWS 2:14–15 RSV

## WHEN ANXIOUS

Therefore I say unto you, Take no thought for your life, what ye shall eat, or what ye shall drink; not yet for your body, what ye shall put on. Is not the life more than meat, and the body than raiment? Behold the fowls of the air: for they sow not, neither do they reap, nor gather into barns; yet your heavenly Father feedeth them. Are ye not much better than they? Which of you by taking thought can add one cubit unto his stature? And why take ye thought for raiment? Consider the lilies of the field, how they grow; they toil not, neither do they spin: and yet I say unto you, That even Solomon in all his glory was not arrayed like one of these. Wherefore, if God so clothe the grass of the field, which to day is, and to morrow is cast into the oven, shall he not much more clothe you, O ye of little faith? Therefore take no thought, saying, What shall we eat? or, What shall we drink? or, Wherewithal shall we be clothed? (For after all these things do the Gentles seek:) for your heavenly Father knoweth that ye have need of all these things. But seek ye first the kingdom of God, and his righteousness; and all these things shall be added unto you.

MATTHEW 6:25–33 KJV

'When they deliver you up, do not be anxious how you are to speak or what you are to say; for what you are to say will be given to you in that hour.'

MATTHEW 10:19 RSV

'Come to me, all who labour and are heavy-laden, and I will give you rest.'

MATTHEW 11:28 RSV

Bear one another's burdens, and so fulfil the law of Christ.

GALATIANS 6:2 RSV

Have no anxiety about anything, but in everything by prayer and supplication with thanksgiving let your requests be made known to God. And the peace of God, which passes all understanding, will keep your hearts and your minds in Christ Jesus.

PHILIPPIANS 4:6–7 RSV

Cast all your anxieties on him, for he cares about you.

1 PETER 5:7 RSV

## IN BEREAVEMENT AND SORROW

'The Lord gave, and the Lord has taken away; blessed be the name of the Lord.'

JOB 1:21 RSV

Yea, though I walk through the valley of the shadow of death, I will fear no evil: for thou art with me; thy rod and thy staff they comfort me.

PSALM 23:4 KJV

Blessed are they that mourn: for they shall be comforted.

MATTHEW 5:4 KJV

Jesus said unto her [Martha], I am the resurrection, and the life: he that believeth in me, though he were dead, yet shall he live. And whosoever liveth and believeth in me shall never die. Believest thou this?

JOHN 11:25–26 KJV

And if I go and prepare a place for you, I will come again, and receive you unto myself; that where I am, there ye may be also.

JOHN 14:3 KJV

Rejoice with those who rejoice; mourn with those who mourn.

ROMANS 12:15 NIV

But in fact Christ has been raised from the dead, the first fruits of those who have fallen asleep.

1 CORINTHIANS 15:20 RSV

For this corruptible must put on incorruption, and this mortal must put on immortality.

1 CORINTHIANS 15:53 KJV

But I would not have you to be ignorant, brethren, concerning them which are asleep, that ye sorrow not, even as others which have no hope . . . For the Lord himself shall descend from heaven with a shout, with the voice of the archangel, and with the trump of God: and the dead in Christ shall rise first. Then we which are

alive and remain shall be caught up together with them in the clouds, to meet the Lord in the air: and so shall we ever be with the Lord. Wherefore comfort one another with these words.
1 THESSALONIANS 4:13, 16–18 KJV

## IN DESPAIR

The Lord is near to those who are discouraged; he saves those who have lost all hope.
PSALM 34:18 GNB

I waited patiently for the Lord; he inclined to me and heard my cry. He drew me up from the desolate pit, out of the miry bog, and set my feet upon a rock, making my steps secure.
PSALM 40:1–2 RSV

Why art though cast down, O my soul? and why art thou disquieted in me? Hope thou in God: for I shall yet praise him for the help of his countenance. O my God, my soul is cast down within me: therefore will I remember thee . . .
PSALM 42:5–6 KJV

Cast me not away from thy presence; and take not thy holy spirit from me. Restore unto me the joy of thy salvation; and uphold me with thy free spirit.
PSALM 51:11–12 KJV

A bruised reed shall he [the Lord's servant] not break, and the smoking flax shall he not quench: he shall bring forth judgment unto truth.
ISAIAH 42:3 KJV

But this I call to mind, and therefore I have hope: The steadfast love of the Lord never ceases, his mercies never come to an end; they are new every morning; great is thy faithfulness.
LAMENTATIONS 3:21–23 RSV

We are afflicted in every way, but not crushed; perplexed, but not driven to despair . . .
2 CORINTHIANS 4:8 RSV

## WHEN LONELY

Turn to me, Lord, and be merciful to me, because I am lonely and weak.
PSALM 25:16 GNB

I lie awake, I am like a lonely bird on the housetop.
PSALM 102:7 RSV

Fear thou not; for I am with thee: be not dismayed; for I am thy God: I will strengthen thee; yea, I will help thee; yea, I will uphold thee with the right hand of my righteousness.
ISAIAH 41:10 KJV

But Zion said, The Lord hath forsaken me, and my Lord hath forgotten me. Can a woman forget her sucking child, that she should not have compassion on the son of her womb? Yea, they may forget, yet will I not forget thee. Behold, I have graven thee upon the palms of my hands; thy walls are continually before me.
ISAIAH 49:14–16 KJV

I will not leave you comfortless: I will come to you.
JOHN 14:18 KJV

No one stood by me the first time I defended myself; all deserted me. May God not count it against them! But the Lord stayed with me and gave me strength, so that I was able to proclaim the full message for all the Gentiles to hear.
2 TIMOTHY 4:16–17 GNB

## IN SUFFERING

And God heard their groaning, and God remembered his covenant with Abraham, with Isaac, and with Jacob. And God saw the people of Israel, and God knew their condition.
EXODUS 2:24–25 RSV

The eternal God is thy refuge, and underneath are the everlasting arms.
DEUTERONOMY 33:27 KJV

Though he slay me, yet will I trust in him: but I will maintain mine own ways before him.
JOB 13:15 KJV

My flesh and my heart faileth: but God is the strength of my heart, and my portion for ever.
PSALM 73:26 KJV

Comfort ye, comfort ye my people, saith your God. Speak ye comfortably to Jerusalem, and cry unto her, that her warfare is accomplished, that her iniquity is pardoned: for she hath received of the Lord's hand double for all her sins.
ISAIAH 40:1–2 KJV

Surely he hath borne our griefs, and carried our sorrows: yet we did esteem him stricken, smitten of God, and afflicted.
ISAIAH 53:4 KJV ᐟ

Though the fig tree do not blossom, nor fruit be on the vines, the produce of the olive fail and the fields yield no food, the flock be cut off from the

fold and there be no herd in the stalls, yet I will rejoice in the Lord, I will joy in the God of my salvation.
HABAKKUK 3:17–18 RSV

We know that in everything God works for good with those who love him, who are called according to his purpose . . . Who shall separate us from the love of Christ? Shall tribulation, or distress, or persecution, or famine, or nakedness, or peril, or sword? As it is written, 'For thy sake we are being killed all the day long; we are regarded as sheep to be slaughtered.' No, in all these things we are more than conquerors through him who loved us. For I am sure that neither death, nor life, nor angels, nor principalities, nor things present, nor things to come, nor powers, nor height, nor depth, nor anything else in all creation, will be able to separate us from the love of God in Christ Jesus our Lord.
ROMANS 8:28, 35–39 RSV

Rejoice in your hope, be patient in tribulation, be constant in prayer.
ROMANS 12:12 RSV

No temptation has overtaken you that is not common to man. God is faithful, and he will not let you be tempted beyond your strength, but with the temptation will also provide the way of escape, that you may be able to endure it.
1 CORINTHIANS 10:13 RSV

Praise be to the God and Father of our Lord Jesus Christ, the Father of compassion and the God of all comfort, who comforts us in all our troubles, so that we can comfort those in any trouble with the comfort we ourselves have received from God.
2 CORINTHIANS 1:3–4 NIV

So we do not lose heart. Though our outer nature is wasting away, our inner nature is being renewed every day. For this slight momentary affliction is preparing for us an eternal weight of glory beyond all comparison, because we look not to the things that are seen but to the things that are unseen; for the things that are seen are transient, but the things that are unseen are eternal.
2 CORINTHIANS 4:16–18 RSV

He said to me, 'My grace is sufficient for you, for my power is made perfect in weakness.' I will all the more gladly boast of my weaknesses, that the power of Christ may rest upon me.
2 CORINTHIANS 12:9 RSV

Let us then with confidence draw near to the throne of grace, that we may receive mercy and find grace to help in time of need.
HEBREWS 4:16 RSV

Looking unto Jesus the author and finisher of our faith; who for the joy that was set before him endured the cross, despising the shame, and is set down at the right hand of the throne of God.
HEBREWS 12:2 KJV

Beloved, do not be surprised at the fiery ordeal which comes upon you to prove you, as though something strange were happening to you. But rejoice in so far as you share Christ's sufferings, that you may also rejoice and be glad when his glory is revealed.
1 PETER 4:12–13 RSV

And God shall wipe away all tears from their eyes; and there shall be no more death, neither sorrow, nor crying, neither shall there be any more pain: for the former things are passed away.
REVELATION 21:4 KJV

## Commitment
See *Covenant; Disciples; Obedience.*

## Communion

Now as they were eating, Jesus took bread, and blessed, and broke it, and gave it to the disciples and said, 'Take, eat; this is my body.' And he took a cup, and when he had given thanks he gave it to them, saying, 'Drink of it, all of you; for this is my blood of the covenant, which is poured out for many for the forgiveness of sins.'
MATTHEW 26:26–28 RSV

And they continued stedfastly in the apostles' doctrine and fellowship, and in breaking of bread, and in prayers.
ACTS 2:42 KJV

The cup of blessing which we bless, is it not a participation in the blood of Christ? The bread which we break, is it not a participation in the body of Christ? Because there is one bread, we who are many are one body, for we all partake of the one bread.
1 CORINTHIANS 10:16–17 RSV

For I received from the Lord what I also delivered to you, that the Lord Jesus on the night when he was betrayed took bread, and when he had given thanks, he broke it, and said, 'This is my body which is for you. Do this in remembrance of me.' In the same way also the cup, after supper, saying, 'This cup is the new covenant in my blood. Do this, as often as you drink it, in remembrance of me.' For as often as you eat this bread and drink the cup, you proclaim the Lord's death until he comes. Whoever, therefore, eats the bread or drinks the cup of the Lord in an unworthy manner will be guilty of profaning the body and blood of the Lord. Let a man examine himself, and so eat of the bread and drink of the cup. For any one who eats and drinks without discerning the body eats and drinks judgment upon himself. That is why many of you are weak and ill, and some have died.

**1 CORINTHIANS 11:23–30 RSV**

See also *Fellowship.*

## Compassion
See *Mercy.*

## Confession

'If anyone declares publicly that he belongs to me, I will do the same for him before my Father in heaven.'

**MATTHEW 10:32 GNB**

That if thou shalt confess with thy mouth the Lord Jesus, and shalt believe in thine heart that God hath raised him from the dead, thou shalt be saved. For with the heart man believeth unto righteousness; and with the mouth confession is made unto salvation.

**ROMANS 10:9–10 KJV**

Every tongue [should] confess that Jesus Christ is Lord, to the glory of God the Father.

**PHILIPPIANS 2:11 RSV**

Whoever confesses that Jesus is the Son of God, God abides in him, and he in God.

**1 JOHN 4:15 RSV**

**OF SIN**

'When a man is guilty in any of these [sins], he shall confess the sin he has committed.'

**LEVITICUS 5:5 RSV**

Blessed is the man to whom the Lord imputes no iniquity, and in whose spirit there is no deceit. When I declared not my sin, my body wasted

away through my groaning all day long. For day and night thy hand was heavy upon me; my strength was dried up as by the heat of summer. I acknowledged my sin to thee, and I did not hide my iniquity; I said, 'I will confess my transgressions to the Lord'; then thou didst forgive the guilt of my sin.

**PSALM 32:3–5 RSV**

You will never succeed in life if you try to hide your sins. Confess them and give them up; then God will show mercy to you.

**PROVERBS 28:13 GNB**

Confess your faults one to another, and pray one for another, that ye may be healed. The effectual fervent prayer of a righteous man availeth much.

**JAMES 5:16 KJV**

If we confess our sins, he is faithful and just and will forgive our sins and cleanse us from all unrighteousness.

**1 JOHN 1:9 RSV**

See also *Repentance.*

## Confidence

Though an host should encamp against me, my heart shall not fear: though war should rise against me, in this will I be confident. One thing have I desired of the Lord, that will I seek after; that I may dwell in the house of the Lord all the days of my life, to behold the beauty of the Lord, and to inquire in his temple.

**PSALM 27:3–4 KJV**

In the fear of the Lord one has strong confidence.

**PROVERBS 14:6 RSV**

The righteous are as bold as a lion.

**PROVERBS 28:1 RSV**

Now when they saw the boldness of Peter and John, and perceived that they were uneducated, common men, they wondered; and they recognised that they had been with Jesus.

**ACTS 4:13 RSV**

For we have not a high priest who is unable to sympathize with our weaknesses, but one who in every respect has been tempted as we are, yet without sin. Let us then with confidence draw near to the throne of grace, that we may receive mercy and find grace to help in time of need.

**HEBREWS 4:15–16 RSV**

Therefore, brethren, since we have confidence to enter the sanctuary by the blood of Jesus . . .
**HEBREWS 10:19 RSV**

Hence we can confidently say, 'The Lord is my helper, I will not be afraid; what can man do to me?'
**HEBREWS 13:6 RSV**

And now, little children, abide in him, so that when he appears we may have confidence and not shrink from him in shame at his coming.
**1 JOHN 2:28 RSV**

Beloved, if our hearts do not condemn us, we have confidence before God.
**1 JOHN 3:21 RSV**

In this is love perfected with us, that we may have confidence for the day of judgment, because as he is so are we in this world.
**1 JOHN 4:17 RSV**

And this is the confidence which we have in him, that if we ask anything according to his will he hears us.
**1 JOHN 5:14 RSV**

See also *Access; Assurance; Courage.*

## Conscience

He [David] . . . got up stealthily and cut off a piece of Saul's cloak; but when he had cut it off, his conscience smote him.
**1 SAMUEL 24:5 NEB**

'So I always take pains to have a clear conscience toward God and toward men.'
**ACTS 24:16 RSV**

When Gentiles who have not the law do by nature what the law requires, they are a law to themselves, even though they do not have the law. They show that what the law requires is written on their hearts, while their conscience also bears witness and their conflicting thoughts accuse or perhaps excuse them.
**ROMANS 2:14–15 RSV**

I am speaking the truth in Christ, I am not lying; my conscience bears me witness in the Holy Spirit.
**ROMANS 9:1 RSV**

Some people are still so accustomed to idols that when they eat such food they think of it as having been sacrificed to an idol, and since their conscience is weak, it is defiled.
**1 CORINTHIANS 8:7 NIV**

To the pure, all things are pure, but to the corrupt and unbelieving nothing is pure; their very minds and consciences are corrupted.
**TITUS 1:15 RSV**

Let us draw near with a true heart in full assurance of faith, with our hearts sprinkled clean from an evil conscience and our bodies washed with pure water.
**HEBREWS 10:22 RSV**

God is greater than our hearts, and he knows everything. Beloved, if our hearts do not condemn us, we have confidence before God.
**1 JOHN 3:20–21 RSV**

See also *Guilt.*

## Contentment

Trust in the Lord, and do good; so you will dwell in the land, and enjoy security.
**PSALM 37:3 RSV**

'If you pour yourself out for the hungry and satisfy the desire of the afflicted, then shall your light rise in the darkness and your gloom be as the noonday. And the Lord will guide you continually, and satisfy your desire with good things, and make your bones strong; and you shall be like a watered garden, like a spring of water, whose waters fail not.'
**ISAIAH 58:10–11 RSV**

Soldiers also asked him [John the Baptist], 'And we, what shall we do?' And he said to them, 'Rob no one by violence or by false accusation, and be content with your wages.'
**LUKE 3:14 RSV**

And Jesus said unto them, I am the bread of life: he that cometh to me shall never hunger; and he that believeth on me shall never thirst.
**JOHN 6:35 KJV**

And do not grumble, as some of them [children of Israel] did—and were killed by the destroying angel.
**1 CORINTHIANS 10:10 NIV**

Not that I complain of want; for I have learned, in whatever state I am, to be content. I know how to be abased, and I know how to abound; in any and all circumstances I have learned the secret of facing plenty and hunger, abundance and want. I can do all things in him who strengthens me.

**PHILIPPIANS 4:11–13 RSV**

There is great gain in godliness with contentment; for we brought nothing into the world, and we cannot take anything out of the world; but if we have food and clothing, with these we shall be content.

**1 TIMOTHY 6:6–8 RSV**

Keep your life free from love of money, and be content with what you have; for he has said, 'I will never fail you nor forsake you.'

**HEBREWS 13:5 RSV**

See also *Joy.*

## Conversion

All the ends of the earth shall remember and turn to the Lord; and all the families of the nations shall worship before him.

**PSALM 22:27 RSV**

Verily I say unto you, Except ye be converted, and become as little children, ye shall not enter into the kingdom of heaven.

**MATTHEW 18:3 KJV**

[The purpose of parables] 'That they may indeed see but not perceive, and may indeed hear but not understand; lest they should turn again, and be forgiven.'

**MARK 4:12 RSV**

[The Lord Jesus to Simon Peter] I have prayed for thee, that thy faith fail not: and when thou art converted, strengthen thy brethren.

**LUKE 22:32 KJV**

'We . . . bring you good news, that you should turn from these vain things to a living God who made the heaven and the earth and the sea and all that is in them.'

**ACTS 14:15 RSV**

' ''That they may turn from darkness to light and from the power of Satan to God, that they may receive forgiveness of sins and a place among those who are sanctified by faith in me.'' '

**ACTS 26:18 RSV**

For they themselves report concerning us what a welcome we had among you, and how you turned to God from idols, to serve a living and true God.

**1 THESSALONIANS 1:9 RSV**

For you were straying like sheep, but have now returned to the Shepherd and Guardian of your souls.

**1 PETER 2:25 RSV**

See also *Faith; New birth; Repentance.*

## Conviction of sin

For I acknowledge my transgressions and my sin is ever before me. Against thee, thee only, have I sinned, and done this evil in thy sight: that thou mightest be justified when thou speakest, and be clear when thou judgest.

**PSALM 51:3–4 RSV**

And I said: 'Woe is me! For I am lost; for I am a man of unclean lips, and I dwell in the midst of a people of unclean lips; for my eyes have seen the King, the Lord of Hosts!'

**ISAIAH 6:5 RSV**

When Simon Peter saw it, he fell down at Jesus' knees, saying, Depart from me; for I am a sinful man, O Lord.

**LUKE 5:8 KJV**

'And when he [the Holy Spirit] comes, he will convince the world concerning sin and righteousness and judgment: concerning sin, because they do not believe in me.'

**JOHN 16:8–9 RSV**

Now when they heard this they were cut to the heart, and said to Peter and the rest of the apostles, 'Brethren, what shall we do?'

**ACTS 2:37 RSV**

## Counsel

Blessed is the man who walks not in the counsel of the wicked, nor stands in the way of sinners, nor sits in the seat of scoffers.

**PSALM 1:1 RSV**

I will instruct you and teach you the way you should go; I will counsel you with my eye upon you. Be not like a horse or a mule, without understanding, which must be curbed with bit and bridle.

**PSALM 32:8–9 RSV**

The Lord brings the counsel of the nations to naught; he frustrates the plans of the peoples. The counsel of the Lord stands for ever, the thoughts of his heart to all generations.

**PSALM 33:10–11 RSV**

The way of a fool is right in his own eyes, but a wise man listens to advice.
**PROVERBS 12:15 RSV**

Listen to advice and accept instruction, that you may gain wisdom for the future.
**PROVERBS 19:20 RSV**

For unto us a child is born, unto us a son is given: and the government shall be upon his shoulder: and his name shall be called Wonderful, Counsellor, The mighty God, The everlasting Father, The Prince of Peace.
**ISAIAH 9:6 KJV**

O Lord, thou art my God; I will exalt thee, I will praise thy name; for thou hast done wonderful things; thy counsels of old are faithfulness and truth.
**ISAIAH 25:1 KJV**

[Paul to the elders at Ephesus] 'For I did not shrink from declaring to you the whole counsel of God.'
**ACTS 20:27 RSV**

See also *Guidance; Way.*

## Courage

[God to Joshua] 'Be strong and of good courage; for you shall cause this people to inherit the land which I swore to their fathers to give them. Only be strong and very courageous, being careful to do according to all the law which Moses my servant commanded you; turn not from it to the right or to the left, that you may have good success wherever you go. This book of the law shall not depart out of your mouth, but you shall meditate on it day and night, that you may be careful to do according to all that is written in it; for then you shall make your way prosperous, and then you shall have good success. Have I not commanded you? Be strong and of good courage; be not frightened, neither be dismayed; for the Lord your God is with you wherever you go.'
**JOSHUA 1:6–9 RSV**

[Hezekiah's encouragement] 'Be strong and courageous. Do not be afraid or discouraged because of the king of Assyria and the vast army with him, for there is a greater power with us than with him. With him is only the arm of flesh, but

with us is the Lord our God to help us fight our battles.'
**2 CHRONICLES 32:7–8 NIV**

Wait for the Lord; be strong, and let your heart take courage; yea, wait for the Lord!
**PSALM 27:14 RSV**

They brought to him a paralytic, lying on his bed; and when Jesus saw their faith he said to the paralytic, 'Take heart, my son; your sins are forgiven.'
**MATTHEW 9:2 RSV**

Jesus turned, and seeing her he said, 'Take heart, daughter; your faith had made you well.' And instantly the woman was made well.
**MATTHEW 9:22 RSV**

These things I have spoken unto you, that in me ye might have peace. In the world ye shall have tribulation; but be of good cheer; I have overcome the world.
**JOHN 16:33 KJV**

'And now, Lord, look upon their threats, and grant to thy servants to speak thy word with all boldness...'
**ACTS 4:29 RSV**

I will know that you stand firm in one spirit, contending as one man for the faith of the gospel without being frightened in any way by those who oppose you.
**PHILIPPIANS 1:27–28 NIV**

For God hath not given us the spirit of fear; but of power, and of love, and of a sound mind.
**2 TIMOTHY 1:7 KJV**

See also *Comfort; Confidence.*

## Covenant

'And I will establish my covenant between me and you and your descendants after you throughout their generations for an everlasting covenant, to be God to you and to your descendants after you. And I will give to you, and to your descendants after you, the land of your sojournings, all the land of Canaan, for an everlasting possession; and I will be their God... This is my covenant, which you shall keep, between me and you and your descendants after you: Every male among you shall be circumcised.'
**GENESIS 17:7–10 RSV**

And Moses took the blood, and sprinkled it on the people, and said, Behold the blood of the covenant, which the Lord hath made with you concerning all these words.
EXODUS 24:8 KJV

The friendship of the Lord is for those who fear him, and he makes known to them his covenant.
PSALM 25:14 RSV

'This is my blood of the covenant, which is poured out for many for the forgiveness of sins.'
MATTHEW 26:28 RSV

[The Gentiles] Strangers to the covenants of promise . . .
EPHESIANS 2:12 RSV

It follows that it is a greater covenant for which Jesus has become our guarantee.
HEBREWS 7:22 JB

'This is the covenant that I will make with the house of Israel after those days, says the Lord: I will put my laws into their minds, and write them on their hearts, and I will be their God, and they shall be my people.'
HEBREWS 8:10 RSV

Therefore he is the mediator of a new covenant, so that those who are called may receive the promised eternal inheritance, since a death has occurred which redeems them from the transgressions under the first covenant.
HEBREWS 9:15 RSV

Now the God of peace, that brought again from the dead our Lord Jesus, that great shepherd of the sheep, through the blood of the everlasting covenant . . .
HEBREWS 13:20 KJV

And I heard a great voice out of heaven saying, Behold, the tabernacle of God is with men, and he will dwell with them, and they shall be his people, and God himself shall be with them, and be their God.
REVELATION 21:3 KJV

## Covetousness
See *Desire, wrong.*

## Creation

In the beginning God created the heaven and the earth.
GENESIS 1:1 KJV

So God created man in his own image, in the image of God created he him; male and female created he them.
GENESIS 1:27 KJV

When I consider thy heavens, the work of thy fingers, the moon and the stars, which thou hast ordained; what is man, that thou art mindful of him? and the son of man, that thou visitest him?
PSALM 8:3–4 KJV

O come, let us worship, and fall down, and kneel before the Lord our Maker.
PSALM 95:6 BCP

Lift up your eyes on high, and behold who hath created these things, that bringeth out their host by number: he calleth them all by names by the greatness of his might, for that he is strong in power; not one faileth . . . Hast thou not known? hast thou not heard, that the everlasting God, the Lord, the creator of the ends of the earth, fainteth not, neither is weary? There is no searching of his understanding.
ISAIAH 40:26, 28 KJV

And he said to them, 'Go into all the world and preach the gospel to the whole creation.'
MARK 16:15 RSV

Ever since the creation of the world his invisible nature, namely, his eternal power and deity, has been clearly perceived in the things that have been made.
ROMANS 1:20 RSV

For the creation waits with eager longing for the revealing of the sons of God; for the creation was subjected to futility, not of its own will but by the will of him who subjected it in hope; because the creation itself will be set free from its bondage to decay and obtain the glorious liberty of the children of God. We know that the whole creation has been groaning in travail together until now; and not only the creation, but we ourselves, who have the first fruits of the Spirit, groan inwardly as we wait for adoption as sons, the redemption of our bodies.
ROMANS 8:19–23 RSV

Therefore, if any one is in Christ, he is a new creation; the old has passed away, behold, the new has come.
2 CORINTHIANS 5:17 RSV

For we are his workmanship, created in Christ

Jesus unto good works, which God hath before ordained that we should walk in them.
**EPHESIANS 2:10 KJV**

[Christ] He is the image of the invisible God, the first-born of all creation; for in him all things were created, in heaven and on earth, visible and invisible, whether thrones or dominions or principalities or authorities—all things were created through him and for him.
**COLOSSIANS 1:15–16 RSV**

Thou art worthy, O Lord, to receive glory and honour and power: for thou hast created all things, and for thy pleasure they are and were created.
**REVELATION 4:11 KJV**

See also *Providence; Revelation; World.*

## Cross

See *Jesus Christ, Death.*

## Deacon

Now in these days when the disciples were increasing in number, the Hellenists murmured against the Hebrews because their widows were neglected in the daily distribution. And the twelve summoned the body of the disciples and said, 'It is not right that we should give up preaching the word of God to serve tables. Therefore, brethren, pick out from among you seven men of good repute, full of the Spirit and of wisdom, whom we may appoint to this duty. But we will devote ourselves to prayer and to the ministry of the word.'
**ACTS 6:1–4 RSV**

Deacons likewise must be serious, not double-tongued, not addicted to much wine, not greedy for gain; they must hold the mystery of the faith with a clear conscience. And let them also be tested first; then if they prove themselves blameless let them serve as deacons. The women likewise must be serious, no slanderers, but temperate, faithful in all things. Let deacons be the husband of one wife, and let them manage their children and their households well; for those who serve well as deacons gain a good standing for themselves and also great confidence in the faith which is in Christ Jesus.
**1 TIMOTHY 3:8–13 RSV**

See also *Elders; Service.*

## Death

But of the tree of the knowledge of good and evil, thou shalt not eat of it: for in the day that thou eatest thereof thou shalt surely die.
**GENESIS 2:17 KJV**

In the sweat of thy face shalt thou eat bread, till thou return unto the ground; for out of it wast thou taken: for dust thou art, and unto dust shalt thou return.
**GENESIS 3:19 JKV**

Precious in the sight of the Lord is the death of his saints.
**PSALM 116:15 RSV**

There is a way which seemeth right unto a man, but the end thereof are the ways of death.
**PROVERBS 14:12 KJV**

'For I have no pleasure in the death of any one, says the Lord God; so turn, and live.'
**EZEKIEL 18:32 RSV**

'Truly, truly, I say to you, if any one keeps my word, he will never see death.'
**JOHN 8:51 RSV**

For he who has died is freed from sin. But if we have died with Christ, we believe that we shall also live with him . . . So you also must consider yourselves dead to sin and alive to God in Christ Jesus.
**ROMANS 6:7–8, 11 RSV**

For the wages of sin is death; but the gift of God is eternal life through Jesus Christ our Lord.
**ROMANS 6:23 KJV**

But if Christ is in you, although your bodies are dead because of sin, your spirits are alive because of righteousness. If the Spirit of him who raised Jesus from the dead dwells in you, he who raised Christ Jesus from the dead will give life to your mortal bodies also through his Spirit which dwells in you.
**ROMANS 8:10–11 RSV**

If we live, we live to the Lord, and if we die, we die to the Lord; so then, whether we live or whether we die, we are the Lord's. For to this end Christ died and lived again, that he might be Lord both of the dead and of the living.
**ROMANS 14:8–9 RSV**

For as in Adam all die, so also in Christ shall all be made alive.
1 CORINTHIANS 15:22 RSV

The last enemy that shall be destroyed is death.
1 CORINTHIANS 15:26 KJV

So when this corruptible shall have put on incorruption, and this mortal shall have put on immortality, then shall be brought to pass the saying that is written, death is swallowed up in victory. O death, where is thy sting? O grave, where is thy victory?
1 CORINTHIANS 15:54–55 KJV

We are of good courage, and we would rather be away from the body and at home with the Lord.
2 CORINTHIANS 5:8 RSV

As for you, you were dead in your transgressions and sins . . .
EPHESIANS 2:1 NIV

For me to live is Christ, and to die is gain.
PHILIPPIANS 1:21 KJV

I am pulled in two directions. I want very much to leave this life and be with Christ, which is a far better thing . . .
PHILIPPIANS 1:23 GNB

You must put to death, then, the earthly desires at work in you, such as sexual immorality, indecency, lust, evil passions, and greed (for greed is a form of idolatry).
COLOSSIANS 3:5 GNB

he Lord himself shall descend from heaven with a shout, with the voice of the archangel, and with the trump of God: and the dead in Christ shall rise first. Then we which are alive and remain shall be caught up together with them in the clouds, to meet the Lord in the air: and so shall we ever be with the Lord. Wherefore comfort one another with these words.
1 THESSALONIANS 4:16–18 KJV

Our Saviour Christ Jesus, who abolished death and brought life and immortality to life through the gospel.
2 TIMOTHY 1:10 RSV

The saying is sure: If we have died with him, we shall also live with him; if we endure, we shall also reign with him.
2 TIMOTHY 2:11 RSV

Since therefore the children share in flesh and blood, he himself likewise partook of the same nature, that through death he might destroy him who has the power of death, that is, the devil.
HEBREWS 2:14 RSV

It is appointed unto men once to die, but after this the judgment.
HEBREWS 9:27 KJV

Then desire when it has conceived gives birth to sin; and sin when it is full-grown brings forth death.
JAMES 1:15 RSV

Be thou faithful unto death, and I will give thee a crown of life.
REVELATION 2:10 KJV

And God shall wipe away all tears from their eyes; and there shall be no more death, neither sorrow, nor crying, neither shall there be any more pain: for the former things are passed away.
REVELATION 21:4 KJV

See also *Comfort; Last things, Resurrection; Life.*

## Deliverance

See *Redemption; Salvation and Saviour.*

## Demons

When evening came, people brought to Jesus many who had demons in them. Jesus drove out the evil spirits with a word and healed all who were sick.
MATTHEW 8:16 GNB

The demons begged Jesus, 'If you are going to drive us out, send us into that herd of pigs.'
MATTHEW 8:31 GNB

Depart from me, ye cursed, into everlasting fire, prepared for the devil and his angels.
MATTHEW 25:41 KJV

And whenever the unclean spirits beheld him, they fell down before him and cried out, 'You are the Son of God.'
MARK 3:11 RSV

Some teachers of the Law who had come from Jerusalem were saying, 'He has Beelzebul in him! It is the chief of the demons who gives him the power to drive them out.'
MARK 3:22 GNB

As Jesus stepped ashore, he was met by a man from the town who had demons in him. For a long time this man had gone without clothes and would not stay at home, but spent his time in the burial caves.

LUKE 8:27 GNB

And he called the twelve together and gave them power and authority over all demons and to cure diseases . . .

LUKE 10:17 RSV

Now he was casting out a demon that was dumb; when the demon had gone out, the dumb man spoke, and the people marvelled.

LUKE 11:14 RSV

For we wrestle not against flesh and blood, but against principalities, against powers, against the rulers of the darkness of this world, against spiritual wickedness in high places.

EPHESIANS 6:12 KJV

He disarmed the principalities and powers and made a public example of them, triumphing over them in him.

COLOSSIANS 2:15 RSV

Thou believest that there is one God; thou doest well: the devils also believe, and tremble.

JAMES 2:19 KJV

See also *Devil; Occult.*

# Depression

And Job spake, and said, Let the day perish wherein I was born.

JOB 3:2–3 KJV

I am worn out with grief; every night my bed is damp from my weeping; my pillow is soaked with tears. I can hardly see; my eyes are so swollen from the weeping caused by my enemies.

PSALM 6:6–7 GNB

How much longer will you forget me, Lord? For ever? How much longer will you hide yourself from me? How long must I endure trouble? How long will sorrow fill my heart day and night? How long will my enemies triumph over me?

PSALM 13:1–2 GNB

For day and night thy hand was heavy upon me; my strength was dried up as by the heat of summer.

PSALM 32:4 RSV

My tears have been my meat day and night, while they continually say unto me, Where is thy God? . . . all thy waves and thy billows are gone over me.

PSALM 42:3, 7 KJV

A man's spirit will endure sickness; but a broken spirit who can bear?

PROVERBS 18:14 RSV

My soul is bereft of peace, I have forgotten what happiness is . . . Remember my affliction and my bitterness, the wormwood and the gall! My soul continually thinks of it and is bowed down within me. But this I call to mind, and therefore I have hope: The steadfast love of the Lord never ceases, his mercies never come to an end; they are new every morning; great is thy faithfulness. 'The Lord is my portion,' says my soul, 'therefore I will hope in him.'

LAMENTATIONS 3:17, 19–24 RSV

See also *Comfort.*

# Desire

See *Christian life, longing for God.*

# Desire, wrong

Thou shalt not covet thy neighbour's house, thou shalt not covet thy neighbour's wife, nor his manservant, nor his maidservant, nor his ox, no. his ass, nor anything that is thy neighbour's.

EXODUS 20:17 KJV

Give me the desire to obey your laws rather than to get rich. Keep me from paying attention to what is worthless; be good to me, as you have promised.

PSALM 119:36–37 GNB

If you try to make a profit dishonestly, you will get your family into trouble.

PROVERBS 15:27 GNB

'For from the least to the greatest of them, every one is greedy for unjust gain; and from prophet to priest, every one deals falsely.'

JEREMIAH 6:13 RSV

And he said to them, 'Take heed, and beware of all covetousness; for a man's life does not consist in the abundance of his possessions.'

LUKE 12:15 RSV

You may be sure that no one who is immoral, indecent, or greedy (for greed is a form of

idolatry) will ever receive a share in the Kingdom of Christ and of God.
**EPHESIANS 5:5 GNB**

But those who want to get rich fall into temptation and are caught in the trap of many foolish and harmful desires, which pull them down to ruin and destruction.
**1 TIMOTHY 6:9 GNB**

You desire and do not have; so you kill. And you covet and cannot obtain; so you fight and wage war.
**JAMES 4:2 RSV**

Love not the world, neither the things that are in the world. If any man love the world, the love of the Father is not in him. For all that is in the world, the lust of the flesh, and the lust of the eyes, and the pride of life, is not of the Father, but is of the world.
**1 JOHN 2:15–16 KJV**

# Devil

Now the serpent was more subtil than any beast of the field which the Lord God had made. And he said unto the woman, Yea, hath God said, Ye shall not eat of every tree of the garden?
**GENESIS 3:1 KJV**

So Satan went forth from the presence of the Lord, and afflicted Job with loathsome sores from the sole of his foot to the crown of his head.
**JOB 2:7 RSV**

Then Jesus was led up by the Spirit into the wilderness to be tempted by the devil.
**MATTHEW 4:1 RSV**

'When any one hears the word of the kingdom and does not understand it, the evil one comes and snatches away what is sown in his heart; this is what was sown along the path.'
**MATTHEW 13:19 RSV**

'You are of your father the devil, and your will is to do your father's desires. He was a murderer from the beginning, and has nothing to do with the truth, because there is no truth in him. When he lies, he speaks according to his own nature, for he is a liar and the father of lies.'
**JOHN 8:44 RSV**

' ''That they may turn from darkness to light and from the power of Satan to God, that they may receive forgiveness of sins and a place among those who are sanctified by faith in me.'' '
**ACTS 26:18 RSV**

Lest Satan should get an advantage of us: for we are not ignorant of his devices.
**2 CORINTHIANS 2:11 KJV**

In their case the god of this world has blinded the minds of the unbelievers, to keep them from seeing the light of the gospel of the glory of Christ, who is the likeness of God.
**2 CORINTHIANS 4:4 RSV**

Even Satan disguises himself as an angel of light.
**2 CORINTHIANS 11:14 RSV**

As for you, you were dead in your transgressions and sins, in which you used to live when you followed the ways of this world and of the ruler of the kingdom of the air, the spirit who is now at work in those who are disobedient.
**EPHESIANS 2:2 NIV**

Put on the whole armour of God, that ye may be able to stand against the wiles of the devil.
**EPHESIANS 6:11 KJV**

Since therefore the children share in flesh and blood, he himself likewise partook of the same nature, that through death he might destroy him who has the power of death, that is, the devil.
**HEBREWS 2:14 RSV**

Be sober, be watchful. Your adversary the devil prowls around like a roaring lion, seeking some one to devour. Resist him, firm in your faith.
**1 PETER 5:8–9 RSV**

The reason the Son of God appeared was to destroy the works of the devil.
**1 JOHN 3:8 RSV**

We know that we are of God, and the whole world is in the power of the evil one.
**1 JOHN 5:19 RSV**

And the great dragon was thrown down, that ancient serpent, who is called the Devil and Satan, the deceiver of the whole world—he was thrown down to the earth, and his angels were thrown down with him. And I heard a loud voice in heaven, saying, 'Now the salvation and the power and the kingdom of our God and the authority of his Christ have come, for the accuser of our brethren has been thrown down, who accuses them day and night before our God.'
**REVELATION 12:9–10 RSV**

Then the Devil, who deceived them, was thrown into the lake of fire and sulphur, where the beast and the false prophet had already been thrown; and they will be tormented day and night for ever.
REVELATION 20:10 GNB

See also *Demons; Victory.*

## Diligence
See *Work.*

## Discernment

[Solomon's prayer] 'Give thy servant therefore an understanding mind to govern thy people, that I may discern between good and evil; for who is able to govern this thy great people?'
1 KINGS 3:9 RSV

And the spirit of the Lord shall rest upon him, the spirit of wisdom and understanding, the spirit of counsel and might, the spirit of knowledge and of the fear of the Lord.
ISAIAH 11:2 KJV

The man without the spirit does not accept the things that come from the Spirit of God, for they are foolishness to him and he cannot understand them, because they are spiritually discerned.
1 CORINTHIANS 2:14 NIV

To another the ability to distinguish between spirits . . .
1 CORINTHIANS 12:10 RSV

Two or three prophets should speak, and the others should weigh carefully what is said.
1 CORINTHIANS 14:29 NIV

And it is my prayer that your love may abound more and more, with knowledge and all discernment.
PHILIPPIANS 1:9 RSV

For the word of God is living and active, sharper than any two-edged sword, piercing to the division of soul and spirit, of joints and marrow, and discerning the thoughts and intentions of the heart.
HEBREWS 4:12 RSV

But solid food is for the mature, for those who have had their faculties trained by practice to distinguish good from evil.
HEBREWS 5:14 RSV

See also *Examination; Self-examination; Wisdom.*

## Disciples

And he called to him his twelve disciples and gave them authority over unclean spirits, to cast them out, and to heal every disease and every infirmity.
MATTHEW 10:1 RSV

'Go therefore and make disciples of all nations, baptizing them in the name of the Father and of the Son and of the Holy Spirit, teaching them to observe all that I have commanded you; and lo, I am with you always, to the close of the age.'
MATTHEW 28:19–20 RSV

'If any one comes to me and does not hate his own father and mother and wife and children and brothers and sisters, yes, and even his own life, he cannot be my disciple. Whoever does not bear his own cross and come after me, cannot be my disciple . . . so therefore, whoever of you does not renounce all that he has cannot be my disciple.'
LUKE 14:26–27, 33 RSV

Jesus then said to the Jews who had believed in him, 'If you continue in my word, you are truly my disciples.'
JOHN 8:31 RSV

By this shall all men know that ye are my disciples, if ye have love one to another.
JOHN 13:35 KJV

'By this my Father is glorified, that you bear much fruit, and so prove to be my disciples.'
JOHN 15:8 RSV

## Discipline

My son, do not despise the Lord's discipline or be weary of his reproof, for the Lord reproves him whom he loves, as a father the son in whom he delights.
PROVERBS 3:11–12 RSV

'If your brother sins against you, go and tell him his fault, between you and him alone. If he listens to you, you have gained your brother. But if he does not listen, take one or two others along with you, that every word may be confirmed by the evidence of two or three witnesses. If he refuses to listen to them, tell it to the church; and if he refuses to listen even to the church, let him be to you as a Gentile and a tax collector. Truly, I say to you, whatever you bind on earth shall be bound

in heaven, and whatever you loose on earth shall be loosed in heaven.'
**MATTHEW 18:15–18 RSV**

Preach the word, be urgent in season and out of season, convince, rebuke, and exhort, be unfailing in patience and in teaching.
**2 TIMOTHY 4:2 RSV**

It is for discipline that you have to endure. God is treating you as sons; for what son is there whom his father does not discipline? If you are left without discipline, in which all have participated, then you are illegitimate children and not sons. Besides this, we have had earthly fathers to discipline us and we respected them. Shall we not much more be subject to the Father of spirits and live? For they disciplined us for a short time at their pleasure, but he disciplines us for our good, that we may share his holiness. For the moment all discipline seems painful rather than pleasant; later it yields the peaceful fruit of righteousness to those who have been trained by it.
**HEBREWS 12:7–11 RSV**

' "Those whom I love, I reprove and chasten; so be zealous and repent." '
**REVELATION 3:19 KJV**

See also *Family, Children and the whole family.*

# Disobedience

'But if you will not obey the voice of the Lord your God or be careful to do all his commandments and his statutes which I command you this day, then all these curses shall come upon you and overtake you.'
**DEUTERONOMY 28:15 RSV**

'But they did not obey or incline their ear, but walked in their own counsels and the stubbornness of their evil hearts, and went backward and not forward. From the day that your fathers came out of the land of Egypt to this day, I have persistently sent all my servants the prophets to them, day after day; yet they did not listen to me, or incline their ear, but stiffened their neck. They did worse than their fathers . . . And you shall say to them, "This is the nation that did not obey the voice of the Lord their God, and did not accept discipline; truth has perished; it is cut off from their lips." '
**JEREMIAH 7:24–26, 28 RSV**

For as by one man's disobedience many were made sinners, so by one man's obedience many will be made righteous.
**ROMANS 5:19 RSV**

The ruler of the kingdom of the air, the spirit who is now at work in those who are disobedient.
**EPHESIANS 2:2 NIV**

[Jesus will appear] with a flaming fire, to punish those who reject God and who do not obey the Good News about our Lord Jesus.
**2 THESSALONIANS 1:8 GNB**

[In the last days] Men will be lovers of self, lovers of money, proud, arrogant, abusive, disobedient to their parents, ungrateful, unholy.
**2 TIMOTHY 3:2 RSV**

See also *Obedience; Punishment; Submission.*

# Divorce
See *Marriage.*

# Doubt

So Sarah laughed to herself, saying, 'After I have grown old, and my husband is old, shall I have pleasure?' The Lord said to Abraham, 'Why did Sarah laugh, and say, "Shall I indeed bear a child, now that I am old?" Is anything too hard for the Lord? At the appointed time I will return to you, in the spring, and Sarah shall have a son.'
**GENESIS 18:12–14 RSV**

I was afraid and thought that he had driven me out of his presence. But he heard my cry, when I called to him for help.
**PSALM 31:22 GNB**

Why sayest thou, O Jacob, and speakest, O Israel, My way is hid from the Lord, and my judgment is passed over from my God? Hast thou not known? hast thou not heard, that the everlasting God, the Lord, the Creator of the ends of the earth, fainteth not, neither is weary? There is no searching of his understanding.
**ISAIAH 40:27–28 KJV**

Now when John heard in prison about the deeds of the Christ, he sent word by his disciples and said to him, 'Are you he who is to come, or shall we look for another?'
**MATTHEW 11:2–3 RSV**

Jesus immediately reached out his hand and

caught him [Peter], saying to him, 'O man of little faith, why did you doubt?'

**MATTHEW 14:31 RSV**

Jesus answered them, 'Truly, I say to you, if you have faith and never doubt, you will not only do what has been done to the fig tree, but even if you say to this mountain, ''Be taken up and cast into the sea,'' it will be done.'

**MATTHEW 21:21 RSV**

And when they saw him they worshipped him; but some doubted.

**MATTHEW 28:17 RSV**

But he [Thomas] said to them, 'Unless I see in his hands the print of the nails, and place my finger in the mark of the nails, and place my hand in his side, I will not believe.'

**JOHN 20:25 RSV**

But let him ask in faith, with no doubting, for he who doubts is like a wave of the sea that is driven and tossed by the wind.

**JAMES 1:6 RSV**

And I heard a loud voice in heaven, saying, 'Now the salvation and the power and the kingdom of our God and the authority of his Christ have come, for the accuser of our brethren has been thrown down, who accuses them day and night before our God.'

**REVELATION 12:10 RSV**

See also *Assurance; Comfort; Unbelief.*

## Dreams

And he [Jacob] dreamed, and behold a ladder set up on the earth, and the top of it reached to heaven: and behold the angels of God ascending and descending on it.

**GENESIS 28:12 KJV**

Now Joseph had a dream, and when he told it to his brothers they only hated him the more.

**GENESIS 37:5 RSV**

'A prophet or an interpreter of dreams may promise a miracle or a wonder, in order to lead you to worship and serve gods that you have not worshipped before. Even if what he promises comes true, do not pay any attention to him. The Lord your God is using him to test you, to see if you love the Lord with all your heart. Follow the Lord and fear him; obey him and keep his commands; worship him and be faithful to him. But put to death any interpreter of dreams or prophet that tells you to rebel against the Lord, who rescued you from Egypt, where you were slaves. Such a man is evil and is trying to lead you away from the life that the Lord has commanded you to live. He must be put to death, in order to rid yourselves of this evil!'

**DEUTERONOMY 13:1–5 GNB**

When the Lord brought us back to Jerusalem, it was like a dream!

**PSALM 126:1 GNB**

I am against the prophets, says the Lord, who dream lies and retail them, misleading my people with wild and reckless falsehoods. It was not I who sent them or commissioned them, and they will do this people no good.

**JEREMIAH 23:32 NEB**

Daniel answered the king, 'No wise men, enchanters, magicians, or astrologers can show to the king the mystery which the king has asked, but there is a God in heaven who reveals mysteries, and he has made known to King Nebuchadnezzar what will be in the latter days. Your dream and the visions of your head as you lay in bed are these . . .'

**DANIEL 2:27–28 RSV**

'And it shall come to pass afterward, that I will pour out my spirit on all flesh; your sons and your daughters shall prophesy, your old men shall dream dreams, and your young men shall see visions.'

**JOEL 2:28 RSV**

But as he considered this, behold, an angel of the Lord appeared to him in a dream, saying, 'Joseph, son of David, do not fear to take Mary your wife, for that which is conceived in her is of the Holy Spirit.'

**MATTHEW 1:20 RSV**

That night Paul had a vision in which he saw a Macedonian standing and begging him, 'Come over to Macedonia and help us!'

**ACTS 16:9 GNB**

## Drunkenness

Show me someone who drinks too much, who has to try out some new drink, and I will show you someone miserable and sorry for himself, always causing trouble and always complaining. His

eyes are bloodshot, and he has bruises that could have been avoided.
**PROVERBS 23:29–30 GNB**

You are doomed! You get up early in the morning to start drinking, and you spend long evenings getting drunk.
**ISAIAH 5:11 GNB**

'Let us eat and drink, for tomorrow we die.'
**ISAIAH 22:13 RSV**

These also reel with wine and stagger with strong drink; the priest and the prophet reel with strong drink, they are confused with wine, they stagger with strong drink; they err in vision, they stumble in giving judgment.
**ISAIAH 28:7 RSV**

Let us conduct ourselves properly, as people who live in the light of day—no orgies or drunkenness . . .
**ROMANS 13:13 GNB**

Now the works of the flesh are plain: . . . drunkenness, carousing, and the like.
**GALATIANS 5:19, 21 RSV**

And be not drunk with wine, wherein is excess; but be filled with the Spirit.
**EPHESIANS 5:18 KJV**

See also *Temperance.*

# Eden, garden of

And the Lord God planted a garden eastward in Eden; and there he put the man whom he had formed. And out of the ground made the Lord God to grow every tree that is pleasant to the sight, and good for food; the tree of life also in the midst of the garden, and the tree of knowledge of good and evil . . . And the Lord God took the man, and put him into the garden of Eden to dress it and to keep it. And the Lord God commanded the man, saying, Of every tree of the garden thou mayest freely eat: but of the tree of the knowledge of good and evil, thou shalt not eat of it: for in the day that thou eatest thereof thou shalt surely die.
**GENESIS 2:8–9, 15–17 KJV**

Therefore the Lord God sent him forth from the garden of Eden, to till the ground from whence he was taken. So he drove out the man; and he placed at the east of the garden of Eden Cherubims, and a flaming sword which turned

every way, to keep the way of the tree of life.
**GENESIS 3:23–24 KJV**

# Education
See *Teachers and teaching.*

# Elders

'Go and gather the elders of Israel together, and say to them, "The Lord, the God of your fathers, the God of Abraham, of Isaac, and of Jacob, has appeared to me." '
**EXODUS 3:16 RSV**

And the disciples determined, every one according to his ability, to send relief to the brethren who lived in Judea; and they did so, sending it to the elders by the hand of Barnabas and Saul.
**ACTS 11:29–30 RSV**

And when they had appointed elders for them in every church, with prayer and fasting, they committed them to the Lord in whom they believed.
**ACTS 14:23 RSV**

[Paul to the elders of the church at Ephesus] 'Take heed to yourselves and to all the flock, in which the Holy Spirit has made you overseers, to care for the church of God which he obtained with the blood of his own Son.'
**ACTS 20:28 RSV**

Now we ask you, brothers, to respect those who work hard among you, who are over you in the Lord and who admonish you. Hold them in the highest regard in love because of their work.
**1 THESSALONIANS 5:12–13 NIV**

This is a true saying: If a man is eager to be a church leader, he desires an excellent work. A church leader must be without fault; he must have only one wife, be sober, self-controlled, and orderly; he must welcome strangers in his home; he must be able to teach; he must not be a drunkard or a violent man, but gentle and peaceful; he must not love money; he must be able to manage his own family well and make his children obey him with all respect.
**1 TIMOTHY 3:1–4 GNB**

Let the elders who rule well be considered worthy of double honour, especially those who labour in preaching and teaching.
**1 TIMOTHY 5:17 RSV**

This is why I left you in Crete, that you might amend what was defective, and appoint elders in every town as I directed you.
TITUS 1:5 RSV

Remember your leaders, those who spoke to you the word of God; consider the outcome of their life, and imitate their faith.
HEBREWS 13:7 RSV

Obey your leaders and submit to them; for they are keeping watch over your souls, as men who will have to give account. Let them do this joyfully, and not sadly, for that would be of no advantage to you.
HEBREWS 13:17 RSV

Is any sick among you? Let him call for the elders of the church; and let them pray over him, anointing him with oil in the name of the Lord.
JAMES 5:14 KJV

I, who am an elder myself, appeal to the church elders among you. I am a witness of Christ's sufferings, and I will share in the glory that will be revealed. I appeal to you to be shepherds of the flock that God gave you and to take care of it willingly, as God wants you to, and not unwillingly. Do your work not for mere pay, but from a real desire to serve. Do not try to rule over those who have been put in your care, but be examples to the flock.
1 PETER 5:1–3 GNB

See also **Deacon; Pastor.**

# Election

'All things have been delivered to me by my Father; and no one knows the Son except the Father, and no one knows the Father except the Son and any one to whom the Son chooses to reveal him.'
MATTHEW 11:27 RSV

Then shall the King say unto them on his right hand, 'Come, ye blessed of my Father, inherit the kingdom prepared for you from the foundation of the world.'
MATTHEW 25:34 KJV

All that the Father giveth me shall come to me; and him that cometh to me I will in no wise cast out.
JOHN 6:37 KJV

'No one can come to me unless the Father who sent me draws him; and I will raise him up at the last day.'
JOHN 6:44 RSV

'You did not choose me, but I chose you and appointed you that you should go and bear fruit and that your fruit should abide.'
JOHN 15:16 RSV

'I have manifested thy name to the men whom thou gavest me out of the world; thine they were, and thou gavest them to me, and they have kept thy word.'
JOHN 17:6 RSV

And when the Gentiles heard this, they were glad and glorified the word of God; and as many as were ordained to eternal life believed.
ACTS 13:48 RSV

For those whom he foreknew he also predestined to be conformed to the image of his Son, in order that he might be the first-born among many brethren. And those whom he predestined he also called; and those whom he called he also justified; and those whom he justified he also glorified . . . Who shall bring any charge against God's elect?
ROMANS 8:29–30, 33 RSV

For he says to Moses, 'I will have mercy on whom I have mercy, and I will have compassion on whom I have compassion.' So it depends not upon man's will or exertion, but upon God's mercy.
ROMANS 9:15–16 RSV

Even before the world was made, God had already chosen us to be his through our union with Christ, so that we would be holy and without fault before him. Because of his love God had already decided that through Jesus Christ he would make us his sons—this was his pleasure and purpose.
EPHESIANS 1:4–5 GNB

You are the people of God; he loved you and chose you for his own. So then, you must clothe yourselves with compassion, kindness, humility, gentleness, and patience.
COLOSSIANS 3:12 GNB

But we are bound to give thanks to God always for you, brethren beloved by the Lord, because God chose you from the beginning to be saved,

through sanctification by the Spirit and belief in the truth.
2 THESSALONIANS 2:13 RSV

Elect according to the foreknowledge of God the Father, through sanctification of the Spirit, unto obedience and sprinkling of the blood of Jesus Christ.
1 PETER 1:2 KJV

But you are a chosen race, a royal priesthood, a holy nation, God's own people, that you may declare the wonderful deeds of him who called you out of darkness into his marvellous light.
1 PETER 2:9 RSV

Therefore, brethren, be the more zealous to confirm your call and election, for if you do this you will never fall.
2 PETER 1:10 RSV

See also *Christian life, Calling of the Christian; Grace.*

## Encouragement

And he [Peter] testified with many other words and exhorted them, saying, 'Save yourselves from this crooked generation.'
ACTS 2:40 RSV

Joseph who was surnamed by the apostles Barnabas (which means, Son of encouragement), a Levite, a native of Cyprus.
ACTS 4:36 RSV

When he [Barnabas] came and saw the grace of God, he was glad; and he exhorted them all to remain faithful to the Lord with steadfast purpose.
ACTS 11:23 RSV

[Paul and Barnabas] Strengthening the souls of the disciples, exhorting them to continue in the faith, and saying that through many tribulations we must enter the kingdom of God.
ACTS 14:22 RSV

Judas and Silas, being themselves prophets, spoke for a long time, encouraging and strengthening the brothers.
ACTS 15:32 JB

If it [a man's gift] is encouraging, let him encourage.
ROMANS 12:8 NIV

You know that we treated each one of you just as a father treats his own children. We encouraged you, we comforted you, and we kept urging you to live the kind of life that pleases God.
1 THESSALONIANS 2:11–12 GNB

And we urge you, brothers, warn those who are idle, encourage the timid, help the weak, be patient with everyone.
1 THESSALONIANS 5:14 NIV

Preach the word, be urgent in season and out of season, convince, rebuke, and exhort, be unfailing in patience and in teaching.
2 TIMOTHY 4:2 RSV

But encourage one another daily, as long as it is called Today, so that none of you may be hardened by sin's deceitfulness.
HEBREWS 3:13 NIV

Let us consider how to stir up one another to love and good works, not neglecting to meet together, as is the habit of some, but encouraging one another, and all the more as you see the Day drawing near.
HEBREWS 10:24–25 RSV

See also *Comfort; Fellowship.*

## Endurance

'But he who endures to the end will be saved.'
MATTHEW 10:22 RSV

'He has no root in himself, but endures for a while, and when tribulation or persecution arises on account of the word, immediately he falls away.'
MATTHEW 13:21 RSV

Endurance produces character, and character produces hope.
ROMANS 5:4 RSV

No temptation has overtaken you that is not common to man. God is faithful, and he will not let you be tempted beyond your strength, but with the temptation will also provide the way of escape, that you may be able to endure it.
1 CORINTHIANS 10:13 RSV

Put on the whole armour of God, that ye may be able to stand against the wiles of the devil . . . praying always with all prayer and supplication in the Spirit, and watching thereunto with all perseverance and supplication for all saints.
EPHESIANS 6:11, 18 KJV

May you be strengthened with all power, according to his glorious might, for all endurance and patience with joy.
COLOSSIANS 1:11 RSV

Share in suffering as a good solider of Christ Jesus.
2 TIMOTHY 2:3 RSV

If we endure, we shall also reign with him; if we deny him, he also will deny us.
2 TIMOTHY 2:12 RSV

Looking unto Jesus the author and finisher of our faith; who for the joy that was set before him endured the cross, despising the shame, and is set down at the right hand of the throne of God.
HEBREWS 12:2 KJV

Blessed is the man who endures trial, for when he has stood the test he will receive the crown of life which God has promised to those who love him.
JAMES 1:12 RSV

See also *Christian life, Continuing in the faith; Victory; Zeal.*

## Enemy

'If you meet your enemy's ox or his ass going astray, you shall bring it back to him. If you see the ass of one who hates you lying under its burden, you shall refrain from leaving him with it, you shall help him to lift it up.'
EXODUS 23:4–5 RSV

When a man's ways please the Lord, he makes even his enemies to be at peace with him.
PROVERBS 16:7 RSV

Do not rejoice when your enemy falls, do not gloat when he is brought down.
PROVERBS 24:17 NEB

If your enemy is hungry, give him bread to eat; and if he is thirsty, give him water to drink; for you will heap coals of fire on his head, and the Lord will reward you.
PROVERBS 25:21–22 RSV

Ye have heard that it hath been said, Thou shalt love thy neighbour, and hate thine enemy. But I say unto you, Love your enemies, bless them that curse you, do good to them that hate you, and pray for them which despitefully use you, and persecute you.
MATTHEW 5:43–44 KJV

For if while we were enemies we were reconciled to God by the death of his Son, much more, now that we are reconciled, shall we be saved by his life.
ROMANS 5:10 RSV

## Enjoyment
See *Joy.*

## Envy

Fret not thy self because of evildoers, neither be thou envious against the workers of iniquity.
PSALM 37:1 KJV

For I was envious of the arrogant, when I saw the prosperity of the wicked.
PSALM 73:3 RSV

Then I saw that all toil and all skill in work come from a man's envy of his neighbour.
ECCLESIASTES 4:4 RSV

For he [Pontius Pilate] knew that it was out of envy that they had delivered him up.
MATTHEW 27:18 RSV

Now the works of the flesh are plain: . . . anger, selfishness, dissension, party spirit, envy . . .
GALATIANS 5:19, 21 RSV

So put away all malice and guile and insincerity and envy and all slander.
1 PETER 2:1 RSV

See also *Jealousy.*

## Eucharist
See *Communion.*

## Evangelism
See *Witness.*

## Evangelists

And on that day a great persecution arose against the church in Jerusalem; and they were all scattered throughout the region of Judea and Samaria, except the apostles . . . Now those who were scattered went about preaching the word. Philip went down to a city of Samaria, and proclaimed to them the Christ . . . When they believed Philip as he preached good news about the kingdom of God and the name of Jesus Christ, they were baptized, both men and women.
ACTS 8:1, 4–5, 12 RSV

Then Philip opened his mouth, and beginning with this scripture he told him the good news of Jesus.
ACTS 8:35 RSV

On the following day we left and arrived in Caesarea. There we stayed at the house of Philip the evangelist.
ACTS 21:8 GNB

And his gifts were that some should be apostles, some prophets, some evangelists . . .
EPHESIANS 4:11 RSV

As for you, always be steady, endure suffering, do the work of an evangelist, fulfil your ministry.
2 TIMOTHY 4:5 RSV

See also *Witness.*

# Evil

For God doth know that in the day ye eat thereof, then your eyes shall be opened, and ye shall be as gods, knowing good and evil.
GENESIS 3:5 KJV

Shall there be evil in a city, and the Lord hath not done it?
AMOS 3:6 KJV

Thou who art of purer eyes than to behold evil and canst not look on wrong.
HABAKKUK 1:13 RSV

Take therefore no thought for the morrow: for the morrow shall take thought for the things of itself. Sufficient unto the day is the evil thereof.
MATTHEW 6:34 KJV

And he [Pontius Pilate] said, 'Why, what evil has he done?' But they shouted all the more, 'Let him be crucified.'
MATTHEW 27:23 RSV

And he said, 'What comes out of a man is what defiles a man. For from within, out of the heart of man, come evil thoughts . . .'
MARK 7:21 RSV

And this is the judgment, that the light has come into the world, and men loved darkness rather than light, because their deeds were evil.
JOHN 3:19 RSV

For I do not do the good I want, but the evil I do not want is what I do.
ROMANS 7:19 RSV

Let love be genuine; hate what is evil, hold fast to what is good.
ROMANS 12:9 RSV

See that none of you repays evil for evil, but always seek to do good to one another and to all.
1 THESSALONIANS 5:15 RSV

Abstain from all appearance of evil.
1 THESSALONIANS 5:22 KJV

For the love of money is the root of all evil.
1 TIMOTHY 6:10 KJV

I am writing to you, young men, because you have overcome the evil one.
1 JOHN 2:13 RSV

# Examination

Search me, O God, and know my heart: try me, and know my thoughts. And see if there be any wicked way in me, and lead me in the way everlasting.
PSALM 139:23–24 KJV

[The Jews at Berea] These were more noble than those in Thessalonica, in that they received the word with all readiness of mind, and searched the scriptures daily, whether those things were so.
ACTS 17:11 KJV

And he who searches the hearts of men knows what is the mind of the Spirit.
ROMANS 8:27 RSV

Prove all things; hold fast that which is good.
1 THESSALONIANS 5:21 KJV

Beloved, do not believe every spirit, but test the spirits to see whether they are of God.
1 JOHN 4:1 RSV

See also *Discernment; Self-examination.*

# Faith

And he [Abraham] believed in the Lord; and he counted it to him for righteousness.
GENESIS 15:6 KJV

The Lord is my rock, and my fortress, and my deliverer, my God, my rock, in whom I take refuge, my shield, and the horn of my salvation, my stronghold.
PSALM 18:2 RSV

Trust in the Lord, and do good; so you will dwell in the land, and enjoy security. Take delight in the Lord, and he will give you the desires of your heart. Commit your way to the Lord; trust in him, and he will act.
PSALM 37:3–5 RSV

Trust in the Lord with all thine heart; and lean not unto thine own understanding.
PROVERBS 3:5 KJV

The righteous shall live by his faith.
HABAKKUK 2:4 RSV

And he said to them, 'Why are you afraid, O men of little faith?'
MATTHEW 8:26 RSV

And Jesus said to him, ' . . . All things are possible to him who believes.' Immediately the father of the child cried out and said, 'I believe; help my unbelief!'
MARK 9:23–24 RSV

And Jesus answered them, 'Have faith in God . . . I tell you, whatever you ask in prayer, believe that you have received it, and it will be yours.'
MARK 11:22, 24 RSV

But as many as received him, to them gave he power to become the sons of God, even to them that believe on his name.
JOHN 1:12 KJV

For God so loved the world, that he gave his only begotten Son, that whosoever believeth in him should not perish, but have everlasting life.
JOHN 3:16 KJV

He who believes in him is not condemned; he who does not believe is condemned already, because he has not believed in the name of the only Son of God.
JOHN 3:18 RSV

Jesus answered them, 'This is the work of God, that you believe in him whom he has sent.'
JOHN 6:29 RSV

Let not your heart be troubled: ye believe in God, believe also in me.
JOHN 14:1 KJV

These [signs] are written that you may believe that Jesus is the Christ, the Son of God, and that believing you may have life in his name.
JOHN 20:31 RSV

And what they said pleased the whole multitude, and they chose Stephen, a man full of faith and of the Holy Spirit.
ACTS 6:5 RSV

And they said, 'Believe in the Lord Jesus, and you will be saved, you and your household.'
ACTS 16:31 RSV

[Christ Jesus] whom God hath set forth to be a propitiation through faith in his blood.
ROMANS 3:25 KJV

Therefore being justified by faith, we have peace with God through our Lord Jesus Christ.
ROMANS 5:1 KJV

That if thou shalt confess with thy mouth the Lord Jesus, and shalt believe in thine heart that God hath raised him from the dead, thou shalt be saved. For with the heart man believeth unto righteousness; and with the mouth confession is made unto salvation.
ROMANS 10:9–10 KJV

So faith comes from what is heard, and what is heard comes by the preaching of Christ.
ROMANS 10:17 RSV

So faith, hope, love abide, these three; but the greatest of these is love.
1 CORINTHIANS 13:13 RSV

We walk by faith, not by sight.
2 CORINTHIANS 5:7 RSV

I have been crucified with Christ; it is no longer I who live, but Christ who lives in me; and the life I now live in the flesh I live by faith in the Son of God, who loved me and gave himself for me.
GALATIANS 2:20 RSV

For by grace are ye saved through faith; and that not of yourselves: it is the gift of God.
EPHESIANS 2:8 KJV

Above all, taking the shield of faith, wherewith ye shall be able to quench all the fiery darts of the wicked.
EPHESIANS 6:16 KJV

Now faith is the substance of things hoped for, the evidence of things not seen.
HEBREWS 11:1 KJV

By faith we understand that the world was created by the word of God, so that what is seen was made out of things which do not appear.
HEBREWS 11:3 RSV

But without faith it is impossible to please him: for he that cometh to God must believe that he is, and that he is a rewarder of them that diligently seek him.

HEBREWS 11:6 KJV

What does it profit, my brethren, if a man says he has faith but has not works? Can his faith save him?

JAMES 2:14 RSV

You see that faith was active along with his works, and faith was completed by works ... For as the body apart from the spirit is dead, so faith apart from works is dead.

JAMES 2:22, 26 RSV

Every one who believes that Jesus is the Christ is a child of God.

1 JOHN 5:1 RSV

For whatever is born of God overcomes the world; and this is the victory that overcomes the world, our faith.

1 JOHN 5:4 RSV

See also **Conversion; Repentance; Righteousness.**

## Faithfulness, faithful

'Know therefore that the Lord your God is God, the faithful God who keeps covenant and steadfast love with those who love him and keep his commandments, to a thousand generations.'

DEUTERONOMY 7:9 RSV

Many a man proclaims his own loyalty, but a faithful man who can find?

PROVERBS 20:6 RSV

The steadfast love of the Lord never ceases, his mercies never come to an end; they are new every morning; great is thy faithfulness.

LAMENTATIONS 3:22–23 RSV

'Who then is the faithful and wise servant, whom his master has set over his household, to give them their food at the proper time?'

MATTHEW 24:45 RSV

His lord said unto him, Well done, thou good and faithful servant: thou hast been faithful over a few things, I will make thee ruler over many things: enter thou into the joy of thy lord.

MATTHEW 25:21 KJV

'He who is faithful in a very little is faithful also in much; and he who is dishonest in a very little is dishonest also in much.'

LUKE 16:10 RSV

God is faithful, and he will not let you be tempted beyond your strength, but with the temptation will also provide the way of escape, that you may be able to endure it.

1 CORINTHIANS 10:13 RSV

But the fruit of the Spirit is ... faithfulness ...

GALATIANS 5:22 RSV

What you have heard from me before many witnesses entrust to faithful men who will be able to teach others also.

2 TIMOTHY 2:2 RSV

If we are faithless, he remains faithful—for he cannot deny himself.

2 TIMOTHY 2:13 RSV

For this reason he had to be made like his brothers in every way, in order that he might become a merciful and faithful high priest in service to God, and that he might make atonement for the sins of the people.

HEBREWS 2:17 NIV

Behold, the devil shall cast some of you into prison, that ye may be tried; and ye shall have tribulation ten days: be thou faithful unto death, and I will give thee a crown of life.

REVELATION 2:10 KJV

See also **Mercy.**

## Fall, *the*

Now the serpent was more subtil than any beast of the field which the Lord God had made. And he said unto the woman, Yea, hath God said, Ye shall not eat of every tree of the garden? ... And the serpent said unto the woman, Ye shall not surely die ... And when the woman saw that the tree was good for food, and that it was pleasant to the eyes, and a tree to be desired to make one wise, she took of the fruit thereof, and did eat, and gave also unto her husband with her; and he did eat. And the eyes of them both were opened, and they knew that they were naked; and they sewed fig leaves together, and made themselves aprons ... and Adam and his wife hid themselves from the presence of the Lord God amongst the trees of the garden.

GENESIS 3:1, 4, 6–8 KJV

Unto the woman he said, I will greatly multiply thy sorrow and thy conception; in sorrow thou shalt bring forth children; and thy desire shall be to thy husband, and he shall rule over thee. And unto Adam he said, Because thou hast hearkened unto the voice of thy wife, and hast eaten of the tree, of which I commanded thee, saying, Thou shalt not eat of it: cursed is the ground for thy sake; in sorrow shalt thou eat of it all the days of thy life . . . in the sweat of thy face shalt thou eat bread, till thou return unto the ground; for out of it wast thou taken: for dust thou art, and unto dust shalt thou return.

GENESIS 3:16–19 KJV

As by one man sin entered into the world, and death by sin . . . so death passed upon all men, for that all have sinned.

ROMANS 5:12 KJV

But the free gift is not like the trespass. For if many died through one man's trespass, much more have the grace of God and the free gift in the grace of that one man Jesus Christ abounded for many. And the free gift is not like the effect of that one man's sin. For the judgment following one trespass brought condemnation, but the free gift following many trespasses brings justification. If, because of one man's trespass, death reigned through that one man, much more will those who receive the abundance of grace and the free gift of righteousness reign in life through the one man Jesus Christ. Then as one man's trespass led to condemnation for all men, so one man's act of righteousness leads to acquittal and life for all men. For as by one man's disobedience many were made sinners, so by one man's obedience many will be made righteous.

ROMANS 5:15–19 RSV

See also *Adam; Eden, garden of.*

## Falling away

The backslider in heart shall be filled with his own ways: and a good man shall be satisfied from himself.

PROVERBS 14:14 KJV

'But they did not obey or incline their ear, but walked in their own counsels and the stubbornness of their evil hearts, and went backward and not forward.'

JEREMIAH 7:24 RSV

'Though our iniquities testify against us, act, O Lord, for thy name's sake; for our backslidings are many, we have sinned against thee.'

JEREMIAH 14:7 RSV

'You, like your ancestors before you, have turned away from my laws and have not kept them. Turn back to me, and I will turn to you. But you ask, "What must we do to turn back to you?"'

MALACHI 3:7 GNB

Then Jesus said to them, 'You will all fall away because of me this night; for it is written, "I will strike the shepherd, and the sheep of the flock will be scattered."'

MATTHEW 26:31 RSV

'If a man does not abide in me, he is cast forth as a branch and withers; and the branches are gathered, thrown into the fire and burned.'

JOHN 15:6 RSV

'I have said all this to you to keep you from falling away.'

JOHN 16:1 RSV

Now the Spirit expressly says that in later times some will depart from the faith by giving heed to deceitful spirits and doctrines of demons.

1 TIMOTHY 4:1 RSV

For how can those who abandon their faith be brought back to repent again? They were once in God's light; they tasted heaven's gift and received their share of the Holy Spirit; they knew from experience that God's word is good, and they had felt the powers of the coming age. And then they abandoned their faith! It is impossible to bring them back to repent again, because they are again crucifying the Son of God and exposing him to public shame.

HEBREWS 6:4–6 GNB

For if we sin deliberately after receiving the knowledge of the truth, there no longer remains a sacrifice for sins.

HEBREWS 10:26 RSV

See also *Rejection; Repentance; Unbelief.*

## Family

### HUSBANDS AND WIVES

Therefore shall a man leave his father and his mother, and shall cleave unto his wife: and they shall be one flesh.

GENESIS 2:24 KJV

A good wife is the crown of her husband, but she who brings shame is like rottenness in his bones.
PROVERBS 12:4 RSV

He who finds a wife finds a good thing, and obtains favour from the Lord.
PROVERBS 18:22 RSV

A good wife who can find? She is far more precious than jewels.
PROVERBS 31:10 RSV

For the unbelieving husband is consecrated through his wife, and the unbelieving wife is consecrated through her husband. Otherwise, your children would be unclean, but as it is they are holy.
1 CORINTHIANS 7:14 RSV

But I want you to understand that the head of every man is Christ, the head of a woman is her husband, and the head of Christ is God.
1 CORINTHIANS 11:3 RSV

Be subject to one another out of reverence for Christ. Wives, be subject to your husbands, as to the Lord, For the husband is the head of the wife as Christ is the head of the church, his body, and is himself its Saviour. As the church is subject to Christ, so let wives also be subject in everything to their husbands. Husbands, love your wives, as Christ loved the church and gave himself up for her ... Even so husbands should love their wives as their own bodies. He who loves his wife loves himself.
EPHESIANS 5:21–25, 28 RSV

In the same way you wives must submit to your husbands, so that if any of them do not believe God's word, your conduct will win them over to believe. It will not be necessary for you to say a word, because they will see how pure and reverent your conduct is. You should not use outward aids to make yourselves beautiful, such as the way you do your hair, or the jewellery you put on, or the dresses you wear. Instead, your beauty should consist of your true inner self, the ageless beauty of a gentle and quiet spirit, which is of the greatest value in God's sight. For the devout women of the past who placed their hope in God used to make themselves beautiful by submitting to their husbands. Sarah was like that; she obeyed Abraham and called him her master. You are now her daughters if you do good and are not afraid of anything. In the same way you husbands must live with your wives with the proper understanding that they are the weaker sex. Treat them with respect, because they also will receive, together with you, God's gift of life. Do this so that nothing will interfere with your prayers.
1 PETER 3:1–7 GNB

See also *Marriage.*

## CHILDREN AND THE WHOLE FAMILY

Honour thy father and thy mother: that thy days may be long upon the land which the Lord thy God giveth thee.
EXODUS 20:12 KJV

'You shall teach them [the words the Lord commands] diligently to your children, and shall talk of them when you sit in your house, and when you walk by the way, and when you lie down, and when you rise.'
DEUTERONOMY 6:7 RSV

[Joshua] But as for me and my house, we will serve the Lord.
JOSHUA 24:15 KJV

She [Hannah] vowed a vow and said, 'O Lord of hosts, if thou wilt indeed look on the affliction of thy maidservant, and remember me, and not forget thy maidservant, but wilt give to thy maidservant a son, then I will give him to the Lord all the days of his life, and no razor shall touch his head.'
1 SAMUEL 1:11 RSV

Lo, children are an heritage of the Lord: and the fruit of the womb is his reward. As arrows are in the hand of a mighty man; so are children of the youth. Happy is the man that hath his quiver full of them: they shall not be ashamed, but they shall speak with the enemies in the gate.
PSALM 127:3–5 KJV

A father who spares the rod hates his son, but one who loves him keeps him in order.
PROVERBS 13:24 NEB

Children's children are a crown to the aged, and parents are the pride of their children.
PROVERBS 17:6 NIV

Train up a child in the way he should go: and when he is old, he will not depart from it.
PROVERBS 22:6 KJV

'Whoever loves his father or mother more than me is not fit to be my disciple; whoever loves his

son or daughter more than me is not fit to be my disciple.'
MATTHEW 10:37 GNB

'But you teach that if a person has something he could use to help his father or mother, but says, "This is Corban" (which means, it belongs to God), he is excused from helping his father or mother.'
MARK 7:11–12 GNB

And they brought young children to him, that he should touch them: and his disciples rebuked those that brought them. But when Jesus saw it, he was much displeased, and said unto them, Suffer the little children to come unto me, and forbid them not: for of such is the kingdom of God. Verily I say unto you, Whosoever shall not receive the kingdom of God as a little child, he shall not enter therein. And he took them up in his arms, put his hands upon them, and blessed them.
MARK 10:13–16 KJV

[Jesus and his parents] And he went down with them and came to Nazareth, and was obedient to them; and his mother kept all these things in her heart. And Jesus increased in wisdom and stature, and in favour with God and man.
LUKE 2:51–52 RSV

Children, obey your parents in the Lord, for this is right. 'Honour your father and mother' (this is the first commandment with a promise).
EPHESIANS 6:1–2 RSV

Fathers, do not provoke your children to anger, but bring them up in the discipline and instruction of the Lord.
EPHESIANS 6:4 RSV

Children, obey your parents in everything, for this pleases the Lord.
COLOSSIANS 3:20 RSV

[A church leader] must be able to manage his own family well and make his children obey him with all respect.
1 TIMOTHY 3:4 GNB

If any one does not provide for his relatives, and especially for his own family, he has disowned the faith and is worse than an unbeliever.
1 TIMOTHY 5:8 RSV

See also *Teachers and teaching.*

# Fasting

'The tenth day of this seventh month is the Day of Atonement. Hold a sacred assembly and deny yourselves, and present an offering made to the Lord by fire.'
LEVITICUS 23:27 NIV

Then David took hold of his clothes, and rent them; and so did all the men who were with him; and they mourned and wept and fasted until evening for Saul and for Jonathan his son and for the people of the Lord and for the house of Israel, because they had fallen by the sword.
2 SAMUEL 1:11–12 RSV

The people ask, 'Why should we fast if the Lord never notices? Why should we go without food if he pays no attention?' The Lord says to them, 'The truth is that at the same time as you fast, you pursue your own interests and oppress your workers. Your fasting makes you violent, and you quarrel and fight. Do you think this kind of fasting will make me listen to your prayers? . . . The kind of fasting I want is this: Remove the chains of oppression and the yoke of injustice, and let the oppressed go free.'
ISAIAH 58:3–4, 6 GNB

'Yet even now,' says the Lord, 'return to me with all your heart, with fasting, with weeping, and with mourning; and rend your hearts and not your garments.'
JOEL 2:12–13 RSV

He [Jesus] fasted for forty days and forty nights, after which he was very hungry.
MATTHEW 4:2 JB

'And when you fast, do not put on a sad face as the hypocrites do. They neglect their appearance so that everyone will see that they are fasting. I assure you, they have already been paid in full. When you go without food, wash your face and comb your fair, so that others cannot know that you are fasting—only your Father, who is unseen, will know. And your Father, who sees what you do in private, will reward you.'
MATTHEW 6:16–18 GNB

Jesus answered, 'Do you expect the guests at a wedding party to be sad as long as the bridegroom is with them? Of course not! But the day will come when the bridegroom will be taken away from them, and then they will fast.'
MATTHEW 9:15 GNB

[A Pharisee] ' ''I fast twice a week, I give tithes of all that I get.'' '
LUKE 18:12 RSV

While they were worshipping the Lord and fasting, the Holy Spirit said, 'Set apart for me Barnabas and Saul for the work to which I have called them.' Then after fasting and praying they laid their hands on them and sent them off.
ACTS 12:2–3 RSV

## Father
See *Family; God, Names, titles and descriptions of God.*

## Fear

And he [Adam] said, I heard thy voice in the garden, and I was afraid, because I was naked; and I hid myself.
GENESIS 3:10 KJV

And Moses hid his face; for he was afraid to look upon God.
EXODUS 3:6 KJV

And the hearts of the people melted, and became as water.
JOSHUA 7:5 RSV

Fear and trembling come upon me, and horror overwhelms me.
PSALM 55:5 RSV

'So do not be afraid of people. Whatever is not covered up will be uncovered, and every secret will be made known.'
MATTHEW 10:26 GNB

'Do not be afraid of those who kill the body but cannot kill the soul; rather be afraid of God, who can destroy both body and soul in hell.'
MATTHEW 10:28, 31 GNB

He said to them, 'Why are you afraid? Have you no faith?'
MARK 4:40 RSV

'People will faint from fear as they wait for what is coming over the whole earth, for the powers in space will be driven from their courses.'
LUKE 21:26 GNB

Yet for fear of the Jews no one spoke openly of him.
JOHN 7:13 RSV

For you did not receive the spirit of slavery to fall back into fear, but you have received the spirit of sonship.
ROMANS 8:15 RSV

And I was with you in weakness and in much fear and trembling.
1 CORINTHIANS 2:3 RSV

There is no fear in love, but perfect love casts out fear. For fear has to do with punishment, and he who fears is not perfected in love.
1 JOHN 4:18 RSV

See also *Comfort.*

## Fear of God
See *Reverence.*

## Fellowship

And they continued stedfastly in the apostles' doctrine and fellowship, and in breaking of bread, and in prayers.
ACTS 2:42 KJV

And all who believed were together and had all things in common.
ACTS 2:44 RSV

God is faithful, by whom you were called into the fellowship of his son, Jesus Christ our Lord.
1 CORINTHIANS 1:9 RSV

The cup of blessing which we bless, is it not a participation in the blood of Christ? The bread which we break, is it not a participation in the body of Christ? Because there is one bread, we who are many are one body, for we all partake of the one bread.
1 CORINTHIANS 10:16–17 RSV

The grace of the Lord Jesus Christ, the love of God, and the fellowship of the Holy Spirit be with you all.
2 CORINTHIANS 13:13 GNB

James and Cephas and John, who were reputed to be pillars, gave to me and Barnabas the right hand of fellowship, that we should go to the Gentiles and they to the circumcised.
GALATIANS 2:9 RSV

Your fellowship in the gospel.
PHILIPPIANS 1:5 KJV

No church entered into partnership with me in giving and receiving except you only.
PHILIPPIANS 4:15 RSV

But rejoice in so far as you share Christ's sufferings, that you may also rejoice and be glad when his glory is revealed.

1 PETER 4:13 RSV

That which we have seen and heard declare we unto you, that ye also may have fellowship with us: and truly our fellowship is with the Father, and with his Son Jesus Christ.

1 JOHN 1:3 KJV

If we say we have fellowship with him while we walk in darkness, we lie and do not live according to the truth; but if we walk in the light, as he is in the light, we have fellowship with one another, and the blood of Jesus his Son cleanses us from all sin.

1 JOHN 1:6–7 RSV

See also *Love; Unity.*

## Fool, foolish

'Please, don't pay any attention to Nabal, that good-for-nothing! He is exactly what his name means—a fool!'

1 SAMUEL 25:25 GNB

The fool hath said in his heart, There is no God.

PSALM 14:1 KJV

The way of a fool is right in his own eyes, but a wise man listens to advice.

PROVERBS 12:15 RSV

As a dog returneth to his vomit, so a fool returneth to his folly.

PROVERBS 26:11 KJV

A fool speaks foolishly and thinks up evil things to do. What he does and what he says are an insult to the Lord, and he never feeds the hungry or gives thirsty people anything to drink.

ISAIAH 32:6 GNB

'And every one who hears these words of mine and does not do them will be like a foolish man who built his house upon the sand.'

MATTHEW 7:26 RSV

But God said unto him, Thou fool, this night thy soul shall be required of thee: then whose shall those things be, which thou hast provided?

LUKE 12:20 KJV

Claiming to be wise, they became fools, and exchanged the glory of the immortal God for images resembling mortal man or birds or animals or reptiles.

ROMANS 1:22–23 RSV

For the word of the cross is folly to those who are perishing, but to us who are being saved it is the power of God.

1 CORINTHIANS 1:18 RSV

But God hath chosen the foolish things of the world to confound the wise; and God hath chosen the weak things of the world to confound the things which are mighty.

1 CORINTHIANS 1:27 KJV

The man without the Spirit does not accept the things that come from the Spirit of God, for they are foolishness to him and he cannot understand them, because they are spiritually discerned.

1 CORINTHIANS 2:14 NIV

See also *Wisdom.*

## Forgiveness

Blessed is he whose transgression is forgiven, whose sin is covered. Blessed is the man to whom the Lord imputes no iniquity, and in whose spirit there is no deceit.

PSALM 32:1–2 RSV

Have mercy upon me, O God, according to thy lovingkindness: according unto the multitude of thy tender mercies blot out my transgressions. Wash me thoroughly from mine iniquity, and cleanse me from my sin.

PSALM 51:1–2 KJV

As far as the east is from the west, so far hath he removed our transgressions from us.

PSALM 103:12 KJV

If thou, O Lord, shouldst mark iniquities, Lord, who could stand? But there is forgiveness with thee, that thou mayest be feared.

PSALM 130:3–4 RSV

'And no longer shall each man teach his neighbour and each his brother, saying "Know the Lord," for they shall all know me, from the least of them to the greatest, says the Lord; for I will forgive their iniquity, and I will remember their sin no more.'

JEREMIAH 31:34 RSV

Who is a God like thee, pardoning iniquity and passing over transgression for the remnant of his inheritance?

MICAH 7:18 RSV

And forgive us our trespasses, as we forgive them that trespass against us.
MATTHEW 6:12 BCP

'If you forgive others the wrongs they have done to you, your Father in heaven will also forgive you. But if you do not forgive others, then your Father will not forgive the wrongs you have done.'
MATTHEW 6:14–15 GNB

'But that you may know that the Son of man has authority on earth to forgive sins'—he then said to the paralytic—'Rise, take up your bed and go home.'
MATTHEW 9:6 RSV

'Therefore I tell you, every sin and blasphemy will be forgiven men, but the blasphemy against the Spirit will not be forgiven.'
MATTHEW 12:31 RSV

And Peter said to them, 'Repent, and be baptized every one of you in the name of Jesus Christ for the forgiveness of your sins; and you shall receive the gift of the Holy Spirit.'
ACTS 2:38 RSV

'To him all the prophets bear witness that every one who believes in him receives forgiveness of sins through his name.'
ACTS 10:43 RSV

In him [Jesus Christ] we have redemption through his blood, the forgiveness of our trespasses, according to the riches of his grace.
EPHESIANS 1:7 RSV

Be kind to one another, tenderhearted, forgiving one another, as God in Christ forgave you.
EPHESIANS 4:32 RSV

Indeed, under the law almost everything is purified with blood, and without the shedding of blood there is no forgiveness of sins.
HEBREWS 9:22 RSV

If we confess our sins, he is faithful and just and will forgive our sins and cleanse us from all unrighteousness.
1 JOHN 1:9 RSV

See also *Atonement; Repentance; Sin.*

## Freedom, free

The Spirit of the Lord is upon me; because the Lord hath anointed me to preach good tidings unto the meek; he hath sent me to bind up the brokenhearted, to proclaim liberty to the captives, and the opening of the prison to them that are bound . . .
ISAIAH 61:1 KJV

Jesus then said to the Jews who had believed in him, 'If you continue in my word, you are truly my disciples, and you will know the truth, and the truth will make you free . . . Truly, truly, I say to you, every one who commits sin is a slave to sin. The slave does not continue in the house for ever; the son continues for ever. So if the Son makes you free, you will be free indeed.'
JOHN 8:31–32, 34–36 RSV

But now that you have been set free from sin and have become slaves to God, the benefit you reap leads to holiness, and the result is eternal life.
ROMANS 6:22 NIV

For the law of the Spirit of life in Christ Jesus has set me free from the law of sin and death. For God has done what the law, weakened by the flesh, could not do: sending his own Son in the likeness of sinful flesh and for sin, he condemned sin in the flesh, in order that the just requirement of the law might be fulfilled in us, who walk not according to the flesh but according to the Spirit.
ROMANS 8:2–4 RSV

The creation itself will be set free from its bondage to decay and obtain the glorious liberty of the children of God.
ROMANS 8:21 RSV

Be careful, however, not to let your freedom of action make those who are weak in the faith fall into sin.
1 CORINTHIANS 8:9 GNB

Now the Lord is the Spirit, and where the Spirit of the Lord is, there is freedom. And we all, with unveiled face, beholding the glory of the Lord, are being changed into his likeness from one degree of glory to another; for this comes from the Lord who is the Spirit.
2 CORINTHIANS 3:17–18 RSV

For freedom Christ has set us free; stand fast therefore, and do not submit again to a yoke of slavery.
GALATIANS 5:1 RSV

As for you, my brothers, you are called to be free. But do not let this freedom become an excuse for

letting your physical desires control you. Instead, let love make you serve one another.
GALATIANS 5:13 GNB

Since therefore the children share in flesh and blood, he himself likewise partook of the same nature, that through death he might destroy him who has the power of death, that is, the devil.
HEBREWS 2:14 RSV

## Friends

Thus the Lord used to speak to Moses face to face, as a man speaks to his friend.
EXODUS 33:11 RSV

The friendship of the Lord is for those who fear him, and he makes known to them his covenant.
PSALM 25:14 RSV

A friend loves at all times, and a brother is born for adversity.
PROVERBS 17:17 RSV

There are friends who pretend to be friends, but there is a friend who sticks closer than a brother.
PROVERBS 18:24 RSV

Faithful are the wounds of a friend; but the kisses of an enemy are deceitful.
PROVERBS 27:6 KJV

'The Son of man came eating and drinking, and they say, ''Behold, a glutton and a drunkard, a friend of tax collectors and sinners!'' Yet wisdom is justified by her deeds.'
MATTHEW 11:19 RSV

Jesus said to him [Judas], 'Friend, why are you here?'
MATTHEW 26:50 RSV

'Greater love has no man than this, that a man lay down his life for his friends. You are my friends if you do what I command you. No longer do I call you servants, for the servant does not know what his master is doing; but I have called you friends, for all that I have heard from my Father I have made known to you.'
JOHN 15:13–15 RSV

The scripture was fulfilled which says, 'Abraham believed God, and it was reckoned to him as righteousness'; and he was called the friend of God.
JAMES 2:23 RSV

## Fruit

He will bless the fruit of your womb.
DEUTERONOMY 7:13 NIV

[John the Baptist to the Pharisees and Sadducees] 'Bear fruit that befits repentance.'
MATTHEW 3:8 RSV

'You will know them by their fruits.'
MATTHEW 7:16 RSV

'I am the vine, you are the branches. He who abides in me, and I in him, he it is that bears much fruit, for apart from me you can do nothing . . . By this my Father is glorified, that you bear much fruit, and so prove to be my disciples.'
JOHN 15:5, 8 RSV

'You did not choose me, but I chose you and appointed you that you should go and bear fruit and that your fruit should abide.'
JOHN 15:16 RSV

But the fruit of the Spirit is love, joy, peace, patience, kindness, goodness, faithfulness, gentleness, self-control; against such there is no law.
GALATIANS 5:22–23 RSV

## Fullness

The earth is the Lord's and the fullness thereof, the world and those who dwell therein.
PSALM 24:1 RSV

And the Word was made flesh, and dwelt among us, (and we beheld his glory, the glory as of the only begotten of the Father,) full of grace and truth.
JOHN 1:14 KJV

And from his fullness have we all received, grace upon grace.
JOHN 1:16 RSV

[The church] which is his body, the fullness of him that filleth all in all.
EPHESIANS 1:23 KJV

[Paul's prayer] That you may be filled with all the fullness of God.
EPHESIANS 3:19 RSV

And be not drunk with wine, wherein is excess; but be filled with the Spirit.
EPHESIANS 5:18 KJV

For in him [Christ] the whole fullness of deity dwells bodily, and you have come to fullness of life in him.

COLOSSIANS 2:9–10 RSV

# Gentiles

Ask of me, and I shall give thee the heathen for thine inheritance, and the uttermost parts of the earth for thy possession.

PSALM 2:8 KJV

And in that day there shall be a root of Jesse, which shall stand for an ensign of the people; to it shall the Gentiles seek: and his rest shall be glorious.

ISAIAH 11:10 KJV

A light to lighten the Gentiles, and to be the glory of thy people Israel.

LUKE 2:32 BCP

The Lord said to him [Ananias], 'Go, because I have chosen him [Paul] to serve me, to make my name known to Gentiles and kings and to the people of Israel.'

ACTS 9:15 GNB

And the believers from among the circumcised who came with Peter were amazed, because the gift of the Holy Spirit had been poured out even on the Gentiles.

ACTS 10:45 RSV

And they glorified God, saying, 'Then to the Gentiles also God has granted repentance unto life.'

ACTS 11:18 RSV

When Gentiles who have not the law do by nature what the law requires, they are a law to themselves, even though they do not have the law.

ROMANS 2:14 RSV

There is neither Jew nor Greek, there is neither bond nor free, there is neither male nor female: for ye are all one in Christ Jesus.

GALATIANS 3:28 KJV

Therefore remember that at one time you Gentiles in the flesh, called the uncircumcision by what is called the circumcision, which is made in the flesh by hands—remember that you were at that time separated from Christ, alienated from the commonwealth of Israel, and strangers to the covenants of promise, having no hope and without God in the world. But now in Christ Jesus you who once were far off have been brought near in the blood of Christ. For he is our peace, who has made us both one, and has broken down the dividing wall of hostility, by abolishing in his flesh the law of commandments and ordinances, that he might create in himself one new man in place of the two, so making peace, and might reconcile us both to God in one body through the cross, thereby bringing the hostility to an end. And he came and preached peace to you who were far off and peace to those who were near; for through him we both have access in one Spirit to the Father. So then you are no longer strangers and sojourners, but you are fellow citizens with the saints and members of the household of God,

EPHESIANS 2:11–19 RSV

After this I looked, and behold, a great multitude which no man could number, from every nation, from all tribes and peoples and tongues, standing before the throne and before the Lamb, clothed in white robes, with palm branches in their hands...

REVELATION 7:9 RSV

# Gentleness

'Take my yoke upon you, and learn from me; for I am gentle and lowly in heart, and you will find rest for your souls.'

MATTHEW 11:29 RSV

I, Paul, myself entreat you, by the meekness and gentleness of Christ—I who am humble when face to face with you, but bold to you when I am away!

2 CORINTHIANS 10:1 RSV

But the fruit of the Spirit is . . . gentleness . . .

GALATIANS 5:22–23 RSV

Brethren, if a man is overtaken in any trespass, you who are spiritual should restore him in a spirit of gentleness.

GALATIANS 6:1 RSV

But we were gentle among you, like a nurse taking care of her children.

1 THESSALONIANS 2:7 RSV

And the servant of the Lord must not strive; but be gentle unto all men, apt to teach, patient.

2 TIMOTHY 2:24 KJV

But the wisdom from above is first pure, then peaceable, gentle, open to reason, full of mercy and good fruits, without uncertainty or insincerity.

JAMES 3:17 RSV

[Paul's instructions to wives] Your beauty should consist of your true inner self, the ageless beauty of a gentle and quiet spirit, which is of the greatest value in God's sight.

1 PETER 3:4 GNB

# Gift

For God so loved the world, that he gave his only begotten Son, that whosoever believeth in him should not perish, but have everlasting life.

JOHN 3:16 KJV

And Peter said to them, 'Repent, and be baptized every one of you in the name of Jesus Christ for the forgiveness of your sins; and you shall receive the gift of the Holy Spirit.'

ACTS 2:38 RSV

'God exalted him at his right hand as Leader and Saviour, to give repentance to Israel and forgiveness of sins.'

ACTS 5:31 RSV

For the wages of sin is death; but the gift of God is eternal life through Jesus Christ our Lord.

ROMANS 6:23 KJV

We have different gifts, according to the grace given us.

ROMANS 12:6 NIV

Now there are varieties of gifts, but the same Spirit; and there are varieties of service, but the same Lord; and there are varieties of working, but it is the same God who inspires them all in every one. To each is given the manifestation of the Spirit for the common good ... All these are inspired by one and the same Spirit, who apportions to each one individually as he wills.

1 CORINTHIANS 12:4–7, 11 RSV

Make love your aim, and earnestly desire the spiritual gifts, especially that you may prophesy.

1 CORINTHIANS 14:1 RSV

Thanks be to God for his inexpressible gift!

2 CORINTHIANS 9:15 RSV

For by grace are ye saved through faith; and that not of yourselves: it is the gift of God.

EPHESIANS 2:8 KJV

Do not neglect the gift you have, which was given you by prophetic utterance when the council of elders laid their hands upon you.

1 TIMOTHY 4:14 RSV

Every good gift and every perfect gift is from above, and cometh down from the Father of lights, with whom is no variableness, neither shadow of turning.

JAMES 1:17 KJV

# Giving

[Melchizedek] 'Blessed be Abram by God Most High, maker of heaven and earth; and blessed be God Most High, who has delivered your enemies into your hand!' And Abram gave him a tenth of everything.

GENESIS 14:18–20 RSV

For all things come of thee, and of thine own have we given thee.

1 CHRONICLES 29:14 KJV

'Bring the full tithes into the storehouse, that there may be food in my house; and thereby put me to the test, says the Lord of hosts, if I will not open the windows of heaven for you and pour down for you an overflowing blessing.'

MALACHI 3:10 RSV

'So when you give something to a needy person, do not make a big show of it, as the hypocrites do in the houses of worship and on the streets. They do it so that people will praise them ... But when you help a needy person, do it in such a way that even your closest friend will not know about it.'

MATTHEW 6:2–3 GNB

And a poor widow came, and put in two copper coins, which make a penny. And he called his disciples to him, and said to them, 'Truly, I say to you, this poor widow has put in more than all those who are contributing to the treasury. For they all contributed out of their abundance; but she out of her poverty has put in everything she had, her whole living.'

MARK 12:42–44 RSV

'Give, and it will be given to you; good measure, pressed down, shaken together, running over, will be put into your lap. For the measure you give will be the measure you get back.'

LUKE 6:38 RSV

On the first day of every week, each of you is to put something aside and store it up, as he may prosper, so that contributions need not be made when I come.

1 CORINTHIANS 16:2 RSV

We want you to know, brethren, about the grace of God which has been shown in the churches of Macedonia, for in a severe test of affliction, their abundance of joy and their extreme poverty have overflowed in a wealth of liberality on their part. For they gave according to their means, as I can testify, and beyond their means, of their own free will, begging us earnestly for the favour of taking part in the relief of the saints—and this, not as we expected, but first they gave themselves to the Lord and to us by the will of God.

2 CORINTHIANS 8:1–5 RSV

Each one must do as he has made up his mind, not reluctantly or under compulsion, for God loves a cheerful giver.

2 CORINTHIANS 9:7 RSV

See also *Stewardship.*

## Glory

Moses said, 'I pray thee, show me thy glory.'

EXODUS 33:18 RSV

But as truly as I live, all the earth shall be filled with the glory of the Lord.

NUMBERS 14:21 KJV

She [the wife of Phinehas] named the child Ichabod, saying, 'the glory has departed from Israel!' because the ark of God had been captured and because of her father-in-law and her husband.

1 SAMUEL 4:21 RSV

And he [Jesus] was transfigured before them, and his face shone like the sun, and his garments became white as light.

MATTHEW 17:2 RSV

'For whoever is ashamed of me and of my words in this adulterous and sinful generation, of him will the Son of man also be ashamed, when he comes in the glory of his Father with the holy angels.'

MARK 8:38 RSV

Jesus performed this first miracle in Cana in Galilee; there he revealed his glory, and his disciples believed in him.

JOHN 2:11 GNB

'And now, Father, glorify thou me in thy own presence with the glory which I had with thee before the world was made.'

JOHN 17:5 RSV

For all have sinned, and come short of the glory of God.

ROMANS 3:23 KJV

I consider that the sufferings of this present time are not worth comparing with the glory that is to be revealed to us.

ROMANS 8:18 RSV

So, whether you eat or drink, or whatever you do, do all to the glory of God.

1 CORINTHIANS 10:31 RSV

For a man ought not to cover his head, since he is the image and glory of God; but woman is the glory of man.

1 CORINTHIANS 11:7 RSV

And we all, with unveiled face, beholding the glory of the Lord, are being changed into his likeness from one degree of glory to another; for this comes from the Lord who is the Spirit.

2 CORINTHIANS 3:18 RSV

The Son is the radiance of God's glory and the exact representation of his being, sustaining all things by his powerful word.

HEBREWS 1:3 NIV

## God

### ALL-KNOWING

O Lord, thou hast searched me and known me! Thou knowest when I sit down and when I rise up; thou discernest my thoughts from afar. Thou searchest out my path and my lying down, and art acquainted with all my ways. Even before a word is on my tongue, lo, O Lord, thou knowest it altogether. Thou dost beset me behind and before, and layest thy hand upon me. Such knowledge is too wonderful for me; it is high, I cannot attain it.

PSALM 139:1–6 RSV

O the depth of the riches both of the wisdom and knowledge of God! how unsearchable are his judgments, and his ways past finding out!

ROMANS 11:33 KJV

Before him no creature is hidden, but all are open and laid bare to the eyes of him with whom we have to do.

HEBREWS 4:13 RSV

## ALL-PRESENT

Whither shall I go from thy Spirit? Or whither shall I flee from thy presence? If I ascend to heaven, thou art there! If I make my bed in Sheol, thou art there! If I take the wings of the morning and dwell in the uttermost parts of the sea, even there thy hand shall lead me, and thy right hand shall hold me.

PSALM 139:7–10 RSV

## ALMIGHTY

[Job to the Lord] 'I know that thou canst do all things, and that no purpose of thine can be thwarted.'

JOB 42:2 RSV

'For with God nothing will be impossible.'

LUKE 1:37 RSV

Alleluia: for the Lord God omnipotent reigneth.

REVELATION 19:6 KJV

## ETERNAL

Before the mountains were brought forth, or ever thou hadst formed the earth and the world, from everlasting to everlasting thou art God.

PSALM 90:2 RSV

Now unto the King eternal, immortal, invisible, the only wise God, be honour and glory for ever and ever. Amen.

1 TIMOTHY 1:17 KJV

## FAITHFUL

'Know therefore that the Lord your God is God, the faithful God who keeps covenant and steadfast love with those who love him and keep his commandments, to a thousand generations.'

DEUTERONOMY 7:9 RSV

The steadfast love of the Lord never ceases, his mercies never come to an end; they are new every morning; great is thy faithfulness.

LAMENTATIONS 3:22–23 RSV

God is faithful, by whom you were called into the fellowship of his Son, Jesus Christ our Lord.

1 CORINTHIANS 1:9 RSV

## GOOD

O taste and see that the Lord is good! Happy is the man who takes refuge in him!

PSALM 34:8 RSV

O give thanks to the Lord, for he is good, for his steadfast love endures for ever.

PSALM 136:1

And Jesus said to him, 'Why do you call me good? No one is good but God alone.'

MARK 10:18 RSV

Or do you presume upon the riches of his kindness and forbearance and patience? Do you not know that God's kindness is meant to lead you to repentance?

ROMANS 2:4 RSV

## HOLY

'Holy, holy, holy is the Lord of hosts; the whole earth is full of his glory.'

ISAIAH 6:3 RSV

Thou who art of purer eyes than to behold evil and canst not look on wrong.

HABAKKUK 1:13 RSV

'Who shall not fear and glorify thy name, O Lord? For thou alone art holy. All nations shall come and worship thee, for thy judgments have been revealed.'

REVELATION 15:4 RSV

## INFINITE

[Solomon's prayer] 'Behold, heaven and the highest heaven cannot contain thee; how much less this house which I have built!'

1 KINGS 8:27 RSV

For thus saith the high and lofty One that inhabiteth eternity, whose name is Holy; I dwell in the high and holy place, with him also that is of a contrite and humble spirit, to revive the spirit of the humble, and to revive the heart of the contrite ones.

ISAIAH 57:15 KJV

'Can a man hide himself in secret places so that I cannot see him? says the Lord. Do I not fill heaven and earth? says the Lord.'

JEREMIAH 23:24 RSV

## JUST

[Abraham pleading for Sodom] 'Far be it from thee to do such a thing, to slay the righteous with the wicked, so that the righteous fare as the wicked! Far be that from thee! Shall not the Judge of all the earth do right?'

GENESIS 18:25 RSV

'The Lord is your mighty defender, perfect and just in all his ways; Your God is faithful and true; he does what is right and fair.'
DEUTERONOMY 32:4 GNB

'He has fixed a day on which he will judge the world in righteousness by a man whom he has appointed, and of this he has given assurance to all men by raising him from the dead.'
ACTS 17:31 RSV

If we confess our sins, he is faithful and just and will forgive our sins and cleanse us from all unrighteousness.
1 JOHN 1:9 RSV

## LOVING

'It was not because you were more in number than any other people that the Lord set his love upon you and chose you, for you were the fewest of all peoples; but it is because the Lord loves you, and is keeping the oath which he swore to your fathers, that the Lord has brought you out with a mighty hand, and redeemed you from the house of bondage, from the hand of Pharaoh king of Egypt. Know therefore that the Lord your God is God, the faithful God who keeps covenant and steadfast love with those who love him and keep his commandments, to a thousand generations.'
DEUTERONOMY 7:7–9 RSV

For God so loved the world, that he gave his only begotten Son, that whosoever believeth in him should not perish, but have everlasting life.
JOHN 3:16 KJV

Herein is love, not that we loved God, but that he loved us, and sent his Son to be the propitiation for our sins.
1 JOHN 4:10 KJV

## MERCIFUL

The Lord passed before him, and proclaimed, 'The Lord, the Lord, a God merciful and gracious, slow to anger, and abounding in steadfast love and faithfulness, keeping steadfast love for thousands, forgiving iniquity and transgression and sin, but who will by no means clear the guilty, visiting the iniquity of the fathers upon the children and the children's children, to the third and the fourth generation.'
EXODUS 34:6–7 RSV

[The Lord] who crowneth thee with lovingkindness and tender mercies.
PSALM 103:4 KJV

But because of his great love for us, God, who is rich in mercy, made us alive with Christ even when we were dead in transgressions—it is by grace you have been saved.
EPHESIANS 2:4–5 NIV

## SELF-EXISTENT

God said to Moses, 'I am who I am.'
EXODUS 3:14 RSV

'For as the Father has life in himself, so he has granted the Son to have life in himself.'
JOHN 5:26 NIV

## SPIRITUAL

'But the hour is coming, and now is, when the true worshippers will worship the Father in spirit and truth, for such the Father seeks to worship him. God is spirit, and those who worship him must worship in spirit and truth.'
JOHN 4:23–24 RSV

## UNCHANGEABLE

'God is not man, that he should lie, or a son of man, that he should repent. Has he said, and will he not do it? Or has he spoken, and will he not fulfil it?'
NUMBERS 23:19 RSV

For I am the Lord, I change not; therefore ye sons of Jacob are not consumed.
MALACHI 3:6 KJV

Every good gift and every perfect gift is from above, and cometh down from the Father of lights, with whom is no variableness, neither shadow of turning.
JAMES 1:17 KJV

## WISE

O Lord, how manifold are thy works! In wisdom hast thou made them all: the earth is full of thy riches.
PSALM 104:24 KJV

Daniel said: 'Blessed be the name of God for ever and ever, to whom belong wisdom and might.'
DANIEL 2:20 RSV

Now unto the King eternal, immortal, invisible, the only wise God, be honour and glory for ever and ever. Amen.
1 TIMOTHY 1:17 KJV

See also *Creation; Providence; Sovereignty of God.*

## Godless

'The triumph of the wicked is short-lived, the glee of the godless lasts but a moment.'
JOB 20:5 NEB

What hope is there for godless men in the hour when God demands their life?
JOB 27:8 GNB

The kings of the earth stand up, and the rulers take counsel together, against the Lord, and against his anointed.
PSALM 2:2 BCP

Let the godless be put to shame, because they have subverted me with guile; as for me, I will meditate on thy precepts.
PSALM 119:78 RSV

With his mouth the godless man would destroy his neighbour, but by knowledge the righteous are delivered.
PROVERBS 11:9 RSV

Let the wicked forsake his way, and the unrighteous man his thoughts: and let him return unto the Lord, and he will have mercy upon him; and to our God, for he will abundantly pardon.
ISAIAH 55:7 KJV

For the wrath of God is revealed from heaven against all ungodliness and unrighteousness of men, who hold the truth in unrighteousness.
ROMANS 1:18 KJV

While we were still weak, at the right time Christ died for the ungodly.
ROMANS 5:6 RSV

See also *Unbeliever.*

## Golden rule
See Matthew 7:12.

## Good

And God saw every thing that he had made, and, behold, it was very good.
GENESIS 1:31 KJV

The song was raised, with trumpets and cymbals and other musical instruments, in praise to the Lord, 'For he is good, for his steadfast love endures for ever.'
2 CHRONICLES 5:13 RSV

Do good in thy good pleasure unto Zion: build thou the walls of Jerusalem.
PSALM 51:18 KJV

And Jesus said to him, 'Why do you call me good? No one is good but God alone.'
MARK 10:18 RSV

'How he [Jesus] went about doing good and healing all that were oppressed by the devil, for God was with him.'
ACTS 10:38 RSV

So the law is holy, and the commandment is holy and just and good.
ROMANS 7:12 RSV

For I know that nothing good dwells within me, that is, in my flesh.
ROMANS 7:18 RSV

We know that in everything God works for good with those who love him, who are called according to his purpose.
ROMANS 8:28 RSV

And be not conformed to this world: but be ye transformed by the renewing of your mind, that ye may prove what is that good, and acceptable, and perfect, will of God.
ROMANS 12:2 KJV

Let love be genuine; hate what is evil, hold fast to what is good.
ROMANS 12:9 RSV

Do not be overcome by evil, but overcome evil with good.
ROMANS 12:21 RSV

But the fruit of the Spirit is love, joy, peace, patience, kindness, goodness, faithfulness, gentleness, self-control.
GALATIANS 5:22 RSV

For we are his workmanship, created in Christ Jesus unto good works, which God hath before ordained that we should walk in them.
EPHESIANS 2:10 KJV

For everything created by God is good and nothing is to be rejected if it is received with thanksgiving; for then it is consecrated by the word of God and prayer.
1 TIMOTHY 4:4 RSV

## Good Samaritan
See appendix, *Parables of Jesus.*

## Gospel

'And because wickedness is multiplied, most men's love will grow cold. But he who endures to the end will be saved. And this gospel of the kingdom will be preached throughout the whole world, as a testimony to all nations; and then the end will come.'

**MATTHEW 24:14 RSV**

Now after John was arrested, Jesus came into Galilee, preaching the gospel of God, and saying, 'The time is fulfilled, and the kingdom of God is at hand; repent, and believe in the gospel.'

**MARK 1:14–15 RSV**

And he said to them, 'Go into all the world and preach the gospel to the whole creation.'

**MARK 16:15 RSV**

[Jesus reading the book of Isaiah] 'The Spirit of the Lord is upon me, because he has anointed me to preach good news to the poor. He has sent me to proclaim release to the captives and recovering of sight to the blind, to set at liberty those who are oppressed, to proclaim the acceptable year of the Lord.' And he closed the book, and gave it back to the attendant, and sat down; and the eyes of all in the synagogue were fixed on him. And he began to say to them, 'Today this scripture has been fulfilled in your hearing.'

**LUKE 4:18–21 RSV**

'But I do not account my life of any value nor as precious to myself, if only I may accomplish my course and the ministry which I received from the Lord Jesus, to testify to the gospel of the grace of God.'

**ACTS 20:24 RSV**

For I am not ashamed of the gospel of Christ: for it is the power of God unto salvation to everyone that believeth; to the Jew first, and also to the Greek. For therein is the righteousness of God revealed from faith to faith; as it is written, The just shall live by faith.

**ROMANS 1:16–17 KJV**

For necessity is laid upon me. Woe to me if I do not preach the gospel!

**1 CORINTHIANS 9:16 RSV**

And now, my brothers, I must remind you of the gospel that I preached to you; the gospel which you received, on which you have taken your stand.

**1 CORINTHIANS 15:1 NEB**

For I delivered to you as of first importance what I also received, that Christ died for our sins in accordance with the scriptures, that he was buried, that he was raised on the third day in accordance with the scriptures, and that he appeared to Cephas, then to the twelve.

**1 CORINTHIANS 15:3–5 RSV**

For if our gospel is veiled, it is veiled only to those who are perishing. In their case the god of this world has blinded the minds of the unbelievers, to keep them from seeing the light of the gospel of the glory of Christ, who is the likeness of God.

**2 CORINTHIANS 4:3–4 RSV**

Let me tell you, my brothers, that the gospel I preach is not of human origin. I did not receive it from any man, nor did anyone teach it to me. It was Jesus Christ himself who revealed it to me.

**GALATIANS 1:11–12 GNB**

And the scripture, foreseeing that God would justify the Gentiles by faith, preached the gospel beforehand to Abraham, saying, 'In you shall all the nations be blessed.'

**GALATIANS 3:8 RSV**

[Paul asks for prayer] That utterance may be given unto me, that I may open my mouth boldly, to make known the mystery of the gospel.

**EPHESIANS 6:19 KJV**

Whatever happens, conduct yourselves in a manner worthy of the gospel of Christ. Then, whether I come and see you or only hear about you in my absence, I will know that you stand firm in one spirit, contending as one man for the faith of the gospel.

**PHILIPPIANS 1:27 NIV**

The glorious gospel of the blessed God, which was committed to my trust.

**1 TIMOTHY 1:11 KJV**

## Grace

'For you are a people holy to the Lord your God; the Lord your God has chosen you to be a people for his own possession, out of all the peoples that are on the face of the earth. It was not because you were more in number than any other people that the Lord set his love upon you and

chose you, for you were the fewest of all peoples; but it is because the Lord loves you, and is keeping the oath which he swore to your fathers, that the Lord has brought you out with a mighty hand, and redeemed you from the house of bondage, from the hand of Pharaoh king of Egypt. Know therefore that the Lord your God is God, the faithful God who keeps covenant and steadfast love with those who love him and keep his commandments, to a thousand generations.'
DEUTERONOMY 7:6–9 RSV

And the Word was made flesh, and dwelt among us, (and we beheld his glory, the glory as of the only begotten of the Father,) full of grace and truth.
JOHN 1:14 KJV

And from his fullness have we all received, grace upon grace. For the law was given through Moses; grace and truth came through Jesus Christ.
JOHN 1:16–17 RSV

And with great power the apostles gave their testimony to the resurrection of the Lord Jesus, and great grace was upon them all.
ACTS 4:33 RSV

Paul and Barnabas . . . spoke to them and urged them to continue in the grace of God.
ACTS 13:43 RSV

Being justified freely by his grace through the redemption that is in Christ Jesus.
ROMANS 3:24 KJV

By whom [the Lord Jesus Christ] also we have access by faith into this grace wherein we stand, and rejoice in hope of the glory of God.
ROMANS 5:2 KJV

Law came in, to increase the trespass; but where sin increased, grace abounded all the more, so that, as sin reigned in death, grace also might reign through righteousness to eternal life through Jesus Christ our Lord. What shall we say then? Are we to continue in sin that grace may abound? By no means!
ROMANS 5:20–6:2 RSV

But by the grace of God I am what I am, and his grace toward me was not in vain. On the contrary, I worked harder than any of them, though it was not I but the grace of God which is with me.
1 CORINTHIANS 15:10 RSV

For ye know the grace of our Lord Jesus Christ, that, though he was rich, yet for your sakes he became poor, that ye through his poverty might be rich.
2 CORINTHIANS 8:9 KJV

'My grace is sufficient for you, for my power is made perfect in weakness.'
2 CORINTHIANS 12:9 RSV

The grace of the Lord Jesus Christ, the love of God, and the fellowship of the Holy Spirit be with you all.
2 CORINTHIANS 13:13 GNB

But because of his great love for us, God, who is rich in mercy, made us alive with Christ even when we were dead in transgressions—it is by grace you have been saved.
EPHESIANS 2:4–5 NIV

For by grace are ye saved through faith; and that not of yourselves: it is the gift of God.
EPHESIANS 2:8 KJV

[Because Jesus can sympathize with our weaknesses] Let us then with confidence draw near to the throne of grace, that we may receive mercy and find grace to help in time of need.
HEBREWS 4:16 RSV

But grow in the grace and knowledge of our Lord and Saviour Jesus Christ. To him be the glory both now and to the day of eternity. Amen.
2 PETER 3:18 RSV

## Great commission
See Matthew 28:18–20.

## Greed
See *Desire, wrong.*

## Grief

For my life is spent with grief, and my years with sighing: my strength faileth because of mine iniquity, and my bones are consumed.
PSALM 31:10 KJV

The sacrifices of God are a broken spirit: a broken and a contrite heart, O God, thou wilt not despise.
PSALM 51:17 KJV

A time to weep, and a time to laugh; a time to mourn, and a time to dance.
ECCLESIASTES 3:4 KJV

And I said: 'Woe is me! For I am lost; for I am a man of unclean lips, and I dwell in the midst of a people of unclean lips; for my eyes have seen the King, the Lord of hosts!'
ISAIAH 6:5 RSV

He is despised and rejected of men; a man of sorrows, and acquainted with grief: and we hid as it were our faces from him; he was despised, and we esteemed him not. Surely he hath borne our griefs, and carried our sorrows: yet we did esteem him stricken, smitten of God, and afflicted.
ISAIAH 53:3–4 KJV

Is there no balm in Gilead; is there no physician there? Why then is not the health of the daughter of my people recovered?
JEREMIAH 8:22 KJV

But the children of the kingdom shall be cast out into outer darkness: there shall be weeping and gnashing of teeth.
MATTHEW 8:12 KJV

And taking with him Peter and the two sons of Zebedee, he began to be sorrowful and troubled. Then he said to them, 'My soul is very sorrowful, even to death; remain here, and watch with me.'
MATTHEW 26:37–38 RSV

He [Jesus] came closer to the city, and when he saw it, he wept over it, saying, 'If you only knew today what is needed for peace! But now you cannot see it!'
LUKE 19:41–42 GNB

And when he rose from prayer, he came to the disciples and found them sleeping for sorrow.
LUKE 22:45 RSV

And the Lord turned, and looked upon Peter. And Peter remembered the word of the Lord, how he had said unto him, Before the cock crow, thou shalt deny me thrice. And Peter went out, and wept bitterly.
LUKE 22:61–62 KJV

Jesus wept.
JOHN 11:35 KJV

Sorrowful, yet always rejoicing.
2 CORINTHIANS 6:10 RSV

For godly grief produces a repentance that leads to salvation and brings no regret, but worldly grief produces death.
2 CORINTHIANS 7:10 RSV

See also **Comfort; Repentance.**

## Growth, spiritual
See **Christian life, Character of the Christian.**

## Guidance

He leadeth me beside the still waters. He restoreth my soul: he leadeth me in the paths of righteousness for his name's sake.
PSALM 23:2–3 KJV

Trust in the Lord, and do good; so you will dwell in the land, and enjoy security. Take delight in the Lord, and he will give you the desires of your heart. Commit your way to the Lord; trust in him, and he will act.
PSALM 37:3–5 RSV

The steps of a man are from the Lord, and he establishes him in whose way he delights.
PSALM 37:23 RSV

'If you pour yourself out for the hungry and satisfy the desire of the afflicted, then shall your light rise in the darkness and your gloom be as the noonday. And the Lord will guide you continually, and satisfy your desire with good things, and make your bones strong.'
ISAIAH 58:10–11 RSV

'When the Spirit of truth comes, he will guide you into all the truth; for he will not speak on his own authority, but whatever he hears he will speak, and he will declare to you the things that are to come.'
JOHN 16:13 RSV

Then it seemed good to the apostles and the elders, with the whole church, to choose men from among them and send them to Antioch with Paul and Barnabas.
ACTS 15:22 RSV

'For it has seemed good to the Holy Spirit and to us to lay upon you no greater burden than these necessary things . . .'
ACTS 15:28 RSV

And be not conformed to this world: but be ye transformed by the renewing of your mind, that ye may prove what is that good, and acceptable, and perfect, will of God.
ROMANS 12:2 KJV

If any of you lacks wisdom, let him ask God, who gives to all men generously and without reproaching, and it will be given him.

JAMES 1:5 RSV

See also **Counsel; Sovereignty of God.**

## Guilt

And they heard the voice of the Lord God walking in the garden in the cool of the day: and Adam and his wife hid themselves from the presence of the Lord God amongst the trees of the garden . . . And he [Adam] said, I heard thy voice in the garden, and I was afraid, because I was naked; and I hid myself.

GENESIS 3:8, 10 KJV

Thou shalt not take the name of the Lord thy God in vain; for the Lord will not hold him guiltless that taketh his name in vain.

EXODUS 20:7 KJV

I acknowledged my sin to thee, and I did not hide my iniquity; I said, 'I will confess my transgressions to the Lord'; then thou didst forgive the guilt of my sin.

PSALM 32:5 RSV

Have mercy upon me, O God, according to thy lovingkindness: according unto the multitude of thy tender mercies blot out my transgressions. Wash me thoroughly from mine iniquity, and cleanse me from my sin. For I acknowledge my transgressions: and my sin is ever before me. Against thee, thee only, have I sinned, and done this evil in thy sight: that thou mightest be justified when thou speakest, and be clear when thou judgest.

PSALM 51:1–4 KJV

And he touched my mouth, and said: 'Behold, this has touched your lips; your guilt is taken away, and your sin forgiven.'

ISAIAH 6:7 RSV

There is therefore now no condemnation for those who are in Christ Jesus.

ROMANS 8:1 RSV

Whoever, therefore, eats the bread or drinks the cup of the Lord in an unworthy manner will be guilty of profaning the body and blood of the Lord.

1 CORINTHIANS 11:27 RSV

For if a man keeps the whole law apart from one single point; he is guilty of breaking all of it.

JAMES 2:10 NEB

See also **Conscience; Conviction of sin; Forgiveness.**

## Happiness
See **Joy.**

## Hardness

And the Lord said to Moses, 'When you go back to Egypt, see that you do before Pharaoh all the miracles which I have put in your power; but I will harden his heart, so that he will not let the people go.'

EXODUS 4:21 RSV

'If there is among you a poor man, one of your brethren, in any of your towns within your land which the Lord your God gives you, you shall not harden your heart or shut your hand against your poor brother.'

DEUTERONOMY 15:7 RSV

Always obey the Lord and you will be happy. If you are stubborn, you will be ruined.

PROVERBS 28:14 GNB

And he said, 'Go, and say to this people: "Hear and hear, but do not understand; see and see, but do not perceive." Make the heart of this people fat, and their ears heavy, and shut their eyes; lest they see with their eyes, and hear with their ears, and understand with their hearts, and turn and be healed.'

ISAIAH 6:9–10 RSV

Jesus replied, 'Moses permitted you to divorce your wives because your hearts were hard. But it was not this way from the beginning.'

MATTHEW 19:8 NIV

And he looked around at them with anger, grieved at their hardness of heart.

MARK 3:5 RSV

[Jesus to the Jews] 'You refuse to come to me that you may have life.'

JOHN 5:40 RSV

'How stubborn you are!' Stephen went on to say. 'How heathen your hearts, how deaf you are to God's message! You are just like your ancestors: you too have always resisted the Holy Spirit!'

ACTS 7:51 GNB

But by your hard and impenitent heart you are storing up wrath for yourself on the day of wrath when God's righteous judgment will be revealed.

ROMANS 2:5 RSV

But their [the Israelites] minds were hardened;
for to this day, when they read the old covenant,
that same veil remains unlifted, because only
through Christ is it taken away.
**2 CORINTHIANS 3:14 RSV**

They [the Gentiles] are darkened in their
understanding, alienated from the life of God
because of the ignorance that is in them, due to
their hardness of heart.
**EPHESIANS 4:18 RSV**

'Today, when you hear his voice do not harden
your hearts as in the rebellion.'
**HEBREWS 3:15 RSV**

See also *Falling away; Rejection; Unbelief.*

## Hate, hatred

Do not I hate them that hate thee, O Lord? And
do I not loathe them that rise up against thee? I
hate them with perfect hatred; I count them my
enemies.
**PSALM 139:21–22 RSV**

There are seven things that the Lord hates and
cannot tolerate: A proud look, a lying tongue,
hands that kill innocent people, a mind that
thinks up wicked plans, feet that hurry off to do
evil, a witness who tells one lie after another, and
a man who stirs up trouble among friends.
**PROVERBS 6:16–19 GNB**

Better is a dinner of herbs where love is than a
fatted ox and hatred with it.
**PROVERBS 15:17 RSV**

Hate evil, and love good, and establish justice in
the gate; it may be that the Lord, the God of
hosts, will be gracious to the remnant of Joseph.
**AMOS 5:15 RSV**

'Then they will deliver you up to tribulation, and
put you to death; and you will be hated by all
nations for my name's sake.'
**MATTHEW 24:9 RSV**

For every one who does evil hates the light, and
does not come to the light, lest his deeds should
be exposed.
**JOHN 3:20 RSV**

'The world cannot hate you, but it does hate me,
because I give evidence that its ways are evil.'
**JOHN 7:7 JB**

'If the world hates you, just remember that it has
hated me first. If you belonged to the world, then
the world would love you as its own. But I chose
you from this world, and you do not belong to it;
that is why the world hates you.'
**JOHN 15:18–19 GNB**

## Healing

And he [Elijah] stretched himself upon the child
three times, and cried unto the Lord, and said, O
Lord my God, I pray thee, let this child's soul
come into him again. And the Lord heard the
voice of Elijah; and the soul of the child came
into him again, and he revived.
**1 KINGS 17:21–22 KJV**

So he [Naaman] went down and dipped himself
seven times in the Jordan, according to the word
of the man of God; and his flesh was restored like
the flesh of a little child, and he was clean.
**2 KINGS 5:14 RSV**

[The Lord's promise to Solomon] 'If my people
who are called by my name humble themselves,
and pray and seek my face, and turn from their
wicked ways, then I will hear from heaven, and
will forgive their sin and heal their land.'
**2 CHRONICLES 7:14 RSV**

Bless the Lord, O my soul, and forget not all his
benefits: who forgiveth all thine iniquities; who
healeth all thy diseases.
**PSALM 103:2–3 KJV**

He sent forth his word, and healed them, and
delivered them from destruction.
**PSALM 107:20 RSV**

Jesus went all over Galilee, teaching in the
synagogues, preaching the Good News about the
Kingdom, and healing people who had all kinds
of disease and sickness.
**MATTHEW 4:23 GNB**

And he called to him his twelve disciples and
gave them authority over unclean spirits, to cast
them out, and to heal every disease and every
infirmity.
**MATTHEW 10:1 RSV**

Then Peter said, Silver and gold have I none; but
such as I have give I thee: in the name of Jesus
Christ of Nazareth rise up and walk. And he took
him by the right hand, and lifted him up: and
immediately his feet and ankle bones received
strength.
**ACTS 3:6–7 KJV**

To another gifts of healing by the one Spirit . . .
1 CORINTHIANS 12:9 RSV

Is any sick among you? Let him call for the elders of the church; and let them pray over him, anointing him with oil in the name of the Lord: and the prayer of faith shall save the sick, and the Lord shall raise him up; and if he have committed sins, they shall be forgiven him. Confess your faults one to another, and pray one for another, that ye may be healed. The effectual fervent prayer of a righteous man availeth much.
JAMES 5:14–16 KJV

See also *Comfort; Illness; Suffering.*

## Heart

Thou shalt love the Lord thy God with all thine heart, and with all thy soul, and with all thy might.
DEUTERONOMY 6:5 KJV

[Samuel to Saul] 'But now your kingdom shall not continue; the Lord has sought out a man after his own heart . . . because you have not kept what the Lord commanded you.'
1 SAMUEL 13:14 RSV

But the Lord said unto Samuel, Look not on his countenance, or on the height of his stature; because I have refused him: for the Lord seeth not as man seeth; for man looketh on the outward appearance, but the Lord looketh on the heart.
1 SAMUEL 16:7 KJV

Create in me a clean heart, O God; and renew a right spirit within me.
PSALM 51:10 RSV

The heart is deceitful above all things, and desperately wicked: who can know it? I the Lord search the heart.
JEREMIAH 17:9–10 KJV

'A new heart I will give you, and a new spirit I will put within you; and I will take out of your flesh the heart of stone and give you a heart of flesh.'
EZEKIEL 36:26 RSV

Blessed are the pure in heart: for they shall see God.
MATTHEW 5:8 KJV

'For where your treasure is, there will your heart be also.'
MATTHEW 6:21 RSV

And he said, 'What comes out of a man is what defiles a man. For from within, out of the heart of man, come evil thoughts, fornication, theft, murder, adultery, coveting, wickedness, deceit, licentiousness, envy, slander, pride, foolishness.'
MARK 7:20–22 RSV

'He who believes in me, as the scripture has said, "Out of his heart shall flow rivers of living water." ' Now this he said about the Spirit, which those who believed in him were to receive.
JOHN 7:38–39 RSV

But thanks be to God, that you who were once slaves of sin have become obedient from the heart to the standard of teaching to which you were committed.
ROMANS 6:17 RSV

And he who searches the hearts of men knows what is the mind of the Spirit, because the Spirit intercedes for the saints according to the will of God.
ROMANS 8:27 RSV

That if thou shalt confess with thy mouth the Lord Jesus, and shalt believe in thine heart that God hath raised him from the dead, thou shalt be saved.
ROMANS 10:9 KJV

And let the peace of God rule in your hearts, to the which also ye are called in one body; and be ye thankful.
COLOSSIANS 3:15 KJV

Now that by your obedience to the truth you have purified yourselves and have come to have a sincere love for your fellow-believers, love one another earnestly with all your heart.
1 PETER 1:22 GNB

By this we shall know that we are of the truth, and reassure our hearts before him whenever our hearts condemn us; for God is greater than our hearts, and he knows everything. Beloved, if our hearts do not condemn us, we have confidence before God.
1 JOHN 3:19–21 RSV

See also *Hardness; Mind; Spirit.*

## Heaven
See *Last things.*

## Hell
See *Last things.*

## Help

Then Samuel took a stone and set it up between Mizpah and Jeshanah, and called its name Ebenezer; for he said, 'Hitherto the Lord has helped us.'
1 SAMUEL 7:12 RSV

God is our refuge and strength, a very present help in trouble.
PSALM 46:1 KJV

I will lift up mine eyes unto the hills, from whence cometh my help. My help cometh from the Lord, which made heaven and earth. He will not suffer thy foot to be moved: he that keepeth thee will not slumber. Behold, he that keepeth Israel shall neither slumber nor sleep. The Lord is thy keeper: the Lord is thy shade upon thy right hand. The sun shall not smite thee by day, nor the moon by night. The Lord shall preserve thee from all evil: he shall preserve thy soul. The Lord shall preserve thy going out and thy coming in from this time forth, and even for evermore.
PSALM 121 KJV

But she [a Canaanite woman] came and knelt before him, saying, 'Lord, help me.'
MATTHEW 15:25 RSV

Apollos then decided to go to Achaia, so the believers in Ephesus helped him by writing to the believers in Achaia, urging them to welcome him. When he arrived, he was a great help to those who through God's grace had become believers.
ACTS 18:27 GNB

'In all things I have shown you that by so toiling one must help the weak, remembering the words of the Lord Jesus, how he said, ''It is more blessed to give than to receive.'' '
ACTS 20:35 RSV

Likewise the Spirit helps us in our weakness; for we do not know how to pray as we ought, but the Spirit himself intercedes for us with sighs too deep for words.
ROMANS 8:26 RSV

And God has appointed in the church first apostles, second prophets, third teachers, then workers of miracles, then healers, helpers, administrators.
1 CORINTHIANS 12:28 RSV

You also must help us by prayer, so that many will give thanks on our behalf for the blessing granted us in answer to many prayers.
2 CORINTHIANS 1:11 RSV

Bear one another's burdens, and so fulfil the law of Christ.
GALATIANS 6:2 RSV

He has said, 'I will never fail you nor forsake you.' Hence we can confidently say, 'The Lord is my helper, I will not be afraid; what can man do to me?'
HEBREWS 13:5–6 RSV

See also **Comfort; Kindness; Service.**

## High priest
See **Priest.**

## Holiness, holy

And he said, Draw not nigh hither: put off thy shoes from off thy feet, for the place whereon thou standest is holy ground.
EXODUS 3:5 KJV

Remember the sabbath day, to keep it holy.
EXODUS 20:8 KJV

'For I am the Lord your God; consecrate yourselves therefore, and be holy, for I am holy.'
LEVITICUS 11:44 RSV

'Holy, holy, holy is the Lord of hosts; the whole earth is full of his glory.'
ISAIAH 6:3 RSV

But now that you have been set free from sin and have become slaves to God, the benefit you reap leads to holiness, and the result is eternal life.
ROMANS 6:22 NIV

Since we have these promises, dear friends, let us purify ourselves from everything that contaminates body and spirit, perfecting holiness out of reverence for God.
2 CORINTHIANS 7:1 NIV

God did not call us to live in immorality, but in holiness.
1 THESSALONIANS 4:7 GNB

For it was fitting that we should have such a high priest, holy, blameless, unstained, separated from sinners, exalted above the heavens.
HEBREWS 7:26 RSV

For they [our human fathers] disciplined us for a

short time at their pleasure, but he disciplines us for our good, that we may share his holiness.
**HEBREWS 12:10 RSV**

Strive for peace with all men, and for the holiness without which no one will see the Lord.
**HEBREWS 12:14 RSV**

But you are a chosen race, a royal priesthood, a holy nation, God's own people, that you may declare the wonderful deeds of him who called you out of darkness into his marvellous light.
**1 PETER 2:9 RSV**

See also *Sanctification.*

# Holy Spirit

And the Spirit of God moved upon the face of the waters.
**GENESIS 1:2 KJV**

'I have filled him [Bezalel] with the Spirit of God, with ability and intelligence, with knowledge and all craftsmanship.'
**EXODUS 31:3 RSV**

The spirit of the Lord came upon him [Othniel], and he became Israel's leader. Othniel went to war, and the Lord gave him victory over the king of Mesopotamia.
**JUDGES 3:10 GNB**

Cast me not away from thy presence; and take not thy holy spirit from me.
**PSALM 51:11 KJV**

And the spirit of the Lord shall rest upon him, the spirit of wisdom and understanding, the spirit of counsel and might, the spirit of knowledge and of the fear of the Lord.
**ISAIAH 11:2 KJV**

'And I will put my spirit within you, and cause you to walk in my statutes and be careful to observe my ordinances.'
**EZEKIEL 36:27 RSV**

'And it shall come to pass afterward, that I will pour out my spirit on all flesh; your sons and your daughters shall prophesy, your old men shall dream dreams, and your young men shall see visions.'
**JOEL 2:28 RSV**

This is the word of the Lord unto Zerubbabel, saying, Not by might, nor by power, but by my spirit, saith the Lord of hosts.
**ZECHARIAH 4:6 KJV**

[John the Baptist] 'I baptize you with water for repentance, but he who is coming after me is mightier than I, whose sandals I am not worthy to carry; he will baptize you with the Holy Spirit and with fire.'
**MATTHEW 3:11 RSV**

And when Jesus was baptized, he went up immediately from the water, and behold, the heavens were opened and he saw the Spirit of God descending like a dove, and alighting on him.
**MATTHEW 3:16 RSV**

'Therefore I tell you, every sin and blasphemy will be forgiven men, but the blasphemy against the Spirit will not be forgiven.'
**MATTHEW 12:31 RSV**

And the angel said to her, 'The Holy Spirit will come upon you, and the power of the Most High will overshadow you; therefore the child to be born will be called holy, the Son of God.'
**LUKE 1:35 RSV**

If ye then, being evil, know how to give good gifts unto your children: how much more shall your heavenly Father give the Holy Spirit to them that ask him?
**LUKE 11:13 KJV**

Jesus answered, Verily, verily, I say unto thee, Except a man be born of water and of the Spirit, he cannot enter into the kingdom of God. That which is born of the flesh is flesh; and that which is born of the Spirit is spirit.
**JOHN 3:5–6 KJV**

'He who believes in me, as the scripture has said, "Out of his heart shall flow rivers of living water." ' Now this he said about the Spirit, which those who believed in him were to receive; for as yet the Spirit had not been given, because Jesus was not yet glorified.
**JOHN 7:38–39 RSV**

And I will pray the Father, and he shall give you another Comforter, that he may abide with you for ever; even the Spirit of truth; whom the world cannot receive, because it seeth him not, neither knoweth him: but ye know him; for he dwelleth with you, and shall be in you.
**JOHN 14:16–17 KJV**

'But the Counsellor, the Holy Spirit, whom the Father will send in my name, he will teach you all things, and bring to your remembrance all that I have said to you.'
JOHN 14:26 RSV

'But when the Counsellor comes, whom I shall send to you from the Father, even the Spirit of truth, who proceeds from the Father, he will bear witness to me.'
JOHN 15:26 RSV

'Nevertheless I tell you the truth: it is to your advantage that I go away, for if I do not go away, the Counsellor will not come to you; but if I go, I will send him to you. And when he comes, he will convince the world concerning sin and righteousness and judgment: concerning sin, because they do not believe in me; concerning righteousness, because I go to the Father, and you will see me no more; concerning judgment, because the ruler of this world is judged . . . When the Spirit of truth comes, he will guide you into all the truth; for he will not speak on his own authority, but whatever he hears he will speak, and he will declare to you the things that are to come. He will glorify me, for he will take what is mine and declare it to you.'
JOHN 16:7–11, 13–14 RSV

'But you shall receive power when the Holy Spirit has come upon you; and you shall be my witnesses in Jerusalem and in all Judea and Samaria and to the end of the earth.'
ACTS 1:8 RSV

When the day of Pentecost had come, they were all together in one place. And suddenly a sound came from heaven like the rush of a mighty wind, and it filled all the house where they were sitting. And there appeared to them tongues as of fire, distributed and resting on each one of them. And they were all filled with the Holy Spirit and began to speak in other tongues, as the Spirit gave them utterance.
ACTS 2:1–4 RSV

And Peter said to them, 'Repent, and be baptized every one of you in the name of Jesus Christ for the forgiveness of your sins; and you shall receive the gift of the Holy Spirit.'
ACTS 2:38 RSV

Then Peter, filled with the Holy Spirit, said to them, 'Rulers of the people and elders . . .'
ACTS 4:8 RSV

Peter said to him, 'Ananias, why did you let Satan take control of you and make you lie to the Holy Spirit by keeping part of the money you received for the property? . . . You have not lied to men—you have lied to God!'
ACTS 5:3–4 GNB

'How stubborn you are!' Stephen went on to say. 'How heathen your hearts, how deaf you are to God's message! You are just like your ancestors: you too have always resisted the Holy Spirit!'
ACTS 7:51 GNB

While they were worshipping the Lord and fasting, the Holy Spirit said, 'Set apart for me Barnabas and Saul for the work to which I have called them.'
ACTS 13:2 RSV

'For it has seemed good to the Holy Spirit and to us to lay upon you no greater burden than these necessary things . . .'
ACTS 15:28 RSV

The love of God is shed abroad in our hearts by the Holy Ghost which is given unto us.
ROMANS 5:5 KJV

For those who live according to the flesh set their minds on the things of the flesh, but those who live according to the Spirit set their minds on the things of the Spirit. To set the mind on the flesh is death, but to set the mind on the Spirit is life and peace.
ROMANS 8:5–6 RSV

But you are not in the flesh, you are in the Spirit, if in fact the Spirit of God dwells in you. Any one who does not have the Spirit of Christ does not belong to him . . . If the Spirit of him who raised Jesus from the dead dwells in you, he who raised Christ Jesus from the dead will give life to your mortal bodies also through his Spirit which dwells in you . . . For if you live according to the flesh you will die, but if by the Spirit you put to death the deeds of the body you will live. For all who are led by the Spirit of God are sons of God. For you did not receive the spirit of slavery to fall back into fear, but you have received the spirit of sonship. When we cry 'Abba! Father!' it is the Spirit himself bearing witness with our spirit that we are children of God.
ROMANS 8:9–11, 13–16 RSV

Likewise the Spirit helps us in our weakness; for we do not know how to pray as we ought, but the

Spirit himself intercedes for us with sighs too deep for words. And he who searches the hearts of men knows what is the mind of the Spirit, because the Spirit intercedes for the saints according to the will of God.

ROMANS 8:26–27 RSV

Never flag in zeal, be aglow with the Spirit, serve the Lord.

ROMANS 12:11 RSV

My speech and my message were not in plausible words of wisdom, but in demonstration of the Spirit and of power.

1 CORINTHIANS 2:4 RSV

For the Spirit searches everything, even the depths of God.

1 CORINTHIANS 2:10 RSV

To each is given the manifestation of the Spirit for the common good.

1 CORINTHIANS 12:7 RSV

Now the Lord is the Spirit, and where the Spirit of the Lord is, there is freedom. And we all, with unveiled face, beholding the glory of the Lord, are being changed into his likeness from one degree of glory to another; for this comes from the Lord who is the Spirit.

2 CORINTHIANS 3:17–18 RSV

But the fruit of the Spirit is love, joy, peace, patience, kindness, goodness, faithfulness, gentleness, self-control; against such there is no law.

GALATIANS 5:22–23 RSV

And grieve not the holy Spirit of God, whereby ye are sealed unto the day of redemption.

EPHESIANS 4:30 KJV

Be filled with the Spirit; speaking to yourselves in psalms and hymns and spiritual songs, singing and making melody in your heart to the Lord; giving thanks always for all things unto God and the Father in the name of our Lord Jesus Christ; submitting yourselves one to another in the fear of God.

EPHESIANS 5:18–21 KJV

And take the helmet of salvation, and the sword of the Spirit, which is the word of God.

EPHESIANS 6:17 KJV

Quench not the Spirit.

1 THESSALONIANS 5:19 KJV

No prophecy of scripture is a matter of one's own interpretation, because no prophecy ever came by the impulse of man, but men moved by the Holy Spirit spoke from God.

2 PETER 1:21 RSV

## Homosexuality

No man is to have sexual relations with another man; God hates that.

LEVITICUS 18:22 GNB

If a man has sexual relations with another man, they have done a disgusting thing, and both shall be put to death. They are responsible for their own death.

LEVITICUS 20:13 GNB

Therefore God gave them over in the sinful desires of their hearts to sexual impurity for the degrading of their bodies with one another.

ROMANS 1:24 NIV

In consequence . . . God has given them up to shameful passions. Their women have exchanged natural intercourse for unnatural, and their men in turn, giving up natural relations with women, burn with lust for one another; males behave indecently with males, and are paid in their own persons the fitting wage of such perversion.

ROMANS 1:26–27 NEB

Do you not know that the wicked will not inherit the kingdom of God? Do not be deceived: Neither the sexually immoral nor idolaters nor adulterers nor male prostitutes nor homosexual offenders . . . will inherit the kingdom of God.

1 CORINTHIANS 6:9–10 NIV

See also *Sex.*

## Honesty

A false balance is an abomination to the Lord, but a just weight is his delight.

PROVERBS 11:1 RSV

'And as for that in the good soil, they are those who, hearing the word, hold it fast in an honest and good heart, and bring forth fruit with patience.'

LUKE 8:15 RSV

We have renounced disgraceful, underhanded ways; we refuse to practise cunning or to tamper with God's word, but by the open statement of the truth we would commend ourselves to every man's conscience in the sight of God.

2 CORINTHIANS 4:2 RSV

Our purpose is to do what is right, not only in the sight of the Lord, but also in the sight of man.

2 CORINTHIANS 8:21 GNB

Let the thief no longer steal, but rather let him labour, doing honest work with his hands, so that he may be able to give to those in need.

EPHESIANS 4:28 RSV

We were not lazy when we were with you. We did not accept anyone's support without paying for it. Instead, we worked and toiled.

2 THESSALONIANS 3:7–8 GNB

See also *Lying; Truth.*

## Hope

Why art thou cast down, O my soul? and why art thou disquieted in me? Hope thou in God: for I shall yet praise him for the help of his countenance.

PSALM 42:5 KJV

Abraham believed and hoped, even when there was no reason for hoping, and so became 'the father of many nations.'

ROMANS 4:18 GNB

We . . . rejoice in hope of the glory of God . . . hope maketh not ashamed; because the love of God is shed abroad in our hearts by the Holy Ghost which is given unto us.

ROMANS 5:2, 5 KJV

Not only the creation, but we ourselves, who have the first fruits of the Spirit, groan inwardly as we wait for adoption as sons, the redemption of our bodies. For in this hope we were saved. Now hope that is seen is not hope. For who hopes for what he sees? But if we hope for what we do not see, we wait for it with patience.

ROMANS 8:23–25 RSV

May the God of hope fill you with all joy and peace in believing, so that by the power of the Holy Spirit you may abound in hope.

ROMANS 15:13 RSV

So faith, hope, love abide, these three; but the greatest of these is love.

1 CORINTHIANS 13:13 RSV

You [Gentiles] were at that time separated from Christ, alienated from the commonwealth of Israel, and strangers to the covenants of promise, having no hope and without God in the world.

EPHESIANS 2:12 RSV

To them God chose to make known how great among the Gentiles are the riches of the glory of this mystery, which is Christ in you, the hope of glory.

COLOSSIANS 1:27 RSV

We who have fled for refuge might have strong encouragement to seize the hope set before us. We have this as a sure and steadfast anchor of the soul, a hope that enters into the inner shrine behind the curtain.

HEBREWS 6:18–19 RSV

Keep alert and set your hope completely on the blessing which will be given you when Jesus Christ is revealed.

1 PETER 1:13 GNB

## Hospitality

I was an hungred, and ye gave me meat: I was thirsty, and ye gave me drink: I was a stranger, and ye took me in.

MATTHEW 25:35 KJV

She [Lydia] was baptized, and her household with her, and then she said to us, 'If you have judged me to be a believer in the Lord, I beg you to come and stay in my house.' And she insisted on our going.

ACTS 16:15 NEB

Contribute to the needs of the saints, practise hospitality.

ROMANS 12:13 RSV

A bishop then must be blameless, the husband of but one wife, vigilant, sober, of good behaviour, given to hospitality . . .

1 TIMOTHY 3:2 KJV

[A widow] . . . well known for her good deeds, such as bringing up children, showing hospitality, washing the feet of the saints, helping those in trouble and devoting herself to all kinds of good deeds.

1 TIMOTHY 5:10 NIV

Do not neglect to show hospitality to strangers,

for thereby some have entertained angels unawares.
HEBREWS 13:2 RSV

Practise hospitality ungrudgingly to one another.
1 PETER 4:9 RSV

## Humility, humble

'This is the man to whom I will look, he that is humble and contrite in spirit, and trembles at my word.'
ISAIAH 66:2 RSV

Blessed are the poor in spirit: for theirs is the kingdom of heaven.
MATTHEW 5:3 KJV

Whosoever therefore shall humble himself as this little child, the same is greatest in the kingdom of heaven.
MATTHEW 18:4 KJV

'But it shall not be so among you; but whoever would be great among you must be your servant.'
MARK 10:43 RSV

Jesus, knowing that the Father had given all things into his hands, and that he had come from God and was going to God, rose from supper, laid aside his garments, and girded himself with a towel. Then he poured water into a basin, and began to wash the disciples' feet, and to wipe them with the towel with which he was girded . . . 'If I then, your Lord and Teacher, have washed your feet, you also ought to wash one another's feet.'
JOHN 13:3–5, 14 RSV

Do nothing from selfishness or conceit, but in humility count others better than yourselves . . . Have this mind among yourselves, which is yours in Christ Jesus, who, though he was in the form of God, did not count equality with God a thing to be grasped, but emptied himself, taking the form of a servant, being born in the likeness of men. And being found in human form he humbled himself and became obedient unto death, even death on a cross. Therefore God has highly exalted him and bestowed on him the name which is above every name, that at the name of Jesus every knee should bow, in heaven and on earth and under the earth, and every tongue confess that Jesus Christ is Lord, to the glory of God the Father.
PHILIPPIANS 2:3, 5–11 RSV

Likewise you that are younger be subject to the elders. Clothe yourselves, all of you, with humility toward one another, for 'God opposes the proud, but gives grace to the humble.' Humble yourselves therefore under the mighty hand of God, that in due time he may exalt you.
1 PETER 5:5–6 RSV

See also *Pride.*

## Husband
See *Marriage.*

## Hypocrisy, hypocrite

'So when you give something to a needy person, do not make a big show of it, as the hypocrites do in the houses of worship and on the streets. They do it so that people will praise them. I assure you, they have already been paid in full . . . When you pray, do not be like the hypocrites! They love to stand up and pray in the houses of worship and on the street corners, so that everyone will see them. I assure you, they have already been paid in full . . . And when you fast, do not put on a sad face as the hypocrites do. They neglect their appearance so that everyone will see that they are fasting. I assure you, they have already been paid in full.'
MATTHEW 6:2, 5, 16 GNB

'You hypocrite, first take the log out of your own eye, and then you will see clearly to take the speck out of your brother's eye.'
MATTHEW 7:5 RSV

[Jesus to the Pharisees and scribes] 'You hypocrites! Well did Isaiah prophesy of you, when he said: "This people honours me with their lips, but their heart is far from me; in vain do they worship me, teaching as doctrines the precepts of men." '
MATTHEW 15:7–9 RSV

'Why do you call me, "Lord, Lord," and yet don't do what I tell you?'
LUKE 6:46 GNB

They [people in the last days] will hold to the outward form of our religion, but reject its real power. Keep away from such people.
2 TIMOTHY 3:5 GNB

See also *Pharisees; Scribes.*

## Idolatry

Thou shalt have no other gods before me. Thou shalt not make unto thee any graven image, or any likeness of any thing that is in heaven above, or that is in the earth beneath, or that is in the water under the earth: thou shalt not bow down thyself to them, nor serve them.
EXODUS 20:3–5 KJV

And he [Aaron] received the gold at their hand, and fashioned it with a graving tool, and made a molten calf.
EXODUS 32:4 RSV

Their idols are silver and gold, made by the hands of men. They have mouths that cannot speak, and eyes that cannot see; they have ears that cannot hear, nostrils, and cannot smell; with their hands they cannot feel, with their feet they cannot walk, and no sound comes from their throats.
PSALM 115:4–7 NEB

Now the works of the flesh are plain . . . idolatry.
GALATIANS 5:19–20 RSV

For they themselves report concerning us what a welcome we had among you, and how you turned to God from idols, to serve a living and true God.
1 THESSALONIANS 1:9 RSV

Little children, keep yourselves from idols.
1 JOHN 5:21 RSV

## Illness

In the thirty-ninth year of his reign Asa was afflicted with a disease in his feet. Though his disease was severe, even in his illness he did not seek help from the Lord, but only from the physicians.
2 CHRONICLES 16:12 NIV

So Satan went forth from the presence of the Lord, and afflicted Job with loathsome sores from the sole of his foot to the crown of his head.
JOB 2:7 RSV

Because of your anger, I am in great pain; my whole body is diseased because of my sins.
PSALM 38:3 GNB

He had healed many, so that all who had diseases pressed upon him to touch him.
MARK 3:10 RSV

So the sisters sent to him, saying, 'Lord, he whom you love is ill.'
JOHN 11:3 RSV

See also **Suffering.**

### HELP IN

The Lord will help them when they are sick and will restore them to health.
PSALM 41:3 GNB

Surely he hath borne our griefs, and carried our sorrows: yet we did esteem him stricken, smitten of God, and afflicted.
ISAIAH 53:4 KJV

A leper came to him and knelt before him, saying, 'Lord, if you will, you can make me clean.' And he stretched out his hand and touched him, saying, 'I will; be clean.' And immediately his leprosy was cleansed.
MATTHEW 8:2–3 RSV

Is any sick among you? Let him call for the elders of the church; and let them pray over him, anointing him with oil in the name of the Lord: and the prayer of faith shall save the sick, and the Lord shall raise him up; and if he have committed sins, they shall be forgiven him. Confess your faults one to another, and pray one for another, that ye may be healed. The effectual fervent prayer of a righteous man availeth much.
JAMES 5:14–16 KJV

See also **Comfort; Healing.**

## Immigrants

'You shall not wrong a stranger or oppress him, for you were strangers in the land of Egypt.'
EXODUS 22:21 RSV

'Do not illtreat foreigners who are living in your land. Treat them as you would a fellow-Israelite, and love them as you love yourselves.'
LEVITICUS 19:33–34 GNB

'He executes justice for the fatherless and the widow, and loves the sojourner, giving him food and clothing. Love the sojourner therefore; for you were sojourners in the land of Egypt.'
DEUTERONOMY 10:18–19 RSV

The Lord watches over the sojourners, he upholds the widow and the fatherless.
PSALM 146:9 RSV

I was an hungred, and ye gave me meat: I was thirsty, and ye gave me drink: I was a stranger,

and ye took me in.
MATTHEW 25:35 KJV

Do not neglect to show hospitality to strangers, for thereby some have entertained angels unawares.
HEBREWS 13:2 RSV

## Incarnation
See *Jesus Christ, Jesus, the man.*

## Inheritance

Then shall the King say unto them on his right hand, Come, ye blessed of my Father, inherit the kingdom prepared for you from the foundation of the world.
MATTHEW 25:34 KJV

'And now I commend you to God, and to the word of his grace that has power to build you up and to give you your inheritance among all the sanctified.'
ACTS 20:32 JB

[Children of God are] heirs, joint heirs of God and fellow heirs with Christ, provided we suffer with him in order that we may also be glorified with him.
ROMANS 8:17 RSV

Do you not know that the wicked will not inherit the kingdom of God? Do not be deceived: Neither the sexually immoral nor idolaters nor adulterers nor male prostitutes nor homosexual offenders nor thieves nor the greedy nor drunkards nor slanderers nor swindlers will inherit the kingdom of God.
1 CORINTHIANS 6:9–10 NIV

I tell you this, brethren: flesh and blood cannot inherit the kingdom of God, nor does the perishable inherit the imperishable.
1 CORINTHIANS 15:50 RSV

So through God you are no longer a slave but a son, and if a son then an heir.
GALATIANS 4:7 RSV

In whom also we have obtained an inheritance, being predestined according to the purpose of him who worketh all things after the counsel of his own will.
EPHESIANS 1:11 KJV

In him you also, who have heard the word of truth, the gospel of your salvation, and have believed in him, were sealed with the promised Holy Spirit, which is the guarantee of our inheritance until we acquire possession of it, to the praise of his glory.
EPHESIANS 1:13–14 RSV

[Paul's prayer] That you may know what is the hope to which he has called you, what are the riches of his glorious inheritance in the saints.
EPHESIANS 1:18 RSV

So that we might be justified by his grace and become heirs in hope of eternal life.
TITUS 3:7 RSV

[God] hath in these last days spoken unto us by his Son, whom he hath appointed heir of all things, by whom also he made the worlds.
HEBREWS 1:2 KJV

By his great mercy we have been born anew . . . to an inheritance which is imperishable, undefiled, and unfading, kept in heaven for you.
1 PETER 1:3–4 RSV

[Husband and wife] Heirs together of the grace of life.
1 PETER 3:7 KJV

## Injustice

'Do not spread false rumours, and do not help a guilty man by giving false evidence.'
EXODUS 23:1 GNB

'You shall do no injustice in judgment; you shall not be partial to the poor or defer to the great, but in righteousness shall you judge your neighbour.'
LEVITICUS 19:15 RSV

'Do not cheat anyone by using false measures of length, weight, or quantity.'
LEVITICUS 19:35 GNB

'Now then, let the fear of the Lord be upon you; take heed what you do, for there is no perversion of justice with the Lord our God, or partiality, or taking bribes.'
2 CHRONICLES 19:7 RSV

'How long will you judge unjustly and show partiality to the wicked?'
PSALM 82:2 RSV

The Lord hates people who use dishonest weights and measures.
PROVERBS 20:10 GNB

'Woe to him who builds his house by unrighteousness, and his upper rooms by injustice; who makes his neighbour serve him for nothing, and does not give him his wages.'
JEREMIAH 22:13 RSV

The Lord is righteous, he does no wrong; every morning he shows forth his justice, each dawn he does not fail; but the unjust knows no shame.
ZEPHANIAH 3:5 RSV

See also *Justice; Oppression.*

## Israel

And he said, Thy name shall be called no more Jacob, but Israel: for as a prince hast thou power with God and with men, and hast prevailed.
GENESIS 32:28 KJV

But thou, Bethlehem Ephratah, though thou be little among the thousands of Judah, yet out of thee shall he come forth unto me that is to be ruler in Israel; whose goings forth have been from of old, from everlasting.
MICAH 5:2 KJV

Jesus said to them, 'You can be sure that when the Son of Man sits on his glorious throne in the New Age, then you twelve followers of mine will also sit on thrones, to rule the twelve tribes of Israel.'
MATTHEW 19:28 GNB

Pilate also wrote a title and put it on the cross; it read, 'Jesus of Nazareth, the King of the Jews.'
JOHN 19:19 RSV

For he is not a real Jew who is one outwardly, nor is true circumcision something external and physical. He is a Jew who is one inwardly, and real circumcision is a matter of the heart, spiritual and not literal. His praise is not from men but from God.
ROMANS 2:28–29 RSV

But it is not as though the word of God has failed. For not all who are descended from Israel belong to Israel, and not all are children of Abraham because they are his descendants; but 'Through Isaac shall your descendants be named.'
ROMANS 9:6–7 RSV

I do not want you to be ignorant of this mystery, brothers, so that you may not be conceited: Israel has experienced a hardening in part until the full number of the Gentiles has come in. And

so all Israel will be saved, as it is written: 'The deliverer will come from Zion; he will turn godlessness away from Jacob.'
ROMANS 11:25–26 NIV

Neither circumcision nor uncircumcision means anything, what counts is a new creation. Peace and mercy to all who follow this rule, even to the Israel of God.
GALATIANS 6:15–16 NIV

For we are the true circumcision, who worship God in spirit, and glory in Christ Jesus, and put no confidence in the flesh.
PHILIPPIANS 3:3 RSV

See also *Gentiles.*

## Jealousy

Thou shalt not bow down thyself to them, nor serve them: for I the Lord thy God am a jealous God, visiting the iniquity of the fathers upon the children unto the third and fourth generation of them that hate me.
EXODUS 20:5 KJV

'You shall worship no other god, for the Lord, whose name is Jealous, is a jealous God.'
EXODUS 34:14 RSV

Anger is cruel and destructive, but it is nothing compared to jealousy.
PROVERBS 27:4 GNB

'Now his elder son was in the field; and as he came and drew near to the house, he heard music and dancing . . . But he was angry and refused to go in. His father came out and entreated him, but he answered his father, ''Lo, these many years I have served you, and I never disobeyed your command; yet you never gave me a kid, that I might make merry with my friends. But when this son of yours came, who has devoured your living with harlots, you killed for him the fatted calf!'' '
LUKE 15:25, 28–30 RSV

Love is not jealous or boastful.
1 CORINTHIANS 13:4 RSV

Now the works of the flesh are plain . . . jealousy . . .
GALATIANS 5:19–29 RSV

But if you have bitter jealousy and selfish ambition in your hearts, do not boast and be false to the truth . . . For where jealousy and

selfish ambition exist, there will be disorder and every vile practice.
JAMES 3:14, 16 RSV

Or do you suppose it is in vain that the scripture says, 'He yearns jealously over the spirit which he has made to dwell in us?'
JAMES 4:5 RSV

See also *Envy.*

# Jesus Christ

## ASCENSION

'Was it not necessary that the Christ should suffer these things and enter into his glory?'
LUKE 24:26 RSV

While he blessed them, he parted from them, and was carried up into heaven.
LUKE 24:52 RSV

Now this he said about the Spirit, which those who believed in him were to receive; for as yet the Spirit had not been given, because Jesus was not yet glorified.
JOHN 7:39 RSV

Jesus said to her [Mary], 'Do not hold me, for I have not yet ascended to the Father; but go to my brethren and say to them, I am ascending to my Father and your Father, to my God and your God.'
JOHN 20:17 RSV

And when he had said this, as they were looking on, he was lifted up, and a cloud took him out of their sight.
ACTS 1:9 RSV

'Being therefore exalted at the right hand of God, and having received from the Father the promise of the Holy Spirit, he has poured out this which you see and hear.'
ACTS 2:33 RSV

He [God] raised him [Christ] from the dead, and set him at his own right hand in the heavenly places, far above all principality, and power, and might, and dominion, and every name that is named, not only in this world, but also in that which is to come: and hath put all things under his feet, and gave him to be the head over all things to the church, which is his body, the fulness of him that filleth all in all.
EPHESIANS 1:20–23 KJV

Therefore God has highly exalted him and bestowed on him the name which is above every name.
PHILIPPIANS 2:9 RSV

## AUTHORITY

He [Jesus] taught . . . as one who had authority, and not as their scribes.
MATTHEW 7:29 RSV

'But that you may know that the Son of man has authority on earth to forgive sins'—he then said to the paralytic—'Rise, take up your bed and go home.'
MATTHEW 9:6 RSV

And Jesus came and said to them, 'All authority in heaven and on earth has been given to me.'
MATTHEW 28:18 RSV

And they were all amazed and said to one another, 'What is this word? For with authority and power he commands the unclean spirits, and they come out.'
LUKE 4:36 RSV

'And he [God the Father] has given him authority to judge because he is the Son of Man.'
JOHN 5:27 NIV

'No-one takes it [my life] from me, but I lay it down of my own accord. I have authority to lay it down and authority to take it up again. This command I received from my Father.'
JOHN 10:18 NIV

## DEATH

[God to the serpent] And I will put enmity between thee and the woman, and between thy seed and her seed; it shall bruise thy head, and thou shalt bruise his heel.
GENESIS 3:15 KJV

He is despised and rejected of men; a man of sorrows, and acquainted with grief: and we hid as it were our faces from him; he was despised, and we esteemed him not. Surely he hath borne our griefs, and carried our sorrows: yet we did esteem him stricken, smitten of God, and afflicted. But he was wounded for our transgressions, he was bruised for our iniquities: the chastisement of our peace was upon him; and with his stripes we are healed. All we like sheep have gone astray; we have turned every one to his own way; and the Lord hath laid on him the iniquity of us all. He was oppressed, and

he was afflicted, yet he opened not his mouth: he is brought as a lamb to the slaughter, and as a sheep before her shearers is dumb, so he openeth not his mouth. He was taken from prison and from judgment: and who shall declare his generation? For he was cut off out of the land of the living: for the transgression of my people was he stricken. And he made his grave with the wicked, and with the rich in his death; because he had done no violence, neither was any deceit in his mouth.
ISAIAH 53:3–9 KJV

From that time forth began Jesus to shew unto his disciples, how that he must go unto Jerusalem, and suffer many things of the elders and chief priests and scribes, and be killed, and be raised again the third day.
MATTHEW 16:21 KJV

'I am the good shepherd. The good shepherd lays down his life for the sheep.'
JOHN 10:11 RSV

This Jesus, delivered up according to the definite plan and foreknowledge of God, you crucified and killed by the hands of lawless men.
ACTS 2:23 RSV

'You killed the author of life, but God raised him from the dead.'
ACTS 3:15 NIV

[Jesus] . . . was delivered for our offences, and was raised again for our justification.
ROMANS 4:25 KJV

While we were still weak, at the right time Christ died for the ungodly. Why, one will hardly die for a righteous man—though perhaps for a good man one will dare even to die. But God shows his love for us in that while we were yet sinners Christ died for us.
ROMANS 5:6–8 RSV

For the word of the cross is folly to those who are perishing, but to us who are being saved it is the power of God.
1 CORINTHIANS 1:18 RSV

But we preach Christ crucified, unto the Jews a stumbling block, and unto the Greeks foolishness; but unto them which are called, both Jews and Greeks, Christ the power of God, and the wisdom of God.
1 CORINTHIANS 1:23–24 KJV

For I delivered to you as of first importance what I also received, that Christ died for our sins in accordance with the scriptures . . .
1 CORINTHIANS 15:3 RSV

I have been crucified with Christ; it is no longer I who live, but Christ who lives in me; and the life I now live in the flesh I live by faith in the Son of God, who loved me and gave himself for me.
GALATIANS 2:20 RSV

But far be it from me to glory except in the cross of our Lord Jesus Christ, by which the world has been crucified to me, and I to the world.
GALATIANS 6:14 RSV

He disarmed the principalities and powers and made a public example of them, triumphing over them in him.
COLOSSIANS 2:15 RSV

Since therefore the children share in flesh and blood, he himself likewise partook of the same nature, that through death he might destroy him who has the power of death, that is, the devil, and deliver all those who through fear of death were subject to lifelong bondage.
HEBREWS 2:14–15 RSV

See also *Atonement; Reconciliation.*

### ETERNAL SON OF GOD

'The Lord possessed me at the beginning of his work, before his deeds of old; I was appointed from eternity, from the beginning, before the world began.'
PROVERBS 8:22–23 NIV

In the beginning was the Word, and the Word was with God, and the Word was God. The same was in the beginning with God.
JOHN 1:1–2 KJV

Jesus said unto them, Verily, verily, I say unto you, Before Abraham was, I am.
JOHN 8:58 KJV

He is the image of the invisible God, the first-born of all creation; for in him all things were created, in heaven and on earth, visible and invisible, whether thrones or dominions or principalities or authorities—all things were created through him and for him. He is before all things, and in him all things hold together. He is the head of the body, the church; he is the beginning, the first-born from the dead, that in everything he might be pre-eminent. For in him all the fullness of God was pleased to dwell.

COLOSSIANS 1:15–19 RSV

His Son, who he appointed heir of all things, and through whom he made the universe. The Son is the radiance of God's glory and the exact representation of his being, sustaining all things by his powerful word. After he had provided purification for sins, he sat down at the right hand of the Majesty in heaven. So he became as much superior to the angels as the name he has inherited is superior to theirs. For to which of the angels did God ever say, 'You are my Son; today I have become your father'? Or again, 'I will be his Father, and he will be my Son'? And again, when God brings his first-born into the world, he says, 'Let all God's angels worship him.' In speaking of the angels he says, 'He makes his angels winds, his servants flames of fire.' But about the Son he says, 'Your throne, O God, will last for ever and ever, and righteousness will be the sceptre of your kingdom.'

HEBREWS 1:2–8 NIV

Jesus Christ is the same yesterday and today and for ever.

HEBREWS 13:8 RSV

'I am the Alpha and the Omega,' says the Lord God, who was and who is and who is to come, the Almighty.

REVELATION 1:8 RSV

## HOLINESS

'Which of you convicts me of sin?'

JOHN 8:46 RSV

For we have not a high priest who is unable to sympathize with our weaknesses, but one who in every respect has been tempted as we are, yet without sin.

HEBREWS 4:15 RSV

For it was fitting that we should have such a high priest, holy, blameless, unstained, separated from sinners, exalted above the heavens.

HEBREWS 7:26 RSV

He committed no sin; no guile was found on his lips.

1 PETER 2:22 RSV

## HUMILITY

Rejoice greatly; O Daughter of Zion! Shout, daughter of Jerusalem! See, your king comes to you, righteous and having salvation, gentle and riding on a donkey, on a colt, the foal of a donkey.

ZECHARIAH 9:9 NIV

For ye know the grace of our Lord Jesus Christ, that, though he was rich, yet for your sakes he became poor, that ye through his poverty might be rich.

2 CORINTHIANS 8:9 KJV

Though he [Jesus] was in the form of God, did not count equality with God a thing to be grasped, but emptied himself, taking the form of a servant, being born in the likeness of men. And being found in human form he humbled himself and became obedient unto death, even death on a cross.

PHILIPPIANS 2:6–8 RSV

## JESUS AS KING

The Lord says to my lord: 'Sit at my right hand, till I make your enemies your footstool.'

PSALM 110:1 RSV

'Behold, the days are coming, says the Lord, when I will raise up for David a righteous Branch, and he shall reign as king and deal wisely, and shall execute justice and righteousness in the land.'

JEREMIAH 23:5 RSV

'In my vision at night I looked, and there before me was one like a son of man, coming with the clouds of heaven. He approached the Ancient of Days and was led into his presence. He was given authority, glory and sovereign power; all peoples, nations and men of every language worshipped him. His dominion is an everlasting dominion that will not pass away, and his kingdom is one that will never be destroyed.'

DANIEL 7:13–14 NIV

Rejoice greatly; O Daughter of Zion! Shout, daughter of Jerusalem! See, your king comes to you, righteous and having salvation, gentle and riding on a donkey, on a colt, the foal of a donkey.

ZECHARIAH 9:9 NIV

Jesus answered, 'My kingship is not of this world; if my kingship were of this world, my servants would fight, that I might not be handed over to the Jews; but my kingship is not from the world.'

JOHN 18:36 RSV

Pilate also wrote a title and put it on the cross; it read, 'Jesus of Nazareth, the King of the Jews.' The chief priests of the Jews then said to Pilate, 'Do not write, "The King of the Jews," but, "This man said, I am King of the Jews." '
JOHN 19:19, 21 RSV

But about the Son he says, 'Your throne, O God, will last for ever and ever, and righteousness will be the sceptre of your kingdom.'
HEBREWS 1:8 NIV

And I heard a loud voice in heaven, saying, 'Now the salvation and the power and the kingdom of our God and the authority of his Christ have come, for the accuser of our brethren has been thrown down, who accuses them day and night before our God.'
REVELATION 12:10 RSV

## JESUS, THE MAN

Therefore the Lord himself shall give you a sign; behold, a virgin shall conceive, and bear a son, and shall call his name Immanuel.
ISAIAH 7:14 KJV

For unto us a child is born, unto us a son is given: and the government shall be upon his shoulder: and his name shall be called Wonderful, Counsellor, The mighty God, The everlasting Father, The Prince of Peace.
ISAIAH 9:6 KJV

And she [Mary] brought forth her firstborn son, and wrapped him in swaddling clothes, and laid him in a manger; because there was no room for them in the inn.
LUKE 2:7 KJV

And the Word was made flesh, and dwelt among us, (and we beheld his glory, the glory as of the only begotten of the Father,) full of grace and truth.
JOHN 1:14 KJV

For God so loved the world, that he gave his only begotten Son, that whosoever believeth in him should not perish, but have everlasting life. For God sent not his Son into the world to condemn the world; but that the world through him might be saved.
JOHN 3:16–17 KJV

But when the time had fully come, God sent forth his Son, born of woman, born under the law, to redeem those who were under the law.
GALATIANS 4:4 RSV

Have this mind among yourselves, which is yours in Christ Jesus, who, though he was in the form of God, did not count equality with God a thing to be grasped, but emptied himself, taking the form of a servant, being born in the likeness of men. And being found in human form he humbled himself and became obedient unto death, even death on a cross.
PHILIPPIANS 2:5–8 RSV

For there is one God, and one mediator between God and men, the man Christ Jesus.
1 TIMOTHY 2:5 KJV

Great indeed, we confess, is the mystery of our religion: He was manifested in the flesh, vindicated in the Spirit, seen by angels, preached among the nations, believed on in the world, taken up in glory.
1 TIMOTHY 3:16 RSV

But we see Jesus, who was made a little lower than the angels for the suffering of death, crowned with glory and honour.
HEBREWS 2:9 KJV

Since therefore the children share in flesh and blood, he himself likewise partook of the same nature, that through death he might destroy him who has the power of death, that is, the devil.
HEBREWS 2:14 RSV

For we have not a high priest who is unable to sympathize with our weaknesses, but one who in every respect has been tempted as we are, yet without sin.
HEBREWS 4:15 RSV

This is how we may recognize the Spirit of God: every spirit which acknowledges that Jesus Christ has come in the flesh is from God.
1 JOHN 4:2 NEB

## JESUS, THE ONE TO BE WORSHIPPED

And when they were come into the house, they saw the young child with Mary his mother, and fell down, and worshipped him: and when they had opened their treasures, they presented unto him gifts; gold, and frankincense, and myrrh.
MATTHEW 2:11 KJV

And Simon Peter answered and said, Thou art the Christ, the Son of the living God.
MATTHEW 16:16 KJV

When Simon Peter saw it, he fell down at Jesus' knees, saying, Depart from me; for I am a sinful man, O Lord.

**LUKE 5:8 KJV**

Thomas answered him, 'My Lord and my God!'

**JOHN 20:28 RSV**

'Worthy is the Lamb who was slain, to receive power and wealth and wisdom and might and honour and glory and blessing!'

**REVELATION 5:12 RSV**

## JESUS AS PRIEST

For there is one God, and one mediator between God and men, the man Christ Jesus.

**1 TIMOTHY 2:5 KJV**

Since then we have a great high priest who has passed through the heavens, Jesus, the Son of God, let us hold fast our confession. For we have not a high priest who is unable to sympathize with our weaknesses, but one who in every respect has been tempted as we are, yet without sin.

**HEBREWS 4:14–16 RSV**

So also Christ did not exalt himself to be made a high priest, but was appointed by him who said to him, 'Thou art my Son, today I have begotten thee'; as he says also in another place, 'Thou art a priest for ever, after the order of Melchizedek.'

**HEBREWS 5:5–6 RSV**

But he holds his priesthood permanently, because he continues for ever. Consequently he is able for all time to save those who draw near to God through him, since he always lives to make intercession for them. For it was fitting that we should have such a high priest, holy, blameless, unstained, separated from sinners, exalted above the heavens.

**HEBREWS 7:24–26 RSV**

Therefore he is the mediator of a new covenant, so that those who are called may receive the promised eternal inheritance, since a death has occurred which redeems them from the transgressions under the first covenant.

**HEBREWS 9:15 RSV**

And every priest stands daily at his service, offering repeatedly the same sacrifices, which can never take away sins. But when Christ had offered for all time a single sacrifice for sins, he sat down at the right hand of God.

**HEBREWS 10:11–12 RSV**

## JESUS AS PROPHET

'The Lord your God will raise up for you a prophet like me from among you, from your brethren—him you shall heed.'

**DEUTERONOMY 18:15 RSV**

And the crowds said, 'This is the prophet Jesus from Nazareth of Galilee.'

**MATTHEW 21:11 RSV**

Fear seized them all; and they glorified God, saying, 'A great prophet has arisen among us!' and 'God has visited his people!'

**LUKE 7:16 RSV**

'Concerning Jesus of Nazareth, who was a prophet mighty in deed and word before God and all the people.'

**LUKE 24:19 RSV**

## LOVE

When he saw the crowds, he had compassion for them, because they were harassed and helpless, like sheep without a shepherd.

**MATTHEW 9:36 RSV**

Now before the feast of the Passover, when Jesus knew that his hour had come to depart out of this world to the Father, having loved his own who were in the world, he loved them to the end.

**JOHN 13:1 RSV**

'As the Father has loved me, so have I loved you; abide in my love.'

**JOHN 15:9 RSV**

For I am sure that neither death, nor life, nor angels, nor principalities, nor things present, nor things to come, nor powers, nor height, nor depth, nor anything else in all creation, will be able to separate us from the love of God in Christ Jesus our Lord.

**ROMANS 8:38–39 RSV**

[Paul's prayer] That you, being rooted and grounded in love, may have power to comprehend with all the saints what is the breadth and length and height and depth, and to know the love of Christ which surpasses knowledge.

**EPHESIANS 3:17–19 RSV**

To him who loves us and freed us from our sins by his blood . . .

REVELATION 1:5 RSV

## OBEDIENCE

'I delight to do thy will, O my God; thy law is within my heart.'

PSALM 40:8 RSV

Again, for the second time, he went away and prayed, 'My Father, if this cannot pass unless I drink it, thy will be done.'

MATTHEW 26:42 RSV

Jesus said to them, 'My food is to do the will of him who sent me, and to accomplish his work.'

JOHN 4:34 RSV

'And he who sent me is with me; he has not left me alone, for I always do what is pleasing to him.'

JOHN 8:29 RSV

And being found in human form he humbled himself and became obedient unto death, even death on a cross.

PHILIPPIANS 2:8 RSV

But even though he was God's Son, he learnt through his sufferings to be obedient.

HEBREWS 5:8 GNB

## RESURRECTION

For thou dost not give me up to Sheol, or let thy godly one see the Pit.

PSALM 16:10 RSV

Yet it pleased the Lord to bruise him; he hath put him to grief: when thou shalt make his soul an offering for sin, he shall see his seed, he shall prolong his days, and the pleasure of the Lord shall prosper in his hand. He shall see of the travail of his soul, and shall be satisfied: by his knowledge shall my righteous servant justify many; for he shall bear their iniquities. Therefore will I divide him a portion with the great, and he shall divide the spoil with the strong; because he hath poured out his soul unto death; and he was numbered with the transgressors; and he bare the sin of many, and made intercession for the transgressors.

ISAIAH 53:10–12 KJV

From that time forth began Jesus to shew unto his disciples, how that he must go unto Jerusalem, and suffer many things of the elders and chief priests and scribes, and be killed, and be raised again the third day.

MATTHEW 16:21 KJV

He is not here: for he is risen, as he said. Come, see the place where the Lord lay.

MATTHEW 28:6 KJV

'This Jesus God raised up, and of that we all are witnesses.'

ACTS 2:32 RSV

'He has fixed a day on which he will judge the world in righteousness by a man whom he has appointed, and of this he has given assurance to all men by raising him from the dead.'

ACTS 17:31 RSV

[Jesus] . . . was delivered for our offences, and was raised again for our justification.

ROMANS 4:25 KJV

By our baptism, then, we were buried with him and shared his death, in order that, just as Christ was raised from death by the glorious power of the Father, so also we might live a new life. For since we have become one with him in dying as he did, in the same way we shall be one with him by being raised to life as he was.

ROMANS 6:4–5 GNB

For we know that Christ being raised from the dead will never die again; death no longer has dominion over him. The death he died he died to sin, once for all, but the life he lives he lives to God. So you also must consider yourselves dead to sin and alive to God in Christ Jesus.

ROMANS 6:9–11 RSV

He was buried . . . he was raised on the third day in accordance with the scriptures, and . . . he appeared to Cephas, then to the twelve.

1 CORINTHIANS 15:4 RSV

Now if Christ is preached as raised from the dead, how can some of you say that there is no resurrection of the dead? But if there is no resurrection of the dead, then Christ has not been raised; if Christ has not been raised, then our preaching is in vain and your faith is in vain. We are even found to be misrepresenting God, because we testified of God that he raised Christ, whom he did not raise if it is true that the dead are not raised. For if the dead are not raised, then Christ has not been raised. If Christ has not been raised, your faith is futile and you are still in your sins. Then those also who have fallen asleep in

Christ have perished. If for this life only we have hoped in Christ, we are of all men most to be pitied. But in fact Christ has been raised from the dead, the first fruits of those who have fallen asleep. For as by a man came death, by a man has come also the resurrection of the dead.
1 CORINTHIANS 15:12–21 RSV

If ye then be risen with Christ, seek those things which are above, where Christ sitteth on the right hand of God.
COLOSSIANS 3:1 KJV

When I saw him, I fell at his feet as though dead. But he laid his right hand upon me and said, 'Do not be afraid. I am the first and the last, and I am the living one; for I was dead and now I am alive for evermore, and I hold the keys of Death and Death's domain.'
REVELATION 1:17–18 NEB

**SECOND COMING**
See *Last things.*

**SEVEN WORDS FROM THE CROSS**

And about the ninth hour Jesus cried with a loud voice, 'Eli, Eli, lama sabachthani?' that is, 'My God, my God, why hast thou forsaken me?'
MATTHEW 27:46 RSV

Then said Jesus, Father, forgive them; for they know not what they do.
LUKE 23:34 KJV

And Jesus said unto him, Verily I say unto thee, To day shalt thou be with me in paradise.
LUKE 23:43 KJV

And when Jesus had cried with a loud voice, he said, Father, into thy hands I commend my spirit: and having said thus, he gave up the ghost.
LUKE 23:46 KJV

When Jesus saw his mother, and the disciple whom he loved standing near, he said to his mother, 'Woman, behold your son!' Then he said to the disciple, 'Behold, your mother!'
JOHN 19:26–27 RSV

After this Jesus, knowing that all was now finished, said (to fulfil the scripture), 'I thirst.'
JOHN 19:28 RSV

When Jesus had received the vinegar, he said, 'It is finished'; and he bowed his head and gave up his spirit.
JOHN 19:30 RSV

# Joy

He [Nehemiah] said . . . 'This day is holy to our Lord; and do not be grieved, for the joy of the Lord is your strength.'
NEHEMIAH 8:10 RSV

Thou dost show me the path of life; in thy presence there is fullness of joy, in thy right hand are pleasures for evermore.
PSALM 16:11 RSV

This is the day which the Lord has made; let us rejoice and be glad in it.
PSALM 118:24 RSV

I rejoice at thy word like one who finds great spoil.
PSALM 119:162 RSV

The Lord has done great things for us, and we are filled with joy.
PSALM 126:3 NIV

They that sow in tears shall reap in joy. He that goeth forth and weepeth, bearing precious seed, shall doubtless come again with rejoicing, bringing his sheaves with him.
PSALM 126:5–6 KJV

With joy you will draw water from the wells of salvation.
ISAIAH 12:3 RSV

And the ransomed of the Lord shall return, and come to Zion with singing; everlasting joy shall be upon their heads; they shall obtain joy and gladness, and sorrow and sighing shall flee away.
ISAIAH 35:10 RSV

Blessed are the poor in spirit: for theirs is the kingdom of heaven . . .
MATTHEW 5:3 KJV

'As for what was sown on rocky ground, this is he who hears the word and immediately receives it with joy; yet he has no root in himself, but endures for a while, and when tribulation or persecution arises on account of the word, immediately he falls away.'
MATTHEW 13:20–21 RSV

'Just so, I tell you, there will be more joy in heaven over one sinner who repents than over ninety-nine righteous persons who need no repentance.'
LUKE 15:7 RSV

'These things I have spoken to you, that my joy may be in you, and that your joy may be full.'
JOHN 15:11 RSV

'Ask and you will receive, that your joy may be complete.'
JOHN 16:24 NEB

And the disciples were filled with joy and with the Holy Spirit.
ACTS 13:52 RSV

Our Lord Jesus Christ: by whom also we have access by faith into this grace wherein we stand, and rejoice in hope of the glory of God.
ROMANS 5:1–2 KJV

May the God of hope fill you with all joy and peace in believing, so that by the power of the Holy Spirit you may abound in hope.
ROMANS 15:13 RSV

I will all the more gladly boast of my weaknesses, that the power of Christ may rest upon me.
2 CORINTHIANS 12:9 RSV

But the fruit of the Spirit is … joy …
GALATIANS 5:22 RSV

Rejoice in the Lord always; again I will say, Rejoice.
PHILIPPIANS 4:4 RSV

As for the rich in this world, charge them not to be haughty, nor to set their hopes on uncertain riches but on God who richly furnishes us with everything to enjoy.
1 TIMOTHY 6:17 RSV

Looking unto Jesus the author and finisher of our faith; who for the joy that was set before him endured the cross, despising the shame, and is set down at the right hand of the throne of God.
HEBREWS 12:2 KJV

Without having seen him you love him; though you do not now see him you believe in him and rejoice with unutterable and exalted joy.
1 PETER 1:8 RSV

No greater joy can I have than this, to hear that my children follow the truth.
3 JOHN 4 RSV

## Judgement
See *Last things*.

## Justice

'Do not take advantage of anyone or rob him. Do not hold back the wages of someone you have hired, not even for one night.'
LEVITICUS 19:13 GNB

'Justice, and only justice, you shall follow, that you may live and inherit the land which the Lord your God gives you.'
DEUTERONOMY 16:20 RSV

Give the king thy justice, O God, and thy righteousness to the royal son! May he judge thy people with righteousness, and thy poor with justice!
PSALM 72:1–2 RSV

To do righteousness and justice is more acceptable to the Lord than sacrifice.
PROVERBS 21:3 RSV

Seek justice, encourage the oppressed. Defend the cause of the fatherless, plead the case of the widow.
ISAIAH 1:17 NIV

We all growl like bears, we moan and moan like doves; we look for justice, but there is none; for salvation, but it is far from us.
ISAIAH 59:11 RSV

Justice is driven away, and right cannot come near. Truth stumbles in the public square, and honesty finds no place there.
ISAIAH 59:14 GNB

The Lord says, 'I love justice and hate oppression and crime. I will faithfully reward my people and make an eternal covenant with them.'
ISAIAH 61:8 GNB

'But let justice roll down like waters, and righteousness like an ever-flowing stream.'
AMOS 5:24 RSV

He hath shewed thee, O man, what is good; and what doth the Lord require of thee, but to do justly, and to love mercy, and to walk humbly with thy God?
MICAH 6:8 KJV

Masters, treat your slaves justly and fairly, knowing that you also have a Master in heaven.
COLOSSIANS 4:1 RSV

See also *Injustice; Righteousness.*

# Justification

And he [Abraham] believed in the Lord; and he counted it to him for righteousness.
GENESIS 15:6 KJV

Then Job answered: 'Truly I know that it is so: But how can a man be just before God?'
JOB 9:1–2 RSV

Blessed is he whose transgression is forgiven, whose sin is covered. Blessed is the man to whom the Lord imputes no iniquity, and in whose spirit there is no deceit.
PSALM 32:1–2 RSV

He is near that justifieth me; who will contend with me? Let us stand together: who is mine adversary? Let him come near to me. Behold, the Lord God will help me; who is he that shall condemn me?
ISAIAH 50:8–9 KJV

I will greatly rejoice in the Lord, my soul shall exult in my God; for he has clothed me with the garments of salvation, he has covered me with the robe of righteousness.
ISAIAH 61:10 RSV

'But the tax collector, standing far off, would not even lift up his eyes to heaven, but beat his breast, saying, ''God, be merciful to me a sinner!'' I tell you, this man went down to his house justified rather than the other; for every one who exalts himself will be humbled, but he who humbles himself will be exalted.'
LUKE 18:13–14 RSV

Being justified freely by his grace through the redemption that is in Christ Jesus.
ROMANS 3:24 KJV

And to one who does not work but trusts him who justifies the ungodly, his faith is reckoned as righteousness.
ROMANS 4:5 RSV

Therefore being justified by faith, we have peace with God through our Lord Jesus Christ.
ROMANS 5:1 KJV

Since, therefore, we are now justified by his blood, much more shall we be saved by him from the wrath of God.
ROMANS 5:9 RSV

For as by one man's disobedience many were made sinners, so by one man's obedience many will be made righteous.
ROMANS 5:19 RSV

And those whom he predestined he also called; and those whom he called he also justified; and those whom he justified he also glorified ... Who shall bring any charge against God's elect? It is God who justifies; who is to condemn? Is it Christ Jesus, who died, yes, who was raised from the dead, who is at the right hand of God, who indeed intercedes for us?
ROMANS 8:30, 33–34 RSV

For our sake he made him to be sin who knew no sin, so that in him we might become the righteousness of God.
2 CORINTHIANS 5:21 RSV

See also *Atonement; Faith; Righteousness.*

# Kindness

'If you pour yourself out for the hungry and satisfy the desire of the afflicted, then shall your light rise in the darkness and your gloom be as the noonday.'
ISAIAH 58:10 RSV

When the Son of man shall come in his glory, and all the holy angels with him, then shall he sit upon the throne of his glory: and before him shall be gathered all nations: and he shall separate them one from another, as a shepherd divideth his sheep from the goats: and he shall set the sheep on his right hand, but the goats on the left. Then shall the King say unto them on his right hand, Come, ye blessed of my Father, inherit the kingdom prepared for you from the foundation of the world: for I was an hungred, and ye gave me meat: I was thirsty, and ye gave me drink: I was a stranger, and ye took me in: naked, and ye clothed me: I was sick, and ye visited me: I was in prison, and ye came unto me ... Verily I say unto you, Inasmuch as ye have done it unto one of the least of these my brethren, ye have done it unto me.
MATTHEW 25:31–36, 40

'A man was going down from Jerusalem to Jericho, and he fell among robbers, who stripped him and beat him, and departed, leaving him half dead ... a Samaritan, as he journeyed, came to where he was; and when he saw him, he had compassion, and went to him and bound up his wounds, pouring on oil and wine; then he set him

on his own beast and brought him to an inn, and took care of him. And the next day he took out two denarii and gave them to the innkeeper, saying, ''Take care of him; and whatever more you spend, I will repay you when I come back.'' '
LUKE 10:30, 33–35 RSV

'In all things I have shown you that by so toiling one must help the weak, remembering the words of the Lord Jesus, how he said, ''It is more blessed to give than to receive.'' '
ACTS 20:35 RSV

But the fruit of the Spirit is love . . . kindness, goodness, faithfulness, gentleness, self-control . . .
GALATIANS 5:22 RSV

Be kind to one another, tenderhearted, forgiving one another, as God in Christ forgave you.
EPHESIANS 4:32 RSV

Let us consider how to stir up one another to love and good works.
HEBREWS 10:24 RSV

See also *Love; Service.*

# Kingdom, kingdom of God

Blessed are the poor in spirit: for theirs is the kingdom of heaven.
MATTHEW 5:3 KJV

Thy kingdom come. Thy will be done, in earth as it is in heaven.
MATTHEW 6:10 BCP

Seek ye first the kingdom of God, and his righteousness; and all these things shall be added unto you.
MATTHEW 6:33 KJV

'Not every one who says to me, ''Lord, Lord,'' shall enter the kingdom of heaven, but he who does the will of my Father who is in heaven.'
MATTHEW 7:21 RSV

Then shall the King say unto them on his right hand, Come, ye blessed of my Father, inherit the kingdom prepared for you from the foundation of the world.
MATTHEW 25:34 KJV

'The time is fulfilled, and the kingdom of God is at hand; repent, and believe in the gospel.'
MARK 1:15 RSV

Verily I say unto you, Whosoever shall not receive the kingdom of God as a little child, he shall not enter therein.
MARK 10:15 KJV

And when he was demanded of the Pharisees, when the kingdom of God should come, he answered them and said, The kingdom of God cometh not with observation; neither shall they say, Lo here! or, lo there! for, behold, the kingdom of God is within you.
LUKE 17:20–21 KJV

Jesus answered and said unto him [Nicodemus], Verily, verily, I say unto thee, Except a man be born again, he cannot see the kingdom of God.
JOHN 3:3 KJV

[Paul and Barnabas] Strengthening the souls of the disciples, exhorting them to continue in the faith, and saying that through many tribulations we must enter the kingdom of God.
ACTS 14:22 RSV

For the kingdom of God does not mean food and drink but righteousness and peace and joy in the Holy Spirit.
ROMANS 14:17 RSV

For the kingdom of God does not consist in talk but in power.
1 CORINTHIANS 4:20 RSV

Do you not know that the wicked will not inherit the kingdom of God? Do not be deceived.
1 CORINTHIANS 6:9 NIV

Then the end will come; Christ will overcome all spiritual rulers, authorities, and powers, and will hand over the Kingdom to God the Father.
1 CORINTHIANS 15:24 GNB

He [God the Father] has delivered us from the dominion of darkness and transferred us to the kingdom of his beloved Son, in whom we have redemption, the forgiveness of sins.
COLOSSIANS 1:13 RSV

Therefore let us be grateful for receiving a kingdom that cannot be shaken, and thus let us offer to God acceptable worship, with reverence and awe.
HEBREWS 12:28 RSV

'The kingdom of the world has become the kingdom of our Lord and of his Christ, and he shall reign for ever and ever.'
REVELATION 11:15 RSV

# Knowledge

And out of the ground made the Lord God to grow every tree that is pleasant to the sight, and good for food; the tree of life also in the midst of the garden, and the tree of knowledge of good and evil.

GENESIS 2:9 KJV

For I know that my redeemer liveth, and that he shall stand at the latter day upon the earth.

JOB 19:25 KJV

'Be still, and know that I am God. I am exalted among the nations, I am exalted in the earth!'

PSALM 46:10 RSV

I am thy servant; give me understanding, that I may know thy testimonies!

PSALM 119:125 RSV

O Lord, thou hast searched me and known me! Thou knowest when I sit down and when I rise up; thou discernest my thoughts from afar. Thou searchest out my path and my lying down, and art acquainted with all my ways. Even before a word is on my tongue, lo, O Lord, thou knowest it altogether. Thou dost beset me behind and before, and layest thy hand upon me. Such knowledge is too wonderful for me; it is high, I cannot attain it.

PSALM 139:1–6 RSV

They shall not hurt nor destroy in all my holy mountain: for the earth shall be full of the knowledge of the Lord, as the waters cover the sea.

ISAIAH 11:9 KJV

'Let us know, let us press on to know the Lord; his going forth is sure as the dawn; he will come to us as the showers, as the spring rains that water the earth.'

HOSEA 6:3 RSV

'All things have been delivered to me by my Father; and no one knows the Son except the Father, and no one knows the Father except the Son and any one to whom the Son chooses to reveal him.'

MATTHEW 11:27 RSV

'I am the good shepherd. As the Father knows me and I know the Father, in the same way I know my sheep and they know me. And I am willing to die for them.'

JOHN 10:14–15 GNB

'And this is eternal life, that they know thee the only true God, and Jesus Christ whom thou hast sent.'

JOHN 17:3 RSV

Knowledge . . . puffs a person up with pride; but love builds up.

1 CORINTHIANS 8:1 GNB

And if I have prophetic powers, and understand all mysteries and all knowledge, and if I have all faith, so as to remove mountains, but have not love, I am nothing . . . For now we see in a mirror dimly, but then face to face. Now I know in part; then I shall understand fully, even as I have been fully understood.

1 CORINTHIANS 13:2, 12 RSV

[Paul's prayer] To know the love of Christ which surpasses knowledge, that you may be filled with all the fullness of God.

EPHESIANS 3:19 RSV

That I may know him and the power of his resurrection, and may share his sufferings, becoming like him in his death.

PHILIPPIANS 3:10 RSV

And so . . . we have not ceased to pray for you, asking that you may be filled with the knowledge of his will in all spiritual wisdom and understanding, to lead a life worthy of the Lord, fully pleasing to him, bearing fruit in every good work and increasing in the knowledge of God.

COLOSSIANS 1:9–10 RSV

But I am not ashamed, for I know whom I have believed, and I am sure that he is able to guard until that Day what has been entrusted to me.

2 TIMOTHY 1:12 RSV

And hereby do we know that we know him, if we keep his commandments.

1 JOHN 2:3 KJV

See also *Discernment; Understanding; Wisdom.*

# Land

'For six years you shall sow your land and gather in its yield; but the seventh year you shall let it rest and lie fallow, that the poor of your people may eat; and what they leave the wild beasts may eat.'

EXODUS 23:10–11 RSV

'And you shall hallow the fiftieth year, and proclaim liberty throughout the land to all its inhabitants; it shall be a jubilee for you, when each of you shall return to his property and each of you shall return to his family. A jubilee shall that fiftieth year be to you; in it you shall neither sow, nor reap what grows of itself, nor gather the grapes from the undressed vines.

LEVITICUS 25:10–11 RSV

Your land must not be sold on a permanent basis, because you do not own it; it belongs to God, and you are like foreigners who are allowed to make use of it.

LEVITICUS 25:23 GNB

'He brought us into this place and gave us this land, a land flowing with milk and honey. And behold, now I bring the first of the fruit of the ground, which thou, O Lord, hast given me.'

DEUTERONOMY 26:9–10 RSV

'And all these blessings shall come upon you and overtake you, if you obey the voice of the Lord your God. Blessed shall you be in the city, and blessed shall you be in the field. Blessed shall be the fruit of your body, and the fruit of your ground, and the fruit of your beasts, the increase of your cattle, and the young of your flock.'

DEUTERONOMY 28:2–4 RSV

[The Lord's promise to Solomon] 'If my people who are called by my name humble themselves, and pray and seek my face, and turn from their wicked ways, then I will hear from heaven, and will forgive their sin and heal their land.'

2 CHRONICLES 7:14 RSV

The earth is the Lord's and the fullness thereof, the world and those who dwell therein.

PSALM 24:1 RSV

There was not a needy person among them, for as many as were possessors of lands or houses sold them, and brought the proceeds of what was sold and laid it at the apostles' feet; and distribution was made to each as any had need.

ACTS 4:34–35 RSV

## Last Supper
See *Communion*.

## Last things

### EVENTS BEFORE THE SECOND COMING

'And you will hear of wars and rumours of wars; see that you are not alarmed; for this must take place, but the end is not yet.'

MATTHEW 24:6 RSV

'Then they will deliver you up to tribulation, and put you to death; and you will be hated by all nations for my name's sake. And then many will fall away, and betray one another, and hate one another. And many false prophets will arise and lead many astray. And because wickedness is multiplied, most men's love will grow cold. But who endures to the end will be saved. And this gospel of the kingdom will be preached throughout the whole world, as a testimony to all nations; and then the end will come.'

MATTHEW 24:9–14 RSV

'For then there will be great tribulation, such as has not been from the beginning of the world until now, no, and never will be. And if those days had not been shortened, no human being would be saved; but for the sake of the elect those days will be shortened.'

MATTHEW 24:21–22 RSV

'Immediately after the tribulation of those days the sun will be darkened, and the moon will not give its light, and the stars will fall from heaven, and the powers of the heavens will be shaken.'

MATTHEW 24:29 RSV

Let no one deceive you in any way; for that day will not come, unless the rebellion comes first, and the man of lawlessness is revealed, the son of perdition, who opposes and exalts himself against every so-called god or object of worship, so that he takes his seat in the temple of God, proclaiming himself to be God.

2 THESSALONIANS 2:3–4 RSV

And then the lawless one will be revealed, whom the Lord Jesus will overthrow with the breath of his mouth and destroy by the splendour of his coming.

2 THESSALONIANS 2:8 NIV

He seized the dragon, that ancient serpent—that is, the Devil, or Satan—and chained him up for a thousand years. The angel threw him into the abyss, locked it, and sealed it, so that he could not deceive the nations any more until the thousand years were over. After that he must be let loose for a little while.

REVELATION 20:2–3 GNB

After the thousand years are over, Satan will be let loose from his prison, and he will go out to

deceive the nations scattered over the whole world, that is, Gog and Magog. Satan will bring them all together for battle, as many as the grains of sand on the sea-shore.
REVELATION 20:7–8 GNB

## HEAVEN

Whom have I in heaven but thee? And there is none upon earth that I desire beside thee.
PSALM 73:25 KJV

Thus saith the Lord, The heaven is my throne, and the earth is my footstool: where is the house that ye build unto me? and where is the place of my rest?
ISAIAH 66:1 KJV

Our Father, which art in heaven, hallowed be thy name. Thy kingdom come. Thy will be done, in earth as it is in heaven.
MATTHEW 6:9–10 BCP

In my Father's house are many mansions: if it were not so, I would have told you. I go to prepare a place for you. And if I go and prepare a place for you, I will come again, and receive you unto myself; that where I am, there ye may be also.
JOHN 14:2–3 KJV

'Father, I desire that they also, whom thou hast given me, may be with me where I am, to behold my glory which thou hast given me in thy love for me before the foundation of the world.'
JOHN 17:24 RSV

And suddenly a sound came from heaven like the rush of a mighty wind, and it filled all the house where they were sitting.
ACTS 2:2 RSV

As it is written, Eye hath not seen, nor ear heard, neither have entered into the heart of man, the things which God hath prepared for them that love him.
1 CORINTHIANS 2:9 KJV

We, however, are citizens of heaven, and we eagerly wait for our Saviour, the Lord Jesus Christ, to come from heaven.
PHILIPPIANS 3:20 GNB

For Christ has entered, not into a sanctuary made with hands, a copy of the true one, but into heaven itself, now to appear in the presence of God on our behalf.
HEBREWS 9:24 RSV

After this I looked, and behold, a great multitude which no man could number, from every nation, from all tribes and peoples and tongues, standing before the throne and before the Lamb, clothed in white robes.
REVELATION 7:9 RSV

'Therefore are they before the throne of God, and serve him day and night within his temple; and he who sits upon the throne will shelter them with his presence.'
REVELATION 7:15 RSV

Then I saw thrones, and those who sat on them were given the power to judge. I also saw the souls of those who had been executed because they had proclaimed the truth that Jesus revealed and the word of God.
REVELATION 20:4 GNB

And I heard a great voice out of heaven saying, Behold, the tabernacle of God is with men, and he will dwell with them, and they shall be his people, and God himself shall be with them, and be their God.
REVELATION 21:3 KJV

There shall no more be anything accursed, but the throne of God and of the Lamb shall be in it, and his servants shall worship him; they shall see his face, and his name shall be on their foreheads. And night shall be no more; they need no light of lamp or sun, for the Lord God will be their light, and they shall reign for ever and ever.
REVELATION 22:3–5 RSV

## HELL

'Enter by the narrow gate; for the gate is wide and the way is easy, that leads to destruction, and those who enter by it are many.'
MATTHEW 7:13 RSV

But the children of the kingdom shall be cast out into outer darkness: there shall be weeping and gnashing of teeth.
MATTHEW 8:12 KJV

'Do not be afraid of those who kill the body but cannot kill the soul; rather be afraid of God, who can destroy both body and soul in hell.'
MATTHEW 10:28 GNB

Then shall he say also unto them on the left hand, Depart from me, ye cursed, into everlasting fire, prepared for the devil and his angels . . . And these shall go away into everlasting punishment: but the righteous into life eternal.

MATTHEW 25:41, 46 KJV

And beside all this, between us and you [heaven and hell] there is a great gulf fixed: so that they which would pass from hence to you cannot; neither can they pass to us, that would come from thence.

LUKE 16:26 KJV

They will suffer the punishment of eternal destruction, separated from the presence of the Lord and from his glorious might.

2 THESSALONIANS 1:9 GNB

'Whoever worships the beast and its image and receives the mark on his forehead or on his hand will himself drink God's wine, the wine of his fury, which he has poured at full strength into the cup of his anger! All who do this will be tormented in fire and sulphur before the holy angels and the Lamb. The smoke of the fire that torments them goes up for ever and ever. There is no relief day or night for those who worship the beast and its image, for anyone who has the mark of its name.'

REVELATION 14:9–11 GNB

Then the Devil, who deceived them, was thrown into the lake of fire and sulphur, where the beast and the false prophet had already been thrown; and they will be tormented day and night for ever and ever.

REVELATION 20:10 GNB

And whosoever was not found written in the book of life was cast into the lake of fire.

REVELATION 20:15 KJV

'But as for the cowardly, the faithless, the polluted, as for murderers, fornicators, sorcerers, idolaters, and all liars, their lot shall be in the lake that burns with fire and sulphur, which is the second death.'

REVELATION 21:8 RSV

## JUDGEMENT

'If anyone declares publicly that he belongs to me, I will do the same for him before my Father in heaven. But if anyone rejects me publicly, I will reject him before my Father in heaven.'

MATTHEW 10:32–33 GNB

When the Son of man shall come in his glory, and all the holy angels with him, then shall he sit upon the throne of his glory: and before him shall be gathered all nations: and he shall separate them one from another, as a shepherd divideth his sheep from the goats: and he shall set the sheep on his right hand, but the goats on the left.

MATTHEW 25:31–33 KJV

'He [God] has fixed a day on which he will judge the world in righteousness by a man whom he has appointed, and of this he has given assurance to all men by raising him from the dead.'

ACTS 17:31 RSV

So you should not pass judgement on anyone before the right time comes. Final judgement must wait until the Lord comes; he will bring to light the dark secrets and expose the hidden purposes of people's minds. And then everyone will receive from God the praise he deserves.

1 CORINTHIANS 4:5 GNB

Do you not know that the saints will judge the world? And if the world is to be judged by you, are you incompetent to try trivial cases? Do you not know that we are to judge angels? How much more, matters pertaining to this life!

1 CORINTHIANS 6:2–3 RSV

For we must all appear before the judgment seat of Christ, so that each one may receive good or evil, according to what he has done in the body.

2 CORINTHIANS 5:10 RSV

It is appointed unto men once to die, but after this the judgment.

HEBREWS 9:27 KJV

And the angels that did not keep their own position but left their proper dwelling have been kept by him in eternal chains in the nether gloom until the judgment of the great day.

JUDE 6 RSV

[They] said to the mountains and rocks, Fall on us, and hide us from the face of him that sitteth on the throne, and from the wrath of the Lamb. For the great day of his wrath is come; and who shall be able to stand?

REVELATION 6:16–17 KJV

And I saw a great white throne, and him that sat on it, from whose face the earth and the heaven fled away; and there was found no place for them. And I saw the dead, small and great, stand before God; and the books were opened: and another book was opened, which is the book of life: and the dead were judged out of those things which were written in the books, according to their works. And the sea gave up the dead which were in it: and they were judged every man according to their works. And death and hell were cast into the lake of fire. This is the second death. And whosoever was not found written in the book of life was cast into the lake of fire.

REVELATION 20:11–15 KJV

## RENEWAL OF ALL THINGS

Jesus said to them, 'You can be sure that when the Son of Man sits on his glorious throne in the New Age, then you twelve followers of mine will also sit on thrones, to rule the twelve tribes of Israel.'

MATTHEW 19:28 GNB

[Jesus Christ] whom the heaven must receive until the times of restitution of all things, which God hath spoken by the mouth of all his holy prophets since the world began.

ACTS 3:21 KJV

The creation itself will be set free from its bondage to decay and obtain the glorious liberty of the children of God.

ROMANS 8:21 RSV

But the day of the Lord will come like a thief, and then the heavens will pass away with a loud noise, and the elements will be dissolved with fire, and the earth and the works that are upon it will be burned up. Since all these things are thus to be dissolved, what sort of persons ought you to be in lives of holiness and godliness, waiting for and hastening the coming of the day of God, because of which the heavens will be kindled and dissolved, and the elements will melt with fire! But according to his promise we wait for new heavens and a new earth in which righteousness dwells.

2 PETER 3:10–13 RSV

And I saw a new heaven and a new earth: for the first heaven and the first earth were passed away; and there was no more sea. And I John saw the holy city, new Jerusalem, coming down from God out of heaven, prepared as a bride adorned for her husband. And I heard a great voice out of heaven saying, Behold, the tabernacle of God is with men, and he will dwell with them, and they shall be his people, and God himself shall be with them, and be their God. And God shall wipe away all tears from their eyes; and there shall be no more death, neither sorrow, nor crying, neither shall there be any more pain: for the former things are passed away. And he that sat upon the throne said, Behold, I make all things new. And he said unto me, write: for these words are true and faithful.

REVELATION 21:1–5 KJV

## RESURRECTION

And they shall come out and see the dead bodies of those who have rebelled against me; their worm shall not die nor their fire be quenched, and they shall be abhorred by all mankind.

ISAIAH 66:24 NEB

'And many of those who sleep in the dust of the earth shall awake, some to everlasting life, and some to shame and everlasting contempt. And those who are wise shall shine like the brightness of the firmament; and those who turn many to righteousness, like the stars for ever.'

DANIEL 12:2–3 RSV

' '''I am the God of Abraham, and the God of Isaac, and the God of Jacob''. He is not God of the dead, but of the living.'

MATTHEW 22:32 RSV

'Do not be surprised at this; the time is coming when all the dead will hear his voice and come out of their graves: those who have done good will rise and live, and those who have done evil will rise and be condemned.'

JOHN 5:28–29 GNB

Martha saith unto him, I know that he shall rise again in the resurrection at the last day. Jesus said unto her, I am the resurrection, and the life: he that believeth in me, though he were dead, yet shall he live.

JOHN 11:24–25 KJV

So it is with the resurrection of the dead. What is sown is perishable, what is raised is imperishable. It is sown in dishonour, it is raised in glory. It is sown in weakness, it is raised in power. It is sown a physical body, it is raised a spiritual body. If there is a physical body, there is also a spiritual body.

1 CORINTHIANS 15:42–44 RSV

In a moment, in the twinkling of an eye, at the last trump: for the trumpet shall sound, and the dead shall be raised incorruptible, and we shall be changed.

1 CORINTHIANS 15:52 KJV

The Lord Jesus Christ, who will change our lowly body to be like his glorious body, by the power which enables him even to subject all things to himself.
PHILIPPIANS 3:20–21 RSV

For the Lord himself shall descend from heaven with a shout, with the voice of the archangel, and with the trump of God: and the dead in Christ shall rise first.
1 THESSALONIANS 4:16 KJV

Then the Devil, who deceived them, was thrown into the lake of fire and sulphur, where the beast and the false prophet had already been thrown; and they will be tormented day and night for ever and ever.
REVELATION 20:10 GNB

## SECOND COMING OF JESUS

'In my vision at night I looked, and there before me was one like a son of man, coming with the clouds of heaven. He approached the Ancient of Days and was led into his presence.'
DANIEL 7:13 NIV

'Immediately after the tribulation of those days the sun will be darkened, and the moon will not give its light, and the stars will fall from heaven, and the powers of the heavens will be shaken; then will appear the sign of the Son of man in heaven, and then all the tribes of the earth will mourn, and they will see the Son of man coming on the clouds of heaven with power and great glory . . . But of that day and hour no one knows, not even the angels of heaven, nor the Son, but the Father only.'
MATTHEW 24:29–30, 36 RSV

And if I go and prepare a place for you, I will come again, and receive you unto myself; that where I am, there ye may be also.
JOHN 14:3 KJV

'Men of Galilee, why do you stand looking into heaven? This Jesus, who was taken up from you into heaven, will come in the same way as you saw him go into heaven.'
ACTS 1:11 RSV

For if we believe that Jesus died and rose again, even so them also which sleep in Jesus will God bring with him. For this we say unto you by the word of the Lord, that we which are alive and remain unto the coming of the Lord shall not prevent them which are asleep. For the Lord himself shall descend from heaven with a shout, with the voice of the archangel, and with the trump of God: and the dead in Christ shall rise first. Then we which are alive and remain shall be caught up together with them in the clouds, to meet the Lord in the air: and so shall we ever be with the Lord.
1 THESSALONIANS 4:14–17 KJV

For yourselves know well that the day of the Lord will come like a thief in the night.
1 THESSALONIANS 5:2 RSV

He will do this when the Lord Jesus appears from heaven with his mighty angels . . . when he comes on that day to receive glory from all his people and honour from all who believe.
2 THESSALONIANS 1:7, 10 GNB

In the same manner Christ also was offered in sacrifice once to take away the sins of many. He will appear a second time, not to deal with sin, but to save those who are waiting for him.
HEBREWS 9:28 GNB

Behold, he is coming with the clouds, and every eye will see him, every one who pierced him; and all tribes of the earth will wail on account of him. Even so. Amen.
REVELATION 1:7 RSV

## STATE BETWEEN DEATH AND RESURRECTION

The wicked shall be turned into hell, and all the nations that forget God.
PSALM 9:17 KJV

There was a certain rich man, which was clothed in purple and fine linen, and fared sumptuously every day: and there was a certain beggar named Lazarus, which was laid at his gate full of sores, and desiring to be fed with the crumbs which fell from the rich man's table: moreover the dogs came and licked his sores. And it came to pass, that the beggar died, and was carried by the angels into Abraham's bosom: the rich man also died, and was buried; and in hell he lift up his eyes, being in torments, and seeth Abraham afar off, and Lazarus in his bosom. And he cried and said, Father Abraham, have mercy on me, and send Lazarus, that he may dip the tip of his finger in water, and cool my tongue; for I am tormented in this flame . . . And beside all this, between us and you there is a great gulf fixed: so that they which would pass from hence to you cannot;

neither can they pass to us, that would come from thence.
**LUKE 16:23–24, 26 KJV**

And Jesus said unto him, Verily I say unto thee, To day shalt thou be with me in paradise.
**LUKE 23:43 KJV**

And whosoever liveth and believeth in me shall never die. Believest thou this?
**JOHN 11:26 KJV**

We are of good courage, and we would rather be away from the body and at home with the Lord.
**2 CORINTHIANS 5:8 RSV**

I am pulled in two directions. I want very much to leave this life and be with Christ, which is a far better thing.
**PHILIPPIANS 1:23 GNB**

For if we believe that Jesus died and rose again, even so them also which sleep in Jesus will God bring with him.
**1 THESSALONIANS 4:14 KJV**

To the assembly of the first-born who are enrolled in heaven, and to a judge who is God of all, and to the spirits of just men made perfect.
**HEBREWS 12:23 RSV**

Then they were each given a white robe and told to rest a little longer, until the number of their fellow servants and their brethren should be complete, who were to be killed as they themselves had been.
**REVELATION 6:11 RSV**

And I heard a voice from heaven saying, 'Write this: Blessed are the dead who die in the Lord henceforth.' 'Blessed indeed,' says the Spirit, 'that they may rest from their labours, for their deeds follow them!'
**REVELATION 14:13 RSV**

## Law

The law of the Lord is perfect, converting the soul: the testimony of the Lord is sure, making wise the simple.
**PSALM 19:7 KJV**

Open thou mine eyes, that I may behold wondrous things out of thy law.
**PSALM 119:18 KJV**

'Do not think that I have come to do away with the Law of Moses and the teachings of the prophets. I have not come to do away with them, but to make their teachings come true.'
**MATTHEW 5:17 GNB**

Now we know that whatever the law says it speaks to those who are under the law, so that every mouth may be stopped, and the whole world may be held accountable to God. For no human being will be justified in his sight by works of the law since through the law comes knowledge of sin.
**ROMANS 3:19–20 RSV**

Do we then make void the law through faith? God forbid: yea, we establish the law.
**ROMANS 3:31 KJV**

For sin shall not have dominion over you: for ye are not under the law, but under grace.
**ROMANS 6:14 KJV**

What then shall we say? That the law is sin? By no means! Yet, if it had not been for the law, I should not have known sin. I should not have known what it is to covet if the law had not said, 'You shall not covet.'
**ROMANS 7:7 RSV**

So the law is holy, and the commandment is holy and just and good.
**ROMANS 7:12 RSV**

For I delight in the law of God, in my inmost self, but I see in my members another law at war with the law of my mind and making me captive to the law of sin which dwells in my members.
**ROMANS 7:22–23 RSV**

For the law of the Spirit of life in Christ Jesus has set me free from the law of sin and death. For God has done what the law, weakened by the flesh, could not do: sending his own Son in the likeness of sinful flesh and for sin, he condemned sin in the flesh, in order that the just requirement of the law might be fulfilled in us, who walk not according to the flesh but according to the Spirit.
**ROMANS 8:2–4 RSV**

Love does no wrong to a neighbour; therefore love is the fulfilling of the law.
**ROMANS 13:10 RSV**

Yet we know that a person is put right with God only through faith in Jesus Christ, never by doing what the Law requires. For no one is put right with God by doing what the Law requires.
**GALATIANS 2:16 GNB**

And so the Law was in charge of us until Christ came, in order that we might then be put right with God through faith.
GALATIANS 3:24 GNB

But when the time had fully come, God sent forth his Son, born of woman, born under the law, to redeem those who were under the law, so that we might receive adoption as sons.
GALATIANS 4:4–5 RSV

'This is the covenant that I will make with the house of Israel after those days, says the Lord: I will put my laws into their minds, and write them on their hearts, and I will be their God, and they shall be my people.'
HEBREWS 8:10 RSV

For since the law has but a shadow of the good things to come instead of the true form of these realities, it can never, by the same sacrifices which are continually offered year after year, make perfect those who draw near.
HEBREWS 10:1 RSV

But he who looks into the perfect law, the law of liberty, and perseveres, being no hearer that forgets but a doer that acts, he shall be blessed in his doing.
JAMES 1:25 RSV

If you really fulfil the royal law, according to the scripture, 'You shall love your neighbour as yourself,' you do well.
JAMES 2:8 RSV

See also *Bible; Ten Commandments; Will of God.*

## Laying on of hands

And Israel stretched out his right hand and laid it upon the head of Ephraim, who was the younger, and his left hand upon the head of Manasseh, crossing his hands, for Manasseh was the first-born. And he blessed Joseph.
GENESIS 48:14–15 RSV

'He [Aaron] shall put both his hands on the goat's head and confess over it all the evils, sins, and rebellions of the people of Israel, and so transfer them to the goat's head. Then the goat is to be driven off into the desert by a man appointed to do it.'
LEVITICUS 16:21 GNB

And Joshua the son of Nun was full of the spirit of wisdom; for Moses had laid his hands upon him: and the children of Israel harkened unto him, and did as the Lord commanded Moses.
DEUTERONOMY 34:9 KJV

And he [Jesus] could do no mighty work there, except that he laid his hands upon a few sick people and healed them.
MARK 6:5 RSV

And he took them up in his arms, put his hands upon them, and blessed them.
MARK 10:16 KJV

These they set before the apostles, and they prayed and laid their hands upon them.
ACTS 6:6 RSV

While they were worshipping the Lord and fasting, the Holy Spirit said, 'Set apart for me Barnabas and Saul for the work to which I have called them.' Then after fasting and praying they laid their hands on them and sent them off.
ACTS 13:2–3 RSV

And when Paul had laid his hands upon them, the Holy Spirit came on them; and they spoke with tongues and prophesied.
ACTS 19:6 RSV

Do not neglect the gift you have, which was given you by prophetic utterance when the council of elders laid their hands upon you.
1 TIMOTHY 4:14 RSV

Be in no hurry to lay hands on someone to dedicate him to the Lord's service.
1 TIMOTHY 5:22 GNB

Let us go forward, then, to mature teaching and leave behind us the first lessons of the Christian message. We should not lay again the foundation of turning away from useless works and believing in God; of the teaching about baptisms and the laying on of hands; of the resurrection of the dead and the eternal judgement.
HEBREWS 6:1–2 GNB

## Laziness

Go to the ant, thou sluggard; consider her ways, and be wise.
PROVERBS 6:6 KJV

How long wilt thou sleep, O sluggard? When wilt thou arise out of thy sleep?
PROVERBS 6:9 KJV

If you are lazy, you will meet difficulty everywhere, but if you are honest, you will have no trouble.
PROVERBS 15:19 GNB

Our brothers, we command you in the name of our Lord Jesus Christ to keep away from all brothers who are living a lazy life and who do not follow the instructions that we gave them. You yourselves know very well that you should do just what we did. We were not lazy when we were with you. We did not accept anyone's support without paying for it. Instead, we worked and toiled; we kept working day and night so as not to be an expense to any of you.
2 THESSALONIANS 3:6–8 GNB

While we were with you, we used to say to you, 'Whoever refuses to work is not allowed to eat.' We say this because we hear that there are some people among you who live lazy lives and who do nothing except meddle in other people's business. In the name of the Lord Jesus Christ we command these people and warn them to lead orderly lives and work to earn their own living.
2 THESSALONIANS 3:10–12 GNB

They [young widows] also learn to waste their time in going round from house to house; but even worse, they learn to be gossips and busybodies, talking of things they should not.
1 TIMOTHY 5:13 GNB

We do not want you to become lazy, but to be like those who believe and are patient, and so receive what God has promised.
HEBREWS 6:12 GNB

See also **Work.**

## Leadership

'And let them judge the people at all times; every great matter they shall bring to you, but any small matter they shall decide themselves; so it will be easier for you, and they will bear the burden with you. If you do this, and God so commands you, then you will be able to endure, and all this people also will go to their place in peace.'
EXODUS 18:22–23 RSV

The Lord said to Moses, 'Send men to spy out the land of Canaan, which I give to the people of Israel; from each tribe of their fathers shall you send a man, every one a leader among them.'
NUMBERS 13:1–2 RSV

[Samuel to Saul] 'But now your kingdom shall not continue; the Lord has sought out a man after his own heart; and the Lord has appointed him to be prince over his people, because you have not kept what the Lord commanded you.'
1 SAMUEL 13:14 RSV

Run to and fro through the streets of Jerusalem, look and take note! Search her squares to see if you can find a man, one who does justice and seeks truth; that I may pardon her.
JEREMIAH 5:1 RSV

'But it shall not be so among you; but whoever would be great among you must be your servant.'
MARK 10:43 RSV

If it [a man's gift] is leadership, let him govern diligently.
ROMANS 12:8 NIV

And, apart from other things, there is the daily pressure upon me of my anxiety for all the churches.
2 CORINTHIANS 11:28 RSV

Now we ask you, brothers, to respect those who work hard among you, who are over you in the Lord and who admonish you. Hold them in the highest regard in love because of their work.
1 THESSALONIANS 5:12–13 NIV

There is a popular saying: 'To aspire to leadership is an honourable ambition.'
1 TIMOTHY 3:1 NEB

What you have heard from me before many witnesses entrust to faithful men who will be able to teach others also.
2 TIMOTHY 2:2 RSV

You should aim not at being 'little tin gods' but as examples of Christian living in the eyes of the flock committed to your charge.
1 PETER 5:3 JBP

See also **Deacon; Elders; Service.**

## Life

And the Lord God formed man of the dust of the ground, and breathed into his nostrils the breath of life; and man became a living soul . . . And out of the ground made the Lord God to grow every tree that is pleasant to the sight, and good for food; the tree of life also in the midst of the

garden, and the tree of knowledge of good and evil.
**GENESIS 2:7, 9 KJV**

Honour thy father and thy mother: that thy days may be long upon the land which the Lord thy God giveth thee.
**EXODUS 20:12 KJV**

'And he humbled you and let you hunger and fed you with manna, which you did not know, nor did your fathers know; that he might make you know that man does not live by bread alone, but that man lives by everything that proceeds out of the mouth of the Lord.'
**DEUTERONOMY 8:3 RSV**

'I call heaven and earth to witness against you this day, that I have set before you life and death, blessing and curse; therefore choose life, that you and your descendants may live.'
**DEUTERONOMY 30:19 RSV**

For I know that my redeemer liveth, and that he shall stand at the latter day upon the earth.
**JOB 19:25 KJV**

Because thy lovingkindness is better than life, my lips shall praise thee.
**PSALM 63:3 KJV**

With long life I will satisfy him, and show him my salvation.
**PSALM 91:16 RSV**

For he who finds me [wisdom] finds life and obtains favour from the Lord.
**PROVERBS 8:35 RSV**

Incline your ear, and come unto me: hear, and your soul shall live; and I will make an everlasting covenant with you, even the sure mercies of David.
**ISAIAH 55:3 KJV**

And he said to me, 'Son of man, can these bones live?' And I answered, 'O Lord God, thou knowest.'
**EZEKIEL 37:3 RSV**

God says to them [the people of Israel], 'You are not my people,' but the day is coming when he will say to them, 'You are the children of the living God!'
**HOSEA 1:10 GNB**

Therefore I say unto you, Take no thought for your life, what ye shall eat, or what ye shall drink; not yet for your body, what ye shall put on. Is not the life more than meat, and the body than raiment?
**MATTHEW 6:25 KJV**

'For the gate is narrow and the way is hard, that leads to life, and those who find it are few.'
**MATTHEW 7:14 RSV**

'For what will it profit a man, if he gains the whole world and forfeits his life?'
**MATTHEW 16:26 RSV**

' ''I am the God of Abraham, and the God of Isaac, and the God of Jacob''. He is not God of the dead, but of the living.'
**MATTHEW 22:32 RSV**

And these shall go away into everlasting punishment: but the righteous into life eternal.
**MATTHEW 25:46 KJV**

'Truly, truly, I say to you, he who hears my word and believes him who sent me, has eternal life; he does not come into judgment, but has passed from death to life.'
**JOHN 5:24 RSV**

And Jesus said unto them, I am the bread of life: he that cometh to me shall never hunger; and he that believeth on me shall never thirst.
**JOHN 6:35 KJV**

Then Simon Peter answered him, Lord, to whom shall we go? thou hast the words of eternal life.
**JOHN 6:68 KJV**

'The thief comes only to steal and kill and destroy; I came that they may have life, and have it abundantly.'
**JOHN 10:10 RSV**

And I give unto them [my sheep] eternal life; and they shall never perish, neither shall any man pluck them out of my hand.
**JOHN 10:28 KJV**

Jesus said unto her, I am the resurrection, and the life: he that believeth in me, though he were dead, yet shall he live.
**JOHN 11:25 KJV**

Jesus saith unto him, I am the way, the truth, and the life: no man cometh unto the Father, but by me.
**JOHN 14:6 KJV**

'Because I live, you also will live.'
JOHN 14:19 GNB

But these are written that you may believe that Jesus is the Christ, the Son of God, and that believing you may have life in his name.
JOHN 20:31 RSV

'For "In him we live and move and have our being"; as even some of your poets have said, "For we are indeed his offspring."'
ACTS 17:28 RSV

For the wages of sin is death; but the gift of God is eternal life through Jesus Christ our Lord.
ROMANS 6:23 KJV

To set the mind on the flesh is death, but to set the mind of the Spirit is life and peace.
ROMANS 8:6 RSV

For if you live according to the flesh you will die, but if by the Spirit you put to death the deeds of the body you will live.
ROMANS 8:13 RSV

Always carrying in the body the death of Jesus, so that the life of Jesus may also be manifested in our bodies.
2 CORINTHIANS 4:10 RSV

I have been crucified with Christ; it is no longer I who live, but Christ who lives in me; and the life I now live in the flesh I live by faith in the Son of God, who loved me and gave himself for me.
GALATIANS 2:20 RSV

[God] made us alive with Christ even when we were dead in transgressions—it is by grace you have been saved.
EPHESIANS 2:5 NIV

For me to live is Christ, and to die is gain.
PHILIPPIANS 1:21 KJV

When Christ, who is our life, shall appear, then shall ye also appear with him in glory.
COLOSSIANS 3:4 KJV

We know that we have passed out of death into life, because we love the brethren.
1 JOHN 3:14 RSV

He that hath the Son hath life; and he that hath not the Son of God hath not life.
1 JOHN 5:12 KJV

See also *Adam; Death; Last things.*

# Light

And God said, Let there be light: and there was light.
GENESIS 1:3 KJV

The Lord is my light and my salvation; whom shall I fear? The Lord is the strength of my life; of whom shall I be afraid?
PSALM 27:1 KJV

Thy word is a lamp unto my feet, and a light unto my path.
PSALM 119:105 KJV

The entrance of thy words giveth light; it giveth understanding unto the simple.
PSALM 119:130 KJV

The people that walked in darkness have seen a great light: they that dwell in the land of the shadow of death, upon them hath the light shined.
ISAIAH 9:2 KJV

I will also give thee for a light to the Gentiles, that thou mayest be my salvation unto the end of the earth.
ISAIAH 49:6 KJV

Arise, shine; for thy light is come, and the glory of the Lord is risen upon thee.
ISAIAH 60:1 KJV

Ye are the light of the world. A city that is set on a hill cannot be hid. Neither do men light a candle, and put it under a bushel, but on a candlestick; and it giveth light unto all that are in the house. Let your light so shine before men, that they may see your good works, and glorify your Father which is in heaven.
MATTHEW 5:14–16 KJV

In him [the Word] was life; and the life was the light of men. And the light shineth in darkness; and the darkness comprehended it not.
JOHN 1:4–5 KJV

He [John the Baptist] came for testimony, to bear witness to the light, that all might believe through him. He was not the light, but came to bear witness to the light. The true light that enlightens every man was coming into the world.
JOHN 1:7–9 RSV

And this is the judgment, that the light has come into the world, and men loved darkness rather than light, because their deeds were evil. For every one who does evil hates the light, and does not come to the light, lest his deeds be exposed. But he who does what is true comes to the light, that it may be clearly seen that his deeds have been wrought in God.

JOHN 3:19–21 RSV

Jesus spoke to them, saying, 'I am the light of the world; he who follows me will not walk in darkness, but will have the light of life.'

JOHN 8:12 RSV

[The Lord Jesus Christ to Paul] ' ''I send you to open their eyes, that they may turn from darkness to light and from the power of Satan to God, that they may receive forgiveness of sins and a place among those who are sanctified by faith in me.'' '

ACTS 26:18 RSV

For it is the God who said, 'Let light shine out of darkness,' who has shone in our hearts to give the light of the knowledge of the glory of God in the face of Christ.

2 CORINTHIANS 4:6 RSV

Be not unequally yoked together with unbelievers: for what fellowship hath righteousness with unrighteousness? and what communion hath light with darkness?

2 CORINTHIANS 6:14 KJV

For once you were darkness, but now you are light in the Lord; walk as children of light (for the fruit of light is found in all that is good and right and true).

EPHESIANS 5:8–9 RSV

But everything exposed by light becomes visible, for it is light that makes everything visible. This is why it is said: 'Wake up, O sleeper, rise from the dead, and Christ will shine upon you.'

EPHESIANS 5:13–14 NIV

So that you may be innocent and pure as God's perfect children, who live in a world of corrupt and sinful people. You must shine among them like stars lighting up the sky.

PHILIPPIANS 2:15 GNB

He [God] alone is immortal; he lives in the light that no one can approach. No one has ever seen him; no one can ever see him. To him be honour and eternal dominion! Amen.

1 TIMOTHY 6:16 GNB

But you are a chosen race, a royal priesthood, a holy nation, God's own people, that you may declare the wonderful deeds of him who called you out of darkness into his marvellous light.

1 PETER 2:9 RSV

This is the message we have heard from him and proclaim to you, that God is light and in him is no darkness at all.

1 JOHN 1:5 RSV

If we say we have fellowship with him while we walk in darkness, we lie and do not live according to the truth; but if we walk in the light, as he is in the light, we have fellowship with one another, and the blood of Jesus his Son cleanses us from all sin.

1 JOHN 1:7 RSV

And night shall be no more; they need no light of lamp or sun, for the Lord God will be their light, and they shall reign for ever and ever.

REVELATION 22:5 RSV

# Loneliness

And he [Elijah] said, I have been very jealous for the Lord God of hosts: for the children of Israel have forsaken thy covenant, thrown down thine altars, and slain thy prophets with the sword; and I, even I only, am left; and they seek my life, to take it away.

1 KINGS 19:10 KJV

'He has put my brethren far from me, and my acquaintances are wholly estranged from me. My kinsfolk and my close friends have failed me.'

JOB 19:13–14 RSV

Then he said to them, 'My soul is very sorrowful, even to death; remain here, and watch with me.'

MATTHEW 26:38 RSV

Then all the disciples forsook him and fled.

MATTHEW 26:56 RSV

And about the ninth hour Jesus cried with a loud voice, 'Eli, Eli lama sabachthani?' that is, 'My God, my God, why hast thou forsaken me?'

MATTHEW 27:46 RSV

You know that everyone in the province of Asia . . . has deserted me.

2 TIMOTHY 1:15 GNB

See also *Comfort*.

## Lord's Prayer

See appendix, *Prayers of the Bible.*

## Love

### OF GOD

'It was not because you were more in number than any other people that the Lord set his love upon you and chose you, for you were the fewest of all peoples; but it is because the Lord loves you, and is keeping the oath which he swore to your fathers, that the Lord has brought you out with a mighty hand, and redeemed you from the house of bondage, from the hand of Pharaoh king of Egypt.'
DEUTERONOMY 7:7–8 RSV

For God so loved the world, that he gave his only begotten Son, that whosoever believeth in him should not perish, but have everlasting life.
JOHN 3:16 KJV

And hope maketh not ashamed; because the love of God is shed abroad in our hearts by the Holy Ghost which is given unto us.
ROMANS 5:5 KJV

But God shows his love for us in that while we were yet sinners Christ died for us.
ROMANS 5:8 RSV

Who shall separate us from the love of Christ? Shall tribulation, or distress, or persecution, or famine, or nakedness, or peril, or sword? As it is written, 'For thy sake we are being killed all the day long; we are regarded as sheep to be slaughtered.' No, in all these things we are more than conquerors through him who loved us. For I am sure that neither death, nor life, nor angels, nor principalities, nor things present, nor things to come, nor powers, nor height, nor depth, nor anything else in all creation, will be able to separate us from the love of God in Christ Jesus our Lord.
ROMANS 8:35–39 RSV

I have been crucified with Christ; it is no longer I who live, but Christ who lives in me; and the life I now live in the flesh I live by faith in the Son of God, who loved me and gave himself for me.
GALATIANS 2:20 RSV

But because of his great love for us, God, who is rich in mercy, made us alive with Christ.
EPHESIANS 2:4–5 NIV

He that loveth not knoweth not God; for God is love. In this was manifested the love of God toward us, because that God sent his only begotten Son into the world, that we might live through him. Herein is love, not that we loved God, but that he loved us, and sent his Son to be the propitiation for our sins.
1 JOHN 4:8–10 KJV

See also *Faithfulness; Grace; Mercy.*

### OF MAN FOR GOD

Thou shalt love the Lord thy God with all thine heart, and with all thy soul, and with all thy might.
DEUTERONOMY 6:5 KJV

'And now, Israel, what does the Lord your God require of you, but to fear the Lord your God, to walk in all his ways, to love him, to serve the Lord your God with all your heart and with all your soul.'
DEUTERONOMY 10:12 RSV

I love the Lord, because he has heard my voice and my supplications.
PSALM 116:1 RSV

If ye love me, keep my commandments.
JOHN 14:15 KJV

He that hath my commandments, and keepth them, he it is that loveth me: and he that loveth me shall be loved of my Father, and I will love him, and will manifest myself to him.
JOHN 14:21 KJV

We know that in everything God works for good with those who love him, who are called according to his purpose.
ROMANS 8:28 RSV

As it is written, Eye hath not seen, nor ear heard, neither have entered into the heart of man, the things which God hath prepared for them that love him.
1 CORINTHIANS 2:9 KJV

If any one has no love for the Lord, let him be accursed. Our Lord, come!
1 CORINTHIANS 16:22 RSV

Without having seen him you love him; though you do not now see him you believe in him and rejoice with unutterable and exalted joy.
1 PETER 1:8 RSV

If any one says, 'I love God,' and hates his brother, he is a liar; for he who does not love his brother whom he has seen, cannot love God whom he has not seen. And this commandment we have from him, that he who loves God should love his brother also.
1 JOHN 4:20–21 RSV

See also *Christian life, Longing for God; Worship.*

**OF MAN FOR MAN**

Honour thy father and thy mother.
EXODUS 20:12 KJV

'You shall not take vengeance or bear any grudge against the sons of your own people, but you shall love your neighbour as yourself: I am the Lord.'
LEVITICUS 19:18 RSV

'Treat them [foreigners] as you would a fellow-Israelite, and love them as you love yourselves.'
LEVITICUS 19:34 GNB

But I say unto you, Love your enemies, bless them that curse you, do good to them that hate you ... For ... love them which love you, what reward have ye? Do not even the publicans the same?
MATTHEW 5:44, 46 KJV

'So, whatever you wish that men would do to you, do so to them; for this is the law and the prophets.'
MATTHEW 7:12 RSV

'See that you don't despise any of these little ones. Their angels in heaven, I tell you, are always in the presence of my Father in heaven.'
MATTHEW 18:10 GNB

A new commandment I give unto you, That ye love one another; as I have loved you, that ye also love one another. By this shall all men know that ye are my disciples, if ye have love one to another.
JOHN 13:34–35 KJV

'Greater love has no man than this, that a man lay down his life for his friends.'
JOHN 15:13 RSV

If I speak in the tongues of men and of angels, but have not love, I am a noisy gong or a clanging cymbal. And if I have prophetic powers, and understand all mysteries and all knowledge, and if I have all faith, so as to remove mountains, but have not love, I am nothing. If I give away all I have, and if I deliver my body to be burned, but have not love, I gain nothing. Love is patient and kind; love is not jealous or boastful; it is not arrogant or rude. Love does not insist on its own way; it is not irritable or resentful; it does not rejoice at wrong, but rejoices in the right. Love bears all things, believes all things, hopes all things, endures all things. So faith, hope, love abide, these three; but the greatest of these is love.
1 CORINTHIANS 13:1–7, 13 RSV

But the fruit of the Spirit is love ...
GALATIANS 5:22 RSV

Husbands, love your wives, as Christ loved the church and gave himself up for her.
EPHESIANS 5:25 RSV

Beloved, let us love one another: for love is of God; and every one that loveth is born of God, and knoweth God ... Beloved, if God so loved us, we ought also to love one another ... If we love one another, God dwelleth in us, and his love is perfected in us.
1 JOHN 4:7, 11 KJV

By this we know that we love the children of God, when we love God and obey his commandments.
1 JOHN 5:2 RSV

See also *Kindness.*

# Lying

Thou shalt not bear false witness against thy neighbour.
EXODUS 20:16 KJV

'God is not man, that he should lie, or a son of man, that he should repent. Has he said, and will he not do it? Or has he spoken, and will he not fulfil it?'
NUMBERS 23:19 RSV

Save me, Lord, from liars and deceivers.
PSALM 120:2 GNB

Everyone deceives his neighbour, and no one speaks the truth; they have taught their tongue to speak lies; they commit iniquity and are too weary to repent.
JEREMIAH 9:5 RSV

'You are of your father the devil, and your will is

to do your father's desires. He was a murderer from the beginning, and has nothing to do with the truth, because there is no truth in him. When he lies, he speaks according to his own nature, for he is a liar and the father of lies.'
**JOHN 8:44 RSV**

Peter said to him, 'Ananias, why did you let Satan take control of you and make you lie to the Holy Spirit by keeping part of the money you received for the property? Before you sold the property, it belonged to you; and after you sold it, the money was yours. Why, then, did you decide to do such a thing? You have not lied to men—you have lied to God!'
**ACTS 5:3–5 GNB**

Do not lie to one another, seeing that you have put off the old nature with its practices.
**COLOSSIANS 3:9 RSV**

If someone says that he knows him, but does not obey his commands, such a person is a liar and there is no truth in him.
**1 JOHN 2:4 GNB**

Who is the liar? Who but he that denies that Jesus is the Christ? He is Antichrist, for he denies both the Father and the Son.
**1 JOHN 2:22 NEB**

## Magnificat
See appendix, *Prayers of the Bible.*

## Man

And God said, Let us make man in our image, after our likeness: and let them have dominion over the fish of the sea, and over the fowl of the air, and over the cattle, and over all the earth, and over every creeping thing that creepeth upon the earth. So God created man in his own image, in the image of God created he him; male and female created he them.
**GENESIS 1:26–27 KJV**

And unto Adam he said, Because thou hast harkened unto the voice of thy wife, and hast eaten of the tree, of which I commanded thee, saying, Thou shalt not eat of it: cursed is the ground for thy sake; in sorrow shalt thou eat of it all the days of thy life.
**GENESIS 3:17 KJV**

The Lord saw how great man's wickedness on the earth had become, and that every inclination of the thoughts of his heart was only evil all the time.
**GENESIS 6:5 NIV**

What is man, that thou art mindful of him? and the son of man, that thou visitest him? For thou hast made him a little lower than the angels, and hast crowned him with glory and honour. Thou madest him to have dominion over the works of thy hands; thou hast put all things under his feet: all sheep and oxen, yea, and the beasts of the field; the fowl of the air, and the fish of the sea, and whatsoever passeth through the paths of the seas.
**PSALM 8:4–8 KJV**

As for man, his days are like grass; he flourishes like a flower of the field; for the wind passes over it, and it is gone, and its place knows it no more.
**PSALM 103:15–16 RSV**

He [Jesus] knew men so well, all of them, that he needed no evidence from others about a man, for he himself could tell what was in a man.
**JOHN 2:25 NEB**

As by one man sin entered into the world, and death by sin . . . so death passed upon all men, for that all have sinned.
**ROMANS 5:12 KJV**

See also *Responsibility of man; Woman.*

## Marriage

And the Lord God said, It is not good that the man should be alone; I will make him an help meet for him.
**GENESIS 2:18 KJV**

Therefore shall a man leave his father and his mother, and shall cleave unto his wife: and they shall be one flesh.
**GENESIS 2:24 KJV**

What therefore God hath joined together, let not man put asunder.
**MATTHEW 19:6 KJV**

'For in the resurrection they neither marry nor are given in marriage, but are like angels in heaven.'
**MATTHEW 22:30 RSV**

A wife is bound to her husband as long as he lives. If the husband dies, she is free to be married to whom she wishes, only in the Lord.
**1 CORINTHIANS 7:39 RSV**

A bishop then must be blameless, the husband of one wife.
1 TIMOTHY 3:2 KJV

Now the Spirit expressly says that in later times some will depart from the faith by giving heed to deceitful spirits and doctrines of demons, through the pretensions of liars whose consciences are seared, who forbid marriage and enjoin abstinence from foods which God created to be received with thanksgiving by those who believe and know the truth.
1 TIMOTHY 4:1–3 RSV

Let marriage be held in honour among all, and let the marriage bed be undefiled; for God will judge the immoral and adulterous.
HEBREWS 13:4 RSV

See also *Family; Sex.*

### ADULTERY

Thou shalt not commit adultery.
EXODUS 20:14 KJV

He who commits adultery has no sense; he who does it destroys himself.
PROVERBS 6:32 RSV

'You have heard that it was said, "Do not commit adultery." But now I tell you: anyone who looks at a woman and wants to possess her is guilty of committing adultery with her in his heart.'
MATTHEW 5:27–28 GNB

### DIVORCE

Has not the one God made and sustained for us the spirit of life? And what does he desire? Godly offspring. So take heed to yourselves, and let none be faithless to the wife of his youth. 'For I hate divorce, says the Lord the God of Israel . . . So take heed to yourselves and do not be faithless.'
MALACHI 2:15–16 RSV

'It was also said, "Anyone who divorces his wife must give her a written notice of divorce." But now I tell you: if a man divorces his wife, even though she has not been unfaithful, then he is guilty of making her commit adultery if she marries again; and the man who marries her commits adultery also.'
MATTHEW 5:31–32 GNB

'Why then,' they asked, 'did Moses command that a man give his wife a certificate of divorce and send her away?' Jesus replied, 'Moses permitted you to divorce your wives because your hearts were hard. But it was not this way from the beginning. I tell you that anyone who divorces his wife, except for marital unfaithfulness, and marries another woman commits adultery.'
MATTHEW 19:7–9 NIV

For married people I have a command which is not my own but the Lord's: a wife must not leave her husband; but if she does, she must remain single or else be reconciled to her husband; and a husband must not divorce his wife.
1 CORINTHIANS 7:10–11 GNB

## Maturity
See *Christian life, Character of the Christian; Perfection.*

## Meditation

This book of the law shall not depart out of your mouth, but you shall meditate on it day and night, that you may be careful to do according to all that is written in it; for then you shall make your way prosperous, and then you shall have good success.
JOSHUA 1:8 RSV

His delight is in the law of the Lord, and on his law he meditates day and night. He is like a tree planted by streams of water, that yields its fruit in its season, and its leaf does not wither. In all that he does, he prospers.
PSALM 1:2–3 RSV

Be angry, but sin not; commune with your own hearts on your beds, and be silent.
PSALM 4:4 RSV

Let the words of my mouth, and the meditation of my heart, be acceptable in thy sight, O Lord, my strength, and my redeemer.
PSALM 19:14 KJV

Be still before the Lord and wait patiently for him; do not fret when men succeed in their ways, when they carry out their wicked schemes.
PSALM 37:7 NIV

I will meditate on thy precepts, and fix my eyes on thy ways.
PSALM 119:15 RSV

I remember the days gone by; I think about all that you have done, I bring to mind all your deeds.
PSALM 143:5 GNB

But Mary kept all these things, and pondered them in her heart.
**LUKE 2:19 KJV**

And we all, with unveiled face, beholding the glory of the Lord, are being changed into his likeness from one degree of glory to another; for this comes from the Lord who is the Spirit.
**2 CORINTHIANS 3:18 RSV**

See also *Mind; Thought.*

# Mercy, merciful

The Lord passed before him, and proclaimed, 'The Lord, the Lord, a God merciful and gracious, slow to anger, and abounding in steadfast love and faithfulness, keeping steadfast love for thousands, forgiving iniquity and transgression and sin, but who will by no means clear the guilty, visiting the iniquity of the fathers upon the children and the children's children, to the third and the fourth generation.'
**EXODUS 34:6–7 RSV**

All the paths of the Lord are steadfast love and faithfulness, for those who keep his covenant and his testimonies.
**PSALM 25:10 RSV**

Have mercy upon me, O God, according to thy lovingkindness: according unto the multitude of thy tender mercies blot out my transgressions.
**PSALM 51:1 KJV**

I will not remove from him my steadfast love, or be false to my faithfulness.
**PSALM 89:33 RSV**

O give thanks to the Lord, for he is good, for his steadfast love endures for ever.
**PSALM 136:1 RSV**

The steadfast love of the Lord never ceases, his mercies never come to an end; they are new every morning.
**LAMENTATIONS 3:22–23 RSV**

'O my God, incline thy ear and hear; open thy eyes and behold our desolations, and the city which is called by thy name; for we do not present our supplications before thee on the ground of our righteousness, but on the ground of thy great mercy.'
**DANIEL 9:18 RSV**

For I desire steadfast love and not sacrifice, the knowledge of God, rather than burnt offerings.
**HOSEA 6:6 RSV**

He hath shewed thee, O man, what is good; and what doth the Lord require of thee, but to do justly, and to love mercy, and to walk humbly with thy God?
**MICAH 6:8 KJV**

Blessed are the merciful: for they shall obtain mercy.
**MATTHEW 5:7 KJV**

'Be merciful just as your Father is merciful.'
**LUKE 6:36 GNB**

'But the tax collector, standing far off, would not even lift up his eyes to heaven, but beat his breast, saying, "God, be merciful to me a sinner!"'
**LUKE 18:13 RSV**

I beseech you therefore, brethren, by the mercies of God, that ye present your bodies a living sacrifice, holy, acceptable unto God, which is your reasonable service.
**ROMANS 12:1 KJV**

You are the people of God; he loved you and chose you for his own. So then, you must clothe yourselves with compassion, kindness, humility, gentleness, and patience.
**COLOSSIANS 3:12 GNB**

See also *Grace.*

# Mind

'Thou dost keep him in perfect peace, whose mind is stayed on thee, because he trusts in thee.'
**ISAIAH 26:3 RSV**

Jesus said unto him, Thou shalt love the Lord thy God with all thy heart, and with all thy soul, and with all thy mind.
**MATTHEW 22:37 KJV**

According to his usual habit Paul went to the synagogue. There during three sabbaths he held discussions with the people, quoting and explaining the Scriptures and proving from them that the Messiah had to suffer and rise from death . . . Some of them were convinced and joined Paul and Silas.
**ACTS 17:2–4 GNB**

For although they knew God they did not honour him as God or give thanks to him, but they

became futile in their thinking and their senseless minds were darkened.
ROMANS 1:21 RSV

For those who live according to the flesh set their minds on the things of the flesh, but those who live according to the Spirit set their minds on the things of the Spirit. To set the mind on the flesh is death, but to set the mind on the Spirit is life and peace.
ROMANS 8:5–6 RSV

O the depth of the riches both of the wisdom and knowledge of God! how unsearchable are his judgments, and his ways past finding out! For who hath known the mind of the Lord? or who hath been his counsellor?
ROMANS 11:33–34 KJV

And be not conformed to this world: but be ye transformed by the renewing of your mind, that ye may prove what is that good, and acceptable, and perfect, will of God.
ROMANS 12:2 KJV

'For who has known the mind of the Lord that he may instruct him?' But we have the mind of Christ.
1 CORINTHIANS 2:16 NIV

Have this mind among yourselves, which is yours in Christ Jesus.
PHILIPPIANS 2:5 RSV

And the peace of God, which passes all understanding, will keep your hearts and minds in Christ Jesus.
PHILIPPIANS 4:7 RSV

Set your minds on things that are above, not on things that are on earth.
COLOSSIANS 3:2 RSV

See also *Heart; Meditation; Understanding.*

## Ministry
See *Service.*

## Miracles

Then Moses stretched out his hand over the sea; and the Lord drove the sea back by a strong east wind all night, and made the sea dry land, and the waters were divided.
EXODUS 14:21 RSV

And Israel saw that great work which the Lord did upon the Egyptians; and the people feared the Lord, and believed the Lord, and his servant Moses.
EXODUS 14:31 KJV

[Elijah's prayer] 'Answer me, O Lord, answer me, that this people may know that thou, O Lord, art God, and that thou hast turned their hearts back.' Then the fire of the Lord fell, and consumed the burnt offering, and the wood, and the stones, and the dust, and licked up the water that was in the trench.
1 KINGS 18:37–38 RSV

Praise the Lord, the God of Israel! He alone does these wonderful things.
PSALM 72:18 GNB

'For false Christs and false prophets will arise and show great signs and wonders, so as to lead astray, if possible, even the elect.'
MATTHEW 24:24 RSV

'For with God nothing will be impossible.'
LUKE 1:37 RSV

Jesus performed this first miracle in Cana in Galilee; there he revealed his glory, and his disciples believed in him.
JOHN 2:11 GNB

'Truly, truly, I say to you, he who believes in me will also do the works that I do; and greater works than these will be do, because I go to the Father.'
JOHN 14:12 RSV

'While thou stretchest out thy hand to heal, and signs and wonders are performed through the name of thy holy servant Jesus.'
ACTS 4:30 RSV

But Peter put them all outside and knelt down and prayed; then, turning to the body he said, 'Tabitha, rise.' And she opened her eyes, and when she saw Peter she sat up.
ACTS 9:40 RSV

To another the working of miracles.
1 CORINTHIANS 12:10 RSV

The things that mark an apostle—signs, wonders and miracles—were done among you with great perseverance.
2 CORINTHIANS 12:12 NIV

God also bore witness by signs and wonders and various miracles and by gifts of the Holy Spirit distributed according to his own will.

HEBREWS 2:4 RSV

See also appendix, *Miracles of Jesus.*

## Money and material goods

He who loves money never has money enough, he who loves wealth never has enough profit; this too is vanity.

ECCLESIASTES 5:9 JB

'Do not lay up for yourselves treasures on earth, where moth and rust consume and where thieves break in and steal.'

MATTHEW 6:19 RSV

'No one can serve two masters; for either he will hate the one and love the other, or he will be devoted to the one and despise the other. You cannot serve God and mammon.'

MATTHEW 6:24 RSV

[The Pharisees] 'Tell us, then, what you think. Is it lawful to pay taxes to Caesar, or not?' But Jesus, aware of their malice, said, 'Why put me to the test, you hypocrites? Show me the money for the tax.' And they brought him a coin. And Jesus said to them, 'Whose likeness and inscription is this?' They said, 'Caesar's.' Then he said to them, 'Render therefore to Caesar the things that are Caesar's, and to God the things that are God's.'

MATTHEW 22:17–21 RSV

[A church leader] must not love money.

1 TIMOTHY 3:3 GNB

There is great gain in godliness with contentment; for we brought nothing into the world, and we cannot take anything out of the world.

1 TIMOTHY 6:6–7 RSV

For the love of money is the root of all evil.

1 TIMOTHY 6:10 KJV

Keep your life free from love of money, and be content with what you have; for he has said, 'I will never fail you nor forsake you.'

HEBREWS 13:5 RSV

See also *Giving; Rich and riches.*

## Mother

see *Family.*

## Murder

Cain said to Abel his brother, 'Let us go out to the field.' And when they were in the field, Cain rose up against his brother Abel, and killed him. Then the Lord said to Cain, 'Where is Abel your brother?' He said, 'I do not know; am I my brother's keeper? And the Lord said, 'What have you done? The voice of your brother's blood is crying to me from the ground.'

GENESIS 4:8–10 RSV

'Whoever sheds the blood of man, by man shall his blood be shed; for God made man in his own image.'

GENESIS 9:6 RSV

'Do not commit murder.'

EXODUS 20:13 GNB

'This is the provision for the manslayer, who by fleeing there [to special cities] may save his life. If any one kills his neighbour unintentionally without having been at enmity with him in time past—as when a man goes into the forest with his neighbour to cut wood, and his hand swings the axe to cut down a tree, and the head slips from the handle and strikes his neighbour so that he dies—he may flee to one of these cities and save his life; lest the avenger of blood in hot anger pursue the manslayer and overtake him . . . and wound him mortally, though the man did not deserve to die, since he was not at enmity with his neighbour in time past.'

DEUTERONOMY 19:4–6 RSV

'But if any man hates his neighbour, and lies in wait for him, and attacks him, and wounds him mortally so that he dies, and the man flees into one of these cities, then the elders of his city shall send and fetch him from there, and hand him over the avenger of blood, so that he may die.'

DEUTERONOMY 19:11–12 RSV

'You have heard that people were told in the past, "Do not commit murder; anyone who does will be brought to trial." But now I tell you: whoever is angry with his brother will be brought to trial.'

MATTHEW 5:21–22 GNB

Any one who hates his brother is a murderer, and you know that no murderer has eternal life abiding in him.

1 JOHN 3:15 RSV

'But as for the cowardly, the faithless, the polluted, as for murderers, fornicators, sorcerers, idolaters, and all liars, their lot shall be in the lake that burns with fire and sulphur, which is the second death.'

REVELATION 21:8 RSV

## Name

He [Abraham] . . . pitched his tent, with Bethel on the west and Ai on the east; and there he built an altar to the Lord and called on the name of the Lord.

GENESIS 12:8 RSV

Then Moses said to God, 'If I come to the people of Israel and say to them, "The God of your fathers has sent me to you," and they ask me, "What is his name?" what shall I say to them?' God said to Moses, 'I am who I am.' And he said, 'Say this to the people of Israel, "The Lord, the God of your fathers, the God of Abraham, the God of Isaac, and the God of Jacob, has sent me to you": this is my name for ever, and thus I am to be remembered throughout all generations.'

EXODUS 3:13–15 RSV

Thou shalt not take the name of the Lord thy God in vain; for the Lord will not hold him guiltless that taketh his name in vain.

EXODUS 20:7 KJV

The name of the Lord is a strong tower; the righteous man runs into it and is safe.

PROVERBS 18:10 RSV

Our Father, which art in heaven, hallowed be thy name.

MATTHEW 6:9 BCP

'For where two or three are gathered in my name, there am I in the midst of them.'

MATTHEW 18:20 RSV

'Go therefore and make disciples of all nations, baptizing them in the name of the Father and of the Son and of the Holy Spirit.'

MATTHEW 28:19 RSV

Repentance and remission of sins should be preached in his name among all nations, beginning at Jerusalem.

LUKE 24:47 KJV

'Whatever you ask in my name, I will do it, that the Father may be glorified in the Son.'

JOHN 14:13 RSV

'But the Counsellor, the Holy Spirit, whom the Father will send in my name, he will teach you all things, and bring to your remembrance all that I have said to you.'

JOHN 14:26 RSV

Then Peter said, Silver and gold have I none; but such as I have give I thee: in the name of Jesus Christ of Nazareth rise up and walk.

ACTS 3:6 KJV

'And there is salvation in no one else, for there is no other name under heaven given among men by which we must be saved.'

ACTS 4:12 RSV

Fear fell upon them all; and the name of the Lord Jesus was extolled.

ACTS 19:17 RSV

Therefore God has highly exalted him and bestowed on him the name which is above every name, that at the name of Jesus every knee should bow, in heaven and on earth and under the earth.

PHILIPPIANS 2:9–10 RSV

And whatsoever ye do in word or deed, do all in the name of the Lord Jesus, giving thanks to God and the Father by him.

COLOSSIANS 3:17 KJV

## Neighbour

Thou shalt not bear false witness against thy neighbour. Thou shalt not covet thy neighbour's house, thou shalt not covet thy neighbour's wife, nor his manservant, nor his maidservant, nor his ox, nor his ass, nor anything that is thy neighbour's.

EXODUS 20:16–17 KJV

'You shall not take vengeance or bear any grudge against the sons of your own people, but you shall love your neighbour as yourself: I am the Lord.'

LEVITICUS 19:18 RSV

But he [a lawyer], desiring to justify himself, said to Jesus, 'And who is my neighbour?' Jesus replied, 'A man was going down from Jerusalem to Jericho, and he fell among robbers, who stripped him and beat him, and departed, leaving him half dead. Now by chance a priest was going down that road; and when he saw him he passed by on the other side. So likewise a Levite, when he came to the place and saw him, passed by on the other side. But a Samaritan, as he journeyed, came to where he was; and when he saw him, he had compassion, and went to him and bound up his wounds, pouring on oil and wine; then he set him on his own beast and brought him to an inn, and took care of him. And the next day he took out two denarii and gave them to the innkeeper, saying, ''Take care of him; and whatever more you spend, I will repay you when I come back.'' Which of these three, do you think, proved neighbour to the man who fell among the robbers?' He said, 'The one who showed mercy on him.' And Jesus said to him, 'Go and do likewise.'

LUKE 10:29–37 RSV

For the whole Law is summed up in one commandment: 'Love your neighbour as you love yourself.'

GALATIANS 5:14 GNB

See also *Love, of man for man.*

## New birth

Create in me a clean heart, O God; and renew a right spirit within me.

PSALM 51:10 KJV

I will sprinkle clean water upon you, and you shall be clean from all your uncleannesses, and from all your idols I will cleanse you. A new heart I will give you, and a new spirit I will put within you; and I will take out of your flesh the heart of stone and give you a heart of flesh. And I will put my spirit within you, and cause you to walk in my statutes and be careful to observe my ordinances.

EZEKIEL 36:25–27 RSV

Jesus answered and said unto him, Verily, verily, I say unto thee, Except a man be born again, he cannot see the kingdom of God. Nicodemus saith unto him, How can a man be born when he is old? Can he enter the second time into his mother's womb, and be born? Jesus answered, Verily, verily, I say unto thee, Except a man be born of water and of the Spirit, he cannot enter into the kingdom of God. That which is born of the flesh is flesh; and that which is born of the Spirit is spirit. Marvel not that I said unto thee, Ye must be born again. The wind bloweth where it listeth, and thou hearest the sound thereof, but canst not tell whence it cometh, and whither it goeth: so is every one that is born of the Spirit.

JOHN 3:3–8 KJV

Therefore if any man be in Christ, he is a new creature: old things are passed away; behold, all things are become new.

2 CORINTHIANS 5:17 KJV

As for you, you were dead in your transgressions and sins, in which you used to live when you followed the ways of this world and of the ruler of the kingdom of the air, the spirit who is now at work in those who are disobedient. All of us also lived among them at one time, gratifying the cravings of our sinful nature and following its desires and thoughts. Like the rest, we were by nature objects of wrath. But because of his great love for us, God, who is rich in mercy, made us alive with Christ even when we were dead in transgressions—it is by grace you have been saved.

EPHESIANS 2:1–5 NIV

[God our Saviour] He saved us, not because of deeds done by us in righteousness, but in virtue of his own mercy, by the washing of regeneration and renewal in the Holy Spirit.

TITUS 3:5 RSV

For through the living and eternal word of God you have been born again as the children of a parent who is immortal, not mortal.

1 PETER 1:23 GNB

Whoever is a child of God does not continue to sin, for God's very nature is in him; and because God is his Father, he cannot continue to sin.

1 JOHN 3:9 GNB

## Nunc Dimittis

See appendix, *Prayers of the Bible.*

## Obedience

'And by your descendants shall all the nations of the earth bless themselves, because you have obeyed my voice.'

GENESIS 22:18 RSV

'But my servant Caleb, because he has a different spirit and has followed me fully, I will bring into the land into which he went, and his descendants shall possess it.'

NUMBERS 14:24 RSV

...ings shall come upon you and ...ou obey the voice of the Lord

...8:2 RSV

...el said, 'Has the Lord as great delight ...offerings and sacrifices, as in obeying the voice of the Lord? Behold, to obey is better than sacrifice, and to hearken than the fat of rams.'

1 SAMUEL 15:22 RSV

'Not every one who says to me, "Lord, Lord," shall enter the kingdom of heaven, but he who does the will of my Father who is in heaven.'

MATTHEW 7:21 RSV

If ye love me, keep my commandments.

JOHN 14:15 KJV

[The high priest] 'We strictly charged you not to teach in this name, yet here you have filled Jerusalem with your teaching and you intend to bring this man's blood upon us.' But Peter and the apostles answered, 'We must obey God rather than men.'

ACTS 5:28–29 RSV

'And we are witnesses to these things, and so is the Holy Spirit whom God has given to those who obey him.'

ACTS 5:32 RSV

But thanks be to God, that you who were once slaves of sin have become obedient from the heart to the standard of teaching to which you were committed.

ROMANS 6:17 RSV

And being found in human form he humbled himself and became obedient unto death, even death on a cross.

PHILIPPIANS 2:8 RSV

But even though he was God's Son, he learnt through his sufferings to be obedient.

HEBREWS 5:8 GNB

But be ye doers of the word, and not hearers only, deceiving your own selves.

JAMES 1:22 KJV

Be obedient to God, and do not allow your lives to be shaped by those desires you had when you were still ignorant. Instead, be holy in all that you do, just as God who called you is holy.

1 PETER 1:14–15 GNB

We receive from him whatever we ask, because we keep his commandments and do what pleases him.

1 JOHN 3:22 RSV

By this we know that we love the children of God, when we love God and obey his commandments.

1 JOHN 5:2 RSV

See also *Blessing; Disobedience; Submission.*

## Occult

' "Do not practise divination or sorcery." '

LEVITICUS 19:26 NIV

'Do not go for advice to people who consult the spirits of the dead. If you do, you will be ritually unclean. I am the Lord your God.'

LEVITICUS 19:31 GNB

'Any man or woman who consults the spirits of the dead shall be stoned to death; any person who does this is responsible for his own death.'

LEVITICUS 20:27 GNB

Let no-one be found among you who sacrifices his son or daughter in the fire, who practises divination or sorcery, interprets omens, engages in witchcraft, or casts spells, or who is a medium or spiritist or who consults the dead. Anyone who does these things is detestable to the Lord.

DEUTERONOMY 18:10–12 NIV

Saul died because he was unfaithful to the Lord; he did not keep the word of the Lord, and even consulted a medium for guidance and did not enquire of the Lord. So the Lord put him to death.

1 CHRONICLES 10:13–14 NIV

And when they say to you, 'Consult the mediums and the wizards who chirp and mutter,' should not a people consult their God? Should they consult the dead on behalf of the living?

ISAIAH 8:19 RSV

Let your astrologers, your star-gazers who foretell your future month by month, persist, and save you! But look, they are gone like chaff; fire burns them up; they cannot snatch themselves from the flames; this is no glowing coal to warm them, no fire for them to sit by.

ISAIAH 47:13–14 NEB

Now for some time a man named Simon had practised sorcery in the city and amazed all the

people of Samaria. He boasted that he was someone great.
**ACTS 8:9 NIV**

A number who had practised sorcery brought their scrolls together and burned them publicly.
**ACTS 19:19 NIV**

Now the works of the flesh are plain: . . . sorcery . . .
**GALATIANS 5:19–20 RSV**

## Old age

'Show respect for old people and honour them. Fear me; I am the Lord.'
**LEVITICUS 19:32 GNB**

'Wisdom is with the aged, and understanding in length of days.'
**JOB 12:12 RSV**

My times are in thy hand.
**PSALM 31:15 KJV**

Do not cast me off in the time of old age; forsake me not when my strength is spent.
**PSALM 71:9 RSV**

The days of our years are three score years and ten; and if by reason of strength they be fourscore years, yet is their strength labour and sorrow; for it is soon cut off, and we fly away . . . So teach us to number our days, that we may apply our hearts unto wisdom.
**PSALM 90:10, 12 KJV**

They [the righteous] are like trees planted in the house of the Lord, that flourish in the Temple of our God, that still bear fruit in old age and are always green and strong.
**PSALM 92:13–14 GNB**  ·

Children's children are a crown to the aged, and parents are the pride of their children.
**PROVERBS 17:6 NIV**

There was a very old prophetess, a widow named Anna, daughter of Phanuel of the tribe of Asher. She had been married for only seven years and was now eighty-four years old. She never left the Temple; day and night she worshipped God, fasting and praying.
**LUKE 2:36–37 GNB**

Here indeed we groan, and long to put on our heavenly dwelling.
**2 CORINTHIANS 5:2 RSV**

For me to live is Christ, and to die is gain.
**PHILIPPIANS 1:21 KJV**

Instruct the older men to be sober, sensible, and self-controlled; to be sound in their faith, love, and endurance. In the same way instruct the older women to behave as women should who live a holy life. They must not be slanderers or slaves to wine. They must teach what is good.
**TITUS 2:2–3 GNB**

## Oppression

'You shall not wrong a stranger or oppress him, for you were strangers in the land of Egypt.'
**EXODUS 22:21 RSV**

'You shall not oppress a hired servant who is poor and needy, whether he is one of your brethren or one of the sojourners who are in your land within your towns.'
**DEUTERONOMY 24:14 RSV**

May the Lord be a tower of strength for the oppressed.
**PSALM 9:9 NEB**

The Lord judges in favour of the oppressed and gives them their rights.
**PSALM 103:6 GNB**

He who oppresses a poor man insults his Maker, but he who is kind to the needy honours him.
**PROVERBS 14:31 RSV**

My eyes are weary with looking upward. O Lord, I am oppressed; be thou my security!
**ISAIAH 38:14 RSV**

He was oppressed, and he was afflicted, yet he opened not his mouth.
**ISAIAH 53:7 KJV**

' "Do not oppress widows, orphans, foreigners who live among you, or anyone else in need. And do not plan ways of harming one another." '
**ZECHARIAH 7:10 GNB**

But you have dishonoured the poor man. Is it not the rich who oppress you, is it not they who drag you into court?
**JAMES 2:6 RSV**

## Parables
See appendix, *Parables of Jesus.*

## Parent
See *Family.*

## Passover

'Tell all the congregation of Israel that on the tenth day of this month they shall take every man a lamb according to their fathers' houses, a lamb for a household ... Your lamb shall be without blemish, a male a year old; you shall take it from the sheep or from the goats; and you shall keep it until the fourteenth day of this month, when the whole assembly of the congregation of Israel shall kill their lambs in the evening. Then they shall take some of the blood, and put it on the two doorposts and the lintel of the houses in which they eat them. They shall eat the flesh that night, roasted; with unleavened bread and bitter herbs they shall eat it ... In this manner you shall eat it: your loins girded, your sandals on your feet, and your staff in your hand; and you shall eat it in haste. It is the Lord's passover. For I will pass through the land of Egypt that night, and I will smite all the first-born in the land of Egypt, both man and beast; and on all the gods of Egypt I will execute judgments: I am the Lord. The blood shall be a sign for you, upon the houses where you are; and when I see the blood, I will pass over you, and no plague shall fall upon you to destroy you, when I smite the land of Egypt.'
EXODUS 12:3, 5–8, 11–13 RSV

'You shall observe this rite as an ordinance for you and for your sons for ever.'
EXODUS 12:24 RSV

Now his parents went to Jerusalem every year at the feast of the Passover.
LUKE 2:41 RSV

They went off and found everything just as Jesus had told them, and they prepared the Passover meal.
LUKE 22:13 GNB

You must remove the old yeast of sin so that you will be entirely pure. Then you will be like a new batch of dough without any yeast, as indeed I know you actually are. For our Passover Festival is ready, now that Christ, our Passover lamb, has been sacrificed.
1 CORINTHIANS 5:7 GNB

See also *Communion*.

## Pastor

And his gifts were that some should be apostles, some prophets, some evangelists, some pastors and teachers, to equip the saints for the work of ministry, for building up the body of Christ.
EPHESIANS 4:11–12 RSV

For you know how, like a father with his children, we exhorted each one of you and encouraged you and charged you.
1 THESSALONIANS 2:11 GNB

As for you, always be steady, endure suffering, do the work of an evangelist, fulfil your ministry.
2 TIMOTHY 4:5 RSV

See also *Elders; Shepherd; Teachers and teaching*.

## Patience

Be still before the Lord and wait patiently for him; do not fret when men succeed in their way, when they carry out their wicked schemes.
PSALM 37:7 NIV

If you stay calm, you are wise, but if you have a hot temper, you only show how stupid you are.
PROVERBS 14:29 GNB

But they that wait upon the Lord shall renew their strength; they shall mount up with wings as eagles; they shall run, and not be weary; and they shall walk, and not faint.
ISAIAH 40:31 KJV

Or do you presume upon the riches of his kindness and forbearance and patience? Do you not know that God's kindness is meant to lead you to repentance?
ROMANS 2:4 RSV

Rejoice in your hope, be patient in tribulation, be constant in prayer.
ROMANS 12:12 RSV

Love is patient and kind ... Love bears all things, believes all things, hopes all things, endures all things.
1 CORINTHIANS 13:4, 7 RSV

But the fruit of the Spirit is ... patience ...
GALATIANS 5:22 RSV

And we urge you, brothers, warn those who are idle, encourage the timid, help the weak, be patient with everyone.
1 THESSALONIANS 5:14 NIV

Be patient, therefore, brethren, until the coming of the Lord. Behold, the farmer waits for the precious fruit of the earth, being patient over it until it receives the early and the late rain. You also be patient. Establish your hearts, for the coming of the Lord is at hand.

**JAMES 5:7–8 RSV**

[To the church in Ephesus] ''I know your works, your toil and your patient endurance, and how you cannot bear evil men but have tested those who call themselves apostles but are not, and found them to be false.'' '

**REVELATION 2:2 RSV**

See also *Endurance*.

## Peace

The Lord lift up his countenance upon thee, and give thee peace.

**NUMBERS 6:26 KJV**

His name shall be called Wonderful, Counsellor, The mighty God, The everlasting Father, The Prince of Peace. Of the increase of his government and peace there shall be no end.

**ISAIAH 9:6–7 KJV**

'Thou dost keep him in perfect peace, whose mind is stayed on thee, because he trusts in thee.'

**ISAIAH 26:3 RSV**

'There is no peace,' says the Lord, 'for the wicked.'

**ISAIAH 48:22 RSV**

And when Jesus was baptized, he went up immediately from the water, and behold, the heavens were opened and he saw the Spirit of God descending like a dove, and alighting on him.

**MATTHEW 3:16 RSV**

Blessed are the peacemakers: for they shall be called the children of God.

**MATTHEW 5:9 KJV**

'Do not think that I have come to bring peace to the world. No, I did not come to bring peace, but a sword.'

**MATTHEW 10:34 GNB**

And he awoke and rebuked the wind, and said to the sea, 'Peace! Be still!' And the wind ceased, and there was a great calm.

**MARK 4:39 RSV**

'Glory to God in highest heaven, and on earth his peace for men on whom his favour rests.'

**LUKE 2:14 NEB**

[Simeon's 'Nunc Dimittis'] Lord, now lettest thou thy servant depart in peace, according to thy word.

**LUKE 2:29 BCP**

'Whenever you go into a house, first say, ''Peace be with this house.'' If a peace-loving man lives there, let your greeting of peace remain on him; if not, take back your greeting of peace.'

**LUKE 10:5–6 GNB**

'Peace I leave with you; my peace I give to you; not as the world gives do I give to you. Let not your hearts be troubled, neither let them be afraid.'

**JOHN 14:27 RSV**

These things I have spoken unto you, that in me ye might have peace. In the world ye shall have tribulation: but be of good cheer; I have overcome the world.

**JOHN 16:33 KJV**

Jesus came and stood among them and said to them, 'Peace be with you.'

**JOHN 20:19 RSV**

Therefore being justified by faith, we have peace with God through our Lord Jesus Christ.

**ROMANS 5:1 KJV**

To set the mind on the flesh is death, but to set the mind on the Spirit is life and peace.

**ROMANS 8:6 RSV**

If possible, so far as it depends upon you, live peaceably with all.

**ROMANS 12:18 RSV**

For God is not a God of confusion but of peace.

**1 CORINTHIANS 14:33 RSV**

But the fruit of the Spirit is . . . peace . . .

**GALATIANS 5:22 RSV**

For he is our peace, who has made us both one, and has broken down the dividing wall of hostility.

**EPHESIANS 2:14 RSV**

And your feet shod with the preparation of the gospel of peace.

**EPHESIANS 6:15 KJV**

And the peace of God, which passes all understanding, will keep your hearts and your minds in Christ Jesus.

**PHILIPPIANS 4:7 RSV**

And let the peace of God rule in your hearts, to the which also ye are called in one body; and be ye thankful.
COLOSSIANS 3:15 KJV

Now may the Lord of peace himself give you peace at all times in all ways.
2 THESSALONIANS 3:16 RSV

See also *Reconciliation.*

## Pentecost
See Acts 2.

## Perfection
[COMPLETENESS, MATURITY]

[David's song of victory] 'This God—his way is perfect; the promise of the Lord proves true; he is a shield for all those who take refuge in him.'
2 SAMUEL 22:31 RSV

The law of the Lord is perfect, converting the soul.
PSALM 19:7 KJV

Be ye therefore perfect, even as your Father which is in heaven is perfect.
MATTHEW 5:48 KJV

Jesus said unto him [the rich young ruler], If thou wilt be perfect, go and sell that thou hast, and give to the poor, and thou shalt have treasure in heaven: and come and follow me.
MATTHEW 19:21 KJV

And be not conformed to this world: but be ye transformed by the renewing of your mind, that ye may prove what is that good, and acceptable, and perfect, will of God.
ROMANS 12:2 KJV

For our knowledge is imperfect and our prophecy is imperfect; but when the perfect comes, the imperfect will pass away.
1 CORINTHIANS 13:9–10 KJV

And his gifts were that some should be apostles, some prophets, some evangelists, some pastors and teacher, to equip the saints for the work of ministry, for building up the body of Christ, until we all attain to the unity of the faith and of the knowledge of the Son of God, to mature manhood, to the measure of the stature of the fullness of Christ.
EPHESIANS 4:11–13 RSV

Not that I have already obtained all this, or have already been made perfect, but I press on to take hold of that for which Christ Jesus took told of me.
PHILIPPIANS 3:12 NIV

All of us who are spiritually mature should have this same attitude. But if some of you have a different attitude, God will make this clear to you.
PHILIPPIANS 3:15 GNB

Him we proclaim, warning every man and teaching every man in all wisdom, that we may present every man mature in Christ.
COLOSSIANS 1:28 RSV

[The purpose of Scripture] That the man of God may be complete, equipped for every good work.
2 TIMOTHY 3:17 RSV

But even though he was God's Son, he learnt through his sufferings to be obedient. When he was made perfect, he became the source of eternal salvation for all those who obey him.
HEBREWS 5:8–9 GNB

But solid food is for the mature, for those who have their faculties trained by practice to distinguish good from evil.
HEBREWS 5:14 RSV

For by a single offering he has perfected for all time those who are sanctified.
HEBREWS 10:14 RSV

## Persecution

'Happy are those who are persecuted because they do what God requires; the Kingdom of heaven belongs to them! Happy are you when people insult you and persecute you and tell all kinds of evil lies against you because you are my followers. Be happy and glad, for a great reward is kept for you in heaven. This is how the prophets who lived before you were persecuted.'
MATTHEW 5:10–12 GNB

But I say unto you, Love your enemies, bless them that curse you, do good to them that hate you, and pray for them which despitefully use you, and persecute you.
MATTHEW 5:44 KJV

'He has no root in himself, but endures for a while, and when tribulation or persecution arises on account of the word, immediately he falls away.'
MATTHEW 13:21 RSV

'But before all this they will lay their hands on you and persecute you, delivering you up to the synagogues and prisons, and you will be brought before kings and governors for my name's sake.'

LUKE 21:12 RSV

'Remember what I told you: "No slave is greater than his master." If they persecuted me, they will persecute you too; if they obeyed my teaching, they will obey yours too.'

JOHN 15:20 GNB

And on that day a great persecution arose against the church in Jerusalem; and they were all scattered throughout the region of Judea and Samaria, except the apostles.

ACTS 8:1 RSV

And he fell to the ground and heard a voice saying to him, 'Saul, Saul, who do you persecute me?'

ACTS 9:4 RSV

Who shall separate us from the love of Christ? Shall tribulation, or distress, or persecution, or famine, or nakedness, or peril, or sword? . . . No, in all these things we are more than conquerors through him who loved us.

ROMANS 8:35, 37 RSV

Bless those who persecute you; bless and do not curse.

ROMANS 12:14 NIV

Indeed all who desire to live a godly life in Christ Jesus will be persecuted.

2 TIMOTHY 3:12 RSV

## Perseverance
See *Christian life, Continuing in the faith.*

## Pharisees

The Pharisees went out and took counsel against him, how to destroy him.

MATTHEW 12:14 RSV

The Pharisees went off and made a plan to trap Jesus with questions.

MATTHEW 22:15 GNB

'But woe to you, scribes and Pharisees, hypocrites! because you shut the kingdom of heaven against men; for you neither enter yourselves, nor allow those who would enter to go in.'

MATTHEW 23:13 RSV

One day when Jesus was teaching, some Pharisees and teachers of the Law were sitting there who had come from every town in Galilee and Judaea and from Jerusalem.

LUKE 5:17 GNB

And the Pharisees and their scribes murmured against his disciples, saying, 'Why do you eat and drink with tax collectors and sinners?' And Jesus answered them, 'Those who are well have no need of a physician, but those who are sick; I have not come to call the righteous, but sinners to repentance.'

LUKE 5:30–31 RSV

When the Pharisee saw this, he said to himself, 'If this man really were a prophet, he would know who this woman is who is touching him; he would know what kind of sinful life she lives!'

LUKE 7:39 GNB

The Pharisee was astonished to see that he did not first wash before dinner. And the Lord said to him, 'Now you Pharisees cleanse the outside of the cup and of the dish, but inside you are full of extortion and wickedness.'

LUKE 11:38–39 RSV

He also told this parable to some who trusted in themselves that they were righteous and despised others: 'Two men went up into the temple to pray, one a Pharisee and the other a tax collector. The Pharisee stood and prayed thus with himself, "God, I thank thee that I am not like other men, extortioners, unjust, adulterers, or even like this tax collector. I fast twice a week, I give tithes of all that I get."'

LUKE 18:9–12 RSV

Many of the Jewish authorities believed in Jesus; but because of the Pharisees they did not talk about it openly, so as not to be expelled from the synagogue.

JOHN 12:42 GNB

But when Paul perceived that one part were Sadducees and the other Pharisees, he cried out in the council, 'Brethren, I am a Pharisee, a son of Pharisees; with respect to the hope and the resurrection of the dead I am on trial.'

ACTS 23:6 RSV

See also *Hypocrisy; Scribes.*

## Possessions
See *Money and material goods.*

## Poverty

'You shall not pervert the justice due to your poor in his suit.'
EXODUS 23:6 RSV

'If there is among you a poor man, one of your brethren, in any of your towns within your land which the Lord you God gives you, you shall not harden your heart or shut your hand against your poor brother.'
DEUTERONOMY 15:7 RSV

'He raises the poor from the dust, he lifts the needy from the dunghill to give them a place with princes, and to assign them a seat of honour.'
1 SAMUEL 2:8 JB

He who oppresses a poor man insults his Maker, but he who is kind to the needy honours him.
PROVERBS 14:31 RSV

He who is kind to the poor lends to the Lord, and he will repay him for his deed.
PROVERBS 19:17 RSV

Blessed are the poor in spirit: for theirs is the kingdom of heaven.
MATTHEW 5:3 KJV

'For you always have the poor with you, but you will not always have me.'
MATTHEW 26:11 RSV

And he called his disciples to him, and said to them, 'Truly, I say to you, this poor widow has put in more than all those who are contributing to the treasury. For they all contributed out of their abundance; but she out of her poverty has put in everything she had, her whole living.'
MARK 12:43–44 RSV

'The Spirit of the Lord is upon me, because he has anointed me to preach good news to the poor.'
LUKE 4:18 RSV

'But when you give a feast, invite the poor, the maimed, the lame, the blind.'
LUKE 14:13 RSV

For ye know the grace of our Lord Jesus Christ, that, though he was rich, yet for your sakes he became poor, that ye through his poverty might be rich.
2 CORINTHIANS 8:9 KJV

Has not God chosen those who are poor in the world to be rich in faith and heirs of the kingdom which he has promised to those who love him? But you have dishonoured the poor man.
JAMES 2:5–6 RSV

See also *Justice; Rich and riches.*

## Power

But they that wait upon the Lord shall renew their strength; they shall mount up with wings as eagles; they shall run, and not be weary; and they shall walk, and not faint.
ISAIAH 40:31 KJV

For thine is the kingdom, and the power, and the glory, for ever. Amen.
MATTHEW 6:13 KJV

But Jesus answered them, 'You are wrong, because you know neither the scriptures nor the power of God.'
MATTHEW 22:29 RSV

'Then will appear the sign of the Son of man in heaven, and then all the tribes of the earth will mourn, and they will see the Son of man coming on the clouds of heaven with power and great glory.'
MATTHEW 24:30 RSV

And Jesus, perceiving in himself that power had gone forth from him, immediately turned about in the crowd, and said, 'Who touched my garments?'
MARK 5:30 RSV

And Jesus returned in the power of the Spirit into Galilee.
LUKE 4:14 KJV

'But you shall receive power when the Holy Spirit has come upon you; and you shall be my witnesses in Jerusalem and in all Judea and Samaria and to the end of the earth.'
ACTS 1:8 RSV

For I am not ashamed of the gospel of Christ: for it is the power of God unto salvation to everyone that believeth; to the Jew first, and also to the Greek.
ROMANS 1:16 KJV

May the God of hope fill you with all joy and peace in believing, so that by the power of the

Holy Spirit you may abound in hope.

ROMANS 15:13 RSV

But we preach Christ crucified, unto the Jews a stumbling block, and unto the Greeks foolishness; but unto them which are called, both Jews and Greeks, Christ the power of God, and the wisdom of God.

1 CORINTHIANS 1:23–24 KJV

But we have this treasure in earthen vessels, that the excellency of the power may be of God, and not of us.

2 CORINTHIANS 4:7 KJV

He said to me, 'My grace is sufficient for you, for my power is made perfect in weakness.' I will all the more gladly boast of my weaknesses, that the power of Christ may rest upon me.

2 CORINTHIANS 12:9 RSV

How very great is his power at work in us who believe. This power working in us is the same as the mighty strength which he used when he raised Christ from death and seated him at his right side in the heavenly world.

EPHESIANS 1:19–20 GNB

Finally, my brethren, be strong in the Lord, and in the power of his might. Put on the whole armour of God, that ye may be able to stand against the wiles of the devil.

EPHESIANS 6:10–11 KJV

That I may know him and the power of his resurrection, and may share his sufferings, becoming like him in his death.

PHILIPPIANS 3:10 RSV

I can do all things in him who strengthens me.

PHILIPPIANS 4:13 RSV

For our gospel came to you not only in word, but also in power and in the Holy Spirit and with full conviction.

1 THESSALONIANS 1:5 RSV

They [people in the last days] will hold to the outward form of our religion, but reject its real power. Keep away from such people.

2 TIMOTHY 3:5 GNB

You, who by God's power are guarded through faith for a salvation ready to be revealed in the last time.

1 PETER 1:4–5 RSV

See also **Authority.**

# Praise

I will bless the Lord at all times; his praise shall continually be in my mouth . . . O magnify the Lord with me, and let us exalt his name together!

PSALM 34:1, 3 RSV

Whoso offereth praise glorifieth me: and to him that ordereth his conversation aright will I shew the salvation of God.

PSALM 50:23 KJV

Make a joyful noise unto the Lord, all ye lands. Serve the Lord with gladness: come before his presence with singing. Know ye that the Lord he is God: it is he that hath made us, and not we ourselves; we are his people, and the sheep of his pasture. Enter into his gates with thanksgiving, and into his courts with praise: be thankful unto him, and bless his name.

PSALM 100:1–4 KJV

The people whom I formed for myself that they might declare my praise.

ISAIAH 43:21 RSV

He hath sent me . . . to appoint unto them that mourn in Zion, to give unto them beauty for ashes, the oil of joy for mourning, the garment of praise for the spirit of heaviness; that they might be called trees of righteousness, the planting of the Lord, that he might be glorified.

ISAIAH 61:1, 3 KJV

Day after day they met as a group in the Temple, and they had their meals together in their homes, eating with glad and humble hearts, praising God, and enjoying the good will of all the people. And every day the Lord added to their group those who were being saved.

ACTS 2:46–47 GNB

Speaking to yourselves in psalms and hymns and spiritual songs, singing and making melody in your heart to the Lord.

EPHESIANS 5:19 KJV

Let us, then, always offer praise to God as our sacrifice through Jesus, which is the offering presented by lips that confess him as Lord.

HEBREWS 13:15 GNB

'Worthy is the Lamb who was slain, to receive power and wealth and wisdom and might and honour and glory and blessing!'

REVELATION 5:12 RSV

See also **Prayer; Worship.**

## Prayer

### ANSWERS TO PRAYER

This poor man cried, and the Lord heard him, and saved him out of all his troubles.
**PSALM 34:6 RSV**

And when he had entered the house, his disciples asked him privately, 'Why could we not cast it out?' And he said to them, 'This kind cannot be driven out by anything but prayer.'
**MARK 9:28–29 RSV**

You also must help us by prayer, so that many will give thanks on our behalf for the blessing granted us in answer to many prayers.
**2 CORINTHIANS 1:11 RSV**

Three times I besought the Lord about this, that it should leave me; but he said to me, 'My grace is sufficient for you, for my power is made perfect in weakness.'
**2 CORINTHIANS 12:8–9 RSV**

Now unto him that is able to do exceeding abundantly above all that we ask or think, according to the power that worketh in us, unto him be glory in the church by Christ Jesus throughout all ages, world without end. Amen.
**EPHESIANS 3:20–21 KJV**

Have no anxiety about anything, but in everything by prayer and supplication with thanksgiving let your requests be made known to God. And the peace of God, which passes all understanding, will keep your hearts and your minds in Christ Jesus.
**PHILIPPIANS 4:6–7 RSV**

Let us then with confidence draw near to the throne of grace, that we may receive mercy and find grace to help in time of need.
**HEBREWS 4:16 RSV**

You ask and do not receive, because you ask wrongly, to spend it on your passions.
**JAMES 4:3 RSV**

The effectual fervent prayer of a righteous man availeth much.
**JAMES 5:16 KJV**

### ENCOURAGEMENTS TO PRAY

[David's thanksgiving] Seek the Lord and his strength, seek his face continually.
**1 CHRONICLES 16:11 KJV**

The Lord watches over the righteous and listens to their cries.
**PSALM 34:15 GNB**

Trust in God at all times, my people. Tell him all your troubles, for he is our refuge.
**PSALM 62:8 GNB**

'Before they call I will answer, while they are yet speaking I will hear.'
**ISAIAH 65:24 RSV**

'But when you pray, go to your room, close the door, and pray to your Father, who is unseen. And your Father, who sees what you do in private, will reward you.'
**MATTHEW 6:6 GNB**

And he told them a parable, to the effect that they ought always to pray and not lose heart.
**LUKE 18:1 RSV**

Pray without ceasing.
**1 THESSALONIANS 5:17 KJV**

Behold, I stand at the door, and knock: if any man hear my voice, and open the door, I will come in to him, and will sup with him and he with me.
**REVELATION 3:20 KJV**

### HOW TO PRAY

'When you pray, do not use a lot of meaningless words, as the pagans do, who think that God will hear them because their prayers are long. Do not be like them. Your Father already knows what you need before you ask him. This, then, is how you should pray . . .'
**MATTHEW 6:7–9 GNB**

Our Father, which art in heaven, hallowed be thy name. Thy kingdom come. Thy will be done, in earth as it is in heaven. Give us this day our daily bread. And forgive us our trespasses, as we forgive them that trespass against us. And lead us not into temptation; but deliver us from evil.
**MATTHEW 6:9–13 BCP**

For thine is the kingdom, and the power, and the glory, for ever. Amen.
**MATTHEW 6:13 KJV**

'Watch and pray that you may not enter into temptation; the spirit indeed is willing, but the flesh is weak.'
**MATTHEW 26:41 RSV**

Likewise the Spirit helps us in our weakness; for

we do not know how to pray as we ought, but the Spirit himself intercedes for us with sighs too deep for words.

**ROMANS 8:26 RSV**

Praying always with all prayer and supplication in the Spirit, and watching thereunto with all perseverance and supplication for all saints; and for me, that utterance may be given unto me, that I may open my mouth boldly, to make known the mystery of the gospel.

**EPHESIANS 6:18–19 KJV**

I exhort, therefore, that, first of all, supplications, prayers, intercessions, and giving of thanks, be made for all men; for kings, and for all that are in authority; that we may lead a quiet and peaceable life in all godliness and honesty.

**1 TIMOTHY 2:1–2 KJV**

If any of you lacks wisdom, let him ask God, who gives to all men generously and without reproaching, and it will be given him. But let him ask in faith, with no doubting, for he who doubts is like a wave of the sea that is driven and tossed by the wind.

**JAMES 1:5–6 RSV**

### PROMISES IN PRAYER

[The Lord's promise to Solomon] 'If my people who are called by my name humble themselves, and pray and seek my face, and turn from their wicked ways, then I will hear from heaven, and will forgive their sin and heal their land.'

**2 CHRONICLES 7:14 RSV**

Take delight in the Lord, and he will give you the desires of your heart.

**PSALM 37:4 RSV**

If I had cherished iniquity in my heart, the Lord would not have listened.

**PSALM 66:18 RSV**

'Ask, and it will be given you; seek, and you will find; knock, and it will be opened to you. For every one who asks receives, and he who seeks finds, and to him who knocks it will be opened.'

**MATTHEW 7:7–8 RSV**

'Again I say to you, if two of you agree on earth about anything they ask, it will be done for them by my Father in heaven. For where two or three are gathered in my name, there am I in the midst of them.'

**MATTHEW 18:19–20 RSV**

'Whatever you ask in prayer, you will receive, if you have faith.'

**MATTHEW 21:22 RSV**

'Whatever you ask in my name, I will do it, that the Father may be glorified in the Son.'

**JOHN 14:13 RSV**

'If you abide in me, and my words abide in you, ask whatever you will, and it shall be done for you.'

**JOHN 15:7 RSV**

'When that day comes you will ask nothing of me. In very truth I tell you, if you ask the Father for anything in my name, he will give it you. So far you have asked nothing in my name. Ask and you will receive, that your joy may be complete.'

**JOHN 16:23–24 NEB**

We receive from him whatever we ask, because we keep his commandments and do what pleases him.

**1 JOHN 3:22 RSV**

And this is the confidence which we have in him, that if we ask anything according to his will he hears us.

**1 JOHN 5:14 RSV**

See also *Praise; Worship.*

## Preaching

How beautiful upon the mountains are the feet of him that bringeth good tidings, that publisheth peace; that bringeth good tidings of good, that publisheth salvation; that saith unto Zion, Thy God reigneth!

**ISAIAH 52:7 KJV**

The Spirit of the Lord God is upon me; because the Lord hath anointed me to preach good tidings unto the meek . . .

**ISAIAH 61:1 KJV**

Repentance and remission of sins should be preached in his name among all nations, beginning at Jerusalem.

**LUKE 24:47 KJV**

[Paul] 'For I did not shrink from declaring to you the whole counsel of God.'

**ACTS 20:27 RSV**

But how are men to call upon him in whom they have not believed? And how are they to believe in him of whom they have never heard? And how are

they to hear without a preacher? And how can men preach unless they are sent? As it is written, 'How beautiful are the feet of those who preach good news!'
ROMANS 10:14–15 RSV

For after that in the wisdom of God the world by wisdom knew not God, it pleased God by the foolishness of preaching to save them that believe ... But we preach Christ crucified, unto the Jews a stumbling block, and unto the Greeks foolishness; but unto them which are called, both Jews and Greeks, Christ the power of God, and the wisdom of God.
1 CORINTHIANS 1:21, 23 KJV

For necessity is laid upon me. Woe to me if I do not preach the gospel!
1 CORINTHIANS 9:16 RSV

Our gospel came to you not only in word, but also in power and in the Holy Spirit and with full conviction.
1 THESSALONIANS 1:5 RSV

Till I come, attend to the public reading of scripture, to preaching, to teaching.
1 TIMOTHY 4:13 RSV

Let the elders who rule well be considered worthy of double honour, especially those who labour in preaching and teaching.
1 TIMOTHY 5:17 RSV

Do your best to present yourself to God as one approved, a workman who has no need to be ashamed, rightly handling the word of truth.
2 TIMOTHY 2:15 RSV

Preach the word, be urgent in season and out of season, convince, rebuke, and exhort, be unfailing in patience and in teaching.
2 TIMOTHY 4:2 RSV

See also *Teachers and teaching.*

## Pride

'Beware lest you say in your heart, "My power and the might of my hand have gotten me this wealth." '
DEUTERONOMY 8:17 RSV

Pride goes before destruction, and a haughty spirit before a fall.
PROVERBS 16:18 RSV

'Whoever exalts himself will be humbled, and whoever humbles himself will be exalted.'
MATTHEW 23:12 RSV

And he said, 'What comes out of a man is what defiles a man. For from within, out of the heart of man, come evil thoughts ... pride ...'
MARK 7:21–22

He hath shewed strength with his arm, he hath scattered the proud in the imaginations of their hearts.
LUKE 1:51 BCP

For by the grace given to me I bid every one among you not to think of himself more highly than he ought to think, but to think with sober judgment, each according to the measure of faith which God has assigned him.
ROMANS 12:3 RSV

Do not be proud, but be willing to associate with people of low position. Do not be conceited.
ROMANS 12:16 NIV

Therefore, as it is written, 'Let him who boasts, boast of the Lord.'
1 CORINTHIANS 1:31 RSV

Therefore let any one who thinks that he stands take heed lest he fall.
1 CORINTHIANS 10:12 RSV

Love is not jealous or boastful.
1 CORINTHIANS 13:4 RSV

And to keep me from being too elated by the abundance of revelations, a thorn was given me in the flesh, a messenger of Satan, to harass me, to keep me from being too elated.
2 CORINTHIANS 12:7 RSV

See also *Humility; Self-righteousness.*

## Priest

'And you shall be to me a kingdom of priests and a holy nation.'
EXODUS 19:6 RSV

'Then bring near to you Aaron your brother, and his sons with him, from among the people of Israel, to serve me as priests.'
EXODUS 28:1 RSV

'Whenever cattle or sheep are sacrificed, the priests are to be given the shoulder, the jaw, and the stomach.'
DEUTERONOMY 18:3 GNB

'And the priests the sons of Levi shall come forward, for the Lord your God has chosen them to minister to him and to bless in the name of the Lord, and by their word every dispute and every assault shall be settled.'
DEUTERONOMY 21:5 RSV

'They shall teach Jacob thy ordinances, and Israel thy law; they shall put incense before thee, and whole burnt offering upon thy altar.'
DEUTERONOMY 33:10 RSV

And they led Jesus to the high priest; and all the chief priests and the elders and the scribes were assembled.
MARK 14:53 RSV

So Judas went off and spoke with the chief priests and the officers of the temple guard about how he could betray Jesus to them.
LUKE 22:4 GNB

And the word of God increased; and the number of the disciples multiplied greatly in Jerusalem, and a great many of the priests were obedient to the faith.
ACTS 6:7 RSV

For every high priest chosen from among men is appointed to act on behalf of men in relation to God, to offer gifts and sacrifices for sins. He can deal gently with the ignorant and wayward, since he himself is beset with weakness. Because of this he is bound to offer sacrifice for his own sins as well as for those of the people. And one does not take the honour upon himself, but he is called by God, just as Aaron was.
HEBREWS 5:1–4 RSV

For every high priest is appointed to offer gifts and sacrifices; hence it is necessary for this priest also to have something to offer.
HEBREWS 8:3 RSV

And every priest stands daily at his service, offering repeatedly the same sacrifices, which can never take away sins. But when Christ had offered for all time a single sacrifice for sins, he sat down at the right hand of God.
HEBREWS 10:11–12 RSV

Like living stones be yourselves built into a spiritual house, to be a holy priesthood, to offer spiritual sacrifices acceptable to God through Jesus Christ . . . you are a chosen race, a royal priesthood, a holy nation, God's own people.
1 PETER 2:5, 9 RSV

See also *Jesus Christ, Jesus as priest.*

## Prodigal son
See *Jesus Christ, Parables of Jesus.*

## Promise

And, behold, I send the promise of my Father upon you: but tarry ye in the city of Jerusalem, until ye be endued with power from on high.
LUKE 24:49 KJV

It is not the natural children who are God's children, but it is the children of the promise who are regarded as Abraham's offspring.
ROMANS 9:8 NIV

For all the promises of God find their Yes in him [Jesus Christ].
2 CORINTHIANS 1:20 RSV

Remember that you were at that time separated from Christ, alienated from the commonwealth of Israel, and strangers to the covenants of promise, having no hope and without God in the world.
EPHESIANS 2:12 RSV

Christ has obtained a ministry which is as much more excellent than the old as the covenant he mediates is better, since it is enacted on better promises.
HEBREWS 8:6 RSV

Let us hold fast the confession of our hope without wavering, for he who promised is faithful.
HEBREWS 10:23 RSV

Blessed is the man who endures trial, for when he has stood the test he will receive the crown of life which God has promised to those who love him.
JAMES 1:12 RSV

Through these he has given us his very great and precious promises, so that through them you may participate in the divine nature and escape the corruption in the world caused by evil desires.
2 PETER 1:4 NIV

The Lord is not slow about his promise as some count slowness, but is forbearing toward you, not wishing that any should perish, but that all should reach repentance . . . But according to his promise we wait for new heavens and a new earth in which righteousness dwells.
2 PETER 3:9, 13 RSV

# Prophets and prophecy

'When a prophet speaks in the name of the Lord, if the word does not come to pass or come true, that is a word which the Lord has not spoken; the prophet has spoken it presumptuously, you need not be afraid of him.'
DEUTERONOMY 18:22 RSV

'From the day that your fathers came out of the land of Egypt to this day, I have persistently sent all my servants the prophets to them, day after day, yet they did not listen to me, or incline their ear, but stiffened their neck.'
JEREMIAH 7:25–26 RSV

Many will say to me in that day, Lord, Lord, have we not prophesied in thy name? And in thy name have cast out devils? And in thy name done many wonderful works? And then will I profess unto them, I never knew you: depart from me, ye that work iniquity.
MATTHEW 7:22–23 KJV

'For false Christs and false prophets will arise and show great signs and wonders, so as to lead astray, if possible, even the elect.'
MATTHEW 24:24 RSV

' "On my menservants and my maidservants in those days I will pour out my Spirit; and they shall prophesy." '
ACTS 2:18 RSV

Now in these days prophets came down from Jerusalem to Antioch. And one of them named Agabus stood up and foretold by the Spirit that there would be a great famine over all the world; and this took place in the days of Claudius.
ACTS 11:27–28 RSV

And God has appointed in the church first apostles, second prophets . . .
1 CORINTHIANS 12:28 RSV

Love never ends; as for prophecies, they will pass away.
1 CORINTHIANS 13:8 RSV

Make love your aim, and earnestly desire the spiritual gifts, especially that you may prophesy.
1 CORINTHIANS 14:1 RSV

For you can all prophesy in turn, so that everybody will learn something and everybody can be encouraged. Prophets can always control their prophetic spirits.
1 CORINTHIANS 14:31–32 JB

[The household of God] Built upon the foundation of the apostles and prophets, Christ Jesus himself being the cornerstone.
EPHESIANS 2:20 RSV

Despise not prophesyings. Prove all things; hold fast that which is good.
1 THESSALONIANS 5:20–21 KJV

No prophecy ever came by the impulse of man, but men moved by the Holy Spirit spoke from God.
2 PETER 1:21 RSV

# Propitiation

Yet it pleased the Lord to bruise him; he hath put him to grief: when thou shalt make his soul an offering for sin, he shall see his seed, he shall prolong his days, and the pleasure of the Lord shall prosper in his hand.
ISAIAH 53:10 KJV

'But the tax collector, standing far off, would not even lift up his eyes to heaven, but beat his breast, saying, "God, be merciful to me a sinner!" '
LUKE 18:13 RSV

[Christ Jesus] Whom God hath set forth to be a propitiation through faith in his blood, to declare his righteousness for the remission of sins that are past, through the forbearance of God.
ROMANS 3:25 KJV

But by becoming a curse for us Christ has redeemed us from the curse that the Law brings; for the scripture says, 'Anyone who is hanged on a tree is under God's curse.'
GALATIANS 3:13 GNB

For this reason he had to be made like his brothers in every way, in order that he might become a merciful and faithful high priest in service to God, and that he might make atonement for the sins of the people.
HEBREWS 2:17 NIV

And over it the cherubims of glory shadowing the mercy seat; of which we cannot now speak particularly.
HEBREWS 9:5 KJV

And he is the propitiation for our sins: and not for ours only, but also for the sins of the whole world.
1 JOHN 2:2 KJV

Herein is love, not that we loved God, but that he loved us, and sent his Son to be the propitiation for our sins.

1 JOHN 4:10 KJV

See also *Anger, of God; Atonement; Reconciliation.*

## Providence

'While the earth remains, seedtime and harvest, cold and heat, summer and winter, day and night, shall not cease.'

GENESIS 8:22 RSV

So Abraham called the name of that place The Lord will provide; as it is said to this day, 'On the mount of the Lord it shall be provided.'

GENESIS 22:14 RSV

For all things come of thee, and of thine own have we given thee.

1 CHRONICLES 29:14 KJV

And Ezra said: 'Thou art the Lord, thou alone; thou hast made heaven, the heaven of heavens, with all their host, the earth and all that is on it, the seas and all that is in them; and thou preservest all of them; and the host of heaven worships thee.'

NEHEMIAH 9:6 RSV

Whatever the Lord pleases he does, in heaven and on earth, in the seas and all deeps. He it is who makes the clouds rise at the end of the earth, who makes lightnings for the rain and brings forth the wind from his storehouses.

PSALM 135:6–7 RSV

The plans of the mind belong to man, but the answer of the tongue is from the Lord.

PROVERBS 16:1 RSV

The lot is cast into the lap, but the decision is wholly from the Lord.

PROVERBS 16:33 RSV

'For only a penny you can buy two sparrows, yet not one sparrow falls to the ground without your Father's consent. As for you, even the hairs of your head have all been counted. So do not be afraid; you are worth much more than many sparrows!'

MATTHEW 10:29–31 GNB

' "In him we live and move and have our being." '

ACTS 17:28 RSV

[God] who worketh all things after the counsel of his own will.

EPHESIANS 1:11 KJV

[Christ] He is before all things, and in him all things hold together.

COLOSSIANS 1:17 RSV

[God] Upholding all things by the word of his power.

HEBREWS 1:3 KJV

See also *Sovereignty of God.*

## Punishment

'Whoever hits a man and kills him is to be put to death.'

EXODUS 2:12 GNB

Be sure your sin will find you out.

NUMBERS 32:23 KJV

'If I say to the wicked, O wicked man, you shall surely die, and you do not speak to warn the wicked to turn from his way, that wicked man shall die in his iniquity, but his blood I will require at your hand.'

EZEKIEL 33:8 RSV

And these shall go away into everlasting punishment: but the righteous into life eternal.

MATTHEW 25:46 KJV

He who believes in him is not condemned; he who does not believe is condemned already, because he has not believed in the name of the only Son of God.

JOHN 3:18 RSV

For those who are factious and do not obey the truth, but obey wickedness, there will be wrath and fury. There will be tribulation and distress for every human being who does evil, the Jew first and also the Greek.

ROMANS 2:8–9 RSV

For the wages of sin is death; but the gift of God is eternal life through Jesus Christ our Lord.

ROMANS 6:23 KJV

He [the man in authority] is God's servant working for your own good. But if you do evil, then be afraid of him, because his power to punish is real.

ROMANS 13:4 GNB

They [those who do not obey the Good News about the Lord Jesus] will suffer the punishment of eternal destruction, separated from the presence of the Lord and from his glorious might.
2 THESSALONIANS 1:9 GNB

What, then, of the person who despises the Son of God? who treats as a cheap thing the blood of God's covenant which purified him from sin? who insults the Spirit of grace? Just think how much worse is the punishment he will deserve!
HEBREWS 10:29 GNB

See also *Anger, of God; Discipline; Last things, Hell.*

## Purity, pure

The statutes of the Lord are right, rejoicing the heart: the commandment of the Lord is pure, enlightening the eyes.
PSALM 19:8 KJV

Thou who art of purer eyes than to behold evil and canst not look on wrong...
HABAKKUK 1:13 RSV

Blessed are the pure in heart: for they shall see God.
MATTHEW 5:8 KJV

Take no part in the sins of others; keep yourself pure.
1 TIMOTHY 5:22 GNB

To the pure, all things are pure, but to the corrupt and unbelieving nothing is pure; their very minds and consciences are corrupted.
TITUS 1:15 RSV

But the wisdom from above is first pure...
JAMES 3:17 RSV

Draw near to God and he will draw near to you. Cleanse your hands, you sinners, and purify your hearts, you men of double mind.
JAMES 4:8 RSV

Now that by your obedience to the truth you have purified yourselves and have come to have a sincere love for your fellow-believers, love one another earnestly with all your heart.
1 PETER 1:22 GNB

## Race

[ETHNIC]

So God created man in his own image, in the image of God created he him; male and female created he them. And God blessed them, and God said unto them, Be fruitful and multiply, and replenish the earth, and subdue it.
GENESIS 1:27–28 KJV

And Peter opened his mouth and said: 'Truly I perceive that God shows no partiality, but in every nation any one who fears him and does what is right is acceptable to him.'
ACTS 10:34–35 RSV

'And he made from one every nation of men to live on all the face of the earth, having determined allotted periods and the boundaries of their habitation.'
ACTS 17:26 RSV

There is neither Jew nor Greek, there is neither bond nor free, there is neither male nor female: for ye are all one in Christ Jesus.
GALATIANS 3:28 KJV

After this I looked, and behold, a great multitude which no man could number, from every nation, from all tribes and peoples and tongues, standing before the throne and before the Lamb.
REVELATION 7:9 RSV

See also *Immigrants.*

## Reconciliation

He shall judge between the nations, and shall decide for many peoples; and they shall beat their swords into ploughshares, and their spears into pruning hooks; nation shall not lift up sword against nation, neither shall they learn war any more.
ISAIAH 2:4 RSV

'If you are bringing your offering to the altar and there remember that your brother has something against you, leave your offering there before the altar, go and be reconciled with your brother first, and then come back and present your offering.'
MATTHEW 5:23–24 JB

For if while we were enemies we were reconciled to God by the death of his Son, much more, now that we are reconciled, shall we be saved by his life. Not only so, but we also rejoice in God through our Lord Jesus Christ, through whom we have now received our reconciliation.
ROMANS 5:10–11 RSV

All this is from God, who through Christ

reconciled us to himself and gave us the ministry of reconciliation; that is, in Christ God was reconciling the world to himself, not counting their trespasses against them, and entrusting to us the message of reconciliation. So we are ambassadors for Christ, God making his appeal through us. We beseech you on behalf of Christ, be reconciled to God.

**2 CORINTHIANS 5:18–20 RSV**

[Christ] might reconcile us both [Jew and Gentile] to God in one body through the cross, thereby bringing the hostility to an end.

**EPHESIANS 2:16 RSV**

Through him [Christ] to reconcile to himself all things, whether on earth or in heaven, making peace by the blood of his cross.

**COLOSSIANS 1:20 RSV**

But now, by means of the physical death of his Son, God has made you his friends, in order to bring you, holy, pure, and faultless, into his presence.

**COLOSSIANS 1:22 GNB**

See also *Atonement; Peace; Propitiation.*

# Redemption

'Say therefore to the people of Israel, "I am the Lord, and I will bring you out from under the burdens of the Egyptians, and I will deliver you from their bondage, and I will redeem you with an outstretched arm and with great acts of judgment." '

**EXODUS 6:6 RSV**

For I know that my redeemer liveth, and that he shall stand at the latter day upon the earth.

**JOB 19:25 KJV**

And the ransomed of the Lord shall return, and come to Zion with singing; everlasting joy shall be upon their heads; they shall obtain joy and gladness, and sorrow and sighing shall flee away.

**ISAIAH 35:10 RSV**

But now thus saith the Lord that created thee, O Jacob, and he that formed thee, O Israel, Fear not: for I have redeemed thee, I have called thee by thy name; thou art mine.

**ISAIAH 43:1 KJV**

'For the Son of man also came not to be served but to serve, and to give his life as a ransom for many.'

**MARK 10:45 RSV**

Being justified freely by his grace through the redemption that is in Christ Jesus.

**ROMANS 3:24 KJV**

Not only the creation, but we ourselves, who have the first fruits of the Spirit, groan inwardly as we wait for adoption as sons, the redemption of our bodies.

**ROMANS 8:23 RSV**

He is the source of your life in Christ Jesus, whom God made our wisdom, our righteousness and sanctification and redemption.

**1 CORINTHIANS 1:30 RSV**

You are not your own; you were bought with a price. So glorify God in your body.

**1 CORINTHIANS 6:20 RSV**

But by becoming a curse for us Christ has redeemed us from the curse that the Law brings; for the scripture says, 'Anyone who is hanged on a tree is under God's curse.'

**GALATIANS 3:13 GNB**

But when the time had fully come, God sent forth his Son, born of woman, born under the law, to redeem those who were under the law, so that we might receive adoption as sons.

**GALATIANS 4.4–5 RSV**

In him we have redemption through his blood, the forgiveness of our trespasses, according to the riches of his grace.

**EPHESIANS 1:7 RSV**

[God's beloved Son] In whom we have redemption, the forgiveness of sins.

**COLOSSIANS 1:14 RSV**

Christ Jesus, who gave himself as a ransom for all.

**1 TIMOTHY 2:5–6 RSV**

[Jesus Christ] who gave himself for us to redeem us from all iniquity and to purify for himself a people of his own who are zealous for good deeds.

**TITUS 2:14 RSV**

He entered once for all into the Holy Place, taking not the blood of goats and calves but his own blood, thus securing an eternal redemption.

**HEBREWS 9:12 RSV**

You know that you were ransomed from the futile ways inherited from your fathers, not with perishable things such as silver or gold, but with the precious blood of Christ, like that of a lamb without blemish or spot.

1 PETER 1:18–19 RSV

## Regeneration
See *New birth.*

## Rejection

'For rebellion is as the sin of divination, and stubbornness is as iniquity and idolatry. Because you have rejected the word of the Lord, he has also rejected you from being king.'

1 SAMUEL 15:23 RSV

The stone which the builders rejected has become the head of the corner.

PSALM 118:22 RSV

The Lord God hath opened mine ear, and I was not rebellious, neither turned away back. I gave my back to the smiters, and my cheeks to them that plucked off the hair: I hid not my face from shame and spitting.

ISAIAH 50:5–6 KJV

He is despised and rejected of men; a man of sorrows, and acquainted with grief: and we hid as it were our faces from him; he was despised, and we esteemed him not.

ISAIAH 53:3 KJV

'But this people has a stubborn and rebellious heart; they have turned aside and gone away.'

JEREMIAH 5:23 RSV

'And if any one will not receive you or listen to your words, shake off the dust from your feet as you leave that house or town.'

MATTHEW 10:14 RSV

And he said to them, 'You have a fine way of rejecting the commandment of God, in order to keep your tradition!'

MARK 7:9 RSV

He came unto his own, and his own received him not.

JOHN 1:11 KJV

'He who rejects me and does not receive my sayings has a judge; the word that I have spoken will be his judge on the last day.'

JOHN 12:48 RSV

Come to him, to that living stone, rejected by men but in God's sight chosen and precious.

1 PETER 2:4 RSV

See also *Hardness; Unbelief.*

## Repentance

[The Lord's promise to Solomon] 'If my people who are called by my name humble themselves, and pray and seek my face, and turn from their wicked ways, then I will hear from heaven, and will forgive their sin and heal their land.'

2 CHRONICLES 7:14 RSV

Let the wicked forsake his way, and the unrighteous man his thoughts: and let him return unto the Lord, and he will have mercy upon him; and to our God, for he will abundantly pardon.

ISAIAH 55:7 KJV

'Therefore, O house of Israel, I will judge you, each one according to his ways, declares the Sovereign Lord. Repent! Turn away from all your offences; then sin will not be your downfall.'

EZEKIEL 18:30 NIV

'Yet even now,' says the Lord, 'return to me with all your heart, with fasting, with weeping, and with mourning; and rend your hearts and not your garments.' Return to the Lord, your God, for he is gracious and merciful, slow to anger, and abounding in steadfast love, and repents of evil.

JOEL 2:12–13 RSV

'Bear fruit that befits repentance.'

MATTHEW 3:8 RSV

'The time is fulfilled, and the kingdom of God is at hand; repent, and believe in the gospel.'

MARK 1:15 RSV

'I have not come to call the righteous, but sinners to repentance.'

LUKE 5:32 RSV

'Unless you repent you will all likewise perish.'

LUKE 13:3 RSV

'Just so, I tell you, there will be more joy in heaven over one sinner who repents than over ninety-nine righteous persons who need no repentance.'

LUKE 15:7 RSV

And when he [the prodigal son] came to himself, he said, How many hired servants of my father's have bread enough and to spare, and I perish

with hunger! I will arise and go to my father, and will say unto him, Father, I have sinned against heaven, and before thee.
LUKE 15:17–18 KJV

Repentance and remission of sins should be preached in his name among all nations, beginning at Jerusalem.
LUKE 24:47 KJV

Repent ye therefore, and be converted, that your sins may be blotted out, when the times of refreshing shall come from the presence of the Lord.
ACTS 3:19 KJV

And they glorified God, saying, 'Then to the Gentiles also God has granted repentance unto life.'
ACTS 11:18 RSV

'The times of ignorance God overlooked, but now he commands all men everywhere to repent . . .'
ACTS 17:30 RSV

'Testifying both to Jews and to Greeks of repentance to God and of faith in our Lord Jesus Christ.'
ACTS 20:21 RSV

Or do you presume upon the riches of his kindness and forbearance and patience? Do you not know that God's kindness is meant to lead you to repentance?
ROMANS 2:4 RSV

For godly grief produces a repentance that leads to salvation and brings no regret, but worldly grief produces death.
2 CORINTHIANS 7:10 RSV

The Lord is not slow about his promise as some count slowness, but is forbearing toward you, not wishing that any should perish, but that all should reach repentance.
2 PETER 3:9 RSV

' "Remember then from what you have fallen, repent and do the works you did at first. If not, I will come to you and remove your lampstand from its place, unless you repent." '
REVELATION 2:5 RSV

See also *Conversion; Faith; Grief.*

## Responsibility of man

Let us hear the conclusion of the whole matter:

Fear God, and keep his commandments; for this is the whole duty of man.
ECCLESIASTES 12:13 KJV

He hath shewed thee, O man, what is good; and what doth the Lord require of thee, but to do justly, and to love mercy, and to walk humbly with thy God?
MICAH 6:8 KJV

Jesus said unto him, Thou shalt love the Lord thy God with all thy heart, and with all thy soul, and with all thy mind. This is the first and great commandment. And the second is like unto it, Thou shalt love thy neighbour as thyself.
MATTHEW 22:37–39 KJV

'For truly in this city there were gathered together against thy holy servant Jesus, whom thou didst anoint, both Herod and Pontius Pilate, with the Gentiles and the peoples of Israel, to do whatever thy hand and thy plan had predestined to take place.'
ACTS 4:27–28 RSV

And when the Gentiles heard this, they were glad and glorified the word of God; and as many as were ordained to eternal life believed.
ACTS 13:48 RSV

None of us lives to himself, and none of us dies to himself. If we live, we live to the Lord, and if we die, we die to the Lord; so then, whether we live or whether we die, we are the Lord's.
ROMANS 14:7–8 RSV

So, whether you eat or drink, or whatever you do, do all to the glory of God.
1 CORINTHIANS 10:31 RSV

Work out your own salvation with fear and trembling; for God is at work in you, both to will and to work for his good pleasure.
PHILIPPIANS 2:12–13 RSV

Therefore, brethren, be the more zealous to confirm your call and election, for if you do this you will never fall.
2 PETER 1:10 RSV

See also *Service; Sovereignty of God.*

## Rest

For thus said the Lord God, the Holy One of Israel, 'In returning and rest you shall be saved; in quietness and trust shall be your strength.'
ISAIAH 30:15 RSV

'Come to me, all who labour and are heavy-laden, and I will give you rest. Take my yoke upon you, and learn from me; for I am gentle and lowly in heart, and you will find rest for your souls. For my yoke is easy, and my burden is light.'
MATTHEW 11:28–30 RSV

And he said to them, 'Come away by yourselves to a lonely place, and rest a while.' For many were coming and going, and they had no leisure even to eat.
MARK 6:31 RSV

Therefore, while the promise of entering his rest remains, let us fear lest any of you be judged to have failed to reach it . . . For we who have believed enter that rest, as he has said, 'As I swore in my wrath, ''They shall never enter my rest,'' ' although his works were finished from the foundation of the world. For he has somewhere spoken of the seventh day in this way, 'And God rested on the seventh day from all his works.' And again in this place he said, 'They shall never enter my rest.' Since therefore it remains for some to enter it, and those who formerly received the good news failed to enter because of disobedience, again he sets a certain day. 'Today,' saying through David so long afterward, in the words already quoted, 'Today, when you hear his voice, do not harden your hearts.' For if Joshua had given them rest, God would not speak later of another day. So then, there remains a sabbath rest for the people of God; for whoever enters God's rest also ceases from his labours as God did from his. Let us therefore strive to enter that rest, that no one fall by the same sort of disobedience.
HEBREWS 4:1, 3–11 RSV

See also *Sabbath.*

## Resurrection
See *Jesus Christ; Last things.*

## Retaliation

'You shall not take vengeance or bear any grudge against the sons of your own people, but you shall love your neighbour as yourself: I am the Lord.'
LEVITICUS 19:18 RSV

'Vengeance is mine, and recompense, for the time when their foot shall slip; for the day of their calamity is at hand, and their doom comes

swiftly.'
DEUTERONOMY 32:35 RSV

Do not think to repay evil for evil, wait for the Lord to deliver you.
PROVERBS 20:22 NEB

'You have heard that it was said, ''An eye for an eye and a tooth for a tooth.'' But I say to you, Do not resist one who is evil. But if any one strikes you on the right cheek, turn to him the other also; and if any one would sue you and take your coat, let him have your cloak as well; and if any one forces you to go one mile, go with him two miles. Give to him who begs from you, and do not refuse him who would borrow from you.'
MATTHEW 5:38–42 RSV

Beloved, never avenge yourselves, but leave it to the wrath of God; for it is written, 'Vengeance is mine, I will repay, says the Lord.' No, 'if your enemy is hungry, feed him; if he is thirsty, give him drink; for by so doing you will heap burning coals upon his head.' Do not be overcome by evil, but overcome evil with good.
ROMANS 12:19–21 RSV

## Revelation

The heavens declare the glory of God; and the firmament sheweth his handywork. Day unto day uttereth speech, and night unto night sheweth knowledge.
PSALM 19:1–2 KJV

For my thoughts are not your thoughts, neither are your ways my ways, saith the Lord. For as the heavens are higher than the earth, so are my ways higher than your ways, and my thoughts than your thoughts. For as the rain cometh down, and the snow from heaven, and returneth not thither, but watereth the earth, and maketh it bring forth and bud, that it may give seed to the sower, and bread to the eater: so shall my word be that goeth forth out of my mouth: it shall not return unto me void but it shall accomplish that which I please, and it shall prosper in the thing whereto I sent it.
ISAIAH 55:8–11 KJV

'All things have been delivered to me by my Father; and no one knows the Son except the Father, and no one knows the Father except the Son and any one to whom the Son chooses to reveal him.'
MATTHEW 11:27 RSV

And Simon Peter answered and said, Thou art the Christ, the Son of the living God. And Jesus answered and said unto him, Blessed art thou, Simon Bar-jona: for flesh and blood hath not revealed it unto thee, but my Father which is in heaven.

**MATTHEW 16:16–17 KJV**

'He did not leave himself without witness, for he did good and gave you from heaven rains and fruitful seasons, satisfying your hearts with food and gladness.'

**ACTS 14:17 RSV**

For what can be known about God is plain to them, because God has shown it to them. Ever since the creation of the world his invisible nature, namely, his eternal power and deity, has been clearly perceived in the things that have been made. So they are without excuse.

**ROMANS 1:19–20 RSV**

As it is written, Eye hath not seen, nor ear heard, neither have entered into the heart of man, the things which God hath prepared for them that love him. But God hath revealed them unto us by his Spirit.

**1 CORINTHIANS 2:9–10 KJV**

Let me tell you, my brothers, that the gospel I preach is not of human origin. I did not receive it from any man, nor did anyone teach it to me. It was Jesus Christ himself who revealed it to me.

**GALATIANS 1:11–12 GNB**

All scripture is inspired by God and profitable for teaching, for reproof, for correction . . .

**2 TIMOTHY 3:16 RSV**

God, who at sundry times and in divers manners spake in time past unto the fathers by the prophets, hath in these last days spoken unto us by his Son, whom he hath appointed heir of all things, by whom also he made the worlds . . .

**HEBREWS 1:1–2 KJV**

See also *Bible; Will of God.*

## Reverence

'That you may fear the Lord your God, you and your son and your son's son, by keeping all his statutes and his commandments, which I command you, all the days of your life.'

**DEUTERONOMY 6:2 RSV**

The fear of the Lord is clean, enduring for ever:

the judgments of the Lord are true and righteous altogether.

**PSALM 19:9 KJV**

For as the heaven is high above the earth, so great is his mercy toward them that fear him.

**PSALM 103:11 KJV**

The fear of the Lord is the beginning of wisdom: a good understanding have all they that do his commandments: his praise endureth for ever.

**PSALM 111:10 KJV**

To honour the Lord is to hate evil; I hate pride and arrogance, evil ways and false words.

**PROVERBS 8:13 GNB**

Let us hear the conclusion of the whole matter: Fear God, and keep his commandments; for this is the whole duty of man.

**ECCLESIASTES 12:12–13 KJV**

And the spirit of the Lord shall rest upon him, the spirit of wisdom and understanding, the spirit of counsel and might, the spirit of knowledge and of the fear of the Lord.

**ISAIAH 11:2 KJV**

And they were filled with awe, and said to one another, 'Who then is this, that even wind and sea obey him?'

**MARK 4:41 RSV**

And so it was that the church throughout Judaea, Galilee, and Samaria had a time of peace. Through the help of the Holy Spirit it was strengthened and grew in numbers, as it lived in reverence for the Lord.

**ACTS 9:31 GNB**

There is no fear of God before their eyes.

**ROMANS 3:18 KJV**

Therefore, knowing the fear of the Lord, we persuade men; but what we are is known to God, and I hope it is known also to your conscience.

**2 CORINTHIANS 5:11 RSV**

Since we have these promises, dear friends, let us purify ourselves from everything that contaminates body and spirit, perfecting holiness out of reverence for God.

**2 CORINTHIANS 7:1 NIV**

Work out your own salvation with fear and trembling; for God is at work in you, both to will and to work for his good pleasure.

**PHILIPPIANS 2:12–13 RSV**

Therefore let us be grateful for receiving a kingdom that cannot be shaken, and thus let us offer to God acceptable worship, with reverence and awe.

**HEBREWS 12:28 RSV**

But in your hearts reverence Christ as Lord. Always be prepared to make a defence to any one who calls you to account for the hope that is in you, yet do it with gentleness and reverence.

**1 PETER 3:15 RSV**

See also **Worship.**

# Revival

[The Lord's promise to Solomon] 'If my people who are called by my name humble themselves, and pray and seek my face, and turn from their wicked ways, then I will hear from heaven, and will forgive their sin and heal their land.'

**2 CHRONICLES 7:14 RSV**

Wilt thou not revive us again: that thy people may rejoice in thee?

**PSALM 85:6 KJV**

Oh, that you would rend the heavens and come down, that the mountains would tremble before you! As when fire sets twigs ablaze and causes water to boil, come down to make your name known to your enemies and cause the nations to quake before you!

**ISAIAH 64:1–2 NIV**

And he said to me, 'Son of man, can these bones live?' And I answered, 'O Lord God, thou knowest.' Again he said to me, 'Prophesy to these bones, and say to them, O dry bones, hear the word of the Lord. Thus says the Lord God to these bones: Behold, I will cause breath to enter you, and you shall live.'

**EZEKIEL 37:3–5 RSV**

'And it shall come to pass afterward, that I will pour out my spirit on all flesh; your sons and your daughters shall prophesy, your old men shall dream dreams, and your young men shall see visions . . .'

**JOEL 2:28 RSV**

O Lord, revive thy work in the midst of the years, in the midst of the years make known; in wrath remember mercy.

**HABAKKUK 3:2 KJV**

Repent ye therefore, and be converted, that your sins may be blotted out, when the times of refreshing shall come from the presence of the Lord.

**ACTS 3:19 KJV**

And when they had prayed, the place in which they were gathered together was shaken; and they were all filled with the Holy Spirit and spoke the word of God with boldness.

**ACTS 4:31 RSV**

And the word of God increased; and the number of the disciples multiplied greatly in Jerusalem, and a great many of the priests were obedient to the faith.

**ACTS 6:7 RSV**

# Reward

After these things the word of the Lord came unto Abram in a vision, saying, Fear not, Abram: I am thy shield, and thy exceeding great reward.

**GENESIS 15:1 KJV**

Moreover by them [the judgements of the Lord] is thy servant warned: and in keeping of them there is great reward.

**PSALM 19:11 KJV**

'Happy are you when people insult you and persecute you and tell all kinds of evil lies against you because you are my followers. Be happy and glad, for a great reward is kept for you in heaven.'

**MATTHEW 5:11–12 GNB**

Then Peter spoke up. 'Look,' he said, 'we have left everything and followed you. What will we have?' Jesus said to them, 'You can be sure that when the Son of Man sits on his glorious throne in the New Age, then you twelve followers of mine will also sit on thrones, to rule the twelve tribes of Israel. And everyone who has left houses or brothers or sisters or father or mother or children or fields for my sake, will receive a hundred times more and will be given eternal life.'

**MATTHEW 19:27–29 GNB**

And these shall go away into everlasting punishment: but the righteous into life eternal.

**MATTHEW 25:46 KJV**

'Love your enemies and do good to them; lend and expect nothing back. You will then have a great reward, and you will be sons of the Most

High God. For he is good to the ungrateful and the wicked.'

LUKE 6:35 GNB

Each man's work will become manifest; for the Day will disclose it, because it will be revealed with fire, and the fire will test what sort of work each one has done. If the work which any man has built on the foundation survives, he will receive a reward.

1 CORINTHIANS 3:13–14 RSV

The scripture says, 'You shall not muzzle an ox when it is treading out the grain,' and 'The labourer deserves his wages.'

1 TIMOTHY 5:18 RSV

But without faith it is impossible to please him: for he that cometh to God must believe that he is, and that he is a rewarder of them that diligently seek him.

HEBREWS 11:6 KJV

See also *Last things, Heaven; Obedience.*

## Rich and riches

'Beware lest you say in your heart, "My power and the might of my hand have gotten me this wealth." You shall remember the Lord your God, for it is he who gives you power to get wealth; that he may confirm his covenant which he swore to your fathers, as at this day.'

DEUTERONOMY 8:17–18 RSV

For I was envious of the arrogant, when I saw the prosperity of the wicked.

PSALM 73:3 RSV

Woe to them that are at ease in Zion, and trust in the mountain of Samaria.

AMOS 6:1 KJV

He hath filled the hungry with good things, and the rich he hath sent empty away.

LUKE 1:53 BCP

There was a certain rich man, which was clothed in purple and fine linen, and fared sumptuously every day: and there was a certain beggar named Lazarus, which was laid at his gate full of sores, and desiring to be fed with the crumbs which fell from the rich man's table: moreover the dogs came and licked his sores. And it came to pass, that the beggar died, and was carried by the angels into Abraham's bosom: the rich man also died, and was buried; and in hell he lift up his eyes, being in torments, and seeth Abraham afar off, and Lazarus in his bosom. And he cried and said, Father Abraham, have mercy on me, and send Lazarus, that he may dip the tip of his finger in water, and cool my tongue; for I am tormented in this flame. But Abraham said, Son, remember that thou in thy lifetime receivedst thy good things, and likewise Lazarus evil things: but now he is comforted, and thou art tormented. And beside all this, between us and you there is a great gulf fixed: so that they which would pass from hence to you cannot; neither can they pass to us, that would come from thence. Then he said, I pray thee therefore, father, that thou wouldest send him to my father's house: for I have five brethren; that he may testify unto them, lest they also come into this place of torment.

LUKE 16:19–28 KJV

On hearing this Jesus said [to the rich young ruler], 'There is still one thing lacking: sell everything you have and distribute to the poor, and you will have riches in heaven; and come, follow me.' At these words his heart sank; for he was a very rich man. When Jesus saw it he said, 'How hard it is for the wealthy to enter the kingdom of God! It is easier for a camel to go through the eye of a needle than for a rich man to enter the kingdom of God.'

LUKE 18:22–25 NEB

The unsearchable riches of Christ.

EPHESIANS 3:8 KJV

As for the rich in this world, charge them not to be haughty, nor to set their hopes on uncertain riches but on God who richly furnishes us with everything to enjoy.

1 TIMOTHY 6:17 RSV

Come now, you rich, weep and howl for the miseries that are coming upon you. Your riches have rotted and your garments are moth-eaten. Your gold and silver have rusted, and their rust will be evidence against you and will eat your flesh like fire. You have laid up treasure for the last days. Behold, the wages of the labourers who mowed your fields, which you kept back by fraud, cry out; and the cries of the harvesters have reached the ears of the Lord of hosts. You have lived on the earth in luxury and in pleasure; you have fattened your hearts in a day of slaughter.

JAMES 5:1–5 RSV

But if any one has the world's goods and sees his brother in need, yet closes his heart against him, how does God's love abide in him?

1 JOHN 3:17 RSV

See also *Desire, wrong; Money and material goods; Poverty.*

# Righteousness

Noah was a righteous man, blameless among the people of his time, and he walked with God.

GENESIS 6:9 NIV

And he [Abraham] believed in the Lord; and he counted it to him for righteousness.

GENESIS 15:6 KJV

Righteousness exalteth a nation: but sin is a reproach to any people.

PROVERBS 14:34 KJV

The effect of righteousness will be peace, and the result of righteousness, quietness and trust for ever.

ISAIAH 32:17 RSV

All our righteousnesses are as filthy rags; and we all do fade as a leaf; and our iniquities, like the wind, have taken us away.

ISAIAH 64:6 KJV

'Let justice roll down like waters, and righteousness like an ever-flowing stream.'

AMOS 5:24 RSV

Blessed are they that mourn: for they shall be comforted. Blessed are the meek: for they shall inherit the earth. Blessed are they which do hunger and thirst after righteousness: for they shall be filled.

MATTHEW 5:6 KJV

'For I tell you, unless your righteousness exceeds that of the scribes and Pharisees, you will never enter the kingdom of heaven.'

MATTHEW 5:20 RSV

But seek ye first the kingdom of God, and his righteousness; and all these things shall be added unto you.

MATTHEW 6:33 KJV

'He has fixed a day on which he will judge the world in righteousness by a man whom he has appointed, and of this he has given assurance to all men by raising him from the dead.'

ACTS 17:31 RSV

For therein [in the gospel] is the righteousness of God revealed from faith to faith: as it is written, The just shall live by faith.

ROMANS 1:17 KJV

As it is written, there is none righteous, no, not one.

ROMANS 3:10 KJV

But now the righteousness of God without the law is manifested, being witnessed by the law and the prophets; even the righteousness of God which is by faith of Jesus Christ unto all and upon all them that believe: for there is no difference: for all have sinned, and come short of the glory of God: being justified freely by his grace through the redemption that is in Christ Jesus: whom God hath set forth to be a propitiation through faith in his blood, to declare his righteousness for the remission of sins that are past, through the forbearance of God; to declare, I say, at this time his righteousness: that he might be just, and the justifier of him which believeth in Jesus.

ROMANS 3:21–26 KJV

If, because of one man's trespass, death reigned through that one man, much more will those who receive the abundance of grace and the free gift of righteousness reign in life through the one man Jesus Christ. Then as one man's trespass led to condemnation for all men, so one man's act of righteousness leads to acquittal and life for all men. For as by one man's disobedience many were made sinners, so by one man's obedience many will be made righteous. Law came in, to increase the trespass; but where sin increased, grace abounded all the more, so that, as sin reigned in death, grace also might reign through righteousness to eternal life through Jesus Christ our Lord.

ROMANS 5:17–21 RSV

He is the source of your life in Christ Jesus, whom God made our wisdom, our righteousness and sanctification and redemption; therefore, as it is written, 'Let him who boasts, boast of the Lord.'

1 CORINTHIANS 1:30 RSV

For our sake he made him to be sin who knew no sin, so that in him we might become the righteousness of God.

2 CORINTHIANS 5:21 RSV

Stand therefore, having your loins girt about with truth, and having on the breastplate of righteousness . . .

**EPHESIANS 6:14 KJV**

In order that I may gain Christ and be found in him, not having a righteousness of my own, based on law, but that which is through faith in Christ, the righteousness from God that depends on faith.

**PHILIPPIANS 3:8–9 RSV**

And the harvest of righteousness is sown in peace by those who make peace.

**JAMES 3:18 RSV**

For Christ also died for sins once for all, the righteous for the unrighteous, that he might bring us to God, being put to death in the flesh but made alive in the spirit.

**1 PETER 3:18 RSV**

See also *Justification.*

## Ritual

And Samuel said, 'Has the Lord as great delight in burnt offerings and sacrifices, as in obeying the voice of the Lord? Behold, to obey is better than sacrifice, and to hearken than the fat of rams.'

**1 SAMUEL 15:22 RSV**

And the Lord said: 'Because this people draw near with their mouth and honour me with their lips, while their hearts are far from me, and their fear of me is a commandment of men learned by rote.'

**ISAIAH 29:13 RSV**

'Even though you offer me your burnt offerings and cereal offerings, I will not accept them, and the peace offerings of your fatted beasts I will not look upon . . . But let justice roll down like waters, and righteousness like an ever-flowing stream.'

**AMOS 5:22, 24 RSV**

'"What a weariness this is," you say, and you sniff at me, says the Lord of hosts. You bring what has been taken by violence or is lame or sick, and this you bring as your offering! Shall I accept that from your hand? says the Lord.'

**MALACHI 1:13 RSV**

'Woe to you, scribes and Pharisees, hypocrites! for you cleanse the outside of the cup and of the plate, but inside they are full of extortion and rapacity. You blind Pharisee! first cleanse the inside of the cup and of the plate, that the outside also may be clean. Woe to you, scribes and Pharisees, hypocrites! for you are like whitewashed tombs, which outwardly appear beautiful, but within they are full of dead men's bones and all uncleanness. So you also outwardly appear righteous to men, but within you are full of hypocrisy and iniquity.'

**MATTHEW 23:25–28 RSV**

He is a Jew who is one inwardly, and real circumcision is a matter of the heart, spiritual and not literal.

**ROMANS 2:29 RSV**

They [people in the last days] will hold to the outward form of our religion, but reject its real power. Keep away from such people.

**2 TIMOTHY 3:5 GNB**

## Sabbath

Remember the sabbath day, to keep it holy. Six days shalt thou labour, and do all thy work: but the seventh day is the sabbath of the Lord thy God: in it thou shalt not do any work, thou, nor thy son, nor thy daughter, thy manservant, nor thy maidservant, nor thy cattle, nor thy stranger that is within thy gates: for in six days the Lord made heaven and earth, the sea, and all that in them is, and rested the seventh day: wherefore the Lord blessed the sabbath day, and hallowed it.

**EXODUS 20:8–11 KJV**

At that time I saw people in Judah pressing juice from grapes on the Sabbath. Others were loading corn, wine, grapes, figs, and other things on their donkeys and taking them into Jerusalem; I warned them not to sell anything on the Sabbath. Some men from the city of Tyre were living in Jerusalem, and they brought fish and all kinds of goods into the city to sell to our people on the Sabbath. I reprimanded the Jewish leaders and said, 'Look at the evil you're doing! You're making the Sabbath unholy. This is exactly why God punished your ancestors when he brought destruction on this city. And yet you insist on bringing more of God's anger down on Israel by profaning the Sabbath.'

**NEHEMIAH 13:15–18 GNB**

The Lord says, 'If you treat the Sabbath as sacred and do not pursue your own interests on that day; if you value my holy day and honour it by not travelling, working, or talking idly on that day, then you will find the joy that comes from serving me. I will make you honoured all over the world, and you will enjoy the land I gave to your ancestor, Jacob.'

**ISAIAH 58:13–14 GNB**

Jesus answered, 'What if one of you has a sheep and it falls into a deep hole on the Sabbath? Will he not take hold of it and lift it out? And a man is worth much more than a sheep! So then, our Law does allow us to help someone on the Sabbath.'

**MATTHEW 12:11–12 GNB**

'The sabbath was made for man, not man for the sabbath; so the Son of man is lord even of the sabbath.'

**MARK 2:27–28 RSV**

On the first day of the week we met to break bread. Paul was due to leave the next day, and he preached a sermon that went on till the middle of the night.

**ACTS 20:7 JB**

On the first day of every week, each of you is to put something aside and store it up, as he may prosper, so that contributions need not be made when I come.

**1 CORINTHIANS 16:2 RSV**

## Sacrifice

Then [after the flood] Noah built an altar to the Lord, and took of every clean animal and of every clean bird, and offered burnt offerings on the altar.

**GENESIS 8:20 RSV**

'Your lamb shall be without blemish, a male a year old; you shall take it from the sheep or from the goats; and you shall keep it until the fourteenth day of this month, when the whole assembly of the congregation of Israel shall kill their lambs in the evening. Then they shall take some of the blood, and put it on the two doorposts and the lintel of the houses in which they eat them.'

**EXODUS 12:5–7 RSV**

And he shall put his hand upon the head of the burnt offering; and it shall be accepted for him to make atonement for him.

**LEVITICUS 1:4 KJV**

And Samuel said, 'Has the Lord as great delight in burnt offerings and sacrifices, as in obeying the voice of the Lord? Behold, to obey is better than sacrifice, and to hearken than the fat of rams.

**1 SAMUEL 15:22 RSV**

For thou desirest not sacrifice; else would I give it: thou delightest not in burnt offering. The sacrifices of God are a broken spirit: a broken and a contrite heart, O God, thou wilt not despise.

**PSALM 51:16–17 KJV**

'I hate, I despise your feasts, and I take no delight in your solemn assemblies. Even though you offer me your burnt offerings and cereal offerings, I will not accept them, and the peace offerings of your fatted beasts I will not look upon. Take away from me the noise of your songs; to the melody of your harps I will not listen. But let justice roll down like waters, and righteousness like an ever-flowing stream.'

**AMOS 5:21–24 RSV**

'Go and learn what this means, ''I desire mercy, and not sacrifice.'' For I came not to call the righteous, but sinners.'

**MATTHEW 9:13 RSV**

I beseech you therefore, brethren, by the mercies of God, that ye present your bodies a living sacrifice, holy, acceptable unto God, which is your reasonable service.

**ROMANS 12:1 KJV**

And every priest stands daily at his service, offering repeatedly the same sacrifices, which can never take away sins. But when Christ had offered for all time a single sacrifice for sins, he sat down at the right hand of God.

**HEBREWS 10:11–12 RSV**

Let us, then, always offer praise to God as our sacrifice through Jesus, which is the offering presented by lips that confess him as Lord. Do not forget to do good and to help one another, because these are the sacrifices that please God.

**HEBREWS 13:15–16 GNB**

See also *Blood; Passover.*

## Sadness
See *Grief.*

## Salvation and Saviour

The Lord is my light and my salvation; whom shall I fear? The Lord is the strength of my life; of whom shall I be afraid?

**PSALM 27:1 KJV**

'And it shall come to pass that all who call upon the name of the Lord shall be delivered; for in Mount Zion and in Jerusalem there shall be those who escape, as the Lord has said, and among the survivors shall be those whom the Lord calls.'

**JOEL 2:32 RSV**

[An angel of the Lord to Joseph] 'You shall call his name Jesus, for he will save his people from their sins.'

**MATTHEW 1:21 RSV**

'Who, then, can be saved?' they [the disciples] asked. Jesus looked straight at them and answered, 'This is impossible for man, but for God everything is possible.'

**MATTHEW 19:25–26 GNB**

'But he who endures to the end will be saved.'

**MATTHEW 24:13 RSV**

For unto you is born this day in the city of David a Saviour, which is Christ the Lord.

**LUKE 2:11 KJV**

Someone said to him, 'Sir, will there be only a few saved?' He said to them, 'Try your best to enter by the narrow door, because, I tell you, many will try to enter and will not succeed.'

**LUKE 13:23–24 JB**

For the Son of man is come to seek and to save that which was lost.

**LUKE 19:10 KJV**

For God sent not his Son into the world to condemn the world; but that the world through him might be saved.

**JOHN 3:17 KJV**

'And there is salvation in no one else, for there is no other name under heaven given among men by which we must be saved.'

**ACTS 4:12 RSV**

'Men, what must I do to be saved?' And they said, 'Believe in the Lord Jesus, and you will be saved, you and your household.'

**ACTS 16:30–31 RSV**

For the word of the cross is folly to those who are perishing, but to us who are being saved it is the power of God.

**1 CORINTHIANS 1:18 RSV**

For he says, 'At the acceptable time I have listened to you, and helped you on the day of salvation.' Behold, now is the acceptable time; behold, now is the day of salvation.

**2 CORINTHIANS 6:2 RSV**

For by grace are ye saved through faith; and that not of yourselves: it is the gift of God.

**EPHESIANS 2:8 KJV**

Work out your own salvation with fear and trembling; for God is at work in you, both to will and to work for his good pleasure.

**PHILIPPIANS 2:12–13 RSV**

God our Saviour, who desires all men to be saved and to come to the knowledge of the truth.

**1 TIMOTHY 2:3–4 RSV**

From childhood you have been acquainted with the sacred writings which are able to instruct you for salvation through faith in Christ Jesus.

**2 TIMOTHY 3:15 RSV**

How shall we escape if we neglect such a great salvation?

**HEBREWS 2:3 RSV**

[We] who by God's power are guarded through faith for a salvation ready to be revealed in the last time.

**1 PETER 1:5 RSV**

And we have seen and do testify that the Father sent the Son to be the Saviour of the world.

**1 JOHN 4:14 KJV**

'Salvation belongs to our God who sits upon the throne, and to the Lamb!'

**REVELATION 7:10 RSV**

See also *Atonement; Christian life, Coming to faith; Sin.*

## Sanctification

Sanctify them through thy truth: thy word is truth.

**JOHN 17:17 KJV**

For just as you once yielded your members to impurity and to greater and greater iniquity, so now yield your members to righteousness for sanctification.

**ROMANS 6:19 RSV**

For I delight in the law of God, in my inmost self, but I see in my members another law at war with the law of my mind and making me captive to the law of sin which dwells in my members.
ROMANS 7:22–23 RSV

I beseech you therefore, brethren, by the mercies of God, that ye present your bodies a living sacrifice, holy, acceptable unto God, which is your reasonable service. And be not conformed to this world: but be ye transformed by the renewing of your mind, that ye may prove what is that good, and acceptable, and perfect, will of God.
ROMANS 12:1–2 KJV

He is the source of your life in Christ Jesus, whom God made our wisdom, our righteousness and sanctification and redemption.
1 CORINTHIANS 1:30 RSV

For this is the will of God, your sanctification: that you abstain from unchastity.
1 THESSALONIANS 4:3 RSV

And the very God of peace sanctify you wholly; and I pray God your whole spirit and soul and body be preserved blameless unto the coming of our Lord Jesus Christ.
1 THESSALONIANS 5:23 KJV

Elect according to the foreknowledge of God the Father, through sanctification of the Spirit, unto obedience and sprinkling of the blood of Jesus Christ.
1 PETER 1:2 KJV

See also *Christian life, Character of the Christian; Holiness.*

## Satan
See *Devil.*

## Scribes

And all the people gathered as one man into the square before the Water Gate; and they told Ezra the scribe to bring the book of the law of Moses which the Lord had given to Israel.
NEHEMIAH 8:1 RSV

'For I tell you, unless your righteousness exceeds that of the scribes and Pharisees, you will never enter the kingdom of heaven.'
MATTHEW 5:20 RSV

He [Jesus] taught . . . as one who had authority, and not as their scribes.
MATTHEW 7:29 RSV

And a scribe came up and said to him, 'Teacher, I will follow you wherever you go.'
MATTHEW 8:19 RSV

But when the chief priests and the scribes saw the wonderful things that he did, and the children crying out in the temple, 'Hosanna to the Son of David!' they were indignant.
MATTHEW 21:15 RSV

'The scribes and the Pharisees sit on Moses' seat; so practise and observe whatever they tell you, but not what they do; for they preach, but do not practise. They bind heavy burdens, hard to bear, and lay them on men's shoulders; but they themselves will not move them with their finger. They do all their deeds to be seen by men; for they make their phylacteries broad and their fringes long, and they love the place of honour at feasts and the best seats in the synagogues, and salutations in the market places, and being called rabbi by men.'
MATTHEW 23:2–7 RSV

And immediately, while he was still speaking, Judas came, one of the twelve, and with him a crowd with swords and clubs, from the chief priests and the scribes and the elders.
MARK 14:43 RSV

See also *Hypocrisy; Pharisees.*

## Second coming
See *Last things.*

## Self-denial

And a poor widow came, and put in two copper coins, which make a penny. And he called his disciples to him, and said to them, 'Truly, I say to you, this poor widow has put in more than all those who are contributing to the treasury. For they all contributed out of their abundance; but she out of her poverty has put in everything she had, her whole living.'
MARK 12:42–44 RSV

And he said to all, 'If any man would come after me, let him deny himself and take up his cross daily and follow me. For whoever would save his life will lose it; and whoever loses his life for my sake, he will save it.'

LUKE 9:23–24 RSV

He must increase, but I must decrease.

JOHN 3:30 KJV

'Whoever loves his own life will lose it; whoever hates his own life in this world will keep it for life eternal.'

JOHN 12:25 GNB

But the fruit of the Spirit is . . . faithfulness, gentleness, self-control . . .

GALATIANS 5:22–23 RSV

See also *Disciples; Service.*

## Self-examination

When I think of thy ways, I turn my feet to thy testimonies.

PSALM 119:59 RSV

Now these are the words of the Lord of Hosts: Consider your way of life.

HAGGAI 1:5 NEB

Let a man examine himself, and so eat of the bread and drink of the cup. For any one who eats and drinks without discerning the body eats and drinks judgment upon himself. That is why many of you are weak and ill, and some have died.

1 CORINTHIANS 11:28–30 RSV

Examine yourselves to make sure you are in the faith; test yourselves. Do you acknowledge that Jesus Christ is really in you? If not, you have failed the test.

2 CORINTHIANS 13:5 JB

If someone thinks he is somebody when really he is nobody, he is only deceiving himself. Each one should judge his own conduct. If it is good, then he can be proud of what he himself has done, without having to compare it with what someone else has done.

GALATIANS 6:3–4 GNB

See also *Examination.*

## Self-righteousness

'After the Lord your God has driven them out for you, do not say to yourselves that he brought you in to possess this land because you deserved it.

No, the Lord is going to drive these people out for you because they are wicked.'

DEUTERONOMY 9:4 GNB

All the ways of a man are pure in his own eyes, but the Lord weighs the spirit.

PROVERBS 16:2 RSV

'Beware of practising your piety before men in order to be seen by them; for then you will have no reward from your Father who is in heaven.'

MATTHEW 6:1 RSV

'So you also outwardly appear righteous to men, but within your are full of hypocrisy and iniquity.'

MATTHEW 23:28 RSV

He also told this parable to some who trusted in themselves that they were righteous and despised others: 'Two men went up into the temple to pray, one a Pharisee and the other a tax collector. The Pharisee stood and prayed thus with himself, ''God, I thank thee that I am not like other men, extortioners, unjust, adulterers, or even like this tax collector. I fast twice a week, I give tithes of all that I get.'' But the tax collector, standing far off, would not even lift up his eyes to heaven, but beat his breast, saying, ''God, be merciful to me a sinner!'' I tell you, this man went down to his house justified rather than the other; for every one who exalts himself will be humbled, but he who humbles himself will be exalted.'

LUKE 18:9–14 RSV

See also *Hypocrisy; Pride; Righteousness.*

## Sermon on the Mount
See Matthew 5–7.

## Service

[God to Moses] He said, 'But I will be with you; and this shall be the sign for you, that I have sent you: when you have brought forth the people out of Egypt, you shall serve God upon this mountain.'

EXODUS 3:12 RSV

It is written, Thou shalt worship the Lord thy God, and him only shalt thou serve.

MATTHEW 4:10 KJV

'A disciple is not above his teacher, nor a servant above his master.'

MATTHEW 10:24 RSV

Whoever would be great among you must be your servant, and whoever would be first among you must be slave of all. For the Son of man also came not to be served but to serve, and to give his life as a ransom for many.

MARK 10:43–45 RSV

'Whoever wants to serve me must follow me, so that my servant will be with me where I am. And my Father will honour anyone who serves me.'

JOHN 12:26 GNB

When he had washed their feet, and taken his garments, and resumed his place, he said to them, 'Do you know what I have done to you? You call me Teacher and Lord; and you are right, for so I am. If I then, your Lord and Teacher, have washed your feet, you also ought to wash one another's feet.'

JOHN 13:12–14 RSV

If it [a man's gift] is serving, let him serve.

ROMANS 12:7 NIV

So then, as we have opportunity, let us do good to all men, and especially to those who are of the household of faith.

GALATIANS 6:10 RSV

Whatever your task, work heartily, as serving the Lord and not men.

COLOSSIANS 3:23 RSV

Whoever renders service, as one who renders it by the strength which God supplies; in order that in everything God may be glorified through Jesus Christ.

1 PETER 4:11 RSV

See also **Help; Kindness.**

# Sex

### GIFT OF

So God created man in his own image, in the image of God created he him; male and female created he them. And God blessed them, and God said unto them, Be fruitful and multiply, and replenish the earth, and subdue it.

GENESIS 1:27–28 KJV

Therefore shall a man leave his father and his mother, and shall cleave unto his wife: and they shall be one flesh. And they were both naked, the man and his wife, and were not ashamed.

GENESIS 2:24–25 KJV

A man should fulfil his duty as a husband, and a woman should fulfil her duty as a wife, and each should satisfy the other's needs. A wife is not the master of her own body, but her husband is; in the same way a husband is not the master of his own body, but his wife is. Do not deny yourselves to each other, unless you first agree to do so for a while in order to spend your time in prayer; but then resume normal marital relations. In this way you will be kept from giving in to Satan's temptation because of your lack of self-control.

1 CORINTHIANS 7:3–5 GNB

See also **Marriage.**

### MISUSE OF

Now Joseph was handsome and good-looking. And after a time his master's wife cast her eyes upon Joseph and said, 'Lie with me.' But he refused and said to his master's wife, '. . . how then can I do this great wickedness, and sin against God?'

GENESIS 39:6–9 RSV

Do you not know that the wicked will not inherit the kingdom of God? Do not be deceived: Neither the sexually immoral nor idolaters nor adulterers nor male prostitutes nor homosexual offenders . . . will inherit the kingdom of God.

1 CORINTHIANS 6:9–10 NIV

You know that your bodies are parts of the body of Christ. Shall I take a part of Christ's body and make it part of the body of a prostitute? Impossible! Or perhaps you don't know that the man who joins his body to a prostitute becomes physically one with her? The scripture says quite plainly, 'The two will become one body.' But he who joins himself to the Lord becomes spiritually one with him. Avoid immorality. Any other sin a man commits does not affect his body; but the man who is guilty of sexual immorality sins against his own body. Don't you know that your body is the temple of the Holy Spirit, who lives in you and who was given to you by God? You do not belong to yourselves but to God.

1 CORINTHIANS 6:15–19 GNB

Now the works of the flesh are plain: immorality, impurity, licentiousness . . .

GALATIANS 5:19 RSV

Since you are God's people, it is not right that any matters of sexual immorality or indecency or greed should even be mentioned among you.

**EPHESIANS 5:3 GNB**

See also *Homosexuality*.

## Shame, ashamed

And they were both naked, the man and his wife, and were not ashamed . . . And [Adam] he said, I heard thy voice in the garden, and I was afraid, because I was naked; and I hid myself.

**GENESIS 2:25, 3:10 KJV**

Look to him, and be radiant; so your faces shall never be ashamed.

**PSALM 34:5 RSV**

'For whoever is ashamed of me and of my words in this adulterous and sinful generation, of him will the Son of man also be ashamed, when he comes in the glory of his Father with the holy angels.'

**MARK 8:38 RSV**

For I am not ashamed of the gospel of Christ: for it is the power of God unto salvation to everyone that believeth; to the Jew first, and also to the Greek.

**ROMANS 1:16 KJV**

But I am not ashamed, for I know whom I have believed, and I am sure that he is able to guard until that Day what has been entrusted to me.

**2 TIMOTHY 1:12 RSV**

Instead, it was a better country they longed for, the heavenly country. And so God is not ashamed for them to call him their God, because he has prepared a city for them.

**HEBREWS 11:16 GNB**

Looking unto Jesus the author and finisher of our faith; who for the joy that was set before him endured the cross, despising the shame, and is set down at the right hand of the throne of God.

**HEBREWS 12:2 KJV**

However, if you suffer because you are a Christian, don't be ashamed of it, but thank God that you bear Christ's name.

**1 PETER 4:16 GNB**

And now, little children, abide in him, so that when he appears we may have confidence and not shrink from him in shame at his coming.

**1 JOHN 2:28 RSV**

## Shepherd

The Lord is my shepherd; I shall not want.

**PSALM 23:1 KJV**

He shall feed his flock like a shepherd: he shall gather the lambs with his arm, and carry them in his bosom, and shall gently lead those that are with young.

**ISAIAH 40:11 KJV**

'My people have been lost sheep; their shepherds have led them astray and caused them to roam on the mountains. They wandered over mountain and hill and forgot their own resting place.'

**JEREMIAH 50:6 NIV**

The word of the Lord came to me: 'Son of man, prophesy against the shepherds of Israel, prophesy, and say to them, even to the shepherds, Thus says the Lord God: Ho, shepherds of Israel who have been feeding yourselves! Should not shepherds feed the sheep?'

**EZEKIEL 34:1–2 RSV**

'And I will set up over them one shepherd, my servant David, and he shall feed them: he shall feed them and be their shepherd.

**EZEKIEL 34:23 RSV**

Then Jesus said to them, 'You will all fall away because of me this night; for it is written, "I will strike the shepherd, and the sheep of the flock will be scattered."'

**MATTHEW 26:31 RSV**

And the shepherds returned, glorifying and praising God for all they had heard and seen, as it had been told them.

**LUKE 2:20 RSV**

'I am the good shepherd. The good shepherd lays down his life for the sheep.'

**JOHN 10:11 RSV**

Now the God of peace, that brought again from the dead our Lord Jesus, that great shepherd of the sheep, through the blood of the everlasting covenant . . .

**HEBREWS 13:20 KJV**

For you were straying like sheep, but have now returned to the Shepherd and Guardian of your souls.

**1 PETER 2:25 RSV**

And when the chief Shepherd is manifested you will obtain the unfading crown of glory.
1 PETER 5:4 RSV

## Sin

Be sure your sin will find you out.
NUMBERS 32:23 KJV

Against thee, thee only, have I sinned, and done this evil in thy sight: that thou mightest be justified when thou speakest, and be clear when thou judgest. Behold, I was shapen in iniquity; and in sin did my mother conceive me.
PSALM 51:4–5 KJV

'Come now, let us reason together,' says the Lord. 'Though your sins are like scarlet, they shall be as white as snow; though they are red as crimson, they shall be like wool.'
ISAIAH 1:18 NIV

All we like sheep have gone astray; we have turned every one to his own way; and the Lord hath laid on him the iniquity of us all.
ISAIAH 53:6 KJV

Your iniquities have made a separation between you and your God, and your sins have hid his face from you so that he does not hear.
ISAIAH 59:2 KJV

Thou who art of purer eyes than to behold evil and canst not look on wrong . . .
HABAKKUK 1:13 RSV

[An angel of the Lord to Joseph] 'You shall call his name Jesus, for he will save his people from their sins.'
MATTHEW 1:21 RSV

The next day he [John the Baptist] saw Jesus coming toward him, and said, 'Behold, the Lamb of God, who takes away the sin of the world!'
JOHN 1:29 RSV

Jesus answered them, 'Truly, truly, I say to you, every one who commits sin is a slave to sin.'
JOHN 8:34 RSV

For all have sinned, and come short of the glory of God.
ROMANS 3:23 KJV

As by one man sin entered into the world, and death by sin . . . so death passed upon all men, for that all have sinned.
ROMANS 5:12 KJV

What shall we say then? Shall we continue in sin, that grace may abound? God forbid. How shall we, that are dead to sin, live any longer therein?
ROMANS 6:1–2 KJV

For the wages of sin is death; but the gift of God is eternal life through Jesus Christ our Lord.
ROMANS 6:23 KJV

For our sake he made him to be sin who knew no sin, so that in him we might become the righteousness of God.
2 CORINTHIANS 5:21 RSV

As for you, you were dead in your transgressions and sins, in which you used to live when you followed the ways of this world and of the ruler of the kingdom of the air, the spirit who is now at work in those who are disobedient. All of us also lived among them at one time, gratifying the cravings of our sinful nature and following its desires and thoughts. Like the rest, we were by nature objects of wrath.
EPHESIANS 2:1–3 NIV

This is a faithful saying, and worthy of all acceptation, that Christ Jesus came into the world to save sinners; of whom I am the chief.
1 TIMOTHY 1:15 KJV

Indeed, under the law almost everything is purified with blood, and without the shedding of blood there is no forgiveness of sins.
HEBREWS 9:22 RSV

He himself bore our sins in his body on the tree, that we might die to sin and live to righteousness.
1 PETER 2:24 RSV

If we walk in the light, as he is in the light, we have fellowship with one another, and the blood of Jesus his Son cleanses us from all sin. If we say we have no sin, we deceive ourselves, and the truth is not in us. If we confess our sins, he is faithful and just and will forgive our sins and cleanse us from all unrighteousness.
1 JOHN 1:7–9 RSV

Every one who commits sin is guilty of lawlessness; sin is lawlessness. You know that he appeared to take away sins, and in him there is no sin.
1 JOHN 3:4–5 RSV

Whoever is a child of God does not continue to sin, for God's very nature is in him; and because

God is his Father, he cannot continue to sin.
1 JOHN 3:9 GNB

See also *Forgiveness; Repentance; Salvation and Saviour.*

## Son of God
See *Jesus Christ.*

## Sorrow
See *Grief.*

## Soul

He restoreth my soul: he leadeth me in the paths of righteousness for his name's sake.
PSALM 23:3 KJV

My soul thirsteth for God, for the living God: when shall I come and appear before God? ... Why art thou cast down, O my soul? and why art thou disquieted in me? Hope thou in God: for I shall yet praise him for the help of his countenance. O my God, my soul is cast down within me: therefore will I remember thee from the land of Jordan.
PSALM 42:2, 5–6 KJV

Bless the Lord, O my soul: and all that is within me, bless his holy name. Bless the Lord, O my soul, and forget not all his benefits.
PSALM 103:1–2 KJV

[The Lord] 'Behold, all souls are mine; the soul of the father as well as the soul of the son is mine: the soul that sins shall die.'
EZEKIEL 18:4 RSV

'Do not be afraid of those who kill the body but cannot kill the soul; rather be afraid of God, who can destroy both body and soul in hell.'
MATTHEW 10:28 GNB

'Take my yoke upon you, and learn from me; for I am gentle and lowly in heart, and you will find rest for your souls.'
MATTHEW 11:29 RSV

Then he said to them, 'My soul is very sorrowful, even to death; remain here, and watch with me.'
MATTHEW 26:38 RSV

[Mary's Magnificat] My soul doth magnify the Lord ...
LUKE 1:46 BCP

See also *Heart; Spirit.*

## Sovereignty of God

Know therefore this day, and consider it in thine heart, that the Lord he is God in heaven above, and upon the earth beneath: there is none else.
DEUTERONOMY 4:39 KJV

And the Lord said to Satan, 'Behold, all that he has is in your power; only upon himself do not put forth your hand.'
JOB 1:12 RSV

Many are the plans in the mind of a man, but it is the purpose of the Lord that will be established.
PROVERBS 19:21 RSV

'For the Son of man goes as it has been determined; but woe to that man by whom he is betrayed!'
LUKE 22:22 RSV

The wind bloweth where it listeth, and thou hearest the sound thereof, but canst not tell whence it cometh, and whither it goeth: so is every one that is born of the Spirit.
JOHN 3:8 KJV

All that the Father giveth me shall come to me; and him that cometh to me I will in no wise cast out.
JOHN 6:37 KJV

'This Jesus, delivered up according to the definite plan and foreknowledge of God, you crucified and killed by the hands of lawless men.'
ACTS 2:23 RSV

We know that in everything God works for good with those who love him, who are called according to his purpose.
ROMANS 8:28 RSV

All these [gifts] are inspired by one and the same Spirit, who apportions to each one individually as he wills.
1 CORINTHIANS 12:11 RSV

[God] who worketh all things after the counsel of his own will.
EPHESIANS 1:11 KJV

Work out your own salvation with fear and trembling; for God is at work in you, both to will and to work for his good pleasure.
PHILIPPIANS 2:12–13 RSV

See also *Election; Providence; Responsibility of Man.*

## Speech

Set a guard over my mouth, O Lord, keep watch over the door of my lips!
**PSALM 141:3 RSV**

A word fitly spoken is like apples of gold in pictures of silver.
**PROVERBS 25:11 KJV**

'You can be sure on Judgement Day everyone will have to give account of every useless word he has ever spoken.'
**MATTHEW 12:36 GNB**

Rather, speaking the truth in love, we are to grow up in every way into him who is the head, into Christ.
**EPHESIANS 4:15 RSV**

Let no evil talk come out of your mouths, but only such as is good for edifying, as fits the occasion, that it may impart grace to those who hear.
**EPHESIANS 4:29 RSV**

Let your speech always be gracious, seasoned with salt, so that you may know how you ought to answer every one.
**COLOSSIANS 4:6 RSV**

And the tongue is like a fire. It is a world of wrong, occupying its place in our bodies and spreading evil through our whole being. It sets on fire the entire course of our existence with the fire that comes to it from hell itself ... But no one has ever been able to tame the tongue. It is evil and uncontrollable, full of deadly poison. We use it to give thanks to our Lord and Father and also to curse our fellow-man, who is created in the likeness of God. Words of thanksgiving and cursing pour out from the same mouth. My brothers, this should not happen!
**JAMES 3:6, 8–10 GNB**

'He that would love life and see good days, let him keep his tongue from evil and his lips from speaking guile.'
**1 PETER 3:10 RSV**

Always be prepared to make a defence to any one who calls you to account for the hope that is in you, yet do it with gentleness and reverence.
**1 PETER 3:15 RSV**

## Spirit

When they had crossed, Elijah said to Elisha, 'Ask what I shall do for you, before I am taken from you.' And Elisha said, 'I pray you, let me inherit a double share of your spirit.'
**2 KINGS 2:9 RSV**

Create in me a clean heart, O God; and renew a right spirit within me.
**PSALM 51:10 KJV**

All the ways of a man are pure in his own eyes, but the Lord weighs the spirit.
**PROVERBS 16:2 RSV**

Blessed are the poor in spirit: for theirs is the kingdom of heaven.
**MATTHEW 5:3 KJV**

'Watch and pray that you may not enter into temptation; the spirit indeed is willing, but the flesh is weak.'
**MATTHEW 26:41 RSV**

And Jesus cried again with a loud voice and yielded up his spirit.
**MATTHEW 27:50 RSV**

'But the hour is coming, and now is, when the true worshippers will worship the Father in spirit and truth, for such the Father seeks to worship him. God is spirit, and those who worship him must worship in spirit and truth.'
**JOHN 4:23–24 RSV**

For you did not receive the spirit of slavery to fall back into fear, but you have received the spirit of sonship. When we cry, 'Abba! Father!' it is the Spirit itself bearing witness with our spirit that we are children of God.
**ROMANS 8:15–16 RSV**

For what person knows a man's thoughts except the spirit of the man which is in him? So also no one comprehends the thoughts of God except the Spirit of God.
**1 CORINTHIANS 2:11 RSV**

The spiritual man makes judgments about all things, but he himself is not subject to any man's judgment.
**1 CORINTHIANS 2:15 NIV**

For if I pray in a tongue, my spirit prays but my mind is unfruitful. What am I to do? I will pray with the spirit and I will pray with the mind also; I will sing with the spirit and I will sing with the mind also.
**1 CORINTHIANS 14:14–15 RSV**

See also *Heart; Holy Spirit; Soul.*

## State, responsibility to

He said to them, 'Render therefore to Caesar the things that are Caesar's, and to God the things that are God's.'
MATTHEW 22:21 RSV

[The high priest] 'We strictly charged you not to teach in this name, yet here you have filled Jerusalem with your teaching and you intend to bring this man's blood upon us.' But Peter and the apostles answered, 'We must obey God rather than men.'
ACTS 5:28–29 RSV

Everyone must obey the state authorities, because no authority exists without God's permission, and the existing authorities have been put there by God. Whoever opposes the existing authority opposes what God has ordered; and anyone who does so will bring judgement on himself. For rulers are not to be feared by those who do good, but by those who do evil. Would you like to be unafraid of the man in authority? Then do what is good, and he will praise you, because he is God's servant working for your own good. But if you do evil, then be afraid of him, because his power to punish is real. He is God's servant and carries out God's punishment on those who do evil. For this reason you must obey the authorities—not just because of God's punishment, but also as a matter of conscience. This is also why you pay taxes, because the authorities are working for God when they fulfil their duties. Pay, then, what you owe them; pay them your personal and property taxes, and show respect and honour for them all.
ROMANS 13:1–7 GNB

[An encouragement to pray] for kings, and for all that are in authority; that we may lead a quiet and peaceable life in all godliness and honesty.
1 TIMOTHY 2:2 KJV

Live as free men, yet without using your freedom as a pretext for evil; but live as servants of God. Honour all men. Love the brotherhood. Fear God. Honour the emperor.
1 PETER 2:16–17 RSV

## Stealing

Thou shalt not steal.
EXODUS 20:15 KJV

'If a man steals an ox or a sheep, and kills it or sells it, he shall pay five oxen for an ox, and four sheep for a sheep. He shall make restitution; if he has nothing, then he shall be sold for his theft.'
EXODUS 22:1 RSV

And [Jesus] said unto them, It is written, My house shall be called the house of prayer; but ye have made it a den of thieves.
MATTHEW 21:13 KJV

'For from within, out of the heart of man, come evil thoughts . . . theft . . .'
MARK 7:21 RSV

He [Judas] said this, not because he cared about the poor, but because he was a thief. He carried the money bag and would help himself from it.
JOHN 12:6 GNB

Neither . . . thieves nor the greedy nor . . . swindlers will inherit the kingdom of God.
1 CORINTHIANS 6:9–10 NIV

Let the thief no longer steal, but rather let him labour, doing honest work with his hands, so that he may be able to give to those in need.
EPHESIANS 4:28 RSV

Bid slaves to be submissive to their masters and to give satisfaction in every respect; they are not to be refractory, nor to pilfer.
TITUS 2:9–10 RSV

But let none of you suffer as a murderer, or a thief, or a wrongdoer, or a mischief-maker.
1 PETER 4:15 RSV

## Stewardship

'For it will be as when a man going on a journey called his servants and entrusted to them his property; to one he gave five talents, to another two, to another one, to each according to his ability . . .'
MATTHEW 25:14–15 RSV

He also said to the disciples, 'There was a rich man who had a steward, and charges were brought to him that this man was wasting his goods. And he called him and said to him, "What is this that I hear about you? Turn in the account of your stewardship, for you can no longer be steward." And the steward said to himself, "What shall I do, since my master is taking the stewardship away from me?" '
LUKE 16:1–3 RSV

This is how one should regard us, as servants of Christ and stewards of the mysteries of God. Moreover it is required of stewards that they be found trustworthy.

1 CORINTHIANS 4:1–2 RSV

For if I preach the gospel, that gives me no ground for boasting. For necessity is laid upon me. Woe to me if I do not preach the gospel! For if I do this of my own will, I have a reward; but if not of my own will, I am entrusted with a commission.

1 CORINTHIANS 9:16–17 RSV

Assuming that you have heard of the stewardship of God's grace that was given to me for you.

EPHESIANS 3:2 RSV

But I am not ashamed, for I know whom I have believed, and I am sure that he is able to guard until that Day what has been entrusted to me ... guard the truth that has been entrusted to you by the Holy Spirit who dwells within us.

2 TIMOTHY 1:12, 14 RSV

As each has received a gift, employ it for one another, as good stewards of God's varied grace.

1 PETER 4:10 RSV

See also *Giving; Time.*

## Strength
See *Power.*

## Submission

Everyone must obey the state authorities, because no authority exists without God's permission, and the existing authorities have been put there by God.

ROMANS 13:1 GNB

Be subject to one another out of reverence for Christ. Wives, be subject to your husbands, as to the Lord ... As the church is subject to Christ, so let wives also be subject in everything to their husbands.

EPHESIANS 5:21–22, 24

Children, obey your parents in the Lord, for this is right. 'Honour your father and mother' (this is the first commandment with a promise).

EPHESIANS 6:1–2 RSV

Slaves, obey your human masters with fear and trembling; and do it with a sincere heart, as though you were serving Christ.

EPHESIANS 6:5 GNB

Obey your leaders and submit to them; for they are keeping watch over your souls, as men who will have to give account. Let them do this joyfully, and not sadly, for that would be of no advantage to you.

HEBREWS 13:17 RSV

Submit yourselves therefore to God. Resist the devil and he will flee from you.

JAMES 4:7 RSV

See also *Obedience.*

## Suffering

Yet man is born unto trouble, as the sparks fly upward.

JOB 5:7 KJV

'He has no root in himself, but endures for a while, and when tribulation or persecution arises on account of the word, immediately he falls away.'

MATTHEW 13:21 RSV

'Then they will deliver you up to tribulation, and put you to death; and you will be hated by all nations for my name's sake.'

MATTHEW 24:9 RSV

'For then there will be great tribulation, such as has not been from the beginning of the world until now, no, and never will be.'

MATTHEW 24:21 RSV

'Was it not necessary that the Christ should suffer these things and enter into his glory?'

LUKE 24:26 RSV

[Paul and Barnabas] Strengthening the souls of the disciples, exhorting them to continue in the faith, and saying that through many tribulations we must enter the kingdom of God.

ACTS 14:22 RSV

There will be tribulation and distress for every human being who does evil, the Jew first and also the Greek.

ROMANS 2:9 RSV

I consider that the sufferings of this present time are not worth comparing with the glory that is to be revealed to us. For the creation waits with eager longing for the revealing of the sons of

God; for the creation was subjected to futility, not of its own will but by the will of him who subjected it in hope; because the creation itself will be set free from its bondage to decay and obtain the glorious liberty of the children of God.
ROMANS 8:18–21 RSV

If one member suffers, all suffer together; if one member is honoured, all rejoice together.
1 CORINTHIANS 12:26 RSV

We are afflicted in every way, but not crushed; perplexed, but not driven to despair; persecuted, but not forsaken; struck down, but not destroyed . . .
2 CORINTHIANS 4:8–9 RSV

Now I rejoice in my sufferings for your sake, and in my flesh I complete what is lacking in Christ's afflictions for the sake of his body, that is, the church.
COLOSSIANS 1:24 RSV

Resist him [the devil], firm in your faith, knowing that the same experience of suffering is required of your brotherhood throughout the world.
1 PETER 5:9 RSV

**PURPOSES OF**

'He delivers the afflicted by the affliction, and opens their ear by adversity.'
JOB 36:15 RSV

It is good for me that I was afflicted, that I might learn thy statutes.
PSALM 119:71 RSV

As Jesus was walking along, he saw a man who had been born blind. His disciples asked him, 'Teacher, whose sin caused him to be born blind? Was it his own or his parents' sin?' Jesus answered, 'His blindness has nothing to do with his sins or his parents' sins. He is blind so that God's power might be seen at work in him.'
JOHN 9:1–3 GNB

We glory in tribulations also: knowing that tribulation worketh patience.
ROMANS 5:3 KJV

[God] comforts us in all our troubles, so that we can comfort those in any trouble with the comfort we ourselves have received from God.
2 CORINTHIANS 1:4 NIV

And to keep me from being too elated by the

abundance of revelations, a thorn was given me in the flesh, a messenger of Satan, to harass me, to keep me from being too elated.
2 CORINTHIANS 12:7 RSV

For they [our human fathers] disciplined us for a short time at their pleasure, but he disciplines us for our good, that we may share his holiness.
HEBREWS 12:10 RSV

In this you rejoice, though now for a little while you may have to suffer various trials, so that the genuineness of your faith, more precious than gold which though perishable is tested by fire, may redound to praise and glory and honour at the revelation of Jesus Christ.
1 PETER 1:6–7 RSV

See also *Comfort.*

## Sunday
See *Sabbath.*

## Swearing
See *Blasphemy.*

## Talents
See *Gift.*

## Teachers and teaching

'You shall teach them [the words the Lord commands] diligently to your children, and shall talk of them when you sit in your house, and when you walk by the way, and when you lie down, and when you rise.'
DEUTERONOMY 6:7 RSV

Teach me, O Lord, the way of thy statutes; and I will keep it to the end.
PSALM 119:33 RSV

'Go therefore and make disciples of all nations . . . teaching them to observe all that I have commanded you . . .'
MATTHEW 28:19–20 RSV

Jesus answered, 'What I teach is not my own teaching, but it comes from God, who sent me.'
JOHN 7:16 GNB

'But the Counsellor, the Holy Spirit, whom the Father will send in my name, he will teach you all things, and bring to your remembrance all that I have said to you.'
JOHN 14:26 RSV

And they continued stedfastly in the apostles' doctrine and fellowship, and in breaking of bread, and in prayers.
**ACTS 2:42 KJV**

'How I did not shrink from declaring to you anything that was profitable, and teaching you in public and from house to house . . .'
**ACTS 20:20 RSV**

Now you are the body of Christ and individually members of it. And God has appointed in the church first apostles, second prophets, third teachers . . .
**1 CORINTHIANS 12:28 RSV**

Let the word of Christ dwell in you richly in all wisdom; teaching and admonishing one another in psalms and hymns and spiritual songs, singing with grace in your hearts to the Lord.
**COLOSSIANS 3:16 KJV**

From childhood you have been acquainted with the sacred writings which are able to instruct you for salvation through faith in Christ Jesus. All scripture is inspired by God and profitable for teaching, for reproof, for correction, and for training in righteousness . . .
**2 TIMOTHY 3:15–16 RSV**

See also *Family; Pastor; Preaching.*

## Teachers, false

'A prophet or an interpreter of dreams may promise a miracle or a wonder, in order to lead you to worship and serve gods that you have not worshipped before. Even if what he promises comes true, do not pay any attention to him. The Lord your God is using him to test you, to see if you love the Lord with all your heart.'
**DEUTERONOMY 13:1–3 GNB**

'Beware of false prophets, who come to you in sheep's clothing but inwardly are ravenous wolves. You will know them by their fruits.'
**MATTHEW 7:15–16 RSV**

' "In vain do they worship me, teaching as doctrines the precepts of men." '
**MATTHEW 15:9 RSV**

And Jesus answered them, 'Take heed that no one leads you astray. For many will come in my name, saying, "I am the Christ," and they will lead many astray.'
**MATTHEW 24:4–5 RSV**

I appeal to you, brethren, to take note of those who create dissensions and difficulties, in opposition to the doctrine which you have been taught; avoid them.
**ROMANS 16:17 RSV**

I am astonished that you are so quickly deserting him who called you in the grace of Christ and turning to a different gospel—not that there is another gospel, but there are some who trouble you and want to pervert the gospel of Christ. But even if we, or an angel from heaven, should preach to you a gospel contrary to that which we preached to you, let him be accursed!
**GALATIANS 1:6–8 RSV**

Now the Spirit expressly says that in later times some will depart from the faith by giving heed to deceitful spirits and doctrines of demons.
**1 TIMOTHY 4:1 RSV**

They profess to know God, but they deny him by their deeds; they are detestable, disobedient, unfit for any good deed.
**TITUS 1:16 RSV**

But false prophets also arose among the people, just as there will be false teachers among you, who will secretly bring in destructive heresies, even denying the Master who bought them, bringing upon themselves swift destruction.
**2 PETER 2:1 RSV**

Beloved, do not believe every spirit, but test the spirits to see whether they are of God; for many false prophets have gone out into the world. By this you know the Spirit of God: every spirit which confesses that Jesus Christ has come in the flesh is of God.
**1 JOHN 4:1–2 RSV**

Beloved, being very eager to write to you of our common salvation, I found it necessary to write appealing to you to contend for the faith which was once for all delivered to the saints. For admission has been secretly gained by some who long ago were designated for this condemnation, ungodly persons who pervert the grace of our God in licentiousness and deny our only Master and Lord, Jesus Christ.
**JUDE 3–4 RSV**

## Temperance

Let us then pursue what makes for peace and for mutual upbuilding . . . it is right not to eat meat or drink wine or do anything that makes your brother stumble.

ROMANS 14:19, 21 RSV

But the fruit of the Spirit is . . . self-control . . .

GALATIANS 5:22–23 RSV

For those who sleep sleep at night, and those who get drunk are drunk at night. But, since we belong to the day, let us be sober.

1 THESSALONIANS 5:7–8 RSV

Deacons likewise must be serious, not double-tongued, not addicted to much wine . . . The women likewise must be . . . temperate, faithful in all things.

1 TIMOTHY 3:8, 11 RSV

Drink no longer water, but use a little wine for thy stomach's sake and thine often infirmities.

1 TIMOTHY 5:23 KJV

See also **Drunkenness**.

## Temptation

'And you shall remember all the way which the Lord your God has led you these forty years in the wilderness, that he might humble you, testing you to know what was in your heart, whether you would keep his commandments, or not.'

DEUTERONOMY 8:2 RSV

And the Lord said to Satan, 'Behold, all that he has is in your power; only upon himself do not put forth your hand.'

JOB 1:12 RSV

Can a man take fire in his bosom, and his clothes not be burned?

PROVERBS 6:27 KJV

Then Jesus was led up by the Spirit into the wilderness to be tempted by the devil.

MATTHEW 4:1 RSV

And lead us not into temptation; but deliver us from evil.

MATTHEW 6:13 BCP

'Watch and pray that you may not enter into temptation; the spirit indeed is willing, but the flesh is weak.'

MATTHEW 26:41 RSV

And he said to his disciples, 'Temptations to sin are sure to come; but woe to him by whom they come!'

LUKE 17:1 RSV

But I am afraid that as the serpent deceived Eve by his cunning, your thoughts will be led astray from a sincere and pure devotion to Christ.

2 CORINTHIANS 11:3 RSV

Brethren, if a man is overtaken in any trespass, you who are spiritual should restore him in a spirit of gentleness. Look to yourself, lest you too be tempted.

GALATIANS 6:1 RSV

It was faith that made Abraham offer his son Isaac as a sacrifice when God put Abraham to the test. Abraham was the one to whom God had made the promise, yet he was ready to offer his only son as a sacrifice.

HEBREWS 11:17 GNB

Let no one say when he is tempted, 'I am tempted by God'; for God cannot be tempted with evil and he himself tempts no one; but each person is tempted when he is lured and enticed by his own desire.

JAMES 1:13–14 RSV

### HELP IN

Keep back thy servant also from presumptuous sins; let them not have dominion over me: then shall I be upright, and I shall be innocent from the great transgression.

PSALM 19:13 KJV

Set a guard over my mouth, O Lord, keep watch over the door of my lips!

PSALM 141:3 RSV

Never set your foot on the path of the wicked, do not walk the way that the evil go.

PROVERBS 4:14 JB

And the Lord said, Simon, Simon, behold, Satan hath desired to have you, that he may shift you as wheat: but I have prayed for thee, that thy faith fail not: and when thou art converted, strengthen thy brethren.

LUKE 22:31–32 KJV

How shall we, that are dead to sin, live any longer therein?

ROMANS 6:2 KJV

No temptation has overtaken you that is not common to man. God is faithful, and he will not let you be tempted beyond your strength, but with the temptation will also provide the way of escape, that you may be able to endure it.

1 CORINTHIANS 10:13 RSV

Put on the whole armour of God, that ye may be able to stand against the wiles of the devil.
**EPHESIANS 6:11 KJV**

Because he himself suffered when he was tempted, he is able to help those who are being tempted.
**HEBREWS 2:18 NIV**

For we have not a high priest who is unable to sympathize with our weaknesses, but one who in every respect has been tempted as we are, yet without sin.
**HEBREWS 4:15 RSV**

Count it all joy, my brethren, when you meet various trials, for you know that the testing of your faith produces steadfastness.
**JAMES 1:2–3 RSV**

In this you rejoice, though now for a little while you may have to suffer various trials, so that the genuineness of your faith, more precious than gold which though perishable is tested by fire, may redound to praise and glory and honour at the revelation of Jesus Christ.
**1 PETER 1:6–7 RSV**

Beloved, do not be surprised at the fiery ordeal which comes upon you to prove you, as though something strange were happening to you. But rejoice in so far as you share Christ's sufferings, that you may also rejoice and be glad when his glory is revealed.
**1 PETER 4:12–13 RSV**

Be sober, be watchful. Your adversary the devil prowls around like a roaring lion, seeking some one to devour. Resist him, firm in your faith, knowing that the same experience of suffering is required of your brotherhood throughout the world.
**1 PETER 5:8–9 RSV**

See also *Victory.*

## Ten Commandments
See Exodus 20; Deuteronomy 5.

## Tests of faith
See *Temptation.*

## Thanksgiving

'Offer to God a sacrifice of thanksgiving, and pay your vows to the Most High.'
**PSALM 50:14 RSV**

O give thanks to the Lord, for he is good, for his steadfast love endures for ever.
**PSALM 136:1 RSV**

He fell on his face at Jesus' feet, giving him thanks. Now he was a Samaritan. Then said Jesus, 'Were not ten cleansed? Where are the nine? Was no one found to return and give praise to God except this foreigner?'
**LUKE 17:16–18 RSV**

But thanks be to God, which giveth us the victory through our Lord Jesus Christ.
**1 CORINTHIANS 15:57 RSV**

Thanks be to God for his inexpressible gift!
**2 CORINTHIANS 9:15 RSV**

I do not cease to give thanks for you, remembering you in my prayers . . .
**EPHESIANS 1:16 RSV**

Nor is it fitting for you to use language which is obscene, profane, or vulgar. Rather you should give thanks to God.
**EPHESIANS 5:4 GNB**

Speaking to yourselves in psalms and hymns and spiritual songs, singing and making melody in your heart to the Lord; giving thanks always for all things unto God and the Father in the name of our Lord Jesus Christ.
**EPHESIANS 5:19–20 KJV**

Have no anxiety about anything, but in everything by prayer and supplication with thanksgiving let your requests be made known to God.
**PHILIPPIANS 4:6 RSV**

In everything give thanks: for this is the will of God in Christ Jesus concerning you.
**1 THESSALONIANS 5:18 KJV**

See also *Joy; Praise; Worship.*

## Thought

We have thought on thy steadfast love, O God, in the midst of thy temple.
**PSALM 48:9 RSV**

How precious to me are thy thoughts, O God! How vast is the sum of them! If I would count them, they are more than the sand. When I awake, I am still with thee.
**PSALM 139:17–18 RSV**

Search me, O God, and know my heart: try me, and know my thoughts. And see if there be any

wicked way in me, and lead me in the way everlasting.
PSALM 139:23–24 KJV

For my thoughts are not your thoughts, neither are your ways my ways, saith the Lord. For as the heavens are higher than the earth, so are my ways higher than your ways, and my thoughts than your thoughts.
ISAIAH 55:8–9 KJV

What think ye of Christ? whose son is he?
MATTHEW 22:42 KJV

For what person knows a man's thoughts except the spirit of the man which is in him? So also no one comprehends the thoughts of God except the Spirit of God.
1 CORINTHIANS 2:11 RSV

Brethren, do not be children in your thinking; be babes in evil, but in thinking be mature.
1 CORINTHIANS 14:20 RSV

We destroy arguments and every proud obstacle to the knowledge of God, and take every thought captive to obey Christ.
2 CORINTHIANS 10:5 RSV

Finally, brethren, whatsoever things are true, whatsoever things are honest, whatsoever things are just, whatsoever things are pure, whatsoever things are lovely, whatsoever things are of good report; if there be any virtue, and if there be any praise, think on these things.
PHILIPPIANS 4:8 KJV

See also *Meditation; Mind.*

# Time

And God said, Let there be lights in the firmament of the heaven to divide the day from the night; and let them be for signs, and for seasons, and for days, and years.
GENESIS 1:14 KJV

Remember the sabbath day, to keep it holy.
EXODUS 20:8 KJV

For everything there is a season, and a time for every matter under heaven: a time to be born, and a time to die.
ECCLESIASTES 3:1–2 RSV

'The time is fulfilled, and the kingdom of God is at hand; repent, and believe in the gospel.'
MARK 1:15 RSV

Jesus said to them, 'My time is not yet come, but your time is always here.'
JOHN 7:6 RSV

Jesus answered, 'Are there not twelve hours in the day? If any one walks in the day, he does not stumble, because he sees the light of this world.'
JOHN 11:9 RSV

He said to them, 'It is not for you to know times or seasons which the Father has fixed by his own authority.'
ACTS 1:7 RSV

[Jesus Christ] Whom the heaven must receive until the times of restitution of all things, which God hath spoken by the mouth of all his holy prophets since the world began.
ACTS 3:21 KJV

For he says, 'At the acceptable time I have listened to you, and helped you on the day of salvation.' Behold, now is the acceptable time; behold, now is the day of salvation.
2 CORINTHIANS 6:2 RSV

But when the time had fully come, God sent forth his Son, born of woman, born under the law, to redeem those who were under the law.
GALATIANS 4:4 RSV

Making the most of the time, because the days are evil.
EPHESIANS 5:16 RSV

Conduct yourselves wisely toward outsiders, making the most of the time.
COLOSSIANS 4:5 RSV

But do not ignore this one fact, beloved, that with the Lord one day is as a thousand years, and a thousand years as one day.
2 PETER 3:8 RSV

See also *Old age; Youth.*

# Tiredness

Of making many books there is no end; and much study is a weariness of the flesh.
ECCLESIASTES 12:12 KJV

Hast thou not known? hast thou not heard, that the everlasting God, the Lord, the Creator of the ends of the earth, fainteth not, neither is weary? There is no searching of his understanding. He giveth power to the faint; and to them that have no might he increaseth strength. Even youths shall faint and be weary, and the young men shall utterly fall: But they that wait upon the Lord shall renew their strength; they shall mount up with wings as eagles; they shall run, and not be weary; and they shall walk, and not faint.

ISAIAH 40:28–31 KJV

The Lord God hath given me the tongue of the learned, that I should know how to speak a word in season to him that is weary: he wakeneth morning by morning, he wakeneth mine ear to hear as the learned.

ISAIAH 50:4 KJV

'Come to me, all who labour and are heavy-laden, and I will give you rest.'

MATTHEW 11:28 RSV

Jesus, tired out by the journey, sat down by the well.

JOHN 4:6 GNB

So we do not lose heart. Though our outer nature is wasting away, our inner nature is being renewed every day.

2 CORINTHIANS 4:16 RSV

And let us not grow weary in well-doing, for in due season we shall reap, if we do not lose heart.

GALATIANS 6:9 RSV

Think of him [Jesus] who submitted to such opposition from sinners: that will help you not to lose heart and grow faint.

HEBREWS 12:3 NEB

See also *Power*.

# Tithing
See *Giving*.

# Tongues, gift of

### SPEAKING IN TONGUES

And they were all filled with the Holy Spirit and began to speak in other tongues, as the Spirit gave them utterance.

ACTS 2:4 RSV

And when Paul had laid his hands upon them, the Holy Spirit came on them; and they spoke with tongues and prophesied.

ACTS 19:6 RSV

Now you are the body of Christ and individually members of it. And God has appointed in the church first apostles, second prophets, third teachers, then workers of miracles, then . . . speakers in various kinds of tongues . . . Do all speak with tongues? . . . But earnestly desire the higher gifts.

1 CORINTHIANS 12:28, 30 RSV

If I speak in the tongues of men and of angels, but have not love, I am a noisy gong or a clanging cymbal . . . as for tongues, they will cease.

1 CORINTHIANS 13:1, 8 RSV

For one who speaks in a tongue speaks not to men but to God; for no one understands him, but he utters mysteries in the Spirit . . . He who speaks in a tongue edifies himself, but he who prophesies edifies the church.

1 CORINTHIANS 14:2, 4 RSV

He who speaks in a tongue should pray for the power to interpret. For if I pray in a tongue, my spirit prays but my mind is unfruitful.

1 CORINTHIANS 14:13–14 RSV

I thank God that I speak in tongues more than all of you. But in the church I would rather speak five intelligible words to instruct others than ten thousand words in a tongue.

1 CORINTHIANS 14:18–19 NIV

We read in the Law: 'I will speak to this nation through men of strange tongues, and by the lips of foreigners; and even so they will not heed me, says the Lord.' Clearly then these 'strange tongues' are not intended as a sign for believers, but for unbelievers, whereas prophecy is designed not for unbelievers but for those who hold the faith.

1 CORINTHIANS 14:21–22 NEB

### INTERPRETATION

To another various kinds of tongues, to another the interpretation of tongues.

1 CORINTHIANS 12:10 RSV

He who prophesies is greater than one who speaks in tongues, unless some one interprets, so that the church may be edified.

1 CORINTHIANS 14:5 RSV

If anyone speaks in a tongue, two—or at the most three—should speak, one at a time, and someone must interpret. If there is no interpreter, the speaker should keep quiet in the church and speak to himself and God.

1 CORINTHIANS 14:27–28 NIV

## Transfiguration

See Matthew 17:1–8

## Trinity

Hear, O Israel: The Lord our God is one Lord . . .

DEUTERONOMY 6:4 KJV

And when Jesus was baptized, he went up immediately from the water, and behold, the heavens were opened and he saw the Spirit of God descending like a dove, and alighting on him; and lo, a voice from heaven, saying, 'This is my beloved Son, with whom I am well pleased.'

MATTHEW 3:16–17 RSV

'Go therefore and make disciples of all nations, baptizing them in the name of the Father and of the Son and of the Holy Spirit . . .'

MATTHEW 28:19 RSV

Now there are varieties of gifts, but the same Spirit; and there are varieties of service, but the same Lord; and there are varieties of working, but it is the same God who inspires them all in every one.

1 CORINTHIANS 12:4–6 RSV

The grace of the Lord Jesus Christ, the love of God, and the fellowship of the Holy Spirit be with you all.

2 CORINTHIANS 13:14 GNB

There is one body and one Spirit, just as you were called to the one hope that belongs to your call, one Lord, one faith, one baptism, one God and Father of us all, who is above all and through all and in all.

EPHESIANS 4:4–6 RSV

Elect according to the foreknowledge of God the Father, through sanctification of the Spirit, unto obedience and sprinkling of the blood of Jesus Christ: Grace unto you, and peace, be multiplied.

1 PETER 1:2 KJV

## Trust

See *Faith*.

## Truth

'But you, Lord, are the true God, you are the living God and the eternal king.'

JEREMIAH 10:10 GNB

And the Word was made flesh, and dwelt among us . . .

JOHN 1:14 KJV

But he who does what is true comes to the light, that it may be clearly seen that his deeds have been wrought in God.

JOHN 3:21 RSV

Jesus then said to the Jews who had believed in him, 'If you continue in my word, you are truly my disciples, and you will know the truth, and the truth will make you free.'

JOHN 8:31–32 RSV

Jesus saith unto him, I am the way, the truth, and the life: no man cometh unto the Father, but by me.

JOHN 14:6 KJV

'When the Spirit of truth comes, he will guide you into all the truth; for he will not speak on his own authority, but whatever he hears he will speak, and he will declare to you the things that are to come.'

JOHN 16:13 RSV

Sanctify them through thy truth: thy word is truth.

JOHN 17:17 KJV

Pilate said to him, 'What is truth?'

JOHN 18:38 RSV

Rather, speaking the truth in love, we are to grow up in every way into him who is the head, into Christ.

EPHESIANS 4:15 RSV

Stand therefore, having your loins girt about with truth . . .

EPHESIANS 6:14 KJV

The household of God, which is the church of the living God, the pillar and bulwark of the truth.

1 TIMOTHY 3:15 RSV

Do your best to present yourself to God as one approved, a workman who has no need to be ashamed, rightly handling the word of truth.

2 TIMOTHY 2:15 RSV

## Unbelief

They [the children of Israel] spoke against God, saying, 'Can God spread a table in the wilderness?' . . . In spite of all this they still sinned; despite his wonders they did not believe.
PSALM 78:19, 32 RSV

And he did not do many mighty works there, because of their unbelief.
MATTHEW 13:58 RSV

'O unbelieving and perverse generation,' Jesus replied, 'how long shall I stay with you? How long shall I put up with you?'
MATTHEW 17:17 NIV

He was amazed at their lack of faith.
MARK 6:6 JB

And Jesus said to him, ' . . . All things are possible to him who believes.' Immediately the father of the child cried out and said, 'I believe; help my unbelief!'
MARK 9:23–24 RSV

Afterwards he appeared to the eleven themselves as they sat at table; and he upbraided them for their unbelief and hardness of heart, because they had not believed those who saw him after he had risen.
MARK 16:14 RSV

'The ones along the path are those who have heard; then the devil comes and takes away the word from their hearts, that they may not believe and be saved.'
LUKE 8:12 RSV

'He [the Holy Spirit] will convince the world . . . concerning sin, because they do not believe in me.'
JOHN 16:8–9 RSV

But he [Thomas] said to them, 'Unless I see in his hands the print of the nails, and place my finger in the mark of the nails, and place my hand in his side, I will not believe' . . . Then he said to Thomas, 'Put your finger here, and see my hands; and put out your hand, and place it in my side; do not be faithless, but believing.'
JOHN 20:25, 27 RSV

See to it, brothers, that none of you has a sinful, unbelieving heart that turns away from the living God.
HEBREWS 3:12 NIV

See also *Doubt; Faith; Hardness.*

## Unbeliever

He who believes in him is not condemned; he who does not believe is condemned already, because he has not believed in the name of the only Son of God. And this is the judgment, that the light has come into the world, and men loved darkness rather than light, because their deeds were evil.
JOHN 3:18–19 RSV

'I told you that you would die in your sins, for you will die in your sins unless you believe that I am he.'
JOHN 8:24 RSV

For although they knew God they did not honour him as God or give thanks to him, but they became futile in their thinking and their senseless minds were darkened.
ROMANS 1:21 RSV

The man without the Spirit does not accept the things that come from the Spirit of God, for they are foolishness to him and he cannot understand them, because they are spiritually discerned.
1 CORINTHIANS 2:14 NIV

In their case the god of this world has blinded the minds of the unbelievers, to keep them from seeing the light of the gospel of the glory of Christ, who is the likeness of God.
2 CORINTHIANS 4:4 RSV

Be ye not unequally yoked together with unbelievers: for what fellowship hath righteousness with unrighteousness? and what communion hath light with darkness?
2 CORINTHIANS 6:14 KJV

As for you, you were dead in your transgressions and sins, in which you used to live when you followed the ways of this world and of the ruler of the kingdom of the air, the spirit who is now at work in those who are disobedient. All of us also lived among them at one time, gratifying the cravings of our sinful nature and following its desires and thoughts. Like the rest, we were by nature objects of wrath.
EPHESIANS 2:1–3 NIV

Remember that you were at that time separated from Christ, alienated from the commonwealth of Israel, and strangers to the covenants of promise, having no hope and without God in the world.

EPHESIANS 2:12 RSV

He that hath the Son hath life; and he that hath not the Son of God hath not life.

1 JOHN 5:12 KJV

See also *Godless; Sin.*

## Understanding

Be not like a horse or a mule, without understanding, which must be curbed with bit and bridle.

PSALM 32:9 RSV

Beg for knowledge; plead for insight. Look for it as hard as you would for silver or some hidden treasure. If you do, you will know what it means to fear the Lord and you will succeed in learning about God. It is the Lord who gives wisdom; from him come knowledge and understanding.

PROVERBS 2:3–6 GNB

Trust in the Lord with all thine heart; and lean not unto thine own understanding.

PROVERBS 3:5 KJV

'The fear of the Lord is the beginning of wisdom, and knowledge of the Holy One is understanding.'

PROVERBS 9:10 NIV

The Lord says, 'My people are stupid; they don't know me. They are like foolish children; they have no understanding. They are experts at doing what is evil, but failures at doing what is good.'

JEREMIAH 4:22 GNB

'When any one hears the word of the kingdom and does not understand it, the evil one comes and snatches away what is sown in his heart ... As for what was sown on good soil, this is he who hears the word and understands it; he indeed bears fruit, and yields, in one case a hundredfold, in another sixty, and in another thirty.'

MATTHEW 13:19, 23 RSV

So Philip ran to him, and heard him reading Isaiah the prophet, and asked, 'Do you understand what you are reading?' And he said, 'How can I, unless someone guides me?' And he invited Philip to come up and sit with him.

ACTS 8:30–31 RSV

Therefore do not be foolish, but understand what the will of the Lord is.

EPHESIANS 5:17 RSV

And the peace of God, which passes all understanding, will keep your hearts and your minds in Christ Jesus.

PHILIPPIANS 4:7 RSV

By faith we understand that the world was created by the word of God, so that what is seen was made out of things which do not appear.

HEBREWS 11:3 RSV

See also *Knowledge; Thought; Wisdom.*

## Unity

Behold, how good and how pleasant it is for brethren to dwell together in unity!

PSALM 133:1 KJV

And though a man might prevail against one who is alone, two will withstand him. A threefold cord is not quickly broken.

ECCLESIASTES 4:12 RSV

Can two walk together, except they be agreed?

AMOS 3:3 KJV

'Again I say to you, if two of you agree on earth about anything they ask, it will be done for them by my Father in heaven. For where two or three are gathered in my name, there am I in the midst of them.'

MATTHEW 18:19–20 RSV

[Jesus' prayer] 'That they may all be one; even as thou, Father, art in me, and I in thee, that they also may be in us, so that the world may believe that thou hast sent me.'

JOHN 17:21 RSV

Now the company of those who believed were of one heart and soul, and no one said that any of the things which he possessed was his own, but they had everything in common.

ACTS 4:32 RSV

Eager to maintain the unity of the Spirit in the bond of peace. There is one body and one Spirit, just as you were called to the one hope that belongs to your call, one Lord, one faith, one baptism, one God and Father of us all, who is above all and through all and in all.

EPHESIANS 4:3–6 RSV

Complete my joy by being of the same mind, having the same love, being in full accord and of one mind.
PHILIPPIANS 2:2 RSV

## Vengeance
See *Retaliation.*

## Victory

Fear not, for I am with you, be not dismayed, for I am your God; I will strengthen you, I will help you, I will uphold you with my victorious right hand.
ISAIAH 41:10 RSV

These things I have spoken unto you, that in me ye might have peace. In the world ye shall have tribulation: but be of good cheer; I have overcome the world.
JOHN 16:33 KJV

What then shall we say to this? If God is for us, who is against us? . . . No, in all these things we are more than conquerors through him who loved us.
ROMANS 8:31, 37 RSV

The God of peace will soon crush Satan under your feet.
ROMANS 16:20 RSV

But thanks be to God, which giveth us the victory through our Lord Jesus Christ.
1 CORINTHIANS 15:57 RSV

For the weapons of our warfare are not worldly but have divine power to destroy strongholds.
2 CORINTHIANS 10:4 RSV

He said to me, 'My grace is sufficient for you, for my power is made perfect in weakness.' I will all the more gladly boast of my weaknesses, that the power of Christ may rest upon me.
2 CORINTHIANS 12:9 RSV

He disarmed the principalities and powers and made a public exhibition of them, triumphing over them in him.
COLOSSIANS 2:15 RSV

He who is in you is greater than he who is in the world.
1 JOHN 4:4 RSV

For whatever is born of God overcomes the world; and this is the victory that overcomes the world, our faith.
1 JOHN 5:4 RSV

'And they have conquered him by the blood of the Lamb and by the word of their testimony, for they loved not their lives even unto death.'
REVELATION 12:11 RSV

See also *Endurance.*

## Vow

Then Jacob made a vow to the Lord: 'If you will be with me and protect me on the journey I am making and give me food and clothing, and if I return safely to my father's home, then you will be my God. This memorial stone which I have set up will be the place where you are worshipped, and I will give you a tenth of everything you give me.'
GENESIS 28:20–22 GNB

'When you make a vow to the Lord your God, you shall not be slack to pay it; for the Lord your God will surely require it of you, and it would be a sin in you. But if you refrain from vowing, it shall be no sin in you. You shall be careful to perform what has passed your lips, for you have voluntarily vowed to the Lord your God what you have promised with your mouth.'
DEUTERONOMY 23:21–23 RSV

From thee comes my praise in the great congregation; my vows I will pay before those who fear him.
PSALM 22:25 RSV

'Offer to God a sacrifice of thanksgiving, and pay your vows to the Most High.'
PSALM 50:14 RSV

It is dangerous to dedicate a gift rashly or to make a vow and have second thoughts.
PROVERBS 20:25 NEB

Keep your feasts, O Judah, fulfil your vows, for never again shall the wicked come against you, he is utterly cut off.
Nahum 1:15 RSV

See also *Blasphemy.*

## War

The Lord is a man of war.
EXODUS 15:3 KJV

'When you go forth to war against your enemies, and see horses and chariots and an army larger than your own, you shall not be afraid of them; for the Lord your God is with you, who brought you out of the land of Egypt.'

DEUTERONOMY 20:1 RSV

[Jehoshaphat's prayer] 'O our God, wilt thou not execute judgment upon them? For we are powerless against this great multitude that is coming against us. We do not know what to do, but our eyes are upon thee.'

2 CHRONICLES 20:12 RSV

Though an host should encamp against me, my heart shall not fear: though war should rise against me, in this will I be confident. One thing have I desired of the Lord, that will I seek after; that I may dwell in the house of the Lord all the days of my life.

PSALM 27:3–4 KJV

A king is not saved by his great army; a warrior is not delivered by his great strength.

PSALM 33:16 RSV

The Lord said, 'Assyria! I use Assyria like a club to punish those with whom I am angry. I sent Assyria to attack a godless nation, people who have made me angry.'

ISAIAH 10:5–6 GNB

'And you will hear of wars and rumours of wars; see that you are not alarmed; for this must take place, but the end is not yet. For nation will rise against nation, and kingdom against kingdom, and there will be famines and earthquakes in various places.'

MATTHEW 24:6–7 RSV

Who shall separate us from the love of Christ? Shall tribulation, or distress, or persecution, or famine, or nakedness, or peril, or sword? As it is written, 'For thy sake we are being killed all the day long; we are regarded as sheep to be slaughtered.' No, in all these things we are more than conquerors through him who loved us.

ROMANS 8:35–37 RSV

[The man in authority] is God's servant working for your own good. But if you do evil, then be afraid of him, because his power to punish is real. He is God's servant and carries out God's punishment on those who do evil.

ROMANS 13:4 GNB

What causes wars, and what causes fightings among you? Is it not your passions that are at war in your members?

JAMES 4:1 RSV

For 'Spiritual warfare' see also *Christian life, Continuing in the faith; Endurance.*

## Water

They shall not hurt nor destroy in all my holy mountain: for the earth shall be full of the knowledge of the Lord, as the waters cover the sea.

ISAIAH 11:9 KJV

With joy you will draw water from the wells of salvation.

ISAIAH 12:13 RSV

Ho, every one that thirsteth, come ye to the waters, and he that hath no money; come ye, buy, and eat.

ISAIAH 55:1 KJV

The Lord, the fountain of living waters.

JEREMIAH 17:13 KJV

'I will sprinkle clean water upon you, and you shall be clean from all your uncleannesses, and from all your idols I will cleanse you.'

EZEKIEL 36:25 RSV

[John the Baptist] 'I baptize you with water for repentance, but he who is coming after me is mightier than I, whose sandals I am not worthy to carry; he will baptize you with the Holy Spirit and with fire.'

MATTHEW 3:11 RSV

Jesus answered, Verily, verily, I say unto thee, Except a man be born of water and of the Spirit, he cannot enter into the kingdom of God.

JOHN 3:5 KJV

'Whoever drinks of the water that I shall give him will never thirst; the water that I shall give him will become in him a spring of water welling up to eternal life.'

JOHN 4:14 RSV

And Jesus said unto them, I am the bread of life: he that cometh to me shall never hunger; and he that believeth on me shall never thirst.

JOHN 6:35 KJV

On the last day of the feast, the great day, Jesus stood up and proclaimed, 'If any one thirst, let him come to me and drink. He who believes in me, as the scripture has said, ''Out of his heart shall flow rivers of living water.'' ' Now this he said about the Spirit, which those who believed in him were to receive; for as yet the Spirit had not been given, because Jesus was not yet glorified.

JOHN 7:37–39 RSV

Christ loved the church and gave himself up for her, that he might sanctify her, having cleansed her by the washing of water with the word.

EPHESIANS 5:25–26 RSV

He [God] saved us, not because of deeds done by us in righteousness, but in virtue of his own mercy, by the washing of regeneration and renewal in the Holy Spirit.

TITUS 3:5 RSV

Let us draw near with a true heart in full assurance of faith, with our hearts sprinkled clean from an evil conscience and our bodies washed with pure water.

HEBREWS 10:22 RSV

## Way

[David's song of victory] 'This God—his way is perfect; the promise of the Lord proves true; he is a shield for all those who take refuge in him.'

2 SAMUEL 22:31 RSV

For the Lord knows the way of the righteous, but the way of the wicked will perish.

PSALM 1:6 RSV

God and upright is the Lord; therefore he instructs sinners in the way. He leads the humble in what is right and teaches the humble his way.

PSALM 25:8–9 RSV

There is a way which seemeth right unto a man, but the end thereof are the ways of death.

PROVERBS 14:12 KJV

And though the Lord give you the bread of adversity, and the water of affliction, yet shall not thy teachers be removed into a corner any more, but thine eyes shall see thy teachers: and thine ears shall hear a word behind thee, saying, This is the way, walk ye in it, when ye turn to the right hand, and when ye turn to the left.

ISAIAH 30:20–21 KJV

Why sayest thou, O Jacob, and speakest, O Israel, My way is hid from the Lord, and my judgment is passed over from my God? Hast thou not known? hast thou not heard, that the everlasting God, the Lord, the Creator of the ends of the earth, fainteth not, neither is weary?

ISAIAH 40:27–28 KJV

'Say to them, As I live, says the Lord God, I have no pleasure in the death of the wicked, but that the wicked turn from his way and live; turn back, turn back from your evil ways; for why will you die, O house of Israel?' . . . 'Yet your people say, ''The way of the Lord is not just''; when it is their own way that is not just.'

EZEKIEL 33:11, 17 RSV

'Enter by the narrow gate; for the gate is wide and the way is easy, that leads to destruction, and those who enter by it are many. For the gate is narrow and the way is hard, that leads to life, and those who find it are few.'

MATTHEW 7:13–14 RSV

Jesus saith unto him, I am the way, the truth, and the life: no man cometh unto the Father, but by me.

JOHN 14:6 KJV

[Paul] 'I do admit this to you: I worship the God of our ancestors by following that Way which they [the Jews] say is false.'

ACTS 24:14 GNB

Therefore, brethren, since we have confidence to enter the sanctuary by the blood of Jesus, by the new and living way which he opened for us through the curtain, that is, through his flesh . . .

HEBREWS 10:19–20 RSV

See also *Guidance.*

## Weakness

Strengthen the weak hands, and make firm the feeble knees.

ISAIAH 35:3 RSV

'When my soul fainted within me, I remembered the Lord; and my prayer came to thee, into thy holy temple.'

JONAH 2:7 RSV

'Watch and pray that you may not enter into temptation; the spirit indeed is willing, but the flesh is weak.'

MATTHEW 26:41 RSV

'In all things I have shown you that by so toiling one must help the weak, remembering the words of the Lord Jesus, how he said, "It is more blessed to give than to receive." '
ACTS 20:35 RSV

Welcome the person who is weak in faith, but do not argue with him about his personal opinions.
ROMANS 14:1 GNB

We who are strong ought to bear with the failings of the weak, and not to please ourselves.
ROMANS 15:1 RSV

But God hath chosen the foolish things of the world to confound the wise; and God hath chosen the weak things of the world to confound the things which are mighty.
1 CORINTHIANS 1:27 KJV

Be careful, however, not to let your freedom of action make those who are weak in the faith fall into sin.
1 CORINTHIANS 8:9 GNB

To the weak I became weak, that I might win the weak. I have become all things to all men, that I might by all means save some.
1 CORINTHIANS 9:22 RSV

It is sown in dishonour, it is raised in glory. It is sown in weakness, it is raised in power.
1 CORINTHIANS 15:43 RSV

But he said to me, 'My grace is sufficient for you, for my power is made perfect in weakness.' I will all the more gladly boast of my weaknesses, that the power of Christ may rest upon me.
2 CORINTHIANS 12:9 RSV

For he was crucified in weakness, but lives by the power of God. For we are weak in him, but in dealing with you we shall live with him by the power of God.
2 CORINTHIANS 13:4 RSV

See also *Power*.

## Widows

'He executes justice for the fatherless and the widow, and loves the sojourner, giving him food and clothing.'
DEUTERONOMY 10:18 RSV

'The Levite, because he has no portion or inheritance with you, and the ... widow, who are within your towns, shall come and eat and be filled; that the Lord your God may bless you in all the work of your hands that you do.'
DEUTERONOMY 14:29 RSV

The Lord watches over the sojourners, he upholds the widow and the fatherless; but the way of the wicked he brings to ruin.
PSALM 146:9 RSV

Seek justice, encourage the oppressed. Defend the cause of the fatherless, plead the case of the widow.
ISAIAH 1:17 NIV

And he sat down opposite the treasury, and watched the multitude putting money into the treasury. Many rich people put in large sums. And a poor widow came, and put in two copper coins, which make a penny. And he called his disciples to him, and said to them, 'Truly, I say to you, this poor widow has put in more than all those who are contributing to the treasury. For they all contributed out of their abundance; but she out of her poverty has put in everything she had, her whole living.'
MARK 12:41–44 RSV

There was a very old prophetess, a widow named Anna, daughter of Phanuel of the tribe of Asher. She had been married for only seven years and was now eighty-four years old. She never left the Temple; day and night she worshipped God, fasting and praying.
LUKE 2:36–37 GNB

Now in these days when the disciples were increasing in number, the Hellenists murmured against the Hebrews because their widows were neglected in the daily distribution.
ACTS 6:1 RSV

A wife is bound to her husband as long as he lives. If the husband dies, she is free to be married to whom she wishes, only in the Lord.
1 CORINTHIANS 7:39 RSV

A widow who is all alone, with no one to take care of her, has placed her hope in God and continues to pray and ask him for his help night and day.
1 TIMOTHY 5:5 GNB

[A widow] ... well known for her good deeds, such as bringing up children, showing hospitality, washing the feet of the saints, helping those in trouble and devoting herself to all kinds of good deeds.
1 TIMOTHY 5:10 NIV

They [young widows] also learn to waste their time in going round from house to house; but even worse, they learn to be gossips and busybodies, talking of things they should not. So I would prefer that the younger widows get married, have children, and take care of their homes, so as to give our enemies no chance of speaking evil of us.

**1 TIMOTHY 5:13–14 GNB**

Religion that is pure and undefiled before God and the Father is this: to visit orphans and widows in their affliction, and to keep oneself unstained from the world.

**JAMES 1:27 RSV**

## Wife

See *Marriage*.

## Will of God

'I delight to do thy will, O my God; thy law is within my heart.'

**PSALM 40:8 RSV**

Yet it pleased the Lord to bruise him; he hath put him to grief: when thou shalt make his soul an offering for sin, he shall see his seed, he shall prolong his days, and the pleasure of the Lord shall prosper in his hand.

**ISAIAH 53:10 KJV**

Jesus said to them, 'My food is to do the will of him who sent me, and to accomplish his work.'

**JOHN 4:34 RSV**

And be not conformed to this world: but be ye transformed by the renewing of your mind, that ye may prove what is that good, and acceptable, and perfect, will of God.

**ROMANS 12:2 KJV**

He made known to us the mystery of his will according to his good pleasure, which he purposed in Christ, to be put into effect when the times will have reached their fulfilment—to bring all things in heaven and on earth together under one head, even Christ.

**EPHESIANS 1:9–10 NIV**

Therefore do not be foolish, but understand what the will of the Lord is.

**EPHESIANS 5:17 RSV**

For this is the will of God, your sanctification: that you abstain from unchastity.

**1 THESSALONIANS 4:3 RSV**

Rejoice evermore. Pray without ceasing. In every thing give thanks: for this is the will of God in Christ Jesus concerning you.

**1 THESSALONIANS 5:16–18 KJV**

And the world passeth away, and the lust thereof: but he that doeth the will of God abideth for ever.

**1 JOHN 2:17 KJV**

And this is his commandment, that we should believe in the name of his Son Jesus Christ and love one another, just as he has commanded us.

**1 JOHN 3:23 RSV**

See also *Accepting the will of God; Guidance.*

## Wisdom

And God gave Solomon wisdom and understanding beyond measure, and largeness of mind like the sand on the seashore, so that Solomon's wisdom surpassed the wisdom of all the people of the east, and all the wisdom of Egypt.

**1 KINGS 4:29–30 RSV**

The fear of the Lord is the beginning of wisdom: a good understanding have all they that do his commandments: his praise endureth for ever.

**PSALM 111:10 KJV**

Happy is the man who finds wisdom, and the man who gets understanding ... She [wisdom] is more precious than jewels, and nothing you desire can compare with her. Long life is in her right hand; in her left hand are riches and honour. Her ways are ways of pleasantness, and all her paths are peace. She is a tree of life to those who lay hold of her.

**PROVERBS 3:13, 15–18 RSV**

And the spirit of the Lord shall rest upon him, the spirit of wisdom and understanding, the spirit of counsel and might, the spirit of knowledge and of the fear of the Lord.

**ISAIAH 11:2 KJV**

'Every one then who hears these words of mine and does them will be like a wise man who built his house upon the rock.'

**MATTHEW 7:24 RSV**

'Behold, I send you out as sheep in the midst of wolves; so be wise as serpents and innocent as doves.'

**MATTHEW 10:16 RSV**

'The Son of man came eating and drinking, and they say, ''Behold, a glutton and a drunkard, a friend of tax collectors and sinners!'' Yet wisdom is justified by her deeds.'
MATTHEW 11:19 RSV

And Jesus increased in wisdom and in stature, and in favour with God and man.
LUKE 2:52 RSV

And the lord commended the unjust steward, because he had done wisely: for the children of this world are in their generation wiser than the children of light.
LUKE 16:8 KJV

'Therefore, brethren, pick out from among you seven men of good repute, full of the Spirit and wisdom, whom we may appoint to this duty.'
ACTS 6:3 RSV

O the depth of the riches both of the wisdom and knowledge of God! how unsearchable are his judgments, and his ways past finding out!
ROMANS 11:33 KJV

For after that in the wisdom of God the world by wisdom knew not God, it pleased God by the foolishness of preaching to save them that believe.
1 CORINTHIANS 1:21 KJV

He is the source of your life in Christ Jesus, whom God made our wisdom . . .
1 CORINTHIANS 1:30 RSV

Yet I do proclaim a message of wisdom to those who are spiritually mature. But it is not the wisdom that belongs to this world or to the powers that rule this world—powers that are losing their power. The wisdom I proclaim is God's secret wisdom, which is hidden from mankind, but which he had already chosen for our glory even before the world was made.
1 CORINTHIANS 2:6–7 GNB

To one is given through the Spirit the utterance of wisdom . . .
1 CORINTHIANS 12:8 RSV

[Paul's prayer] That the God of our Lord Jesus Christ, the Father of glory, may give you a spirit of wisdom and of revelation in the knowledge of him.
EPHESIANS 1:17 RSV

[Christ] in whom are hid all the treasures of wisdom and knowledge.
COLOSSIANS 2:3 RSV

If any of you lacks wisdom, let him ask God, who gives to all men generously and without reproaching, and it will be given him.
JAMES 1:5 RSV

But the wisdom from above is first pure, then peaceable, gentle, open to reason, full of mercy and good fruits, without uncertainty or insincerity.
JAMES 3:17 RSV

See also *Fool; Knowledge; Understanding.*

## Witness

And I heard the voice of the Lord saying, 'Whom shall I send, and who will go for us?' Then I said, 'Here I am! Send me.'
ISAIAH 6:8 RSV

[Jesus to Simon Peter and Andrew] And he said to them, 'Follow me, and I will make you fishers of men.'
MATTHEW 4:19 RSV

Then he said to his disciples, 'The harvest is plentiful, but the labourers are few; pray therefore the Lord of the harvest to send out labourers into his harvest.'
MATTHEW 9:37–38 RSV

'Go therefore and make disciples of all nations, baptizing them in the name of the Father and of the Son and of the Holy Spirit, teaching them to observe all that I have commanded you; and lo, I am with you always, to the close of the age.'
MATTHEW 28:19–20 RSV

And [Jesus] said unto them, Thus it is written, and thus it behoved Christ to suffer, and to rise from the dead the third day: and that repentance and remission of sins should be preached in his name among all nations, beginning at Jerusalem. And ye are witnesses of these things.
LUKE 24:46–48 KJV

'But when the Counsellor comes, whom I shall send to you from the Father, even the Spirit of truth, who proceeds from the Father, he will bear witness to me; and you also are witnesses, because you have been with me from the beginning.'
JOHN 15:26–27 RSV

'But you shall receive power when the Holy Spirit has come upon you; and you shall be my witnesses in Jerusalem and in all Judea and Samaria and to the end of the earth.'
ACTS 1:8 RSV

[Peter and John] 'We cannot but speak of what we have seen and heard.'
ACTS 4:20 RSV

So we are ambassadors for Christ, God making his appeal through us. We beseech you on behalf of Christ, be reconciled to God.
2 CORINTHIANS 5:20 RSV

[Paul asks for prayer] That utterance may be given unto me, that I may open my mouth boldly, to make known the mystery of the gospel.
EPHESIANS 6:19 KJV

See also *Evangelists; Preaching.*

# Woman

And the Lord God said, It is not good that the man should be alone; I will make him an help meet for him ... And the Lord God caused a deep sleep to fall upon Adam, and he slept: and he took one of his ribs, and closed up the flesh instead thereof. And the rib, which the Lord God had taken from man, made a woman, and brought her unto the man. And Adam said, This is now bone of my bones, and flesh of my flesh: she shall be called Woman, because she was taken out of Man.
GENESIS 2:18, 21–23 KJV

Unto the woman he said, I will greatly multiply thy sorrow and thy conception; in sorrow thou shalt bring forth children; and thy desire shall be to thy husband, and he shall rule over thee.
GENESIS 3:16 KJV

And Adam called his wife's name Eve; because she was the mother of all living.
GENESIS 3:20 KJV

There were also many women there, looking on from afar, who had followed Jesus from Galilee, ministering to him.
MATTHEW 27:55 RSV

Now when he rose early on the first day of the week, he appeared first to Mary Magdalene, from whom he had cast out seven demons.
MARK 16:9 RSV

She [Elizabeth] exclaimed with a loud cry, 'Blessed are you among women, and blessed is the fruit of your womb!'
LUKE 1:42 RSV

Many of the Samaritans in that town believed in Jesus because the woman had said, 'He told me everything I have ever done.'
JOHN 4:39 GNB

But I want you to understand that the head of every man is Christ, the head of a woman is her husband, and the head of Christ is God.
1 CORINTHIANS 11:3 RSV

For man was not made from woman, but woman from man.
1 CORINTHIANS 11:8 RSV

As in all the churches of the saints, the women should keep silence in the churches. For they are not permitted to speak, but should be subordinate, as even the law says.
1 CORINTHIANS 14:33–34 RSV

There is neither Jew nor Greek, there is neither bond nor free, there is neither male nor female: for ye are all one in Christ Jesus.
GALATIANS 3:28 KJV

Let a woman learn in silence with all submissiveness. I permit no woman to teach or to have authority over men; she is to keep silent ... the woman was deceived and became a transgressor. Yet woman will be saved through bearing children, if she continues in faith and love and holiness, with modesty.
1 TIMOTHY 2:11–12, 14–15 RSV

See also *Man.*

# Word of God
See *Bible; Jesus Christ.*

# Work

And the Lord God took the man, and put him into the garden of Eden to dress it and to keep it.
GENESIS 2:15 KJV

In the sweat of thy face shalt thou eat bread, till thou return unto the ground.
GENESIS 3:19 KJV

Six days shalt thou labour, and do all thy work: but the seventh day is the sabbath of the Lord thy God: in it thou shalt not do any work.
EXODUS 20:9–10

Man goes forth to his work and to his labour until the evening.

**PSALM 104:23 RSV**

Except the Lord build the house, they labour in vain that build it: except the Lord keep the city, the watchman waketh but in vain.

**PSALM 127:1 KJV**

Commit your work to the Lord, and your plans will be established.

**PROVERBS 16:3 RSV**

Whatsoever thy hand findeth to do, do it with thy might; for there is no work, nor device, nor knowledge, nor wisdom, in the grave, whither thou goest.

**ECCLESIASTES 9:10 KJV**

'For the kingdom of heaven is like a householder who went out early in the morning to hire labourers for his vineyard.'

**MATTHEW 20:1 RSV**

The labourer is worthy of his hire.

**LUKE 10:7 KJV**

Slaves, obey your human masters with fear and trembling; and do it with a sincere heart, as though you were serving Christ. Do this not only when they are watching you, because you want to gain their approval; but with all your heart do what God wants, as slaves of Christ. Do your work as slaves cheerfully, as though you served the Lord, and not merely men. Remember that the Lord will reward everyone, whether slave or free, for the good work he does. Masters, behave in the same way towards your slaves and stop using threats. Remember that you and your slaves belong to the same Master in heaven, who judges everyone by the same standard.

**EPHESIANS 6:5–9 GNB**

And whatsoever ye do in word or deed, do all in the name of the Lord Jesus, giving thanks to God and the Father by him.

**COLOSSIANS 3:17 KJV**

If any one does not provide for his relatives, and especially for his own family, he has disowned the faith and is worse than an unbeliever.

**1 TIMOTHY 5:8 RSV**

The scripture says, 'You shall not muzzle an ox when it is treading out the grain,' and 'The labourer deserves his wages.'

**1 TIMOTHY 5:18 RSV**

See also *Laziness.*

# Works, good

Let your light so shine before men, that they may see your good works, and glorify your Father which is in heaven.

**MATTHEW 5:16 KJV**

'Why do you call me, "Lord, Lord," and yet don't do what I tell you?'

**LUKE 6:46 GNB**

Then they said to him, 'What must we do, to be doing the works of God?' Jesus answered them, 'This is the work of God, that you believe in him whom he has sent.'

**JOHN 6:28–29 RSV**

'I turned first to the inhabitants of Damascus, and then to Jerusalem and all the country of Judaea, and to the Gentiles, and sounded the call to repent and turn to God, and to prove their repentance by deeds.'

**ACTS 26:20 NEB**

Therefore, my beloved brethren, be steadfast, immovable, always abounding in the work of the Lord, knowing that in the Lord your labour is not in vain.

**1 CORINTHIANS 15:58 RSV**

For by grace are ye saved through faith; and that not of yourselves: it is the gift of God: not of works, lest any man should boast. For we are his workmanship, created in Christ Jesus unto good works, which God hath before ordained that we should walk in them.

**EPHESIANS 2:8–10 KJV**

[The purpose of scripture] That the man of God may be complete, equipped for every good work.

**2 TIMOTHY 3:17 RSV**

Let us consider how to stir up one another to love and good works.

**HEBREWS 10:24 RSV**

But be ye doers of the word, and not hearers only, deceiving your own selves.

**JAMES 1:22 KJV**

What does it profit, my brethren, if a man says he has faith but has not works? Can his faith save him? . . . Faith by itself, if it has no works, is dead. But some one will say, 'You have faith and I have works.' Show me your faith apart from your works, and I by my works will show you my faith.

JAMES 2:14, 17–18 RSV

You see that a man is justified by works and not by faith alone.

JAMES 2:24 RSV

For as the body apart from the spirit is dead, so faith apart from works is dead.

JAMES 2:26 RSV

See also **Service.**

# World

### CREATED UNIVERSE

The earth is the Lord's and the fullness thereof, the world and those who dwell therein.

PSALM 24:1 RSV

'The God who made the world and everything in it, being Lord of heaven and earth, does not live in shrines made by man.'

ACTS 17:24 RSV

[The Son] He is the one through whom God created the universe.

HEBREWS 1:2 GNB

See also **Creation.**

### MAN

For God so loved the world, that he gave his only begotten Son, that whosoever believeth in him should not perish, but have everlasting life. For God sent not his Son into the world to condemn the world; but that the world through him might be saved.

JOHN 3:16–17 KJV

### MAN REBELLING AGAINST GOD

'If the world hates you, just remember that it has hated me first. If you belonged to the world, then the world would love you as its own. But I chose you from this world, and you do not belong to it; that is why the world hates you.'

JOHN 15:18–19 GNB

'And now I am no more in the world, but they are in the world, and I am coming to thee. Holy Father, keep them in thy name which thou hast given me, that they may be one, even as we are one.'

JOHN 17:11 RSV

They are not of the world, even as I am not of the world.

JOHN 17:16 KJV

Love not the world, neither the things that are in the world. If any man love the world, the love of the Father is not in him. For all that is in the world, the lust of the flesh, and the lust of the eyes, and the pride of life, is not of the Father, but is of the world. And the world passeth away, and the lust thereof: but he that doeth the will of God abideth for ever.

1 JOHN 2:15–17 KJV

# Worry

See **Comfort, when anxious.**

# Worship

Thou shalt have no other gods before me. Thou shalt not make unto thee any graven image, or any likeness of any thing that is in heaven above, or that is in the earth beneath, or that is in the water under the earth.

EXODUS 20:3–4 KJV

Give unto the Lord the glory due unto his name: bring an offering, and come before him: worship the Lord in the beauty of holiness.

1 CHRONICLES 16:29 KJV

O come, let us worship, and fall down, and kneel before the Lord our Maker.

PSALM 95:6 BCP

And when they were come into the house, they saw the young child with Mary his mother, and fell down, and worshipped him: and when they had opened their treasures, they presented unto him gifts; gold, and frankincense, and myrrh.

MATTHEW 2:11 KJV

It is written, Thou shalt worship the Lord thy God, and him only shalt thou serve.

MATTHEW 4:10 KJV

'But the hour is coming, and now is, when the true worshippers will worship the Father in spirit and truth, for such the Father seeks to worship him. God is spirit, and those who worship him must worship in spirit and truth.'

JOHN 4:23–24 RSV

Day after day they met as a group in the Temple, and they had their meals together in their homes, eating with glad and humble hearts, praising

God, and enjoying the good will of all the people. And every day the Lord added to their group those who were being saved.

**ACTS 2:46–47 GNB**

At the name of Jesus every knee should bow, in heaven and on earth and under the earth.

**PHILIPPIANS 2:10 RSV**

Lead a life worthy of the Lord, fully pleasing to him, bearing fruit in every good work and increasing in the knowledge of God.

**COLOSSIANS 1:10 RSV**

Let the word of Christ dwell in you richly in all wisdom; teaching and admonishing one another in psalms and hymns and spiritual songs, singing with grace in your hearts to the Lord. And whatsoever ye do in word or deed, do all in the name of the Lord Jesus, giving thanks to God and the Father by him.

**COLOSSIANS 3:16–17 KJV**

Thou art worthy, O Lord, to receive glory and honour and power: for thou hast created all things, and for thy pleasure they are and were created.

**REVELATION 4:11 KJV**

See also *Praise; Reverence; Service.*

## Youth

Honour thy father and thy mother: that thy days may be long upon the land which the Lord thy God giveth thee.

**EXODUS 20:12 KJV**

Would you like to enjoy life? Do you want long life and happiness? Then hold back from speaking evil and from telling lies. Turn away from evil and do good; strive for peace with all your heart.

**PSALM 34:12–14 GNB**

How can a young man keep his way pure? By guarding it according to thy word.

**PSALM 119:9 RSV**

A foolish son brings grief to his father and bitter regrets to his mother.

**PROVERBS 17:25 GNB**

Remember now thy Creator in the days of thy youth, while the evil days come not, nor the years draw nigh, when thou shalt say, I have no pleasure in them.

**ECCLESIASTES 12:1 KJV**

Even youths shall faint and be weary, and the young men shall utterly fall: But they that wait upon the Lord shall renew their strength.

**ISAIAH 40:30–31 KJV**

It is good for a man that he bear the yoke in his youth.

**LAMENTATIONS 3:27 RSV**

Jesus said unto him [the rich young ruler], If thou wilt be perfect, go and sell that thou hast, and give to the poor, and thou shalt have treasure in heaven: and come and follow me.

**MATTHEW 19:21 KJV**

And he said, A certain man had two sons: and the younger of them said to his father, Father, give me the portion of goods that falleth to me. And he divided unto them his living. And not many days after the younger son gathered all together, and took his journey into a far country, and there wasted his substance with riotous living. And when he had spent all, there arose a mighty famine in that land; and he began to be in want. And he went and joined himself to a citizen of that country; and he sent him into his fields to feed swine. And he would fain have filled his belly with the husks that the swine did eat: and no man gave unto him. And when he came to himself, he said, How many hired servants of my father's have bread enough and to spare, and I perish with hunger! I will arise and go to my father, and will say unto him, Father, I have sinned against heaven, and before thee, and am no more worthy to be called thy son: make me as one of thy hired servants. And he arose, and came to his father. But when he was yet a great way off, his father saw him, and had compassion, and ran, and fell on his neck, and kissed him. And the son said unto him, Father, I have sinned against heaven, and in thy sight, and am no more worthy to be called thy son. But the father said to his servants, Bring forth the best robe, and put it on him; and put a ring on his hand, and shoes on his feet: and bring hither the fatted calf, and kill it; and let us eat, and be merry: for this my son was dead, and is alive again; he was lost, and is found. And they began to be merry.

**LUKE 15:11–24 KJV**

Let no one despise your youth, but set the believers an example in speech and conduct, in love, in faith, in purity.

**1 TIMOTHY 4:12 RSV**

Avoid the passions of youth, and strive for righteousness, faith, love, and peace, together with those who with a pure heart call out to the Lord for help.

2 TIMOTHY 2:22 GNB

I write to you, young men, because you are strong, and the word of God abides in you, and you have overcome the evil one.

1 JOHN 2:14 RSV

See also *Family*.

# Zeal

For zeal for thy house has consumed me, and the insults of those who insult thee have fallen on me.

PSALM 69:9 RSV

For I can testify about them [the Israelites] that they are zealous for God, but their zeal is not based on knowledge. Since they did not know the righteousness that comes from God and sought to establish their own, they did not submit to God's righteousness.

ROMANS 10:2–3 NIV

Never flag in zeal, be aglow with the Spirit, serve the Lord.

ROMANS 12:11 RSV

For necessity is laid upon me. Woe to me if I do not preach the gospel!

1 CORINTHIANS 9:16 RSV

Therefore, my beloved brethren, be ye steadfast, unmoveable, always abounding in the work of the Lord, forasmuch as ye know that your labour is not in vain in the Lord.

1 CORINTHIANS 15:58 RSV

And let us not grow weary in well-doing, for in due season we shall reap, if we do not lose heart. So then, as we have opportunity, let us do good to all men, and especially to those who are of the household of faith.

GALATIANS 6:9–10 RSV

As to zeal a persecutor of the church, as to righteousness under the law blameless. But whatever gain I had, I counted as loss for the sake of Christ.

PHILIPPIANS 3:6–7 RSV

I press on toward the goal for the prize of the upward call of God in Christ Jesus.

PHILIPPIANS 3:14 RSV

[Jesus Christ] who gave himself for us to redeem us from all iniquity and to purify for himself a people of his own who are zealous for good works.

TITUS 2:14 RSV

Now that by your obedience to the truth you have purified yourselves and have come to have a sincere love for your fellow-believers, love one another earnestly with all your heart.

1 PETER 1:22 GNB

Beloved, being very eager to write to you of our common salvation, I found it necessary to write appealing to you to contend for the faith which was once for all delivered to the saints.

JUDE 3 RSV

' ''Those whom I love, I reprove and chasten; so be zealous and repent.'' '

REVELATION 3:19 RSV

# Part 2

BOOK BY BOOK

# OLD TESTAMENT

## Genesis

In the beginning God created the heaven and the earth. And the earth was without form, and void; and darkness was upon the face of the deep. And the Spirit of God moved upon the face of the waters. And God said, Let there be light: and there was light.

1:1–3 KJV

And God said, Let us make man in our image, after our likeness: and let them have dominion over the fish of the sea, and over the fowl of the air, and over the cattle, and over all the earth, and over every creeping thing that creepeth upon the earth. So God created man in his own image, in the image of God created he him; male and female created he them. And God blessed them, and God said unto them, Be fruitful and multiply, and replenish the earth, and subdue it: and have dominion over the fish of the sea, and over the fowl of the air, and over every living thing that moveth upon the earth.

1:26–28 KJV

And God saw everything that he had made, and, behold, it was very good. And the evening and morning were the sixth day.

GENESIS 1:31 KJV

And the Lord God formed man of the dust of the ground, and breathed into his nostrils the breath of life; and man became a living soul. And the Lord God planted a garden eastward in Eden; and there he put the man whom he had formed. And out of the ground made the Lord God to grow every tree that is pleasant to the sight, and good for food; the tree of life also in the midst of the garden, and the tree of knowledge of good and evil.

2:7–9 KJV

And the Lord God took the man, and put him into the garden of Eden to dress it and to keep it. And the Lord God commanded the man, saying, Of every tree of the garden thou mayest freely eat: but of the tree of the knowledge of good and evil, thou shalt not eat of it: for in the day that thou

eatest thereof thou shalt surely die. And the Lord God said, It is not good that the man should be alone; I will make him an help meet for him.

2:15–18 KJV

And the Lord God caused a deep sleep to fall upon Adam, and he slept: and he took one of his ribs, and closed up the flesh instead thereof. And the rib, which the Lord God had taken from man, made he a woman, and brought her unto the man. And Adam said, This is now bone of my bones, and flesh of my flesh: she shall be called Woman, because she was taken out of Man. Therefore shall a man leave his father and his mother, and shall cleave unto his wife: and they shall be one flesh. And they were both naked, the man and his wife, and were not ashamed. Now the serpent was more subtil than any beast of the field which the Lord God had made. And he said unto the woman, Yea, hath God said, Ye shall not eat of every tree of the garden? And the woman said unto the serpent, We may eat of the fruit of the trees of the garden: but of the fruit of the tree which is in the midst of the garden, God hath said, Ye shall not eat of it, neither shall ye touch it, lest ye die. And the serpent said unto the woman, Ye shall not surely die: for God doth know that in the day ye eat thereof, then your eyes shall be opened, and ye shall be as gods, knowing good and evil. And when the woman saw that the tree was good for food, and that it was pleasant to the eyes, and a tree to be desired to make one wise, she took of the fruit thereof, and did eat, and gave also unto her husband with her; and he did eat. And the eyes of them both were opened, and they knew that they were naked; and they sewed fig leaves together, and made themselves aprons. And they heard the voice of the Lord God walking in the garden in the cool of the day: and Adam and his wife hid themselves from the presence of the Lord God amongst the trees of the garden. And the Lord God called unto Adam, and said unto him, Where art thou? And he said, I heard thy voice in the garden, and I was afraid, because I was naked; and I hid myself.

2:21–3:10 KJV

And the Lord God said unto the woman, What is this that thou hast done? And the woman said, The serpent beguiled me, and I did eat. And the Lord God said unto the serpent, Because thou hast done this, thou art cursed above all cattle, and above every beast of the field; upon thy belly shalt thou go, and dust shalt thou eat all the days of thy life. And I will put enmity between thee and the woman, and between thy seed and her seed; it shall bruise thy head, and thou shalt bruise his heel. Unto the woman he said, I will greatly multiply thy sorrow and thy conception; in sorrow thou shalt bring forth children; and thy desire shall be to thy husband, and he shall rule over thee. And unto Adam he said, Because thou hast hearkened unto the voice of thy wife, and hast eaten of the tree, of which I commanded thee, saying, Thou shalt not eat of it: cursed is the ground for thy sake; in sorrow shalt thou eat of it all the days of thy life ... in the sweat of thy face shalt thou eat bread, till thou return unto the ground; for out of it wast thou taken: for dust thou art, and unto dust shalt thou return.
3:13–20 KJV

Cain said to Abel his brother, 'Let us go out to the field.' And when they were in the field, Cain rose up against his brother Abel, and killed him. Then the Lord said to Cain, 'Where is Abel your brother?' He said, 'I do not know; am I my brother's keeper?' And the Lord said, 'What have you done? The voice of your brother's blood is crying to me from the ground.'
4:8–10 RSV

And Enoch walked with God: and he was not; for God took him.
5:24 KJV

The sons of God saw the daughters of men that they were fair; and they took them wives of all which they chose. And the Lord said, My spirit shall not always strive with man, for that he also is flesh.
6:2–3 KJV

The Lord saw how great man's wickedness on the earth had become, and that every inclination of the thoughts of his heart was only evil all the time. The Lord was grieved that he had made man on the earth, and his heart was filled with pain. So the Lord said, 'I will wipe mankind, whom I have created, off from the face of the earth—men and animals, and creatures that move along the ground, and birds of the air—for I am grieved that I have made them.' But Noah found favour in the eyes of the Lord. This is the account of Noah. Noah was a righteous man, blameless among the people of his time, and he walked with God.
6:5–9 NIV

'For behold, I will bring a flood of water upon the earth, to destroy all flesh in which is the breath of life from under heaven; everything that is on the earth shall die. But I will establish my covenant with you; and you shall come into the ark, you, your sons, your wife, and your sons' wives with you. And of every living thing of all flesh, you shall bring two of every sort into the ark, to keep them alive with you; they shall be male and female.'
6:17–19 RSV

Then [after the flood] Noah built an altar to the Lord, and took of every clean animal and of every clean bird, and offered burnt offerings on the altar.
8:20 RSV

'While the earth remains, seedtime and harvest, cold and heat, summer and winter, day and night, shall not cease.'
8:22 RSV

'Whoever sheds the blood of man, by man shall his blood be shed; for God made man in his own image.'
9:6 RSV

'I establish my covenant with you, that never again shall all flesh be cut off by the waters of a flood, and never again shall there be a flood to destroy the earth.' And God said, 'This is the sign of the covenant which I make between me and you and every living creature that is with you, for all future generations: I set my bow in the cloud, and it shall be a sign of the covenant between me and the earth.'
9:11–13 RSV

They said, 'Now let's build a city with a tower that reaches the sky, so that we can make a name for ourselves and not be scattered all over the earth.' Then the Lord came down to see the city and the tower which those men had built, and he said, 'Now then, these are all one people and they speak one language; this is just the beginning of what they are going to do. Soon they will be able to do anything they want! Let us go down and mix up their language so that they will not understand one another.' So the Lord scattered them all over the earth, and they stopped building the city. The city was called Babylon, because there the Lord mixed up the language of all the people, and from there he scattered them all over the earth.

11:4–9 GNB

Now the Lord had said unto Abram, Get thee out of thy country, and from thy kindred, and from thy father's house, unto a land that I will shew thee: and I will make of thee a great nation, and I will bless thee, and make thy name great; and thou shalt be a blessing: and I will bless them that bless thee, and curse him that curseth thee: and in thee shall all families of the earth be blessed. So Abram departed, as the Lord had spoken unto him; and Lot went with him: and Abram was seventy and five years old when he departed out of Haran.

12:1–4 KJV

And Melchizedek king of Salem brought out bread and wine; he was priest of God Most High. And he blessed him and said, 'Blessed be Abram by God Most High, maker of heaven and earth; and blessed be God Most High, who has delivered your enemies into your hand!' And Abram gave him a tenth of everything.

14:18–20 RSV

After these things the word of the Lord came unto Abram in a vision, saying, Fear not, Abram: I am thy shield, and thy exceeding great reward. And Abram said, Lord God, what wilt thou give me, seeing I go childless, and the steward of my house is this Eliezer of Damascus?

15:1–2 KJV

And he [the Lord] brought him [Abraham] forth abroad, and said, Look now toward heaven, and tell the stars, if thou be able to number them: and he said unto him, So shall thy seed be. And he believed in the Lord; and he counted it to him for righteousness.

15:5–6 KJV

'And I will establish my covenant between me and you and your descendants after you throughout their generations for an everlasting covenant, to be God to you and to your descendants after you. And I will give to you, and to your descendants after you, the land of your sojournings, all the land of Canaan, for an everlasting possession; and I will be their God . . . This is my covenant, which you shall keep,

between me and you and your descendants after you: Every male among you shall be circumcised.'

17:7–10 RSV

So Sarah laughed to herself, saying, 'After I have grown old, and my husband is old, shall I have pleasure?' The Lord said to Abraham, 'Why did Sarah laugh, and say, "Shall I indeed bear a child, now that I am old?" Is anything too hard for the Lord? At the appointed time I will return to you, in the spring, and Sarah shall have a son.'

18:12–14 RSV

[Abraham pleading for Sodom] 'Suppose there are fifty righteous within the city; wilt thou then destroy the place and not spare it for the fifty righteous who are in it? Far be it from thee to do such a thing, to slay the righteous with the wicked, so that the righteous fare as the wicked! Far be that from thee! Shall not the Judge of all the earth do right?'

18:24–25 RSV

But Lot's wife behind him looked back, and she became a pillar of salt.

19:26 RSV

After these things God tested Abraham, and said to him, 'Abraham!' And he said, 'Here am I.' He said, 'Take your son, your only son Isaac, whom you love, and go to the land of Moriah, and offer him there as a burnt offering upon one of the mountains of which I shall tell you.'

22:1–2 RSV

And Isaac said to his father Abraham, 'My father!' And he said, 'Here am I, my son.' He said, 'Behold, the fire and the wood; but where is the lamb for a burnt offering?' Abraham said, 'God will provide himself the lamb for a burnt offering, my son.'

22:7–8 RSV

And Abraham lifted up his eyes and looked, and behold, behind him was a ram, caught in a thicket by his horns; and Abraham went and took the ram, and offered it up as a burnt offering instead of his son. So Abraham called the name of that place The Lord will provide; as it is said to this day, 'On the mount of the Lord it shall be provided.'

22:13–14 RSV

'By myself I have sworn, says the Lord, because you have done this, and have not withheld your son, your only son, I will indeed bless you, and I will multiply your descendants as the stars of heaven and as the sand which is on the seashore. And your descendants shall possess the gate of their enemies, and by your descendants shall all the nations of the earth bless themselves, because you have obeyed my voice.'

22:16–18 RSV

Jacob said, 'Swear to me first.' So he [Esau] swore to him, and sold his birthright to Jacob.

25:33 RSV

So Jacob went near to Isaac his father, who felt him and said, 'The voice is Jacob's voice, but the hands are the hands of Esau.' And he did not recognise him, because his hands were hairy like his brother Esau's hands; so he blessed him.

27:22–23 RSV

And he [Jacob] dreamed, and behold a ladder set up on the earth, and the top of it reached to heaven: and behold the angels of God ascending and descending on it.

28:12 KJV

And Jacob was left alone; and there wrestled a man with him until the breaking of the day. And when he saw that he prevailed not against him, he touched the hollow of his thigh; and the hollow of Jacob's thigh was out of joint, as he wrestled with him. And he said, Let me go, for the day breaketh. And he said, I will not let thee go, except thou bless me. And he said unto him, what is thy name? And he said, Jacob. And he said, Thy name shall be called no more Jacob, but Israel: for as a prince hast thou power with God and with men, and hast prevailed.

32:24–28 KJV

So Joseph said to his brothers, 'Come near to me, I pray you.' And they came near. And he said, 'I am your brother, Joseph, whom you sold into Egypt. And now do not be distressed, or angry with yourselves, because you sold me here; for God sent me before you to preserve life.'

45:4–5 RSV

'As for you, you meant evil against me; but God meant it for good, to bring it about that many people should be kept alive, as they are today.'

50:20 RSV

# Exodus

The woman conceived and bore a son; and when she saw that he was a goodly child, she hid him three months. And when she could hide him no longer she took for him a basket made of bulrushes, and daubed it with bitumen and pitch; and she put the child in it and placed it among the reeds at the river's bank.

2:2–3 RSV

'Who made you a prince and a judge over us? Do you mean to kill me as you killed the Egyptian?'

2:14 RSV

And God heard their groaning, and God remembered his covenant with Abraham, with Isaac, and with Jacob. And God saw the people of Israel, and God knew their condition.

2:24–25 RSV

And the angel of the Lord appeared unto him in a flame of fire out of the midst of a bush: and he looked, and, behold, the bush burned with fire, and the bush was not consumed.

3:2 KJV

And he said, Draw not nigh hither: put off thy shoes from off thy feet, for the place whereon thou standest is holy ground.

3:5 KJV

And Moses hid his face; for he was afraid to look upon God.

3:6 KJV

And I am come down to deliver them out of the hand of the Egyptians, and to bring them up out of that land unto a good land and a large, unto a land flowing with milk and honey.

3:8 KJV

But Moses said to God, 'Who am I that I should go to Pharaoh, and bring the sons of Israel out of Egypt?' He said, 'But I will be with you; and this shall be the sign for you, that I have sent you: when you have brought forth the people out of Egypt, you shall serve God upon this mountain.' Then Moses said to God, 'If I come to the people of Israel and say to them, "The God of your fathers has sent me to you," and they ask me, "What is his name?" what shall I say to them?' God said to Moses, 'I am who I am.' And he said, 'Say this to the people of Israel, "The Lord, the God of your fathers, the God of Abraham, the

God of Isaac, and the God of Jacob, has sent me to you'': this is my name for ever, and thus I am to be remembered throughout all generations.
3:11–15 RSV

Moses said, 'No, Lord, don't send me. I have never been a good speaker, and I haven't become one since you began to speak to me. I am a poor speaker, slow and hesitant.' The Lord said to him, 'Who gives man his mouth? Who makes him deaf or dumb? Who gives him sight or makes him blind? It is I, the Lord. Now, go! I will help you to speak, and I will tell you what to say.'
4:10–12 GNB

'Say therefore to the people of Israel, ''I am the Lord, and I will bring you out from under the burdens of the Egyptians, and I will deliver you from their bondage, and I will redeem you with an outstretched arm and with great acts of judgment.'' '
6:6 RSV

'Your lamb shall be without blemish, a male a year old; you shall take it from the sheep or from the goats; and you shall keep it until the fourteenth day of this month, when the whole assembly of the congregation of Israel shall kill their lambs in the evening. Then they shall take some of the blood, and put it on the two doorposts and the lintel of the houses in which they eat them.'
12:5–7 RSV

'In this manner you shall eat it: your loins girded, your sandals on your feet, and your staff in your hand; and you shall eat it in haste. It is the Lord's passover. For I will pass through the land of Egypt that night, and I will smite all the first-born in the land of Egypt, both man and beast; and on all the gods of Egypt I will execute judgments: I am the Lord. The blood shall be a sign for you, upon the houses where you are; and when I see the blood, I will pass over you, and no plague shall fall upon you to destroy you, when I smite the land of Egypt.'
12:11–13 RSV

And the Lord went before them by day in a pillar of a cloud, to lead them the way; and by night in a pillar of fire, to give them light; to go by day and night.
13:21 KJV

Then Moses stretched out his hand over the sea; and the Lord drove the sea back by a strong east wind all night, and made the sea dry land, and the waters were divided.
14:21 RSV

And the children of Israel said unto them, Would to God we had died by the hand of the Lord in the land of Egypt, when we sat by the flesh pots, and when we did eat bread to the full; for ye have brought us forth into this wilderness, to kill this whole assembly with hunger.
16:3 KJV

'Moreover choose able men from all the people, such as fear God, men who are trustworthy and who hate a bribe; and place such men over the people as rulers of thousands, of hundreds, of fifties, and of tens. And let them judge the people at all times; every great matter they shall bring to you, but any small matter they shall decide themselves; so it will be easier for you, and they will bear the burden with you. If you do this, and God so commands you, then you will be able to endure, and all this people also will go to their place in peace.'
18:21–23 RSV

And God spake all these words, saying, I am the Lord thy God, which have brought thee out of the land of Egypt, out of the house of bondage. Thou shalt have no other gods before me. Thou shalt not make unto thee any graven image, or any likeness of any thing that is in heaven above, or that is in the earth beneath, or that is in the water under the earth: thou shalt not bow down thyself to them, nor serve them: for I the Lord thy God am a jealous God, visiting the iniquity of the fathers upon the children unto the third and fourth generation of them that hate me; and shewing mercy unto thousands of them that love me, and keep my commandments. Thou shalt not take the name of the Lord thy God in vain; for the Lord will not hold him guiltless that taketh his name in vain. Remember the sabbath day, to keep it holy. Six days shalt thou labour, and do all thy work: but the seventh day is the sabbath of the Lord thy God: in it thou shalt not do any work, thou, nor thy son, nor thy daughter, thy manservant, nor thy maidservant, nor thy cattle, nor thy stranger that is within thy gates: for in six days the Lord made heaven and earth, the sea, and all that in them is, and rested the seventh day: wherefore the Lord blessed the sabbath day, and hallowed it. Honour thy father and thy mother: that thy days may be long upon the land which the Lord thy God giveth thee. Thou shalt not kill. Thou shalt not commit adultery. Thou shalt not steal. Thou shalt not bear false witness against thy neighbour. Thou shalt not covet thy neighbour's house, thou shalt not covet thy neighbour's wife, nor his manservant, nor his maidservant, nor his ox, nor his ass, nor anything that is thy neighbour's.

20:1–17 KJV

'If any harm follows, then you shall give life for life, eye for eye, tooth for tooth.

21:23–24 RSV

'You shall not wrong a stranger or oppress him, for you were strangers in the land of Egypt.'

22:21 RSV

'Do not spread false rumours, and do not help a guilty man by giving false evidence.'

23:1 GNB

'For six years you shall sow your land and gather in its yield; but the seventh year you shall let it rest and lie fallow, that the poor of your people may eat; and what they leave the wild beasts may eat.'

23:10–11 RSV

And he received the gold at their hand, and fashioned it with a graving tool, and made a molten calf.

32:4 RSV

Thus the Lord used to speak to Moses face to face, as a man speaks to his friend.

33:11 RSV

And the Lord said to Moses, 'This very thing that you have spoken I will do; for you have found favour in my sight, and I know you by name.' Moses said, 'I pray thee, show me thy glory.' And he said, 'I will make all my goodness pass before you, and will proclaim before you my name "The Lord"; and I will be gracious to whom I will be gracious, and will show mercy on whom I will show mercy. But,' he said, 'you cannot see my face; for man shall not see me and live.' And the Lord said, 'Behold, there is a place by me where you shall stand upon the rock; and while my glory passes by I will put you in a cleft of the rock, and I will cover you with my hand until I have passed by; then I will take away my hand, and you shall see my back; but my face shall not be seen.'

33:17–23 RSV

The Lord passed before him, and proclaimed,

'The Lord, the Lord, a God merciful and gracious, slow to anger, and abounding in steadfast love and faithfulness, keeping steadfast love for thousands, forgiving iniquity and transgression and sin, but who will by no means clear the guilty, visiting the iniquity of the fathers upon the children and the children's children, to the third and the fourth generation.'

34:6–7 RSV

# Leviticus

And he shall put his hand upon the head of the burnt offering; and it shall be accepted for him to make atonement for him.

1:4 KJV

'The man shall put his hand on the head of the animal and kill it at the entrance of the Tent of the Lord's presence. The Aaronite priests shall throw the blood against all four sides of the altar.'

3:2 GNB

'So the priest shall make atonement for him for his sin, and he shall be forgiven.'

4:26 RSV

'When a man is guilty in any of these, he shall confess the sin he has committed.'

5:5 RSV

'For I am the Lord your God; consecrate yourselves therefore, and be holy, for I am holy.'

11:44 RSV

'But the goat chosen by lot as the scapegoat shall be presented alive before the Lord to be used for making atonement by sending it into the desert as a scapegoat.'

16:10 NIV

'He [Aaron] shall put both his hands on the goat's head and confess over it all the evils, sins, and rebellions of the people of Israel, and so transfer them to the goat's head. Then the goat is to be driven off into the desert by a man appointed to do it. The goat will carry all their sins away with him into some uninhabited land.'

16:21 GNB

'And it shall be a statute to you for ever that in the seventh month, on the tenth day of the month, you shall afflict yourselves, and shall do no work, either the native or the stranger who sojourns among you; for on this day shall atonement be made for you, to cleanse you; from all your sins you shall be clean before the Lord.'

16:29–30 RSV

'For the life of the flesh is in the blood; and I have given it for you upon the altar to make atonement for your souls; for it is the blood that makes atonement, by reason of the life.'

17:11 RSV

'You shall not take vengeance or bear any grudge against the sons of your own people, but you shall love your neighbour as yourself: I am the Lord.'

19:18 RSV

'And you shall hallow the fiftieth year, and proclaim liberty throughout the land to all its inhabitants; it shall be a jubilee for you, when each of you shall return to his property and each of you shall return to his family. A jubilee shall that fiftieth year be to you; in it you shall neither sow, nor reap what grows of itself, nor gather the grapes from the undressed vines.'

25:10–11 RSV

# Numbers

The Lord bless thee, and keep thee: the Lord make his face shine upon thee, and be gracious unto thee: the Lord lift up his countenance upon thee, and give thee peace.

6:24–26 KJV

And whenever the cloud was taken up from over the tent, after that the people of Israel set out; and in the place where the cloud settled down, there the people of Israel encamped.

9:17 RSV

And the people complained in the hearing of the Lord about their misfortunes; and when the Lord heard it, his anger was kindled, and the fire of the Lord burned among them, and consumed some outlying parts of the camp.

11:1 RSV

But Moses said to him [Joshua], ' . . . Would that all the Lord's people were prophets, that the Lord would put his spirit upon them!'

11:29 RSV

Now the man Moses was very meek, above all the men which were upon the face of the earth.

12:3 KJV

'God is not man, that he should lie, or a son of man, that he should repent. Has he said, and will he not do it? Or has he spoken, and will he not fulfil it?'

23:19 RSV

Be sure your sin will find you out.

32:23 KJV

# Deuteronomy

'And now, O Israel, give heed to the statutes and the ordinances which I teach you, and do them; that you may live, and go in and take possession of the land which the Lord, the God of your fathers, gives you.'

4:1 RSV

'But from there you will seek the Lord your God, and you will find him, if you search after him with all your heart and with all your soul.'

4:29 RSV

And Moses called all Israel, and said unto them, Hear, O Israel, the statutes and judgments which I speak in your ears this day, that ye may learn them, and keep, and do them.

5:1 KJV

Hear, O Israel: The Lord our God is one Lord: and thou shalt love the Lord thy God with all thine heart, and with all thy soul, and with all thy might.

6:4–5 KJV

'You shall teach them [the words the Lord commands] diligently to your children, and shall talk of them when you sit in your house, and when you walk by the way, and when you lie down, and when you rise.'

6:7 RSV

'For you are a people holy to the Lord your God; the Lord your God has chosen you to be a people for his own possession, out of all the peoples that are on the face of the earth. It was not because you were more in number than any other people that the Lord set his love upon you and chose you, for you were the fewest of all peoples; but it is because the Lord loves you, and is keeping the oath which he swore to your fathers, that the Lord has brought you out with a mighty hand, and redeemed you from the house of bondage, from the hand of Pharaoh king of Egypt. Know therefore that the Lord your God is God, the faithful God who keeps covenant and steadfast love with those who love him and keep his commandments, to a thousand generations.'

7:6–9 RSV

'And you shall remember all the way which the Lord your God has led you these forty years in the wilderness, that he might humble you, testing you to know what was in your heart, whether you would keep his commandments, or not. And he humbled you and let you hunger and fed you with manna, which you did not know, nor did your fathers know; that he might make you know that man does not live by bread alone, but that man lives by everything that proceeds out of the mouth of the Lord.'

8:2–3 RSV

'The Lord your God will raise up for you a prophet like me from among you, from your brethren—him you shall heed.'

18:15 RSV

Thou shalt not muzzle the ox when he treadeth out the corn.

25:4 KJV

'He brought us into this place and gave us this land, a land flowing with milk and honey. And behold, now I bring the first of the fruit of the ground, which thou, O Lord, hast given me.'

26:9–10 RSV

'And all these blessings shall come upon you and overtake you, if you obey the voice of the Lord your God. Blessed shall you be in the city, and blessed shall you be in the field. Blessed shall be the fruit of your body, and the fruit of your ground, and the fruit of your beasts, the increase of your cattle, and the young of your flock.'

28:2–4 RSV

'But if you will not obey the voice of the Lord your God or be careful to do all his commandments and his statutes which I command you this day, then all these curses shall come upon you and overtake you. Cursed shall you be in the city, and cursed shall you be in the field.'

28:15–16 RSV

'The secret things belong to the Lord our God but the things that are revealed belong to us and to our children for ever, that we may do all the words of this law.'

29:29 RSV

'I call heaven and earth to witness against you this day, that I have set before you life and death, blessing and curse; therefore choose life, that you and your descendants may live.'

30:19 RSV

'The Lord is your mighty defender, perfect and just in all his ways; Your God is faithful and true; he does what is right and fair.'

32:4 GNB

'He found him in a desert land, and in the howling waste of the wilderness; he encircled him, he cared for him, he kept him as the apple of his eye.'

32:10 RSV

This is the blessing with which Moses the man of God blessed the children of Israel before his death.

33:1 RSV

As thy days, so shall thy strength be.

33:25 KJV

The eternal God is thy refuge, and underneath are the everlasting arms.

33:27 KJV

So Moses the servant of the Lord died there in the land of Moab, according to the word of the Lord.

34:5 KJV

And Joshua the son of Nun was full of the spirit of wisdom; for Moses had laid his hands upon him: and the children of Israel hearkened unto him, and did as the Lord commanded Moses.

34:9 KJV

# Joshua

'As I was with Moses, so I will be with you; I will not fail you or forsake you. Be strong and of good courage; for you shall cause this people to inherit the land which I swore to their fathers to give them. Only be strong and very courageous, being careful to do according to all the law which Moses my servant commanded you; turn not from it to the right or to the left, that you may have good success wherever you go. This book of the law shall not depart out of your mouth, but you shall mediate on it day and night, that you may be careful to do according to all that is written in it; for then you shall make your way prosperous, and then you shall have good success. Have I not commanded you? Be strong and of good courage; be not frightened, neither be dismayed; for the Lord your God is with you wherever you go.'

1:5–9 RSV

And Joshua said to the people, 'Sanctify yourselves; for tomorrow the Lord will do wonders among you.'

3:5 RSV

So the people shouted, and the trumpets were blown. As soon as the people heard the sound of the trumpet, the people raised a great shout, and the wall [of Jericho] fell down flat, so that the people went up into the city, every man straight before him, and they took the city.

6:20 RSV

Thus the Lord gave Israel all the land which he had sworn to give to their forefathers; they occupied it and settled in it. The Lord gave them security on every side as he had sworn to their forefathers. Of all their enemies not a man could withstand them; the Lord delivered all their enemies into their hands. Not a word of the Lord's promises to the house of Israel went unfulfilled; they all came true.

21:43–45 NEB

# Judges

And the people of Israel did what was evil in the sight of the Lord and served the Baals; and they forsook the Lord, the God of their fathers, who had brought them out of the land of Egypt; they went after other gods, from among the gods of the peoples who were round about them, and bowed down to them; and they provoked the Lord to anger.

2:11–12 RSV

Then the Lord raised up judges, who saved them out of the power of those who plundered them.

2:16 RSV

The spirit of the Lord came upon him [Othniel], and he became Israel's leader. Othniel went to

war, and the Lord gave him victory over the king of Mesopotamia.

3:10 GNB

And the angel of the Lord appeared to him [Gideon] and said to him, 'The Lord is with you, you mighty man of valour.'

6:12 RSV

He [the angel of the Lord] replied, 'Why do you ask my name? It is beyond understanding.'

13:18 NIV

And he [Samson] said unto them, Out of the eater came forth meat, and out of the strong came forth sweetness.

14:14 KJV

Delilah lulled Samson to sleep in her lap and then called a man, who cut off Samson's seven locks of hair. Then she began to torment him, for he had lost his strength . . . He did not know that the Lord had left him.

16:19–20 GNB

In those days there was no king in Israel, but every man did what was right in his own eyes.

17:6 KJV

# Ruth

Ruth said, 'Entreat me not to leave you or to return from following you; for where you go I will go, and where you lodge I will lodge; your people shall be my people, and your God my God; where you die I will die, and there will I be buried. May the Lord do so to me and more also if even death parts me from you.'

1:16–17 RSV

The women said to Naomi: 'Praise be to the Lord, who this day has not left you without a kinsman-redeemer. May he become famous throughout Israel!'

4:14 NIV

# 1 Samuel

She [Hannah] vowed a vow and said, 'O Lord of hosts, if thou wilt indeed look on the affliction of thy maidservant, and remember me, and not forget thy maidservant, but wilt give to thy maidservant a son, then I will give him to the

Lord all the days of his life, and no razor shall touch his head.'

1:11 RSV

' ''Those who honour me I will honour, and those who despise me shall be lightly esteemed.'' '

2:30 RSV

The Lord called Samuel: and he answered, Here am I.

3:4 KJV

Eli said unto Samuel, Go, lie down: and it shall be, if he call thee, that thou shalt say, Speak, Lord; for thy servant heareth.

3:9 KJV

She [the wife of Phinehas] named the child Ichabod, saying, 'The glory has departed from Israel!' because the ark of God had been captured and because of her father-in-law and her husband.

4:21 RSV

Then Samuel took a stone and set it up between Mizpah and Jeshanah, and called its name Ebenezer; for he said, 'Hitherto the Lord has helped us.'

7:12 RSV

Is Saul also among the prophets?

10:11 KJV

And Samuel said, 'Has the Lord as great delight in burnt offerings and sacrifices, as in obeying the voice of the Lord? Behold, to obey is better than sacrifice, and to hearken than the fat of rams. For rebellion is as the sin of divination, and stubbornness is as iniquity and idolatry. Because you have rejected the word of the Lord, he has also rejected you from being king.'

15:22–23 RSV

But the Lord said unto Samuel, Look not on his countenance, or on the height of his stature; because I have refused him: for the Lord seeth not as man seeth; for man looketh on the outward appearance, but the Lord looketh on the heart.

16:7 KJV

David said moreover, The Lord that delivered me out of the paw of the lion, and out of the paw of the bear, he will deliver me out of the hand of this Philistine. And Saul said unto David, Go, and the Lord be with thee.

17:37 KJV

Saul hath slain his thousands, and David his ten thousands.

18:7 KJV

# 2 Samuel

[David's lament for Saul and Jonathan] The beauty of Israel is slain upon thy high places: how are the mighty fallen! Tell it not in Gath, publish it not in the streets of Askelon; lest the daughters of the Philistines rejoice, lest the daughters of the uncircumcised triumph.

1:19–20 KJV

I am distressed for thee, my brother Jonathan: very pleasant hast thou been unto me: thy love to me was wonderful, passing the love of women.

1:26 KJV

And as the ark of the Lord came into the city of David, Michal Saul's daughter looked through a window, and saw king David leaping and dancing before the Lord; and she despised him in her heart.

6:16 KJV

Nathan said to David, 'You are the man. Thus says the Lord, the God of Israel, ''I anointed you king over Israel, and I delivered you out of the hand of Saul; and I gave you your master's house, and your master's wives into your bosom, and gave you the house of Israel and of Judah; and if this were too little, I would add to you as much more. Why have you despised the word of the Lord, to do what is evil in his sight? You have smitten Uriah the Hittite with the sword, and have taken his wife to be your wife, and have slain him with the sword of the Ammonites.'' '

12:7–9 RSV

And the king was much moved, and went up to the chamber . . . and wept: and as he went, thus he said, O my son Absalom, my son, my son Absalom! would God I had died for thee, O Absalom, my son, my son!

18:33 KJV

[David's song of victory] 'This God—his way is perfect; the promise of the Lord proves true; he is a shield for all those who take refuge in him.'

22:31 RSV

# 1 Kings

[Solomon's prayer] 'Give thy servant therefore an understanding mind to govern thy people, that I may discern between good and evil; for who is able to govern this thy great people?'
**3:9 RSV**

And God gave Solomon wisdom and understanding beyond measure, and largeness of mind like the sand on the seashore, so that Solomon's wisdom surpassed the wisdom of all the people of the east, and all the wisdom of Egypt.
**4:29–30 RSV**

For when Solomon was old his wives turned away his heart after other gods; and his heart was not wholly true to the Lord his God, as was the heart of David his father.
**11:4 RSV**

And the ravens brought him [Elijah] bread and meat in the morning, and bread and meat in the evening; and he drank from the brook. And after a while the brook dried up, because there was no rain in the land.
**17:6–7 RSV**

'For thus says the Lord the God of Israel, "The jar of meal shall not be spent, and the cruse of oil shall not fail, until the day that the Lord sends rain upon the earth." '
**17:14 RSV**

And he [Elijah] stretched himself upon the child three times, and cried unto the Lord, and said, O Lord my God, I pray thee, let this child's soul come into him again. And the Lord heard the voice of Elijah; and the soul of the child came into him again, and he revived.
**17:21–22 KJV**

And Elijah came unto all the people, and said, How long halt ye between two opinions? If the Lord be God, follow him: but if Baal, then follow him. And the people answered him not a word.
**18:21 KJV**

[Elijah's prayer] 'Answer me, O Lord, answer me, that this people may know that thou, O Lord, art God, and that thou hast turned their hearts back.' Then the fire of the Lord fell, and consumed the burnt offering, and the wood, and the stones, and the dust, and licked up the water that was in the trench. And when all the people saw it, they fell on their faces; and they said, 'The Lord, he is God; the Lord, he is God.' And Elijah said to them, 'Seize the prophets of Baal; let not one of them escape.'
**18:37–40 RSV**

And he [Elijah] said, I have been very jealous for the Lord God of hosts: for the children of Israel have forsaken thy covenant, thrown down thine altars, and slain thy prophets with the sword; and I, even I only, am left; and they seek my life, to take it away.
**19:10 KJV**

And behold, the Lord passed by, and a great and strong wind rent the mountains, and broke in pieces the rocks before the Lord, but the Lord was not in the wind; and after the wind an earthquake, but the Lord was not in the earthquake; and after the earthquake a fire, but the Lord was not in the fire; and after the fire a still small voice.
**19:11–12 RSV**

# 2 Kings

When they had crossed, Elijah said to Elisha, 'Ask what I shall do for you, before I am taken from you.' And Elisha said, 'I pray you, let me inherit a double share of your spirit.'
**2:9 RSV**

And as they [Elijah and Elisha] still went on and talked, behold, a chariot of fire and horses of fire separated the two of them. And Elijah went up by a whirlwind into heaven.
**2:11 RSV**

So he [Naaman] went down and dipped himself seven times in the Jordan, according to the word of the man of God; and his flesh was restored like the flesh of a little child, and he was clean.
**5:14 RSV**

And he [Azariah] did what was right in the eyes of the Lord, according to all that his father Amaziah had done. Nevertheless the high places were not taken away; the people still sacrificed and burned incense on the high places.
**15:3–4 RSV**

Hezekiah received the letter from the hand of the messengers, and read it; and Hezekiah went up to the house of the Lord, and spread it before the Lord. And Hezekiah prayed before the Lord, and said; 'O Lord the God of Israel, who art enthroned above the cherubim, thou art the God, thou alone, of all the kingdoms of the earth; thou hast made heaven and earth. Incline thy ear, O Lord, and hear; open thy eyes, O Lord, and see; and hear the words of Sennacherib, which he has sent to mock the living God. Of a truth, O Lord, the kings of Assyria have laid waste the nations and their lands, and have cast their gods into the fire; for they were no gods, but the work of men's hands, wood and stone; therefore they were destroyed. So now, O Lord our God, save us, I beseech thee, from his hand, that all the kingdoms of the earth may know that thou, O Lord, art God alone.'

19:14–19 RSV

# 1 Chronicles

[David's thanksgiving] Seek the Lord and his strength, seek his face continually.

16:11 KJV

Give unto the Lord the glory due unto his name: bring an offering, and come before him: worship the Lord in the beauty of holiness.

16:29 KJV

[David's prayer] Thine, O Lord, is the greatness, and the power, and the glory, and the victory, and the majesty: for all that is in the heaven and in the earth is thine; thine is the kingdom, O Lord, and thou art exalted as head above all.

29:11 KJV

But who am I, and what is my people, that we should be able to offer so willingly after this sort? For all things come of thee, and of thine own have we given thee.

29:14 KJV

# 2 Chronicles

[It was the duty of the trumpeters and singers to make themselves heard in unison in praise and thanksgiving to the Lord], and when the song was raised, with trumpets and cymbals and other musical instruments, in praise to the Lord, 'For he is good, for his steadfast love endures for ever,' the house, the house of the Lord, was filled with a cloud.

5:13 RSV

[The Lord's promise to Solomon] 'If my people who are called by my name humble themselves, and pray and seek my face, and turn from their wicked ways, then I will hear from heaven, and will forgive their sin and heal their land.'

7:14 RSV

'For the eyes of the Lord run to and fro throughout the whole earth, to show his might in behalf of those whose heart is blameless toward him.'

16:9 RSV

[Jehoshaphat's prayer] 'O our God, wilt thou not execute judgment upon them? For we are powerless against this great multitude that is coming against us. We do not know what to do, but our eyes are upon thee.'

20:12 RSV

# Ezra

Then rose up the heads of the fathers' houses of Judah and Benjamin, and the priests and the Levites, everyone whose spirit God had stirred to go up to rebuild the house of the Lord which is in Jerusalem.

1:5 RSV

Then the people who had been living in the land tried to discourage and frighten the Jews and keep them from building. They also bribed Persian government officials to work against them. They kept on doing this throughout the reign of Cyrus and into the reign of Darius.

4:4–5 GNB

They finished the Temple on the third day of the month Adar in the sixth year of the reign of Darius the emperor. Then the people of Israel—the priests, the Levites, and all the others who had returned from exile—joyfully dedicated the Temple.

6:15–16 GNB

Ezra was a scholar with a thorough knowledge of the Law which the Lord, the God of Israel, had given to Moses. Because Ezra had the blessing of the Lord his God, the emperor gave him everything he asked for.

7:6 GNB

For Ezra had set his heart to study the law of the Lord, and to do it, and to teach his statutes and ordinances in Israel.

7:10 RSV

# Nehemiah

I [Nehemiah] answered the king, 'If it pleases the king and if your servant has found favour in his sight, let him send me to the city in Judah where my fathers are buried so that I can rebuild it.'

2:5 NIV

Then I said to them, 'You see the trouble we are in, how Jerusalem lies in ruins with its gates burned. Come, let us build the wall of Jerusalem, that we may no longer suffer disgrace.' And I told them of the hand of my God which had been upon me for good, and also of the words which the king had spoken to me. And they said, 'Let us rise up and build.'

2:17–18 RSV

Sanballat, Tobiah, and the people of Arabia, Ammon, and Ashdod heard that we were making progress in rebuilding the wall of Jerusalem and that the gaps in the wall were being closed, and they were very angry. So they all plotted together to come and attack Jerusalem and create confusion, but we prayed to our God and kept men on guard against them day and night.

4:7–9 GNB

After fifty-two days of work the entire wall was finished on the twenty-fifth day of the month of Elul. When our enemies in the surrounding nations heard this, they realized that they had lost face, since everyone knew that the work had been done with God's help.

6:15–16 GNB

And all the people gathered as one man into the square before the Water Gate; and they told Ezra the scribe to bring the book of the law of Moses which the Lord had given to Israel. And Ezra the priest brought the law before the assembly, both

men and women and all who could hear with understanding, on the first day of the seventh month.

8:1–2 RSV

'All these now join their brothers the nobles, and bind themselves with a curse and an oath to follow the Law of God given through Moses the servant of God and to obey carefully all the commands, regulations and decrees of the Lord our God.'

10:29 NIV

When the city wall of Jerusalem was dedicated, the Levites were brought in from wherever they were living, so that they could join in celebrating the dedication with songs of thanksgiving and with the music of cymbals and harps.

12:27 GNB

# Esther

The king loved Esther more than all the women, and she found grace and favour in his sight more than all the virgins, so that he set the royal crown on her head and made her queen instead of Vashti.

2:17 RSV

Haman was furious when he realized that Mordecai was not going to kneel and bow to him, and when he learnt that Mordecai was a Jew, he decided to do more than punish Mordecai alone. He made plans to kill every Jew in the whole Persian Empire.

3:5–6 GNB

Letters were sent by couriers to all the king's provinces, to destroy, to slay, and to annihilate all Jews, young and old, women and children, in one day, the thirteenth day of the twelfth month, which is the month of Adar, and to plunder their goods.

3:13 RSV

[Mordecai to Esther] And who knoweth whether thou art come to the kingdom for such a time as this?

4:14 KJV

Esther sent Mordecai this reply: 'Go and gather all the Jews in Susa together; hold a fast and pray for me. Don't eat or drink anything for three days and nights. My servant-girls and I will be doing the same. After that, I will go to the king, even though it is against the law. If I must die for doing it; I will die.'

**4:15–16 GNB**

Then Queen Esther answered, 'If I have found favour in your sight, O king, and if it please the king, let my life be given me at my petition, and my people at my request. For we are sold, I and my people, to be destroyed, to be slain, and to be annihilated. If we had been sold merely as slaves, men and women, I would have held my peace; for our affliction is not to be compared with the loss to the king.'

**7:3–4 RSV**

The king's edict granted the Jews in every city the right to assemble and protect themselves; to destroy, kill and annihilate any armed force of any nationality or province that might attack them and their women and children; and to plunder the property of their enemies.

**8:11 NIV**

Mordecai had these events written down and sent letters to all the Jews, near and far, throughout the Persian Empire, telling them to observe the fourteenth and fifteenth days of Adar as holidays every years. These were the days on which the Jews had rid themselves of their enemies; this was a month that had been turned from a time of grief and despair into a time of joy and happiness. They were told to observe these days with feasts and parties, giving gifts of food to one another and to the poor.

**9:20–22 GNB**

It was resolved that every Jewish family of every future generation in every province and every city should remember and observe the days of Purim for all time to come.

**9:28 GNB**

# Job

Now there was a day when the sons of God came to present themselves before the Lord, and Satan also came among them.

**1:6 RSV**

And the Lord said to Satan, 'Have you considered my servant Job, that there is none like him on the earth, a blameless and upright man,

who fears God and turns away from evil?' Then Satan answered the Lord, 'Does Job fear God for nought?'

**1:8–9 RSV**

And the Lord said to Satan, 'Behold, all that he has is in your power; only upon himself do not put forth your hand.'

**1:12 RSV**

And he [Job] said, 'Naked I came from my mother's womb, and naked shall I return; the Lord gave, and the Lord has taken away; blessed be the name of the Lord.'

**1:21 RSV**

So Satan went forth from the presence of the Lord, and afflicted Job with loathsome sores from the sole of his foot to the crown of his head.

**2:7 RSV**

And Job spake, and said, Let the day perish wherein I was born.

**3:2–3 KJV**

[Eliphaz] 'Consider now: Who, being innocent, has ever perished? Where were the upright ever destroyed? As I have observed, those who plough evil and those who sow trouble reap it.'

**4:7–8 NIV**

Yet man is born to trouble, as the sparks fly upward.

**5:7 KJV**

Then Job answered: 'Truly I know that is so: But how can a man be just before God?'

**9:1–2 RSV**

[Zophar] Canst thou by searching find out God? canst thou find out the Almighty unto perfection? It is as high as heaven; what canst thou do? deeper than hell; what canst thou know? The measure thereof is longer than the earth, and broader than the sea.

**11:7–9 KJV**

Though he slay me, yet will I trust in him: but I will maintain mine own ways before him.

**13:15 KJV**

I have heard many such things: miserable comforters are ye all.

**16:2 KJV**

For I know that my redeemer liveth, and that he shall stand at the latter day upon the earth: and though after my skin worms destroy this body, yet in my flesh shall I see God.

19:25–26 KJV

'He [Man] sings before men, and says: "I sinned, and perverted what was right, and it was now requited to me. He has redeemed my soul from going down into the Pit, and my life shall see the light." '

33:27–28 RSV

[The Lord] Where wast thou when I laid the foundations of the earth? Declare, if thou hast understanding.

38:4 KJV

[Job to the Lord] 'I know that thou canst do all things, and that no purpose of thine can be thwarted.'

42:2 RSV

'I had heard of thee by the hearing of the ear, but now my eye sees thee; therefore I despise myself, and repent in dust and ashes.'

42:5–6 RSV

And the Lord restored the fortunes of Job, when he had prayed for his friends; and the Lord gave Job twice as much as he had before.

42:10 RSV

# Psalms

Blessed is the man who walks not in the counsel of the wicked, nor stands in the way of sinners, nor sits in the seat of scoffers; but his delight is in the law of the Lord, and on his law he meditates day and night. He is like a tree planted by streams of water, that yields its fruit in its season, and its leaf does not wither. In all that he does, he prospers.

1:1–3 RSV

For the Lord knows the way of the righteous, but the way of the wicked will perish.

1:6 RSV

Why do the heathen so furiously rage together, and why do the people imagine a vain thing? The kings of the earth stand up, and the rulers take counsel together, against the Lord, and against his anointed.

2:1–2 BCP

I will declare the decree: the Lord hath said unto me, Thou art my Son; this day have I begotten thee.

2:7 KJV

Be angry, but sin not; commune with your own hearts on your beds, and be silent.

4:4 RSV

O Lord our Lord, how excellent is thy name in all the earth! who hast set thy glory above the heavens. Out of the mouth of babes and sucklings hast thou ordained strength because of thine enemies, that thou mightest still the enemy and the avenger. When I consider thy heavens, the work of thy fingers, the moon and the stars, which thou hast ordained; what is man, that thou art mindful of him? and the son of man, that thou visitest him? For thou hast made him a little lower than the angels, and hast crowned him with glory and honour. Thou madest him to have dominion over the works of thy hands; thou hast put all things under his feet: all sheep and oxen, yea, and the beasts of the field; the fowl of the air, and the fish of the sea, and whatsoever passeth through the paths of the seas. O Lord our Lord, how excellent is thy name in all the earth!

8 KJV

The fool hath said in his heart, There is no God.

14:1 KJV

For thou dost not give me up to Sheol, or let thy godly one see the Pit. Thou dost show me the path of life; in thy presence there is fullness of joy, in thy right hand are pleasures for evermore.

16:10–11 RSV

The heavens declare the glory of God; and the firmament sheweth his handywork. Day unto day uttereth speech, and night unto night sheweth knowledge.

19:1–2 KJV

The law of the Lord is perfect, converting the soul: the testimony of the Lord is sure, making wise the simple. The statutes of the Lord are right, rejoicing the heart: the commandment of the Lord is pure, enlightening the eyes. The fear of the Lord is clean, enduring for ever: the judgments of the Lord are true and righteous altogether. More to be desired are they than gold, yea, than much fine gold: sweeter also than honey and the honeycomb. Moreover by them is thy servant warned: and in keeping of them there is great reward. Who can understand his errors?

Cleanse thou me from secret faults. Keep back thy servant also from presumptuous sins; let them not have dominion over me: then shall I be upright, and I shall be innocent from the great transgression. Let the words of my mouth, and the meditation of my heart, be acceptable in thy sight, O Lord, my strength, and my redeemer.

19:7–14 KJV

My God, my God, why hast thou forsaken me?

22:1 KJV

They have pierced my hands and my feet. I can count all my bones; people stare and gloat over me. They divide my garments among them and cast lots for my clothing.

22:16–18 NIV

The Lord is my shepherd; I shall not want. He maketh me to lie down in green pastures; he leadeth me beside the still waters. He restoreth my soul: he leadeth me in the paths of righteousness for his name's sake. Yea, though I walk through the valley of the shadow of death, I will fear no evil: for thou art with me; thy rod and thy staff they comfort me. Thou preparest a table before me in the presence of mine enemies: thou anointest my head with oil; my cup runneth over. Surely goodness and mercy shall follow me all the days of my life: and I will dwell in the house of the Lord for ever.

23 KJV

The earth is the Lord's and the fullness thereof, the world and those who dwell therein.

24:1 RSV

Who shall ascend the hill of the Lord? And who shall stand in his holy place? He who has clean hands and a pure heart, who does not lift up his soul to what is false, and does not swear deceitfully.

24:3–4 RSV

Lift up your heads, O ye gates; and be ye lift up, ye everlasting doors; and the King of glory shall come in. Who is this King of glory? The Lord strong and mighty, the Lord mighty in battle. Lift up your heads, O ye gates; even lift them up, ye everlasting doors; and the King of glory shall come in. Who is this King of glory? The Lord of hosts, he is the King of glory.

24:7–10 KJV

The Lord is my light and my salvation; whom shall I fear? The Lord is the strength of my life; of whom shall I be afraid?

27:1 KJV

Though an host should encamp against me, my heart shall not fear: though war should rise against me, in this will I be confident. One thing have I desired of the Lord, that will I seek after; that I may dwell in the house of the Lord all the days of my life, to behold the beauty of the Lord, and to inquire in his temple.

27:3–4 KJV

I believe that I shall see the goodness of the Lord in the land of the living! Wait for the Lord; be strong, and let your heart take courage; yea, wait for the Lord!

27:13–14 RSV

Blessed is he whose transgression is forgiven, whose sin is covered. Blessed is the man to whom the Lord imputes no iniquity, and in whose spirit there is no deceit. When I declared not my sin, my body wasted away through my groaning all day long. For day and night thy hand was heavy upon me; my strength was dried up as by the heat of summer. I acknowledged my sin to thee, and I did not hide my iniquity; I said, 'I will confess my transgressions to the Lord'; then thou didst forgive the guilt of my sin.'

32:1–5 RSV

I will instruct you and teach you the way you should go; I will counsel you with my eye upon you. Be not like a horse or a mule, without understanding, which must be curbed with bit and bridle.

32:8–9 RSV

I will bless the Lord at all times; his praise shall continually be in my mouth. My soul makes its boast in the Lord; let the afflicted hear and be glad. O magnify the Lord with me, and let us exalt his name together! I sought the Lord, and he answered me, and delivered me from all my fears. Look to him, and be radiant; so your faces shall never be ashamed. This poor man cried, and the Lord heard him, and saved him out of all his troubles.

34:1–6 RSV

O taste and see that the Lord is good! Happy is the man who takes refuge in him! O fear the Lord, you his saints, for those who fear him have no want!

34:8–9 RSV

Trust in the Lord, and do good; so you will dwell in the land, and enjoy security. Take delight in the Lord, and he will give you the desires of your heart. Commit your way to the Lord; trust in him, and he will act.

37:3–5 RSV

I waited patiently for the Lord; he inclined to me and heard my cry. He drew me up from the desolate pit, out of the miry bog, and set my feet upon a rock, making my steps secure. He put a new song in my mouth, a song of praise to our God. Many will see and fear, and put their trust in the Lord.

40:1–3 RSV

Then I said, Lo, I come; in the roll of the book it is written of me; I delight to do thy will, O my God; thy law is within my heart.'

40:7–8 RSV

As the hart panteth after the water brooks, so panteth my soul after thee, O God. My soul thirsteth for God, for the living God: when shall I come and appear before God? My tears have been my meat day and night, while they continually say unto me, Where is thy God?

42:1–3 KJV

Why art thou cast down, O my soul? and why art thou disquieted in me? Hope thou in God: for I shall yet praise him for the help of his countenance. O my God, my soul is cast down within me: therefore will I remember thee from the land of Jordan, and of the Hermonites, from the hill Mizar. Deep calleth unto deep at the noise of thy waterspouts: all thy waves and thy billows are gone over me.

42:5–7 KJV

Thy throne, O God, is for ever and ever: the sceptre of thy kingdom is a right sceptre.

45:6 KJV

God is our refuge and strength, a very present help in trouble. Therefore will we not fear, though the earth be removed, and though the mountains be carried into the midst of the sea.

46:1–2 KJV

God is in the midst of her [the city of God]; she shall not be moved: God shall help her, and that right early.

46:5 KJV

He makes wars cease to the end of the earth; he breaks the bow, and shatters the spear, he burns the chariots with fire! 'Be still, and know that I am God. I am exalted among the nations, I am exalted in the earth!' The Lord of hosts is with us; the God of Jacob is our refuge.

46:9–11 RSV

O clap your hands, all ye people; shout unto God with the voice of triumph.

47:1 KJV

For every beast of the forest is mine, and the cattle upon a thousand hills.

50:10 KJV

'Offer to God a sacrifice of thanksgiving, and pay your vows to the Most High; and call upon me in the day of trouble; I will deliver you, and you shall glorify me.'

50:14–15 RSV

Have mercy upon me, O God, according to thy lovingkindness: according unto the multitude of thy tender mercies blot out my transgressions. Wash me thoroughly from mine iniquity, and cleanse me from my sin. For I acknowledge my transgressions: and my sin is ever before me. Against thee, thee only, have I sinned, and done this evil in thy sight: that thou mightest be justified when thou speakest, and be clear when thou judgest. Behold, I was shapen in iniquity; and in sin did my mother conceive me.

51:1–5 KJV

Purge me with hyssop, and I shall be clean: wash me, and I shall be whiter than snow.

51:7 KJV

Create in me a clean heart, O God; and renew a right spirit within me. Cast me not away from thy presence; and take not thy holy spirit from me. Restore unto me the joy of thy salvation; and uphold me with thy free spirit. Then will I teach transgressors thy ways; and sinners shall be converted unto thee.

51:10–13 KJV

O Lord, open thou my lips; and my mouth shall shew forth thy praise. For thou desirest not sacrifice; else would I give it: thou delightest not in burnt offering. The sacrifices of God are a broken spirit: a broken and a contrite heart, O God, thou wilt not despise. Do good in thy good pleasure unto Zion: build thou the walls of Jerusalem.

51:15–18 KJV

From the end of the earth will I cry unto thee, when my heart is overwhelmed: lead me to the rock that is higher than I.

61:2 KJV

Because thy lovingkindness is better than life, my lips shall praise thee. Thus will I bless thee while I live: I will lift up my hands in thy name.

63:3–4 KJV

I am full of heaviness: I looked for some to have pity on me, but there was no man, neither found I any to comfort me. They gave me gall to eat: and when I was thirsty they gave me vinegar to drink.

69:20–21 BCP

Give the king thy justice, O God, and thy righteousness to the royal son! May he judge thy people with righteousness, and thy poor with justice!

72:1–2 RSV

Whom have I in heaven but thee? And there is none upon earth that I desire beside thee. My flesh and my heart faileth: but God is the strength of my heart, and my portion for ever.

73:25–26 KJV

How dear is thy dwelling-place, thou Lord of Hosts! I pine, I faint with longing for the courts of the Lord's temple; my whole being cries out with joy to the living God.

84:1–2 NEB

For a day in thy courts is better than a thousand elsewhere. I would rather be a doorkeeper in the house of my God than dwell in the tents of wickedness.

84:10 RSV

Glorious things are spoken of thee, O city of God.

87:3 KJV

Before the mountains were brought forth, or ever thou hadst formed the earth and the world, from everlasting to everlasting thou art God.

90:2 RSV

He who dwells in the shelter of the Most High will rest in the shadow of the Almighty. I will say of the Lord, 'He is my refuge and my fortress, my God, in whom I trust.'

91:1–2 NIV

It is good to praise the Lord and make music to your name, O Most High, to proclaim your love in the morning and your faithfulness at night.

92:1–2 NIV

O come, let us sing unto the Lord; let us heartily rejoice in the strength of our salvation. Let us come before his presence with thanksgiving, and shew ourselves glad in him with psalms. For the Lord is a great God, and a great King above all gods. In his hand are all the corners of the earth; and the strength of the hills is his also. The sea is his, and he made it; and his hands prepared the dry land. O come, let us worship, and fall down, and kneel before the Lord our Maker. For he is the Lord our God, and we are the people of his pasture, and the sheep of his hand.

95:1–7 BCP

O sing unto the Lord a new song; for he hath done marvellous things: his right hand, and his holy arm, hath gotten him the victory.

98:1 KJV

Make a joyful noise unto the Lord, all ye lands. Serve the Lord with gladness: come before his presence with singing. Know ye that the Lord he is God: it is he that hath made us, and not we ourselves; we are his people, and the sheep of his pasture. Enter into his gates with thanksgiving, and into his courts with praise: be thankful unto him, and bless his name.

100:1–4 KJV

Bless the Lord, O my soul: and all that is within me, bless his holy name. Bless the Lord, O my soul, and forget not all his benefits: who forgiveth all thine iniquities; who healeth all thy diseases; who redeemeth thy life from destruction; who crowneth thee with lovingkindness and tender mercies; who satisfieth thy mouth with good things; so that thy youth is renewed like the eagle's.

103:1–5 KJV

The Lord is merciful and gracious, slow to anger, and plenteous in mercy. He will not always chide: neither will he keep his anger for ever.

103:8–9 KJV

For as the heaven is high above the earth, so great is his mercy toward them that fear him. As far as the east is from the west, so far hath he removed our transgressions from us.

103:11–12 KJV

O Lord, how manifold are thy works! In wisdom hast thou made them all: the earth is full of thy riches.

104:24 KJV

They that go down to the sea in ships, that do business in great waters; these see the works of the Lord, and his wonders in the deep.
107:23–24 KJV

The Lord says to my lord: 'Sit at my right hand, till I make your enemies your footstool.'
110:1 RSV

The Lord has sworn and will not change his mind, 'You are a priest for ever after the order of Melchizedek.'
110:4 RSV

The fear of the Lord is the beginning of wisdom: a good understanding have all they that do his commandments: his praise endureth for ever.
111:10 KJV

What shall I render to the Lord for all his bounty to me? I will lift up the cup of salvation and call on the name of the Lord, I will pay my vows to the Lord in the presence of all his people. Precious in the sight of the Lord is the death of his saints.
116:12–15 RSV

The stone which the builders rejected has become the head of the corner.
118:22 RSV

This is the day which the Lord has made; let us rejoice and be glad in it.
118:24 RSV

How can a young man keep his way pure? By guarding it according to thy word.
119:9 RSV

I have laid up thy word in my heart, that I might not sin against thee.
119:11 RSV

Open thou mine eyes, that I may behold wondrous things out of thy law.
119:18 KJV

It is good for me that I was afflicted, that I might learn thy statutes.
119:71 RSV

O how love I thy law! It is my meditation all the day.
119:97 KJV

Thy word is a lamp unto my feet, and a light unto my path.
119:105 KJV

The entrance of thy words giveth light; it giveth understanding unto the simple.
119:130 KJV

I will lift up mine eyes unto the hills, from whence cometh my help. My help cometh from the Lord, which made heaven and earth. He will not suffer thy foot to be moved: he that keepeth thee will not slumber. Behold, he that keepeth Israel shall neither slumber nor sleep. The Lord is thy keeper: the Lord is thy shade upon thy right hand. The sun shall not smite thee by day, nor the moon by night. The Lord shall preserve thee from all evil: he shall preserve thy soul. The Lord shall preserve thy going out and thy coming in from this time forth, and even for evermore.
121 KJV

I was glad when they said unto me, Let us go into the house of the Lord.
122:1 KJV

Pray for the peace of Jerusalem! 'May they prosper who love you!'
122:6 RSV

The Lord has done great things for us, and we are filled with joy.
126:3 NIV

They that sow in tears shall reap in joy. He that goeth forth and weepeth, bearing precious seed, shall doubtless come again with rejoicing, bringing his sheaves with him.
126:5–6 KJV

Except the Lord build the house,they labour in vain that build it: except the Lord keep the city, the watchman waketh but in vain. It is vain for you to rise up early, to sit up late, to eat the bread of sorrows: for so he giveth his beloved sleep. Lo, children are an heritage of the Lord: and the fruit of the womb is his reward. As arrows are in the hand of a mighty man; so are children of the youth. Happy is the man that hath his quiver full of them: they shall not be ashamed, but they shall speak with the enemies in the gate.
127 KJV

If thou, O Lord, shouldst mark iniquities, Lord, who could stand? But there is forgiveness with thee, that thou mayest be feared.
130:3–4 RSV

Behold, how good and how pleasant it is for brethren to dwell together in unity!
133:1 KJV

O give thanks to the Lord, for he is good, for his steadfast love endures for ever.

136:1 RSV

By the rivers of Babylon, there we sat down, yea, we wept, when we remembered Zion.

137:1 KJV

O Lord, thou hast searched me and known me! Thou knowest when I sit down and when I rise up; thou discernest my thoughts from afar. Thou searchest out my path and my lying down, and art acquainted with all my ways. Even before a word is on my tongue, lo, O Lord, thou knowest it altogether. Thou dost beset me behind and before, and layest thy hand upon me. Such knowledge is too wonderful for me; it is high, I cannot attain it. Whither shall I go from thy Spirit? Or whither shall I flee from thy presence? If I ascend to heaven, thou art there! If I make my bed in Sheol, thou art there! If I take the wings of the morning and dwell in the uttermost parts of the sea, even there thy hand shall lead me, and thy right hand shall hold me.

139:1–10 RSV

Search me, O God, and know my heart: try me, and know my thoughts. And see if there be any wicked way in me, and lead me in the way everlasting.

139:23–24 KJV

Enter not into judgement with thy servant; for no man living is righteous before thee.

143:2 RSV

Praise him upon the loud cymbals: praise him upon the high sounding cymbals. Let everything that hath breath praise the Lord. Praise ye the Lord.

150:5–6 KJV

# Proverbs

The fear of the Lord is the beginning of knowledge: but fools despise wisdom and instruction. My son, hear the instruction of thy father, and forsake not the law of thy mother. For they shall be an ornament of grace unto thy head, and chains about thy neck.

1:7–9 KJV

Trust in the Lord with all thine heart; and lean not unto thine own understanding. In all thy ways acknowledge him, and he shall direct thy paths. Be not wise in thine own eyes: fear the Lord, and depart from evil.

3:5–7 KJV

My son, do not despise the Lord's discipline or be weary of his reproof, for the Lord reproves him whom he loves, as a father the son in whom he delights.

3:11–12 RSV

Let your fountain be blessed, and rejoice in the wife of your youth, a lovely hind, a graceful doe. Let her affection fill you at all times with delight, be infatuated always with her love.

5:18–19 RSV

Go to the ant, thou sluggard; consider her ways, and be wise.

6:6 KJV

There are seven things that the Lord hates and cannot tolerate: A proud look, a lying tongue, hands that kill innocent people, a mind that thinks up wicked plans, feet that hurry off to do evil, a witness who tells one lie after another, and a man who stirs up trouble among friends.

6:16–19 GNB

'The Lord possessed me at the beginning of his work, before his deeds of old; I was appointed from eternity, from the beginning, before the world began.'

8:22–23 NIV

Wisdom has built her house, she has set up her seven pillars.

9:1 RSV

A false balance is an abomination to the Lord, but a just weight is his delight.

11:1 RSV

The way of a fool is right in his own eyes, but a wise man listens to advice.

12:15 RSV

There is a way which seemeth right unto a man, but the end thereof are the ways of death.

14:12 KJV

Righteousness exalteth a nation: but sin is a reproach to any people.

14:34 KJV

Better is a dinner of herbs where love is than a fatted ox and hatred with it.

15:17 RSV

Commit your work to the Lord, and your plans will be established.

16:3 RSV

Pride goes before destruction, and a haughty spirit before a fall.

16:18 RSV

He who is slow to anger is better than the mighty, and he who rules his spirit than he who takes a city. The lot is cast into the lap, but the decision is wholly from the Lord.

16:32–33 RSV

There are friends who pretend to be friends, but there is a friend who sticks closer than a brother.

18:24 RSV

He who is kind to the poor lends to the Lord, and he will repay him for his deed.

19:17 RSV

Many are the plans in the mind of a man, but it is the purpose of the Lord that will be established.

19:21 RSV

To do righteousness and justice is more acceptable to the Lord than sacrifice.

21:3 RSV

Better to live on the roof than share the house with a nagging wife.

21:9 GNB

Train up a child in the way he should go: and when he is old, he will not depart from it.

22:6 KJV

A word fitly spoken is like apples of gold in pictures of silver.

25:11 KJV

Faithful are the wounds of a friend; but the kisses of an enemy are deceitful.

27:6 KJV

Iron sharpeneth iron; so a man sharpeneth the countenance of his friend.

27:17 KJV

Where there is no vision, the people perish: but he that keepeth the law, happy is he.

29:18 KJV

A good wife who can find? She is far more precious than jewels.

31:10 RSV

# Ecclesiastes

Vanity of vanities, says the Preacher, vanity of vanities! All is vanity.

1:2 RSV

All things are full of weariness; a man cannot utter it; the eye is not satisfied with seeing, nor the ear filled with hearing. What has been is what will be, and what has been done is what will be done; and there is nothing new under the sun.

1:8–9 RSV

I have seen all the deeds that are done here under the sun; they are all emptiness and chasing the wind.

1:14 NEB

For everything there is a season, and a time for every matter under heaven: a time to be born, and a time to die.

3:1–2 RSV

He has made everything beautiful in its time; also he has put eternity into man's mind, yet so that he cannot find out what God has done from the beginning to the end. I know that there is nothing better for them than to be happy and enjoy themselves as long as they live; also that it is God's gift to man that every one should eat and drink and take pleasure in all his toil. I know that whatever God does endures for ever; nothing can be added to it, nor anything taken from it; God has made it so, in order that men should fear before him.

3:11–14 RSV

I said in mine heart, God shall judge the righteous and the wicked: for there is a time there for every purpose and for every work.

3:17 KJV

And though a man might prevail against one who is alone, two will withstand him. A threefold cord is not quickly broken.

4:12 RSV

Be not rash with thy mouth, and let not thine heart be hasty to utter any thing before God: for God is in heaven, and thou upon earth: therefore let thy words be few.

5:2 KJV

Though a sinner does evil a hundred times and prolongs his life, yet I know that it will be well with those who fear God, because they fear before him; but it will not be well with the wicked, neither will he prolong his days like a shadow, because he does not fear before God.
8:12–13 RSV

Go, eat your bread with enjoyment, and drink your wine with a merry heart; for God has already approved what you do.
9:7 RSV

Whatsoever thy hand findeth to do, do it with thy might; for there is no work, nor device, nor knowledge, nor wisdom, in the grave, whither thou goest.
9:10 KJV

Cast thy bread upon the waters: for thou shalt find it after many days.
11:1 KJV

Remember now thy creator in the days of thy youth, while the evil days come not, nor the years draw nigh, when thou shalt say, I have no pleasure in them.
12:1 KJV

Of making many books there is no end; and much study is a weariness of the flesh. Let us hear the conclusion of the whole matter: Fear God, and keep his commandments; for this is the whole duty of man.
12:12–13 KJV

# Song of Solomon

The Song of Songs, which is Solomon's.
1:1 RSV

I am very dark, but comely, O daughters of Jerusalem, like the tents of Kedar, like the curtains of Solomon.
1:5 RSV

If thou know not, O thou fairest among women, go thy way forth by the footsteps of the flock, and feed thy kids beside the shepherds' tents.
1:8 KJV

I am the rose of Sharon, and the lily of the valleys.
2:1 KJV

He brought me to the banqueting house, and his banner over me was love.
2:4 KJV

I adjure you, O daughters of Jerusalem, by the gazelles or the hinds of the field, that you stir not up nor awaken love until it please.
2:7 RSV

'Arise, my love, my fair one, and come away; for lo, the winter is past, the rain is over and gone. The flowers appear on the earth, the time of singing has come, and the voice of the turtledove is heard in our land.'
2:10–12 RSV

My beloved is mine and I am his, he pastures his flock among the lilies. Until the day breathes and the shadows flee, turn, my beloved, be like a gazelle, or a young stag upon rugged mountains.
2:16–17 RSV

Behold, thou art fair, my love; behold, thou art fair.
4:1 KJV

I opened to my beloved; but my beloved had withdrawn himself, and was gone: my soul failed when he spake: I sought him, but I could not find him; I called him, but he gave me no answer. The watchmen that went about the city found me, they smote me, they wounded me; the keepers of the walls took away my veil from me. I charge you, O daughters of Jerusalem, if ye find my beloved, that ye tell him, that I am sick of love.
5:6–8 KJV

My beloved is white and ruddy, the chiefest among ten thousand.
5:10 KJV

Love is as strong as death; jealousy is cruel as the grave: the coals thereof are coals of fire, which hath a most vehement flame. Many waters cannot quench love, neither can the floods drown it: if a man would give all the substance of his house for love, it would utterly be contemned.
8:6–7 KJV

Thou that dwellest in the gardens, the companions hearken to thy voice: cause me to hear it. Make haste, my beloved, and be thou like to a roe or to a young hart upon the mountains of spices.
8:13–14 KJV

# Isaiah

Hear, O heavens, and give ear, O earth; for the Lord has spoken: 'Sons I have reared and brought up, but they have rebelled against me. The ox knows its owner, and the ass its master's crib; but Israel does not know, my people does not understand.

1:2–3 RSV

Israel, your head is already covered with wounds, and your heart and mind are sick. From head to foot there is not a healthy spot on your body. You are covered with bruises and sores and open wounds. Your wounds have not been cleaned or bandaged. No ointment has been put on them.

1:5–6 GNB

Wash and make yourselves clean. Take your evil deeds out of my sight! Stop doing wrong, learn to do right! Seek justice, encourage the oppressed. Defend the cause of the fatherless, plead the case of the widow. 'Come now, let us reason together,' says the Lord. 'Though your sins are like scarlet, they shall be as white as snow; though they are red as crimson, they shall be like wool.'

1:16–18 NIV

He shall judge between the nations, and shall decide for many peoples; and they shall beat their swords into ploughshares, and their spears into pruning hooks; nation shall not lift up sword against nation, neither shall they learn war any more.

2:4 RSV

In the year that King Uzziah died I saw the Lord sitting upon a throne, high and lifted up; and his train filled the temple. Above him stood the seraphim; each had six wings: with two he covered his face, and with two he covered his feet, and with two he flew. And one called to another and said: 'Holy, holy, holy is the Lord of hosts; the whole earth is full of his glory.'

6:1–3 RSV

And I said: 'Woe is me! For I am lost; for I am a man of unclean lips, and I dwell in the midst of a people of unclean lips; for my eyes have seen the King, the Lord of hosts!' Then flew one of the seraphim to me, having in his hand a burning coal which he had taken with tongs from the altar. And he touched my mouth, and said:

'Behold, this has touched your lips; your guilt is taken away, and your sin forgiven.' And I heard the voice of the Lord saying, 'Whom shall I send, and who will go for us?' Then I said, 'Here I am! Send me.' And he said, 'Go, and say to this people: "Hear and hear, but do not understand; see and see, but do not perceive." Make the heart of this people fat, and their ears heavy, and shut their eyes; lest they see with their eyes, and hear with their ears, and understand with their hearts, and turn and be healed.'

6:5–10 RSV

'And though a tenth remains in the land, it will again be laid waste. But as the terebinth and oak leave stumps when they are cut down, so the holy seed will be the stump in the land.'

6:13 NIV

Therefore the Lord himself shall give you a sign; behold, a virgin shall conceive, and bear a son, and shall call his name Immanuel.

7:14 KJV

Bind up the testimony, seal the teaching among my disciples. I will wait for the Lord, who is hiding his face from the house of Jacob, and I will hope in him. Behold, I and the children whom the Lord has given me are signs and portents in Israel from the Lord of hosts, who dwells on Mount Zion.

8:16–18 RSV

The people who walked in darkness have seen a great light: they that dwell in the land of the shadow of death, upon them hath the light shined.

9:2 KJV

For unto us a child is born, unto us a son is given: and the government shall be upon his shoulder: and his name shall be called Wonderful, Counsellor, The mighty God, The everlasting Father, The Prince of Peace. Of the increase of his government and peace there shall be no end, upon the throne of David, and upon his kingdom, to order it, and to establish it with judgment and with justice from henceforth even for ever. The zeal of the Lord of hosts will perform this.

9:6–7 KJV

The Lord said, 'Assyria! I use Assyria like a club to punish those with whom I am angry. I sent Assyria to attack a godless nation, people who have made me angry.'

10:5–6 GNB

And there shall come forth a rod out of the stem of Jesse, and a Branch shall grow out of his roots. And the spirit of the Lord shall rest upon him, the spirit of wisdom and understanding, the spirit of counsel and might, the spirit of knowledge and of the fear of the Lord.

11:1–2 KJV

The wolf also shall dwell with the lamb, and the leopard shall lie down with the kid; and the calf and the young lion and the fatling together; and a little child shall lead them.

11:6 KJV

They shall not hurt nor destroy in all my holy mountain: for the earth shall be full of the knowledge of the Lord, as the waters cover the sea.

11:9 KJV

With joy you will draw water from the wells of salvation.

12:3 RSV

How art thou fallen from heaven, O Lucifer, son of the morning!

14:12 KJV

'Thou dost keep him in perfect peace, whose mind is stayed on thee, because he trusts in thee.'

26:3 RSV

For precept must be upon precept, precept upon precept; line upon line, line upon line; here a little, and there a little: for with stammering lips and another tongue will he speak to this people.

28:10–11 KJV

And the Lord said: '. . . this people draw near with their mouth and honour me with their lips, while their hearts are far from me, and their fear of me is a commandment of men learned by rote.'

29:13 RSV

For thus said the Lord God, the Holy One of Israel, 'In returning and rest you shall be saved; in quietness and trust shall be your strength.'

30:15 RSV

And a man shall be as an hiding place from the wind, and a covert from the tempest; as rivers of water in a dry place, as the shadow of a great rock in a weary land.

32:2 KJV

Then the eyes of the blind shall be opened, and the ears of the deaf shall be unstopped. Then shall the lame man leap as an hart, and the tongue of the dumb sing: for in the wilderness shall waters break out, and streams in the desert.

35:5–6 KJV

And the ransomed of the Lord shall return, and come to Zion with singing; everlasting joy shall be upon their heads; they shall obtain joy and gladness, and sorrow and sighing shall flee away.

35:10 RSV

Comfort ye, comfort ye my people, saith your God. Speak ye comfortably to Jerusalem, and cry unto her, that her warfare is accomplished, that her iniquity is pardoned: for she hath received of the Lord's hand double for all her sins. The voice of him that crieth in the wilderness, Prepare ye the way of the Lord, make straight in the desert a highway for our God. Every valley shall be exalted, and every mountain and hill shall be made low: and the crooked shall be made straight, and the rough places plain: and the glory of the Lord shall be revealed, and all flesh shall see it together: for the mouth of the Lord hath spoken it.

40:1–5 KJV

The grass withereth, the flower fadeth: but the word of our God shall stand for ever. O Zion, that bringest good tidings, get thee up into the high mountain; O Jerusalem, that bringest good tidings, lift up thy voice with strength; lift it up, be not afraid; say unto the cities of Judah, Behold your God! Behold, the Lord God will come with strong hand, and his arm shall rule for him: behold, his reward is with him, and his work before him. He shall feed his flock like a shepherd: he shall gather the lambs with his arm, and carry them in his bosom, and shall gently lead those that are with young.

40:8–11 KJV

Who hath directed the Spirit of the Lord, or being his counsellor hath taught him? With whom took he counsel, and who instructed him, and taught him in the path of judgment, and taught him knowledge, and shewed to him the way of understanding? Behold, the nations are as a drop of a bucket, and are counted as the small dust of the balance: behold, he taketh up the isles as a very little thing.

40:13–15 KJV

Have ye not known? have ye not heard? hath it not been told you from the beginning? have ye not understood from the foundations of the earth? It is he that sitteth upon the circle of the earth, and the inhabitants thereof are as grasshoppers; that stretcheth out the heavens as a curtain, and spreadeth them out as a tent to dwell in: that bringeth the princes to nothing; he maketh the judges of the earth as vanity.
40:21–23 KJV

To whom then will ye liken me, or shall I be equal? said the Holy One. Lift up your eyes on high, and behold who hath created these things, that bringeth out their host by number: he calleth them all by names by the greatness of his might, for that he is strong in power; not one faileth. Why sayest thou, O Jacob, and speakest, O Israel, My way is hid from the Lord, and my judgment is passed over from my God? Hast thou not known? hast thou not heard, that the everlasting God, the Lord, the Creator of the ends of the earth, fainteth not, neither is weary? There is no searching of his understanding. He giveth power to the faint; and to them that have no might he increaseth strength. Even youths shall faint and be weary, and the young men shall utterly fall: But they that wait upon the Lord shall renew their strength; they shall mount up with wings as eagles; they shall run, and not be weary; and they shall walk, and not faint.
40:25–31 KJV

Fear thou not; for I am with thee: be not dismayed; for I am thy God: I will strengthen thee; yea, I will help thee; yea, I will uphold thee with the right hand of my righteousness.
41:10 KJV

A bruised reed shall he [the Lord's servant] not break, and the smoking flax shall he not quench: he shall bring forth judgment unto truth.
42:3 KJV

But now thus saith the Lord that created thee, O Jacob, and he that formed thee, O Israel, Fear not: for I have redeemed thee, I have called thee by thy name; thou art mine. When thou passest through the waters, I will be with thee: and through the rivers, they shall not overflow thee: when thou walkest through the fire, thou shalt not be burned; neither shall the flame kindle upon thee. For I am the Lord thy God, the Holy One of Israel, thy Saviour.
43:1–3 KJV

Look unto me, and be ye saved, all the ends of the earth: for I am God, and there is none else.
45:22 KJV

O that thou hadst hearkened to my commandments! Then had thy peace been as a river, and thy righteousness as the waves of the sea.
48:18 KJV

'There is no peace,' says the Lord, 'for the wicked.'
48:22 RSV

I will also give thee for a light to the Gentiles, that thou mayest be my salvation unto the end of the earth.
49:6 KJV

The Lord God hath given me the tongue of the learned, that I should know how to speak a word in season to him that is weary: he wakeneth morning by morning, he wakeneth mine ear to hear as the learned. The Lord God hath opened mine ear, and I was not rebellious, neither turned away back. I gave my back to the smiters, and my cheeks to them that plucked off the hair: I hid not my face from shame and spitting. For the Lord God will help me; therefore shall I not be confounded: therefore have I set my face like a flint, and I know that I shall not be ashamed. He is near that justifieth me; who will contend with me? Let us stand together: who is mine adversary? Let him come near to me. Behold, the Lord God will help me; who is he that shall condemn me? Lo, they all shall wax old as a garment; the moth shall eat them up.
50:4–9 KJV

How beautiful upon the mountains are the feet of him that bringeth good tidings, that publisheth peace; that bringeth good tidings of good, that publisheth salvation; that saith unto Zion, thy God reigneth! Thy watchmen shall lift up the voice; with the voice together shall they sing: for they shall see eye to eye, when the Lord shall bring again Zion. Break forth into joy, sing together, ye waste places of Jerusalem: for the Lord hath comforted his people, he hath redeemed Jerusalem. The Lord hath made bare his holy arm in the eyes of all the nations; and all the ends of the earth shall see the salvation of our God.
52:7–10 KJV

Who hath believed our report? and to whom is

the arm of the Lord revealed? For he shall grow up before him as a tender plant, and as a root out of a dry ground: he hath no form nor comeliness; and when we shall see him, there is no beauty that we should desire him. He is despised and rejected of men; a man of sorrows, and acquainted with grief: and we hid as it were our faces from him; he was despised, and we esteemed him not. Surely he hath borne our griefs, and carried our sorrows: yet we did esteem him stricken, smitten of God, and afflicted. But he was wounded for our transgressions, he was bruised for our iniquities: the chastisement of our peace was upon him; and with his stripes we are healed. All we like sheep have gone astray; we have turned every one to his own way; and the Lord hath laid on him the iniquity of us all. He was oppressed, and he was afflicted, yet he opened not his mouth: he is brought as a lamb to the slaughter, and as a sheep before her shearers is dumb, so he openeth not his mouth. He was taken from prison and from judgment: and who shall declare his generation? For he was cut off out of the land of the living: for the transgression of my people was he stricken. And he made his grave with the wicked, and with the rich in his death; because he had done no violence, neither was any deceit in his mouth. Yet it pleased the Lord to bruise him; he hath put him to grief: when thou shalt make his soul an offering for sin, he shall see his seed, he shall prolong his days, and the pleasure of the Lord shall prosper in his hand. He shall see of the travail of his soul, and shall be satisfied: by his knowledge shall my righteous servant justify many; for he shall bear their iniquities. Therefore will I divide him a portion with the great, and he shall divide the spoil with the strong; because he hath poured out his soul unto death; and he was numbered with the transgressors; and he bare the sin of many, and made intercession for the transgressors.

**53 KJV**

Ho, every one that thirsteth, come ye to the waters, and he that hath no money; come ye, buy, and eat; yea, come, buy wine and milk without money and without price. Wherefore do ye spend money for that which is not bread? and your labour for that which satisfieth not? Hearken diligently unto me, and eat ye that which is good, and let your soul delight itself in fatness. Incline your ear, and come unto me: hear, and

your soul shall live; and I will make an everlasting covenant with you, even the sure mercies of David.

**55:1–3 KJV**

Seek ye the Lord while he may be found, call ye upon him while he is near. Let the wicked forsake his way, and the unrighteous man his thoughts: and let him return unto the Lord, and he will have mercy upon him; and to our God, for he will abundantly pardon. For my thoughts are not your thoughts, neither are your ways my ways, saith the Lord. For as the heavens are higher than the earth, so are my ways higher than your ways, and my thoughts than your thoughts. For as the rain cometh down, and the snow from heaven, and returneth not thither, but watereth the earth, and maketh it bring forth and bud, that it may give seed to the sower, and bread to the eater: so shall my word be that goeth forth out of my mouth: it shall not return unto me void but it shall accomplish that which I please, and it shall prosper in the thing whereto I sent it.

**55:6–11 KJV**

For thus saith the high and lofty One that inhabiteth eternity, whose name is Holy; I dwell in the high and holy place, with him also that is of a contrite and humble spirit, to revive the spirit of the humble, and to revive the heart of the contrite ones.

**57:15 KJV**

'The kind of fasting I want is this: Remove the chains of oppression and the yoke of injustice, and let the oppressed go free.'

**58:6 GNB**

Behold, the Lord's hand is not shortened, that it cannot save, or his ear dull, that it cannot hear; but your iniquities have made a separation between you and your God, and your sins have hid his face from you so that he does not hear.

**59:1–2 RSV**

Arise, shine; for thy light is come, and the glory of the Lord is risen upon thee.

**60:1 KJV**

The Spirit of the Lord God is upon me; because the Lord hath anointed me to preach good tidings unto the meek; he hath sent me to bind up the brokenhearted, to proclaim liberty to the captives, and the opening of the prison to them that are bound; to proclaim the acceptable year of the Lord, and the day of vengeance of our God;

to comfort all that mourn; to appoint unto them that mourn in Zion, to give unto them beauty for ashes, the oil of joy for mourning, the garment of praise for the spirit of heaviness; that they might be called trees of righteousness, the planting of the Lord, that he might be glorified.

61:1–3 KJV

# Jeremiah

'Before I formed you in the womb I knew you, and before you were born I consecrated you; I appointed you a prophet to the nations.' Then I said, 'Ah, Lord God! Behold, I do not know how to speak, for I am only a youth.' But the Lord said to me, 'Do not say, ''I am only a youth''; for to all to whom I send you you shall go, and whatever I command you you shall speak. Be not afraid of them, for I am with you to deliver you, says the Lord.' Then the Lord put forth his hand and touched my mouth; and the Lord said to me, 'Behold, I have put my words in your mouth. See, I have set you this day over nations and over kingdoms, to pluck up and to break down, to destroy and to overthrow, to build and to plant.'

1:5–10 RSV

Then the Lord said to me, 'You have seen well, for I am watching over my word to perform it.'

1:12 RSV

'But this people has a stubborn and rebellious heart; they have turned aside and gone away.'

5:23 RSV

'The prophets prophesy lies, the priests rule by their own authority, and my people love it this way. But what will you do in the end?'

5:31 NIV

'For from the least to the greatest of them, every one is greedy for unjust gain; and from prophet to priest, every one deals falsely. They have healed the wound of my people lightly, saying, ''Peace, peace,'' when there is no peace.'

6:13–14 RSV

Thus saith the Lord, Stand ye in the ways, and see, and ask for the old paths, where is the good way, and walk therein, and ye shall find rest for your souls. But they said, We will not walk therein.

6:16 KJV

The harvest is past, the summer is ended, and we are not saved.

8:20 KJV

Is there no balm in Gilead; is there no physician there? Why then is not the health of the daughter of my people recovered?

8:22 KJV

Everyone deceives his neighbour, and no one speaks the truth; they have taught their tongue to speak lies; they commit iniquity and are too weary to repent.

9:5 RSV

Thus says the Lord: 'Let not the wise man glory in his wisdom, let not the mighty man glory in his might, let not the rich man glory in his riches; but let him who glories glory in this, that he understands and knows me, that I am the Lord who practise steadfast love, justice, and righteousness in the earth; for in these things I delight, says the Lord.'

9:23–24 RSV

Can the Ethiopian change his skin, or the leopard his spots?

13:23 KJV

The heart is deceitful above all things, and desperately wicked: who can know it? I the Lord search the heart.

17:9–10

Cursed be the day on which I was born! The day when my mother bore me, let it not be blessed! Cursed be the man who brought the news to my father, 'A son is born to you,' making him very glad. Let that man be like the cities which the Lord overthrew without pity; let him hear a cry in the morning and an alarm at noon, because he did not kill me in the womb; so my mother would have been my grave, and her womb for ever great. Why did I come forth from the womb to see toil and sorrow, and spend my days in shame?

20:14–18 RSV

'Behold, the days are coming, says the Lord, when I will raise up for David a righteous Branch, and he shall reign as king and deal wisely, and shall execute justice and righteousness in the land. In his days Judah will be saved, and Israel will dwell securely. And this is the name by which he will be called: ''The Lord is our righteousness.'' '

23:5–6 RSV

'For I know the plans I have for you, says the Lord, plans for welfare and not for evil, to give you a future and a hope. Then you will call upon me and come and pray to me, and I will hear you. You will seek me and find me; when you seek me with all your heart, I will be found by you, says the Lord, and I will restore your fortunes and gather you from all the nations and all the places where I have driven you, says the Lord, and I will bring you back to the place from where I sent you into exile.'

**29:11–14 RSV**

'Behold, the days are coming, says the Lord, when I will make a new covenant with the house of Israel and the house of Judah, not like the covenant which I made with their fathers when I took them by the hand to bring them out of the land of Egypt, my covenant which they broke, though I was their husband, says the Lord. But this is the covenant which I will make with the house of Israel after those days, says the Lord: I will put my law within them, and I will write it upon their hearts; and I will be their God, and they shall be my people. And no longer shall each man teach his neighbour and each his brother, saying ''Know the Lord,'' for they shall all know me, from the least of them to the greatest, says the Lord; for I will forgive their iniquity, and I will remember their sin no more.'

**31:31–34 RSV**

# Lamentations

Is it nothing to you, all ye that pass by? Behold, and see if there be any sorrow like unto my sorrow, which is done unto me, wherewith the Lord hath afflicted me in the day of this fierce anger.

**1:12 KJV**

My soul is bereft of peace, I have forgotten what happiness is.

**3:17 RSV**

Remember my affliction and my bitterness, the wormwood and the gall! My soul continually thinks of it and is bowed down within me. But this I call to mind, and therefore I have hope: The steadfast love of the Lord never ceases, his mercies never come to an end; they are new every morning; great is thy faithfulness. 'The Lord is my portion,' says my soul, 'therefore I will hope in him.' The Lord is good to those who wait for him, to the soul that seeks him. It is good that one should wait quietly for the salvation of the Lord. It is good for a man that he bear the yoke in his youth.

**3:19–27 RSV**

# Ezekiel

And from the midst of it came the likeness of four living creatures. And this was their appearance: they had the form of men, but each had four faces, and each of them had four wings.

**1:5–6 RSV**

Now as I looked at the living creatures, I saw a wheel upon the earth beside the living creatures, one for each of the four of them. As for the appearance of the wheels and their construction: their appearance was like the gleaming of a chrysolite; and the four had the same likeness, their construction being as it were a wheel within a wheel.

**1:15–16 RSV**

Such was the appearance of the likeness of the glory of the Lord. And when I saw it, I fell upon my face, and I heard the voice of one speaking. And he said to me, 'Son of man, stand upon your feet, and I will speak with you.' And when he spoke to me, the Spirit entered into me and set me upon my feet; and I heard him speaking to me. And he said to me, 'Son of man, I send you to the people of Israel, to a nation of rebels, who have rebelled against me; they and their fathers have transgressed against me to this very day. The people also are impudent and stubborn: I send you to them; and you shall say to them, ''Thus says the Lord God.'' And whether they hear or refuse to hear (for they are a rebellious house) they will know that there has been a prophet among them. And you, son of man, be not afraid of them, nor be afraid of their words.'

**1:28–2:6 RSV**

'They [false prophets] have spoken falsehood and divined a lie; they say, ''Says the Lord,'' when the Lord has not sent them, and yet they expect him to fulfil their word.'

**13:6 RSV**

[The Lord] 'Behold, all souls are mine; the soul of the father as well as the soul of the son is mine: the soul that sins shall die.'

18:4 RSV

'I will manifest my holiness among you in the sight of the nations. And you shall know that I am the Lord, when I bring you into the land of Israel, the country which I swore to give to your fathers. And there you shall remember your ways and all the doings with which you have polluted yourselves; and you shall loathe yourselves for all the evils that you have committed. And you shall know that I am the Lord, when I deal with you for my name's sake, not according to your evil ways, nor according to your corrupt doings, O house of Israel, says the Lord God.'

20:41–44 RSV

'So you, son of man, I have made a watchman for the house of Israel; whenever you hear a word from my mouth, you shall give them warning from me. If I say to the wicked, O wicked man, you shall surely die, and you do not speak to warn the wicked to turn from his way, that wicked man shall die in his iniquity, but his blood I will require at your hand. But if you warn the wicked to turn from his way, and he does not turn from his way; he shall die in his iniquity, but you will have saved your life.'

33:7–9 RSV

'Say to them, As I live, says the Lord God, I have no pleasure in the death of the wicked, but that the wicked turn from his way and live; turn back, turn back from your evil ways; for why will you die, O house of Israel?'

33:11 RSV

'Yet your people say, "The way of the Lord is not just"; when it is their own way that is not just. When the righteous turns from his righteousness, and commits iniquity, he shall die for it. And when the wicked turns from his wickedness, and does what is lawful and right, he shall live by it. Yet you say, "The way of the Lord is not just." O house of Israel, I will judge each of you according to his ways.' In the twelfth year of our exile, in the tenth month, on the fifth day of the month, a man who had escaped from Jerusalem came to me and said, 'The city has fallen.'

33:17–21 RSV

The word of the Lord came to me: 'Son of man, prophesy against the shepherds of Israel, prophesy, and say to them, even to the shepherds, Thus says the Lord God: Ho, shepherds of Israel who have been feeding yourselves! Should not shepherds feed the sheep?'

34:1–2 RSV

'And I will set up over them one shepherd, my servant David, and he shall feed them: he shall feed them and be their shepherd. And I, the Lord, will be their God, and my servant David shall be prince among them; I, the Lord, have spoken.'

34:23–24 RSV

'Therefore say to the house of Israel, Thus says the Lord God: It is not for your sake, O house of Israel, that I am about to act, but for the sake of my holy name, which you have profaned among the nations to which you came. And I will vindicate the holiness of my great name, which has been profaned among the nations, and which you have profaned among them; and the nations will know that I am the Lord, says the Lord God, when through you I vindicate my holiness before their eyes. For I will take you from the nations, and gather you from all the countries, and bring you into your own land. I will sprinkle clean water upon you, and you shall be clean from all your uncleannesses, and from all your idols I will cleanse you. A new heart I will give you, and a new spirit I will put within you; and I will take out of your flesh the heart of stone and give you a heart of flesh. And I will put my spirit within you, and cause you to walk in my statutes and be careful to observe my ordinances. You shall dwell in the land which I gave to your fathers; and you shall be my people, and I will be your God.'

36:22–28 RSV

The hand of the Lord was upon me, and he brought me out by the Spirit of the Lord, and set me down in the midst of the valley; it was full of bones. And he led me round among them; and behold, there were very many upon the valley; and lo, they were very dry. And he said to me, 'Son of man, can these bones live?' And I answered, 'O Lord God, thou knowest.' Again he said to me, 'Prophesy to these bones, and say to them, O dry bones, hear the word of the Lord. Thus says the Lord God to these bones: Behold, I will cause breath to enter you, and you shall live.'

37:1–5 RSV

The name of the city from that day shall be, The Lord is there.

48:35 KJV

# Daniel

Daniel answered the king, 'No wise men, enchanters, magicians, or astrologers can show to the king the mystery which the king has asked, but there is a God in heaven who reveals mysteries, and he has made known to King Nebuchadnezzar what will be in the latter days. Your dream and the visions of your head as you lay in bed are these.'

2:27–28 RSV

The king said [to Daniel], 'Your God is the greatest of all gods, the Lord over kings, and the one who reveals mysteries. I know this because you have been able to explain this mystery.' Then he gave Daniel a high position, presented him with many splendid gifts, put him in charge of the province of Babylon, and made him the head of all the royal advisors.

2:47–48 GNB

And the herald proclaimed aloud, 'You are commanded, O peoples, nations, and languages, that when you hear the sound of the horn, pipe, lyre, trigon, harp, bagpipe, and every kind of music, you are to fall down and worship the golden image that King Nebuchadnezzar has set up; and whoever does not fall down and worship shall immediately be cast into a burning fiery furnace.' Therefore, as soon as all the peoples heard . . . every kind of music, all the peoples, nations, and languages fell down and worshipped the golden image which King Nebuchadnezzar had set up.

3:4–7 RSV

Shadrach, Meshach, and Abednego answered the king, 'O Nebuchadnezzar, we have no need to answer you in this matter. If it be so, our God whom we serve is able to deliver us from the burning fiery furnace; and he will deliver us out of your hand, O king. But if not, be it known to you, O king, that we will not serve your gods or worship the golden image which you have set up.' Then Nebuchadnezzar was full of fury, and the expression of his face was changed against

Shadrach, Meshach, and Abednego. He ordered the furnace heated seven times more than it was wont to be heated. And he ordered certain mighty men of his army to bind Shadrach, Meshach, and Abednego, and to cast them into the burning fiery furnace.

3:16–20 RSV

Then King Nebuchadnezzar was astonished and rose up in haste. He said to his counsellors, 'Did we not cast three men bound into the fire?' They answered the king, 'True, O king.' He answered, 'But I see four men loose, walking in the midst of the fire, and they are not hurt; and the appearance of the fourth is like a son of the gods.' Then Nebuchadnezzar came near to the door of the burning fiery furnace and said, 'Shadrach, Meshach, and Abednego, servants of the Most High God, come forth, and come here!'

3:24–26 RSV

Nebuchadnezzar said, 'Blessed be the God of Shadrach, Meshach, and Abednego, who has sent his angel and delivered his servants, who trusted in him, and set at naught the king's command, and yielded up their bodies rather than serve and worship any god except their own God.'

3:28 RSV

Immediately the word was fulfilled upon Nebuchadnezzar. He was driven from among men, and ate grass like an ox, and his body was wet with the dew of heaven till his hair grew as long as eagles' feathers, and his nails were like birds' claws.

4:33 RSV

Immediately the fingers of a man's hand appeared and wrote on the plaster of the wall of the king's palace, opposite the lampstand; and the king saw the hand as it wrote.

5:5 RSV

'This is the writing that was inscribed: Mene, Mene, Tekel, and Parsin. This is the interpretation of the matter: Mene, God has numbered the days of your kingdom and brought it to an end; Tekel, you have been weighed in the balances and found wanting; Peres, your kingdom is divided and given to the Medes and Persians.'

5:25–28 RSV

Then the king commanded, and Daniel was brought and cast into the den of lions. The king said to Daniel, 'May your God, whom you serve continually, deliver you!'
6:16 RSV

'As I looked, thrones were set in place, and the Ancient of Days took his seat. His clothing was as white as snow; the hair of his head was white like wool. His throne was flaming with fire, and its wheels were all ablaze. A river of fire was flowing, coming out from before him. Thousands upon thousands attended him; ten thousand times ten thousand stood before him. The court was seated, and the books were opened.'
7:9–10 NIV

'In my vision at night I looked, and there before me was one like a son of man, coming with the clouds of heaven. He approached the Ancient of Days and was led into his presence. He was given authority, glory and sovereign power; all peoples, nations and men of every language worshipped him. His dominion is an everlasting dominion that will not pass away, and his kingdom is one that will never be destroyed.'
7:13–14 NIV

'Now, therefore, O our God, hearken to the prayer of thy servant and to his supplications, and for thy own sake, O Lord, cause thy face to shine upon thy sanctuary, which is desolate. O my God, incline thy ear and hear; open thy eyes and behold our desolations, and the city which is called by thy name; for we do not present our supplications before thee on the ground of our righteousness, but on the ground of thy great mercy. O Lord, hear; O Lord, forgive; O Lord, give heed and act; delay not, for thy own sake, O my God, because thy city and thy people are called by thy name.'
9:17–19 RSV

'At that time shall arise Michael, the great prince who has charge of your people. And there shall be a time of trouble, such as never has been since there was a nation till that time; but at that time your people shall be delivered, every one whose name shall be found written in the book. And many of those who sleep in the dust of the earth shall awake, some to everlasting life, and some to shame and everlasting contempt. And those who are wise shall shine like the brightness of the firmament; and those who turn many to righteousness, like the stars for ever and ever. But you, Daniel, shut up the words, and seal the book, until the time of the end. Many shall run to and fro, and knowledge shall increase.'
12:1–4 RSV

# Hosea

When the Lord first spoke through Hosea, the Lord said to Hosea, 'Go, take to yourself a wife of harlotry and have children of harlotry, for the land commits great harlotry by forsaking the Lord.'
1:2 RSV

The people of Israel will become like the sand of the sea, more than can be counted or measured. Now God says to them, 'You are not my people,' but the day is coming when he will say to them, 'You are the children of the living God!'
1:10 GNB

[The Lord] 'And I will betroth you to me for ever; I will betroth you to me in righteousness and in justice, in steadfast love, and in mercy. I will betroth you to me in faithfulness; and you shall know the Lord.'
2:19–20 RSV

'My people are destroyed for lack of knowledge; because you have rejected knowledge, I reject you from being a priest to me. And since you have forgotten the law of your God, I also will forget your children.'
4:6 RSV

'Let us know, let us press on to know the Lord; his going forth is sure as the dawn; he will come to us as the showers, as the spring rains that water the earth.'
6:3 RSV

For I desire steadfast love and not sacrifice, the knowledge of God, rather than burnt offerings.
6:6 RSV

When Israel was a child, I loved him, and out of Egypt I called my son.
11:1 RSV

I will heal their faithlessness; I will love them freely, for my anger has turned from them. I will be as the dew to Israel; he shall blossom as the lily, he shall strike root as the poplar; his shoots shall spread out; his beauty shall be like the olive, and his fragrance like Lebanon.

14:4–5 RSV

# Joel

What the locust swarm has left the great locusts have eaten; what the great locusts have left the young locusts have eaten; what the young locusts have left other locusts have eaten.

1:4 NIV

'Yet even now,' says the Lord, 'return to me with all your heart, with fasting, with weeping, and with mourning; and rend your hearts and not your garments.' Return to the Lord, your God, for he is gracious and merciful, slow to anger, and abounding in steadfast love, and repents of evil.

2:12–23 RSV

And I will restore to you the years that the locust hath eaten.

2:25 KJV

'And it shall come to pass afterward, that I will pour out my spirit on all flesh; your sons and your daughters shall prophesy, your old men shall dream dreams, and your young men shall see visions. Even upon the menservants and maidservants in those days, I will pour out my spirit. And I will give portents in the heavens and on the earth, blood and fire and columns of smoke. The sun shall be turned to darkness, and the moon to blood, before the great and terrible day of the Lord comes. And it shall come to pass that all who call upon the name of the Lord shall be delivered; for in Mount Zion and in Jerusalem there shall be those who escape, as the Lord has said, and among the survivors shall be those whom the Lord calls.'

2:28–32 RSV

# Amos

And he said: 'The Lord roars from Zion, and utters his voice from Jerusalem; the pastures of the shepherds mourn, and the top of Carmel withers.'

1:2 RSV

Can two walk together, except they be agreed?

3:3 KJV

The Sovereign Lord never does anything without revealing his plan to his servants, the prophets. When a lion roars, who can avoid being afraid? When the Sovereign Lord speaks, who can avoid proclaiming his message?

3:7–8 GNB

'I hate, I despise your feasts, and I take no delight in your solemn assemblies. Even though you offer me your burnt offerings and cereal offerings, I will not accept them, and the peace offerings of your fatted beasts I will not look upon. Take away from me the noise of your songs; to the melody of your harps I will not listen. But let justice roll down like waters, and righteousness like an ever-flowing stream.'

5:21–24 RSV

Woe to them that are at ease in Zion, and trust in the mountain of Samaria.

6:1 KJV

'The days are coming,' says the Lord, 'when corn will grow faster than it can be harvested, and grapes will grow faster than the wine can be made. The mountains will drip with sweet wine, and the hills will flow with it. I will bring my people back to their land. They will rebuild their ruined cities and live there; they will plant vineyards and drink the wine; they will plant gardens and eat what they grow. I will plant my people on the land I gave them, and they will not be pulled up again.' The Lord your God has spoken.

9:13–15 GNB

# Obadiah

For soon the day of the Lord will come on all the nations: you shall be treated as you have treated others, and your deeds will recoil on your own head.

15 NEB

'But on Mount Zion will be deliverance; it will be holy, and the house of Jacob will possess its inheritance.'

17 NIV

Saviours shall go up to Mount Zion to rule Mount Esau; and the kingdom shall be the Lord's.

21 RSV

# Jonah

Now the word of the Lord came to Jonah the son of Amittai, saying, 'Arise, go to Nineveh, that great city, and cry against it; for their wickedness has come up before me.' But Jonah rose to flee to Tarshish from the presence of the Lord.

1:1–3 RSV

And the Lord appointed a great fish to swallow up Jonah; and Jonah was in the belly of the fish three days and three nights.

1:17 RSV

'When my soul fainted within me, I remembered the Lord; and my prayer came to thee, into thy holy temple.'

2:7 RSV

Then the word of the Lord came to Jonah the second time, saying, 'Arise, go to Nineveh, that great city, and proclaim to it the message that I tell you.' So Jonah arose and went to Nineveh, according to the word of the Lord. Now Nineveh was an exceedingly great city, three days' journey in breadth ... And he cried, 'Yet forty days, and Nineveh shall be overthrown!' And the people of Nineveh believed God; they proclaimed a fast, and put on sackcloth, from the greatest of them to the least of them.

3:1–5 RSV

When God saw what they did, how they turned from their evil way, God repented of the evil which he had said he would do to them; and he did not do it. But it displeased Jonah exceedingly, and he was angry.

3:10–4:1 RSV

But God said to Jonah, 'Do you do well to be angry for the plant?' And he said, 'I do well to be angry, angry enough to die.' And the Lord said, 'You pity the plant, for which you did not labour, nor did you make it grow, which came into being in a night, and perished in a night. And should not I pity Nineveh, that great city, in which there are more than a hundred and twenty thousand persons who do not know their right hand from their left, and also much cattle?'

4:9–11 RSV

# Micah

But as for me, I am filled with power, with the Spirit of the Lord, and with justice and might, to declare to Jacob his transgression and to Israel his sin.

3:8 RSV

It shall come to pass in the latter days that the mountain of the house of the Lord shall be established as the highest of the mountains, and shall be raised up above the hills; and peoples shall flow to it, and many nations shall come, and say: 'Come, let us go up to the mountain of the Lord, to the house of the God of Jacob; that he may teach us his ways and we may walk in his paths.' For out of Zion shall go forth the law, and the word of the Lord from Jerusalem. He shall judge between many peoples, and shall decide for strong nations afar off; and they shall beat their swords into ploughshares, and their spears into pruning hooks; nation shall not lift up sword against nation, neither shall they learn war any more; but they shall sit every man under his vine and under his fig tree, and none shall make them afraid for the mouth of the Lord of hosts has spoken. For all the peoples walk each in the name of its god, but we will walk in the name of the Lord our God for ever and ever.

4:1–5 RSV

But thou, Bethlehem Ephratah, though thou be little among the thousands of Judah, yet out of thee shall he come forth unto me that is to be ruler in Israel; whose goings forth have been from of old, from everlasting. Therefore will he give them up, until the time that she which travaileth hath brought forth: then the remnant of his brethren shall return unto the children of Israel. And he shall stand and feed in the strength of the Lord, in the majesty of the name of the Lord his God; and they shall abide: for now shall he be great unto the ends of the earth.

5:2–4 KJV

He hath shewed thee, O man, what is good; and what doth the Lord require of thee, but to do justly, and to love mercy, and to walk humbly with thy God?

6:8 KJV

Who is a God like thee, pardoning iniquity and passing over transgression for the remnant of his inheritance? He does not retain his anger for ever because he delights in steadfast love. He will again have compassion upon us, he will tread our iniquities under foot. Thou wilt cast all our sins into the depths of the sea. Thou wilt show faithfulness to Jacob and steadfast love to Abraham, as thou hast sworn to our fathers from the days of old.

7:18–20 RSV

# Nahum

An oracle concerning Nineveh. The book of the vision of Nahum the Elkoshite. The Lord is a jealous and avenging God; the Lord takes vengeance and is filled with wrath. The Lord takes vengeance on his foes and maintains his wrath against his enemies.

1:1–2 NIV

Behold, I am against you, says the Lord of hosts, and I will burn your chariots in smoke, and the sword shall devour your young lions; I will cut off your prey from the earth, and the voice of your messengers shall no more be heard. Woe to the bloody city, all full of lies and booty—no end to the plunder!

2:13–3:1 RSV

# Habakkuk

Look among the nations, and see; wonder and be astounded. For I am doing a work in your days that you would not believe if told. For lo, I am rousing the Chaldeans, that bitter and hasty nation, who march through the breadth of the earth, to seize habitations not their own.

1:5–6 RSV

Art thou not from everlasting, O Lord my God, my Holy One? We shall not die. O Lord, thou hast ordained them as a judgment; and thou, O Rock, hast established them for chastisement. Thou who art of purer eyes than to behold evil and canst not look on wrong, why dost thou look on faithless men, and art silent when the wicked swallows up the man more righteous than he?

1:12–13 RSV

I will take my stand to watch, and station myself on the tower, and look forth to see what he will say to me, and what I will answer concerning my complaint. And the Lord answered me: 'Write the vision; make it plain upon tablets, so he may run who reads it. For still the vision awaits its time; it hastens to the end—it will not lie. If it seem slow, wait for it; it will surely come, it will not delay. Behold, he whose soul is not upright in him shall fail, but the righteous shall live by his faith.'

2:1–4 RSV

O Lord, revive thy work in the midst of the years, in the midst of the years make known; in wrath remember mercy.

3:2 KJV

I hear, and my body trembles, my lips quiver at the sound; rottenness enters into my bones, my steps totter beneath me. I will quietly wait for the day of trouble to come upon people who invade us. Though the fig tree do not blossom, nor fruit be on the vines, the produce of the olive fail and the fields yield no food, the flock be cut off from the fold and there be no herd in the stalls, yet I will rejoice in the Lord, I will joy in the God of my salvation. God, the Lord, is my strength; he makes my feet like hinds' feet, he makes me tread upon my high places.

3:16–19 RSV

# Zephaniah

'I will utterly sweep away everything from the face of the earth,' says the Lord. 'I will sweep away man and beast; I will sweep away the birds of the air and the fish of the sea. I will overthrow the wicked; I will cut off mankind from the face of the earth,' says the Lord.

1:2–3 RSV

'Yea, at that time I will change the speech of the peoples to a pure speech, that all of them may call on the name of the Lord and serve him with one accord.'

3:9 RSV

'But I will leave within you the meek and humble, who trust in the name of the Lord. The remnant of Israel will do no wrong; they will speak no lies, nor will deceit be found in their mouths. They will eat and lie down and no-one will make them afraid.'

3:12–13 NIV

'At that time I will bring you home, at the time when I gather you together; yea, I will make you renowned and praised among all the peoples of the earth, when I restore your fortunes before you eyes,' says the Lord.

3:20 RSV

# Haggai

These are the words of the Lord of Hosts: This nation says to itself that it is not yet time for the house of the Lord to be rebuilt. Then this word came through Haggai the prophet: Is it a time for you to live in your own well-roofed houses, while this house lies in ruins? Now these are the words of the Lord of Hosts: Consider your way of life.

1:2–5 NEB

' "Yet now take courage, O Zerubbabel, says the Lord; take courage, O Joshua, son of Jehozadak, the high priest; take courage, all you people of the land, says the Lord; work, for I am with you, says the Lord of hosts, according to the promise that I made you when you came out of Egypt. My Spirit abides among you; fear not. For thus says the Lord of hosts: Once again, in a little while, I will shake the heavens and the earth and the sea and the dry land; and I will shake all nations, so that the treasures of all nations shall come in, and I will fill this house with splendour, says the Lord of hosts. The silver is mine, and the gold is mine, says the Lord of hosts. The latter splendour of this house shall be greater than the former, says the Lord of hosts; and in this place I will give prosperity, says the Lord of hosts." '

2:4–9 RSV

# Zechariah

These are the words of the Lord of Hosts: I am very jealous for Jerusalem and Zion. I am full of anger against the nations that enjoy their ease, because, while my anger was but mild, they heaped evil on evil. Therefore these are the words of the Lord: I have come back to Jerusalem with compassion, and my house shall be rebuilt in her, says the Lord of Hosts, and the measuring-line shall be stretched over Jerusalem.

1:14–16 NEB

This is the word of the Lord unto Zerubbabel, saying, Not by might, nor by power, but by my spirit, saith the Lord of hosts.

4:6 KJV

For who hath despised the day of small things? For they shall rejoice, and shall see the plummet in the hand of Zerubbabel with those seven; they are the eyes of the Lord, which run to and fro through the whole earth.

4:10 KJV

'Tell him [Joshua, the high priest] that the Lord Almighty says, "The man who is called The Branch will flourish where he is and rebuild the Lord's Temple. He is the one who will build it and receive the honour due to a king, and he will rule his people. A priest will stand by his throne, and they will work together in peace and harmony." '

6:12–13 GNB

The Lord gave this message to Zechariah: 'Long ago I gave these commands to my people: "You must see that justice is done, and must show kindness and mercy to one another. Do not oppress widows, orphans, foreigners who live among you, or anyone else in need. And do not plan ways of harming one another." '

7:8–10 GNB

Rejoice greatly; O Daughter of Zion! Shout, daughter of Jerusalem! See, your king comes to you, righteous and having salvation, gentle and riding on a donkey, on a colt, the foal of a donkey. I will take away the chariots from Ephraim and the war-horses from Jerusalem, and the battle-bow will be broken. He will proclaim peace to the nations. His rule will extend from sea to sea and from the River to the ends of the earth.

9:9–10 NIV

And they weighed out as my wages thirty shekels of silver.

11:13 RSV

And I will pour upon the house of David, and upon the inhabitants of Jerusalem, the spirit of grace and of supplications: and they shall look upon me whom they have pierced, and they shall mourn for him, as one mourneth for his only son, and shall be in bitterness for him, as one that is in bitterness for his firstborn.

12:10 KJV

And one shall say unto him, What are these wounds in thine hands? Then he shall answer, Those with which I was wounded in the house of my friends. Awake, O sword, against my shepherd, and against the man that is my fellow, saith the Lord of hosts: smite the shepherd, and the sheep shall be scattered: and I will turn mine hand upon the little ones.

**13:6–7 KJV**

# Malachi

Have we not all one father? Has not one God created us? Why then are we faithless to one another, profaning the covenant of our fathers?

**2:10 RSV**

You have wearied the Lord with your words. Yet you say, 'How have we wearied him?' By saying, 'Everyone who does evil is good in the sight of the Lord, and he delights in them.' Or by asking, 'Where is the god of Justice?' 'Behold, I send my messenger to prepare the way before me, and the Lord whom you seek will suddenly come to his temple; the messenger of the covenant in whom you delight, behold, he is coming, says the Lord of hosts. But who can endure the day of his coming, and who can stand when he appears?'

**2:17–3:2 RSV**

For I am the Lord, I change not; therefore ye sons of Jacob are not consumed.

**3:6 KJV**

'Bring the full tithes into the storehouse, that there may be food in my house; and thereby put me to the test, says the Lord of hosts, if I will not open the windows of heaven for you and pour down for you an overflowing blessing.'

**3:10 RSV**

Then the people who feared the Lord spoke to one another, and the Lord listened and heard what they said. In his presence, there was written down in a book a record of those who feared the Lord and respected him.

**3:16 GNB**

But unto you that fear my name shall the Sun of righteousness arise with healing in his wings; and ye shall go forth, and grow up as calves of the stall.

**4:2 KJV**

# NEW TESTAMENT

## Matthew

[An angel of the Lord to Joseph] 'You shall call his name Jesus, for he will save his people from their sins.
1:21 RSV

Now when Jesus was born in Bethlehem of Judea in the days of Herod the king, behold, there came wise men from the east to Jerusalem, saying, Where is he that is born King of the Jews? for we have seen his star in the east, and are come to worship him.
2:1–2 KJV

And when they were come into the house, they saw the young child with Mary his mother, and fell down, and worshipped him: and when they had opened their treasures, they presented unto him gifts; gold, and frankincense, and myrrh.
2:11 KJV

[John the Baptist] 'I baptize you with water for repentance, but he who is coming after me is mightier than I, whose sandals I am not worthy to carry; he will baptize you with the Holy Spirit and with fire.'
3:11 RSV

And when Jesus was baptized, he went up immediately from the water, and behold, the heavens were opened and he saw the Spirit of God descending like a dove, and alighting on him; and lo, a voice from heaven, saying, 'This is my beloved Son, with whom I am well pleased.' Then Jesus was led up by the Spirit into the wilderness to be tempted by the devil.
3:16–4:1 RSV

As he walked by the Sea of Galilee, he saw two brothers, Simon who is called Peter and Andrew his brother, casting a net into the sea; for they were fishermen. And he said to them, 'Follow me, and I will make you fishers of men.' Immediately they left their nets and followed him.
4:18–20 RSV

And seeing the multitudes, he went up into a mountain: and when he was set, his disciples came unto him: and he opened his mouth, and taught them, saying, Blessed are the poor in spirit: for theirs is the kingdom of heaven. Blessed are they that mourn: for they shall be comforted. Blessed are the meek: for they shall inherit the earth. Blessed are they which do hunger and thirst after righteousness: for they shall be filled. Blessed are the merciful: for they shall obtain mercy. Blessed are the pure in heart: for they shall see God. Blessed are the peacemakers: for they shall be called the children of God. Blessed are they which are persecuted for righteousness' sake: for theirs is the kingdom of heaven. Blessed are ye, when men shall revile you, and persecute you, and shall say all manner of evil against you falsely, for my sake.
5:1–11 KJV

Ye are the salt of the earth: but if the salt have lost his savour, wherewith shall it be salted? It is thenceforth good for nothing, but to be cast out, and to be trodden under foot of men. Ye are the light of the world. A city that is set on a hill cannot be hid. Neither do men light a candle, and put it under a bushel, but on a candlestick; and it giveth light unto all that are in the house. Let your light so shine before men, that they may see your good works, and glorify your Father which is in heaven.
5:13–16 KJV

'Think not that I have come to abolish the law and the prophets; I have come not to abolish them but to fulfil them.'
5:17 RSV

'For I tell you, unless your righteousness exceeds that of the scribes and Pharisees, you will never enter the kingdom of heaven.'
5:20 RSV

Ye have heard that it hath been said, Thou shalt love thy neighbour, and hate thine enemy. But I say unto you, Love your enemies, bless them that curse you, do good to them that hate you, and pray for them which despitefully use you, and persecute you; that ye may be the children of your Father which is in heaven: for he maketh his sun to rise on the evil and on the good, and sendeth rain on the just and on the unjust. For if ye love them which love you, what reward have ye? Do not even the publicans the same? And if ye salute your brethren only, what do ye more than others? Do not even the publicans so? Be ye therefore perfect, even as your Father which in heaven is perfect.

5:43–48 KJV

'Beware of practising your piety before men in order to be seen by them; for then you will have no reward from your Father who is in heaven.'

6:1 RSV

'When you pray, do not be like the hypocrites! They love to stand up and pray in the houses of worship and on the street corners, so that everyone will see them. I assure you, they have already been paid in full. But when you pray, go to your room, close the door, and pray to your Father, who is unseen. And your Father, who sees what you do in private, will reward you. When you pray, do not use a lot of meaningless words, as the pagans do, who think that God will hear them because their prayers are long. Do not be like them. Your Father already knows what you need before you ask him. This, then, is how you should pray.'

6:5–9 GNB

Our Father, which art in heaven, hallowed be thy name. Thy kingdom come. Thy will be done, in earth as it is in heaven. Give us this day our daily bread. And forgive us our trespasses, as we forgive them that trespass against us. And lead us not into temptation; but deliver us from evil.

6:9–13 BCP

For thine is the kingdom, and the power, and the glory, for ever. Amen.

6:13 KJV

'Do not lay up for yourselves treasures on earth, where moth and rust consume and where thieves break in and steal, but lay up for yourselves treasures in heaven, where neither moth nor rust consumes and where thieves do not break in and steal. For where your treasure is, there will your heart be also.'

6:19–21 RSV

'No one can serve two masters; for either he will hate the one and love the other, or he will be devoted to the one and despise the other. You cannot serve God and mammon.'

6:24 RSV

Therefore I say unto you, Take no thought for your life, what ye shall eat, or what ye shall drink; not yet for your body, what ye shall put on. Is not the life more than meat, and the body than raiment? Behold the fowls of the air: for they sow not, neither do they reap, nor gather into barns; yet your heavenly Father feedeth them. Are ye not much better than they? Which of you by taking thought can add one cubit unto his stature? And why take ye thought for raiment? Consider the lilies of the field, how they grow; they toil not, neither do they spin: and yet I say unto you, That even Solomon in all his glory was not arrayed like one of these. Wherefore, if God so clothe the grass of the field, which to day is, and to morrow is cast into the oven, shall he not much more clothe you, O ye of little faith? Therefore take no thought, saying, What shall we eat? or, What shall we drink? or, Wherewithal shall we be clothed? (For after all these things do the Gentles seek:) for your heavenly Father knoweth that ye have need of all these things. But seek ye first the kingdom of God, and his righteousness; and all these things shall be added unto you. Take therefore no thought for the morrow: for the morrow shall take thought for the things of itself. Sufficient unto the day is the evil thereof.

6:25–34 KJV

Judge not, that ye be not judged.

7:1 KJV

'Why do you see the speck that is in your brother's eye, but do not notice the log that is in your own eye?'

7:3 RSV

'Do not give dogs what is holy; and do not throw your pearls before swine, lest they trample them under foot and turn to attack you. Ask, and it will be given you; seek, and you will find; knock, and it will be opened to you. For every one who asks receives, and he who seeks finds, and to him who knocks it will be opened.'

7:6–8 RSV

'So, whatever you wish that men would do to you, do so to them; for this is the law and the

prophets. Enter by the narrow gate; for the gate is wide and the way is easy, that leads to destruction, and those who enter by it are many. For the gate is narrow and the way is hard, that leads to life, and those who find it are few. Beware of false prophets, who come to you in sheep's clothing but inwardly are ravenous wolves. You will know them by their fruits.'
7:12–16 RSV

'Not every one who says to me, "Lord, Lord," shall enter the kingdom of heaven, but he who does the will of my Father who is in heaven.'
7:21 RSV

'But that you may know that the Son of man has authority on earth to forgive sins'—he then said to the paralytic—'Rise, take up your bed and go home.'
9:6 RSV

'And no one puts a piece of unshrunk cloth on an old garment, for the patch tears away from the garment, and a worse tear is made. Neither is new wine put into old wineskins; if it is, the skins burst, and the wine is spilled, and the skins are destroyed; but new wine is put into fresh wineskins, and so both are preserved.'
9:16–17 RSV

When he saw the crowds, he had compassion for them, because they were harassed and helpless, like sheep without a shepherd. Then he said to his disciples, 'The harvest is plentiful, but the labourers are few; pray therefore the Lord of the harvest to send out labourers into his harvest.'
9:36–38 RSV

And he called to him his twelve disciples and gave them authority over unclean spirits, to cast them out, and to heal every disease and every infirmity. The names of the twelve apostles are these: first, Simon, who is called Peter, and Andrew his brother; James the son of Zebedee, and John his brother; Philip and Bartholomew; Thomas and Matthew the tax collector; James the son of Alphaeus, and Thaddaeus; Simon the Cananaean, and Judas Iscariot, who betrayed him.
10:1–4 RSV

'All things have been delivered to me by my Father; and no one knows the Son except the Father, and no one knows the Father except the Son and any one to whom the Son chooses to reveal him. Come to me, all who labour and are heavy-laden, and I will give you rest. Take my yoke upon you, and learn from me; for I am gentle and lowly in heart, and you will find rest for your souls. For my yoke is easy, and my burden is light.'
11:27–30 RSV

Jesus said to them, 'A prophet is not without honour except in his own country and in his own house.' And he did not do many mighty works there, because of their unbelief.
13:57–58 RSV

When Jesus came into the coasts of Caesarea Philippi, he asked his disciples, saying, Whom do men say that I the Son of man am? And they said, Some say that thou art John the Baptist: some, Elias; and others, Jeremias, or one of the prophets. He saith unto them, But whom say ye that I am? And Simon Peter answered and said, Thou art the Christ, the Son of the living God. And Jesus answered and said unto him, Blessed art thou, Simon Bar-jona: for flesh and blood hath not revealed it unto thee, but my Father which is in heaven. And I say also unto thee, That thou art Peter, and upon this rock I will build my church; and the gates of hell shall not prevail against it. And I will give unto thee the keys of the kingdom of heaven: and whatsoever thou shalt bind on earth shall be bound in heaven: and whatsoever thou shalt loose on earth shall be loosed in heaven.
16:13–19 KJV

From that time forth began Jesus to shew unto his disciples, how that he must go unto Jerusalem, and suffer many things of the elders and chief priests and scribes, and be killed, and be raised again the third day. Then Peter took him, and began to rebuke him, saying, Be it far from thee, Lord: this shall not be unto thee. But he turned, and said unto Peter, Get thee behind me, Satan: thou art an offence unto me.
16:21–23 KJV

Verily I say unto you, Except ye be converted, and become as little children, ye shall not enter into the kingdom of heaven. Whosoever therefore shall humble himself as this little child, the same is greatest in the kingdom of heaven.
18:3–4 KJV

'Again I say to you, if two of you agree on earth about anything they ask, it will be done for them by my Father in heaven. For where two or three are gathered in my name, there am I in the midst of them.'

18:19–20 RSV

Master, which is the great commandment in the law? Jesus said unto him, Thou shalt love the Lord thy God with all thy heart, and with all thy soul, and with all thy mind. This is the first and great commandment. And the second is like unto it, Thou shalt love thy neighbour as thyself. On these two commandments hang all the law and the prophets.

22:36–40 KJV

'But woe to you, scribes and Pharisees, hypocrites! because you shut the kingdom of heaven against men; for you neither enter yourselves, nor allow those who would enter to go in.'

23:13 RSV

As he sat on the Mount of Olives, the disciples came to him privately, saying, 'Tell us, when will this be, and what will be the sign of your coming and of the close of the age?' And Jesus answered them, 'Take heed that no one leads you astray. For many will come in my name, saying ''I am the Christ,'' and they will lead many astray. And you will hear of wars and rumours of wars; see that you are not alarmed; for this must take place, but the end is not yet. For nation will rise against nation, and kingdom against kingdom, and there will be famines and earthquakes in various places.'

24:3–7 RSV

When the Son of man shall come in his glory, and all the holy angels with him, then shall he sit upon the throne of his glory: and before him shall be gathered all nations: and he shall separate them one from another, as a shepherd divideth his sheep from the goats: and he shall set the sheep on his right hand, but the goats on the left. Then shall the King say unto them on his right hand, Come, ye blessed of my Father, inherit the kingdom prepared for you from the foundation of the world: for I was an hungred, and ye gave me meat: I was thirsty, and ye gave me drink: I was a stranger, and ye took me in: naked, and ye clothed me: I was sick, and ye visited me: I was in prison, and ye came unto me.

25:31–36 KJV

And the King shall answer and say unto them, Verily I say unto you, Inasmuch as ye have done it unto one of the least of these my brethren, ye have done it unto me. Then shall he say also unto them on the left hand, Depart from me, ye cursed, into everlasting fire, prepared for the devil and his angels.

25:40–41 KJV

And these shall go away into everlasting punishment: but the righteous into life eternal.

25:46 KJV

Now as they were eating, Jesus took bread, and blessed, and broke it, and gave it to the disciples and said, 'Take, eat; this is my body.' And he took a cup, and when he had given thanks he gave it to them, saying, 'Drink of it, all of you; for this is my blood of the covenant, which is poured out for many for the forgiveness of sins.' I tell you I shall not drink again of this fruit of the vine until that day when I drink it new with you in my Father's kingdom.'

26:26–29 RSV

And the high priest said to him, 'I adjure you by the living God, tell us if you are the Christ, the Son of God.' Jesus said to him, 'You have said so. But I tell you, hereafter you will see the Son of man seated at the right hand of Power, and coming on the clouds of heaven.' Then the high priest tore his robes, and said, 'He has uttered blasphemy. Why do we still need witnesses? You have now heard his blasphemy.'

26:63–65 RSV

And they stripped him and put a scarlet robe upon him, and plaiting a crown of thorns they put it on his head, and put a reed in his right hand. And kneeling before him they mocked him, saying, 'Hail, King of the Jews!' And they spat upon him, and took the reed and struck him on the head. And when they had mocked him, they stripped him of the robe, and put his own clothes on him, and led him away to crucify him.

27:28–31 RSV

Now from the sixth hour there was darkness over all the land until the ninth hour. And about the ninth hour Jesus cried with a loud voice, 'Eli, Eli, lama sabachthani?' that is, 'My God, my God, why hast thou forsaken me?'

27:45–46 RSV

He is not here: for he is risen, as he said. Come, see the place where the Lord lay.

28:6 KJV

And when they saw him they worshipped him; but some doubted. And Jesus came and said to them, 'All authority in heaven and on earth has been given to me. Go therefore and make disciples of all nations, baptizing them in the name of the Father and of the Son and of the Holy Spirit, teaching them to observe all that I have commanded you; and lo, I am with you always, to the close of the age.'

28:17–20 RSV

# Mark

This is the Good News about Jesus Christ, the Son of God.

1:1 GNB

Now after John was arrested, Jesus came into Galilee, preaching the gospel of God, and saying, 'The time is fulfilled, and the kingdom of God is at hand; repent, and believe in the gospel.'

1:14–15 RSV

'The sabbath was made for man, not man for the sabbath; so the Son of man is lord even of the sabbath.'

2:27–28 RSV

And he said, 'He who has ears to hear, let him hear.' And when he was alone, those who were about him with the twelve asked him concerning the parables. And he said to them, 'To you has been given the secret of the kingdom of God, but for those outside everything is in parables; so that they may indeed see but not perceive, and may indeed hear but not understand; lest they should turn again, and be forgiven.'

4:9–12 RSV

And he said, 'What comes out of a man is what defiles a man. For from within, out of the heart of man, come evil thoughts, fornication, theft, murder, adultery, coveting, wickedness, deceit, licentiousness, envy, slander, pride, foolishness.'

7:20–22 RSV

And they brought young children to him, that he should touch them: and his disciples rebuked those that brought them. But when Jesus saw it, he was much displeased, and said unto them, Suffer the little children to come unto me, and forbid them not: for of such is the kingdom of God. Verily I say unto you, Whosoever shall not receive the kingdom of God as a little child, he shall not enter therein. And he took them up in his arms, put his hands upon them, and blessed them.

10:13–16 KJV

And Jesus called them to him and said to them, 'You know that those who are supposed to rule over the Gentiles lord it over them, and their great men exercise authority over them. But it shall not be so among you; but whoever would be great among you must be your servant, and whoever would be first among you must be slave of all. For the Son of man also came not to be served but to serve, and to give his life as a ransom for many.'

10:42–45 RSV

Afterwards he appeared to the eleven themselves as they sat at table; and he upbraided them for their unbelief and hardness of heart, because they had not believed those who saw him after he had risen. And he said to them, 'Go into all the world and preach the gospel to the whole creation.'

16:14–15 RSV

# Luke

It seemed good to me also, having followed all things closely for some time past, to write an orderly account for you, most excellent Theophilus, that you may know the truth concerning the things of which you have been informed.

1:3–4 RSV

[The angel Gabriel to Mary] And he came to her and said, 'Hail, O favoured one, the Lord is with you!' But she was greatly troubled at the saying, and considered in her mind what sort of greeting this might be. And the angel said to her, 'Do not be afraid, Mary, for you have found favour with God. And behold, you will conceive in your womb and bear a son, and you shall call his name Jesus. He will be great, and will be called the Son of the Most High; and the Lord God will give to him the throne of his father David, and he will reign over the house of Jacob for ever; and of his kingdom there will be no end.' And Mary said to the angel, 'How shall this be, since I have no husband?' And the angel said to her, 'The Holy Spirit will come upon you, and the power of the Most High will overshadow you; therefore the child to be born will be called holy, the Son of God. And behold, your kinswoman Elizabeth in her old age has also conceived a son; and this is the sixth month with her who was called barren. For with God nothing will be impossible.' And Mary said, 'Behold, I am the handmaid of the Lord; let it be to me according to your word.'

1:28–38 RSV

[Mary's 'Magnificat'] My soul doth magnify the Lord, and my spirit hath rejoiced in God my Saviour, for he hath regarded the lowliness of his hand-maiden. For behold from henceforth all generations shall call me blessed; for he that is mighty hath magnified me, and holy is his name. And his mercy is on them that fear him throughout all generations. He hath shewed strength with his arm, he hath scattered the proud in the imaginations of their hearts, he hath put down the mighty from their seat, and hath exalted the humble and meek. He hath filled the hungry with good things, and the rich he hath sent empty away. He remembering his mercy hath holpen his servant Israel, as he promised to our forefathers, Abraham and his seed, for ever.

1:46–55 BCP

[Zechariah's 'Benedictus'] And thou, child, shalt be called the Prophet of the highest; for thou shalt go before the face of the Lord to prepare his ways, to give knowledge of salvation unto his people for the remission of their sins, through the tender mercy of our God, whereby the day-spring from on high hath visited us; to give light to them that sit in darkness, and in the shadow of death, and to guide our feet into the way of peace.

1:76–79 BCP

And it came to pass in those days, that there went out a decree from Caesar Augustus, that all the world should be taxed.

2:1 KJV

And she [Mary] brought forth her firstborn son, and wrapped him in swaddling clothes, and laid him in a manger; because there was no room for them in the inn.

2:7 KJV

And the angel said unto them [the shepherds], Fear not: for, behold, I bring you good tidings of great joy, which shall be to all people. For unto you is born this day in the city of David a Saviour, which is Christ the Lord. And this shall be a sign unto you; ye shall find the babe wrapped in swaddling clothes, lying in a manger. And suddenly there was with the angel a multitude of the heavenly host praising God, and saying, Glory to God in the highest, and on earth peace, good will toward men.

2:10–14 KJV

[Simeon's 'Nunc Dimittis'] Lord, now lettest thou thy servant depart in peace, according to thy word; for mine eyes have seen thy salvation, which thou hast prepared before the face of all people, to be a light to lighten the Gentiles, and to be the glory of thy people Israel.

2:29–32 BCP

And Simeon blessed them, and said unto Mary his mother, Behold, this child is set for the fall and rising again of many in Israel; and for a sign which shall be spoken against; (yea, a sword shall pierce through thy own soul also,) that the thoughts of many hearts may be revealed.

2:34–35 KJV

He said to them, 'How is it that you sought me? Did you not know that I must be in my Father's house?' And they did not understand the saying which he spoke to them. And he went down with them and came to Nazareth, and was obedient to them; and his mother kept all these things in her heart. And Jesus increased in wisdom and in stature, and in favour with God and man.

2:49–52 RSV

And he [Jesus] came to Nazareth, where he had been brought up; and he went to the synagogue, as his custom was, on the sabbath day. And he stood up to read; and there was given to him the book of the prophet Isaiah. He opened the book and found the place where it was written, 'The Spirit of the Lord is upon me, because he has anointed me to preach good news to the poor. He has sent me to proclaim release to the captives and recovering of sight to the blind, to set at liberty those who are oppressed, to proclaim the acceptable year of the Lord.' And he closed the book, and gave it back to the attendant, and sat down; and the eyes of all in the synagogue were fixed on him. And he began to say to them, 'Today this scripture has been fulfilled in your hearing.'

4:16–21 RSV

When Simon Peter saw it, he fell down at Jesus' knees, saying, Depart from me; for I am a sinful man, O Lord.

5:8 KJV

And the Pharisees and their scribes murmured against his disciples, saying, 'Why do you eat and drink with tax collectors and sinners?' And Jesus answered them, 'Those who are well have no need of a physician, but those who are sick; I have not come to call the righteous, but sinners to repentance.'

5:30–32 RSV

Woe unto you, when all men shall speak well of you! for so did their fathers to the false prophets.

6:26 KJV

And he said to all, 'If any man would come after me, let him deny himself and take up his cross daily and follow me. for whoever would save his life will lose it; and whoever loses his life for my sake, he will save it.'

9:23–24 RSV

But he [a lawyer], desiring to justify himself, said to Jesus, 'And who is my neighbour?' Jesus replied, 'A man was going down from Jerusalem to Jericho, and he fell among robbers, who stripped him and beat him, and departed, leaving him half dead. Now by chance a priest was going down that road; and when he saw him he passed by on the other side. So likewise a Levite, when he came to the place and saw him, passed by on the other side. But a Samaritan, as he journeyed, came to where he was; and when he saw him, he had compassion, and went to him and bound up his wounds, pouring on oil and wine; then he set him on his own beast and brought him to an inn, and took care of him. And the next day he took out two denarii and gave them to the innkeeper, saying, ''Take care of him; and whatever more you spend, I will repay you when I come back.'' Which of these three, do you think, proved neighbour to the man who fell among the robbers?' He said, 'The one who showed mercy on him.' And Jesus said to him, 'Go and do likewise.'

10:29–37 RSV

But Martha was cumbered about much serving, and came to him, and said, Lord, dost thou not care that my sister hath left me to serve alone? Bid her therefore that she help me. And Jesus answered and said unto her, Martha, Martha, thou art careful and troubled about many things: but one thing is needful: and Mary hath chosen that good part, which shall not be taken away from her.

10:41–42 KJV

O Jerusalem, Jerusalem, which killest the prophets, and stonest them that are sent unto thee; how often would I have gathered thy children together, as a hen doth gather her brood under her wings, and ye would not! Behold, your house is left unto you desolate: and verily I say unto you, Ye shall not see me, until the time come when ye shall say, Blessed is he that cometh in the name of the Lord.

13:34–35 KJV

And he said, A certain man had two sons: and the younger of them said to his father, Father, give me the portion of goods that falleth to me. And he divided unto them his living. And not many days after the younger son gathered all together, and took his journey into a far country, and there wasted his substance with riotous living. And when he had spent all, there arose a mighty famine in that land; and he began to be in want. And he went and joined himself to a citizen of that country; and he sent him into his fields to feed swine. And he would fain have filled his belly with the husks that the swine did eat: and no man gave unto him. And when he came to himself, he said, How many hired servants of my father's have bread enough and to spare, and I perish with hunger! I will arise and go to my father, and will say unto him, Father, I have sinned against heaven, and before thee, and am no more worthy to be called thy son: make me as one of thy hired servants. And he arose, and came to his father. But when he was yet a great way off, his father saw him, and had compassion, and ran, and fell on his neck, and kissed him. And the son said unto him, Father, I have sinned against heaven, and in thy sight, and am no more worthy to be called thy son. But the father said to his servants, Bring forth the best robe, and put it on him; and put a ring on his hand, and shoes on his feet: and bring hither the fatted calf, and kill it; and let us eat, and be merry: for this my son was dead, and is alive again; he was lost, and is found. And they began to be merry.

15:11–24 KJV

And the Lord said, Simon, Simon, behold, Satan hath desired to have you, that he may sift you as wheat: but I have prayed for thee, that thy faith fail not: and when thou art converted, strengthen thy brethren. And he said unto him, Lord, I am ready to go with thee, both into prison, and to death. And he said, I tell thee, Peter, the cock shall not crow this day, before that thou shalt thrice deny that thou knowest me.

22:31–34 KJV

An angel from heaven appeared to him and strengthened him. In great anguish he prayed even more fervently; his sweat was like drops of blood falling to the ground.

22:43–44 GNB

And Peter said, Man, I know not what thou sayest. And immediately, while he yet spake, the cock crew. And the Lord turned, and looked upon Peter. And Peter remembered the word of the Lord, how he had said unto him, Before the cock crow, thou shalt deny me thrice. And Peter went out, and wept bitterly.

22:60–62 KJV

Then said Jesus, Father, forgive them; for they know not what they do.

23:34 KJV

And Jesus said unto him, Verily I say unto thee, To day shalt thou be with me in paradise.

23:43 KJV

And when Jesus had cried with a loud voice, he said, Father, into thy hands I commend my spirit: and having said thus, he gave up the ghost.

23:46 KJV

They [the two on the Emmaus road] said to each other, 'Did not our hearts burn within us while he talked to us on the road, while he opened to us the scriptures?'

24:32 RSV

And [Jesus] said unto them, Thus it is written, and thus it behoved Christ to suffer, and to rise from the dead the third day: and that repentance and remission of sins should be preached in his name among all nations, beginning at Jerusalem. And ye are witnesses of these things. And, behold, I send the promise of my Father upon you: but tarry ye in the city of Jerusalem, until ye be endued with power from on high.

24:46–49 KJV

# John

In the beginning was the Word, and the Word was with God, and the Word was God. The same was in the beginning with God. All things were made by him; and without him was not any thing made that was made. In him was life; and the life was the light of men. And the light shineth in darkness; and the darkness comprehended it not.

1:1–5 KJV

He came unto his own, and his own received him not. But as many as received him, to them gave he power to become the sons of God, even to them that believe on his name: which were born, not of blood, nor of the will of the flesh, nor of the will of man, but of God.

1:11–13 KJV

And the Word was made flesh, and dwelt among us, (and we beheld his glory, the glory as of the only begotten of the Father,) full of grace and truth.

1:14 KJV

And from his fullness have we all received, grace upon grace. For the law was given through Moses; grace and truth came through Jesus Christ. No one has ever seen God; the only Son, who is in the bosom of the Father, he has made him known.

1:16–18 RSV

The next day he [John the Baptist] saw Jesus coming toward him, and said, 'Behold, the Lamb of God, who takes away the sin of the world!'

1:29 RSV

Jesus answered and said unto him, Verily, verily, I say unto thee, Except a man be born again, he cannot see the kingdom of God. Nicodemus saith unto him, How can a man be born when he is old? Can he enter the second time into his mother's womb, and be born? Jesus answered, Verily, verily, I say unto thee, Except a man be born of water and of the Spirit, he cannot enter into the kingdom of God. That which is born of the flesh is flesh; and that which is born of the Spirit is spirit. Marvel not that I said unto thee, Ye must be born again. The wind bloweth where it listeth, and thou hearest the sound thereof, but canst not tell

whence it cometh, and wither it goeth: so is every one that is born of the Spirit.
**3:3–8 KJV**

For God so loved the world, that he gave his only begotten Son, that whosoever believeth in him should not perish, but have everlasting life. For God sent not his Son into the world to condemn the world; but that the world through him might be saved.
**3:16–17 KJV**

He that believeth on the Son hath everlasting life; and he that believeth not the Son shall not see life; but the wrath of God abideth on him.
**3:36 KJV**

Jesus said to her [the Samaritan woman], 'Everyone who drinks of this water will thirst again, but whoever drinks of the water that I shall give him will never thirst; the water that I shall give him will become in him a spring of water welling up to eternal life.'
**4:13–14 RSV**

'But the hour is coming, and now is, when the true worshippers will worship the Father in spirit and truth, for such the Father seeks to worship him. God is spirit, and those who worship him must worship in spirit and truth.'
**4:23–24 RSV**

'For as the Father has life in himself, so he has granted the Son to have life in himself. And he has given him authority to judge because he is the Son of Man.'
**5:26–27 NIV**

One of his disciples, Andrew, Simon Peter's brother, said to him, 'There is a lad here who has five barley loaves and two fish; but what are they among so many?'
**6:8–9 RSV**

And Jesus said unto them, I am the bread of life: he that cometh to me shall never hunger; and he that believeth on me shall never thirst.
**6:35 KJV**

All that the Father giveth me shall come to me; and him that cometh to me I will in no wise cast out.
**6:37 KJV**

'No one can come to me unless the Father who

sent me draws him; and I will raise him up at the last day.'
**6:44 RSV**

I am the living bread which came down from heaven: if any man eat of this bread, he shall live for ever: and the bread that I will give is my flesh, which I will give for the life of the world.
**6:51 KJV**

Then said Jesus unto the twelve, Will ye also go away? Then Simon Peter answered him, Lord, to whom shall we go? thou hast the words of eternal life. And we believe and are sure that thou art that Christ, the Son of the living God.
**6:67–69 KJV**

On the last day of the feast, the great day, Jesus stood up and proclaimed, 'If any one thirst, let him come to me and drink. He who believes in me, as the scripture has said, "Out of his heart shall flow rivers of living water." ' Now this he said about the Spirit, which those who believed in him were to receive; for as yet the Spirit had not been given, because Jesus was not yet glorified.
**7:37–39 RSV**

He that is without sin among you, let him first cast a stone at her.
**8:7 KJV**

Jesus spoke to them, saying, 'I am the light of the world; he who follows me will not walk in darkness, but will have the light of life.'
**8:12 RSV**

If the Son therefore shall make you free, ye shall be free indeed.
**8:36 KJV**

Jesus said unto them, Verily, verily, I say unto you, Before Abraham was, I am.
**8:58 KJV**

'The thief comes only to steal and kill and destroy; I came that they may have life, and have it abundantly. I am the good shepherd. The good shepherd lays down his life for the sheep.'
**10:10–11 RSV**

And I give unto them [my sheep] eternal life; and they shall never perish, neither shall any man pluck them out of my hand.
**10:28 KJV**

So the sisters sent to him, saying, 'Lord, he whom you love is ill.' But when Jesus heard it he said, 'This illness is not unto death; it is for the glory of God, so that the Son of God may be glorified by means of it.'

11:3–4 RSV

Jesus saith unto her, Thy brother shall rise again. Martha saith unto him, I know that he shall rise again in the resurrection at the last day. Jesus said unto her, I am the resurrection, and the life: he that believeth in me, though he were dead, yet shall he live. And whosoever liveth and believeth in me shall never die. Believest thou this? She saith unto him, Yea, Lord: I believe that thou art the Christ, the Son of God, which should come into the world.

11:23–27 KJV

The same came therefore to Philip, which was of Bethsaida of Galilee, and desired him, saying, Sir, we would see Jesus.

12:21 KJV

Verily, verily, I say unto you, Except a corn of wheat fall into the ground and die, it abideth alone: but if it die, it bringeth forth much fruit.

12:24 KJV

Now before the feast of the Passover, when Jesus knew that his hour had come to depart out of this world to the Father, having loved his own who were in the world, he loved them to the end.

13:1 RSV

Jesus, knowing that the Father had given all things into his hands, and that he had come from God and was going to God, rose from supper, laid aside his garments, and girded himself with a towel. Then he poured water into a basin, and began to wash the disciples' feet, and to wipe them with the towel with which he was girded.

13:3–5 RSV

A new commandment I give unto you, That ye love one another; as I have loved you, that ye also love one another. By this shall all men know that ye are my disciples, if ye have love one to another.

13:34–35 KJV

Let not your heart be troubled: ye believe in God, believe also in me. In my Father's house are many mansions: if it were not so, I would have told you. I go to prepare a place for you. And if I go and prepare a place for you, I will come again, and receive you unto myself; that where I am, there ye may be also. And whither I go ye know, and the way ye know. Thomas saith unto him, Lord, we know not whither thou goest; and how can we know the way? Jesus saith unto him, I am the way, the truth, and the life: no man cometh unto the Father, but by me.

14:1–6 KJV

If ye love me, keep my commandments. And I will pray the Father, and he shall give you another Comforter, that he may abide with you for ever; even the Spirit of truth; whom the world cannot receive, because it seeth him not, neither knoweth him: but ye know him; for he dwelleth with you, and shall be in you.

14:15–17 KJV

'But the Counsellor, the Holy Spirit, whom the Father will send in my name, he will teach you all things, and bring to your remembrance all that I have said to you. Peace I leave with you; my peace I give to you; not as the world gives do I give to you. Let not your hearts be troubled, neither let them be afraid.'

14:26–27 RSV

'I am the true vine, and my Father is the vinedresser. Every branch of mine that bears no fruit, he takes away, and every branch that does bear fruit he prunes, that it may bear more fruit. You are already made clean by the word which I have spoken to you. Abide in me, and I in you. As the branch cannot bear fruit by itself, unless it abides in the vine, neither can you, unless you abide in me. I am the vine, you are the branches. He who abides in me, and I in him, he it is that bears much fruit, for apart from me you can do nothing.'

15:1–5 RSV

'Greater love has no man than this, that a man lay down his life for his friends. You are my friends if you do what I command you. No longer do I call you servants, for the servant does not know what his master is doing; but I have called you friends, for all that I have heard from my Father I have made known to you. You did not choose me, but I chose you and appointed you that you should go and bear fruit and that your fruit should abide.'

15:13–16 RSV

'Nevertheless I tell you the truth: it is to your advantage that I go away, for if I do not go away, the Counsellor will not come to you; but if I go, I will send him to you. And when he comes, he will convince the world concerning sin and righteousness and judgment; concerning sin, because they do not believe in me; concerning righteousness, because I go to the Father, and you will see me no more; concerning judgment, because the ruler of this world is judged. I have yet many things to say to you, but you cannot bear them now. When the Spirit of truth comes, he will guide you into all the truth; for he will not speak on his own authority, but whatever he hears he will speak, and he will declare to you the things that are to come. He will glorify me, for he will take what is mine and declare it to you.'

16:7–14 RSV

These things I have spoken unto you, that in me ye might have peace. In the world ye shall have tribulation: but be of good cheer; I have overcome the world.

16:33 KJV

When Jesus had spoken these words, he lifted up his eyes to heaven and said, 'Father, the hour has come; glorify thy Son that the Son may glorify thee, since thou hast given him power over all flesh, to give eternal life to all whom thou hast given him. And this is eternal life, that they know thee the only true God, and Jesus Christ whom thou hast sent. I glorified thee on earth, having accomplished the work which thou gavest me to do; and now, Father, glorify thou me in thy own presence with the glory which I had with thee before the world was made.'

17:1–5 RSV

Jesus answered, 'My kingship is not of this world; if my kingship were of this world, my servants would fight, that I might not be handed over to the Jews; but my kingship is not from the world.' Pilate said to him, 'So you are a king?' Jesus answered, 'You say that I am a king. For this I was born, and for this I have come into the world, to bear witness to the truth. Every one who is of the truth hears my voice.' Pilate said to him, 'What is truth?'

18:36–38 RSV

There they crucified him, and with him two others, one on either side, and Jesus between them. Pilate also wrote a title and put it on the cross; it read, 'Jesus of Nazareth, the King of the Jews.' Many of the Jews read this title, for the place where Jesus was crucified was near the city; and it was written in Hebrew, in Latin, and in Greek. The chief priests of the Jews then said to Pilate, 'Do not write, "The King of the Jews," but, "This man said, I am King of the Jews."' Pilate answered, 'What I have written I have written.'

19:18–22 RSV

When Jesus saw his mother, and the disciple whom he loved standing near, he said to his mother, 'Woman, behold your son!' Then he said to the disciple, 'Behold, your mother!' And from that hour the disciple took her to his own home. After this Jesus, knowing that all was now finished, said (to fulfil the scripture), 'I thirst.' A bowl full of vinegar stood there; so they put a sponge full of the vinegar on hyssop and held it to his mouth. When Jesus had received the vinegar, he said, 'It is finished'; and he bowed his head and gave up his spirit.

19:26–30 RSV

Supposing him to be the gardener, she said to him, 'Sir, if you have carried him away, tell me where you have laid him, and I will take him away.' Jesus said to her, 'Mary.' She turned and said to him in Hebrew, 'Rabboni!' (which means Teacher). Jesus said to her, 'Do not hold me, for I have not yet ascended to the Father; but go to my brethren and say to them, I am ascending to my Father and your Father, to my God and your God.'

20:15–17 RSV

Then he said to Thomas, 'Put your finger here, and see my hands; and put out your hand, and place it in my side; do not be faithless, but believing.' Thomas answered him, 'My Lord and my God!' Jesus said to him, 'Have you believed because you have seen me? Blessed are those who have not seen and yet believe.' Now Jesus did many other signs in the presence of the disciples, which are not written in this book; but these are written that you may believe that Jesus is the Christ, the Son of God, and that believing you may have life in his name.

20:27–31 RSV

He said to him the third time, 'Simon, son of John, do you love me?' Peter was grieved because he said to him the third time, 'Do you love me?' And he said to him, 'Lord, you know everything;

you know that I love you.' Jesus said to him, 'Feed my sheep.'

21:17 RSV

But there are also many other things which Jesus did; were every one of them to be written, I suppose that the world itself could not contain the books that would be written.

21:25 RSV

# Acts

Dear Theophilus: In my first book I [Luke] wrote about all the things that Jesus did and taught from the time be began his work until the day he was taken up to heaven. Before he was taken up, he gave instructions by the power of the Holy Spirit to the men he had chosen as his apostles.

1:1–2 GNB

So when they had come together, they asked him, 'Lord, will you at this time restore the kingdom to Israel?' He said to them, 'It is not for you to know times or seasons which the Father has fixed by his own authority. But you shall receive power when the Holy Spirit has come upon you; and you shall be my witnesses in Jerusalem and in all Judea and Samaria and to the end of the earth.' And when he had said this, as they were looking on, he was lifted up, and a cloud took him out of their sight. And while they were gazing into heaven as he went, behold, two men stood by them in white robes, and said, 'Men of Galilee, why do you stand looking into heaven? This Jesus, who was taken up from you into heaven, will come in the same way as you saw him go into heaven.'

1:6–11 RSV

When the day of Pentecost had come, they were all together in one place. And suddenly a sound came from heaven like the rush of a mighty wind, and it filled all the house where they were sitting. And there appeared to them tongues as of fire, distributed and resting on each one of them. And they were all filled with the Holy Spirit and began to speak in other tongues, and the Spirit gave them utterance.

2:1–4 RSV

[Peter's sermon] 'Men of Israel, hear these words: Jesus of Nazareth, a man attested to you by God with mighty works and wonders and signs which God did through him in your midst, as you yourselves know—this Jesus, delivered up according to the definite plan and foreknowledge of God, you crucified and killed by the hands of lawless men. But God raised him up, having loosed the pangs of death, because it was not possible for him to be held by it.'

2:22–24 RSV

Now when they heard this they were cut to the heart, and said to Peter and the rest of the apostles, 'Brethren, what shall we do?' And Peter said to them, 'Repent, and be baptized every one of you in the name of Jesus Christ for the forgiveness of your sins; and you shall receive the gift of the Holy Spirit. For the promise is to you and to your children and to all that are far off, every one whom the Lord our God calls to him.'

ACTS 2:37–39 RSV

And they continued stedfastly in the apostles' doctrine and fellowship, and in breaking of bread, and in prayers.

ACTS 2:42 KJV

'And there is salvation in no one else, for there is no other name under heaven given among men by which we must be saved.'

4:12 RSV

[The high priest] 'We strictly charged you not to teach in this name, yet here you have filled Jerusalem with your teaching and you intend to bring this man's blood upon us.' But Peter and the apostles answered, 'We must obey God rather than men.'

5:28–29 RSV

Now in these days when the disciples were increasing in number, the Hellenists murmured against the Hebrews because their widows were neglected in the daily distribution. And the twelve summoned the body of the disciples and said, 'It is not right that we should give up preaching the word of God to serve tables. Therefore, brethren, pick out from among you seven men of good repute, full of the Spirit and of wisdom, whom we may appoint to this duty. But we will devote ourselves to prayer and to the ministry of the word.'

6:1–4 RSV

Then they cast him [Stephen] out of the city and stoned him; and the witnesses laid down their garments at the feet of a young man named Saul.

7:58 RSV

But Saul, still breathing threats and murder against the disciples of the Lord, went to the high priest and asked him for letters to the synagogues at Damascus, so that if he found any belonging to the Way, men or women, he might bring them bound to Jerusalem. Now as he journeyed he approached Damascus, and suddenly a light from heaven flashed about him. And he fell to the ground and heard a voice saying to him, 'Saul, Saul, why do you persecute me?' And he said, 'Who are you, Lord?' And he said, 'I am Jesus, whom you are persecuting; but rise and enter the city, and you will be told what you are to do.'

9:1–6 RSV

And the believers from among the circumcised who came with Peter were amazed, because the gift of the Holy Spirit had been poured out even on the Gentiles.

10:45 RSV

[Paul and Barnabas] Strengthening the souls of the disciples, exhorting them to continue in the faith, and saying that through many tribulations we must enter the kingdom of God.

14:22 RSV

'For it has seemed good to the Holy Spirit and to us to lay upon you no greater burden than these necessary things: that you abstain from what has been sacrificed to idols and from blood and from what is strangled and from unchastity. If you keep yourselves from these, you will do well.'

15:28–29 RSV

'Men, what must I do to be saved?' And they said, 'Believe in the Lord Jesus, and you will be saved, you and your household.'

ACTS 16:30–31 RSV

[The Jews at Berea] These were more noble than those in Thessalonica, in that they received the word with all readiness of mind, and searched the scriptures daily, whether those things were so.

17:11 KJV

So Paul, standing in the middle of the Areopagus, said: 'Men of Athens, I perceive that in every way you are very religious. For as I passed along, and observed the objects of your worship, I found also an altar with this inscription, "To an unknown god." What therefore you worship as unknown, this I proclaim to you. The God who made the world and everything in it, being Lord of heaven and earth, does not live in shrines made by man, nor is he served by human hands, as though he needed anything, since he himself gives to all men life and breath and everything. And he made from one every nation of men to live on all the face of the earth, having determined allotted periods and the boundaries of their habitation, that they should seek God, in the hope that they might feel after him and find him. Yet he is not far from each one of us, for "In him we live and move and have our being"; as even some of your poets have said, "For we are indeed his offspring." Being then God's offspring, we ought not to think that the Deity is like gold, or silver, or stone, a representation by the art and imagination of man. The times of ignorance God overlooked, but now he commands all men everywhere to repent, because he has fixed a day on which he will judge the world in righteousness by a man whom he has appointed, and of this he has given assurance to all men by raising him from the dead.'

ACTS 17:22–31 RSV

The following night the Lord stood by him and said, 'Take courage, for as you have testified about me at Jerusalem, so you must bear witness also at Rome.'

23:11

And he lived there [in Rome] two whole years at his own expense, and welcomed all who came to him, preaching the kingdom of God and teaching about the Lord Jesus Christ quite openly and unhindered.

28:30 RSV

# Romans

For I am not ashamed of the gospel of Christ: for it is the power of God unto salvation to everyone that believeth; to the Jew first, and also to the Greek. For therein is the righteousness of God revealed from faith to faith; as it is written, The just shall live by faith. For the wrath of God is revealed from heaven against all ungodliness and unrighteousness of men, who hold the truth in unrighteousness.

1:16–18 KJV

Or do you presume upon the riches of his kindness and forbearance and patience? Do you not know that God's kindness is meant to lead you to repentance? But by your hard and impenitent heart you are storing up wrath for yourself on the day of wrath when God's righteous judgment will be revealed.

2:4–5 RSV

All who have sinned without the law will also perish without the law, and all who have sinned under the law will be judged by the law. For it is not the hearers of the law who are righteous before God, but the doers of the law who will be justified. When Gentiles who have not the law do by nature what the law requires, they are a law to themselves, even though they do not have the law.

2:12–14 RSV

Now we know that whatever the law says it speaks to those who are under the law, so that every mouth may be stopped, and the whole world may be held accountable to God. For no human being will be justified in his sight by works of the law since through the law comes knowledge of sin.

3:19–20 RSV

But now the righteousness of God without the law is manifested, being witnessed by the law and the prophets; even the righteousness of God which is by faith of Jesus Christ unto all and upon all them that believe: for there is no difference: for all have sinned, and come short of the glory of God: being justified freely by his grace through the redemption that is in Christ Jesus: whom God hath set forth to be a propitiation through faith in his blood, to declare his righteousness for the remission of sins that are past, through the forbearance of God; to declare, I say, at this time his righteousness: that he might be just, and the justifier of him which believeth in Jesus.

3:21–26 KJV

Therefore being justified by faith, we have peace with God through our Lord Jesus Christ: by whom also we have access by faith into this grace wherein we stand, and rejoice in hope of the glory of God. And not only so, but we glory in tribulations also: knowing that tribulation worketh patience; and patience, experience; and experience, hope: and hope maketh not ashamed; because the love of God is shed abroad in our hearts by the Holy Ghost which is given unto us.

ROMANS 5:1–5 KJV

While we were still weak, at the right time Christ died for the ungodly. Why, one will hardly die for a righteous man—though perhaps for a good man one will dare even to die. But God shows his love for us in that while we were yet sinners Christ died for us. Since, therefore, we are now justified by his blood, much more shall we be saved by him from the wrath of God. For if while we were enemies we were reconciled to God by the death of his Son, much more, now that we are reconciled, shall we be saved by his life. Not only so, but we also rejoice in God through our Lord Jesus Christ, through whom we have now received our reconciliation.

5:6–11 RSV

As by one man sin entered into the world, and death by sin . . . so death passed upon all men, for that all have sinned.

ROMANS 5:12 KJV

What shall we say then? Shall we continue in sin, that grace may abound? God forbid. How shall we, that are dead to sin, live any longer therein? Know ye not, that so many of us as were baptized into Jesus Christ were baptized into his death? Therefore we are buried with him by baptism into death: that like as Christ was raised up from the dead by the glory of the Father, even so we also should walk in newness of life.

6:1–4 KJV

We know that our old self was crucified with him so that the sinful body might be destroyed, and we might no longer be enslaved to sin. For he who has died is freed from sin. But if we have died with Christ, we believe that we shall also live with him.

6:6–8 RSV

In the same way, count yourselves dead to sin but alive to God in Christ Jesus. Therefore do not let sin reign in your mortal body so that you obey its evil desires.

6:11–12 NIV

For sin shall not have dominion over you: for ye are not under the law, but under grace.

6:14 KJV

For the wages of sin is death; but the gift of God is eternal life through Jesus Christ our Lord.

6:23 KJV

For I know that nothing good dwells within me, that is, in my flesh. I can will what is right, but I cannot do it. For I do not do the good I want, but the evil I do not want is what I do.

**7:18–19 RSV**

So I find it to be a law that when I want to do right, evil lies close at hand. For I delight in the law of God, in my inmost self, but I see in my members another law at war with the law of my mind and making me captive to the law of sin which dwells in my members. Wretched man that I am! Who will deliver me from this body of death? Thanks be to God through Jesus Christ our Lord! So then, I of myself serve the law of God with my mind, but with my flesh I serve the law of sin.

**7:21–25 RSV**

There is therefore now no condemnation for those who are in Christ Jesus. For the law of the Spirit of life in Christ Jesus has set me free from the law of sin and death. For God has done what the law, weakened by the flesh, could not do: sending his own Son in the likeness of sinful flesh and for sin, he condemned sin in the flesh, in order that the just requirement of the law might be fulfilled in us, who walk not according to the flesh but according to the Spirit.

**8:1–4 RSV**

For as many as are led by the Spirit of God, they are the sons of God. For ye have not received the spirit of bondage again to fear; but ye have received the Spirit of adoption, whereby we cry, Abba, Father. The Spirit itself beareth witness with our spirit, that we are the children of God.

**8:14–16 KJV**

For we know that the whole creation groaneth and travaileth in pain together until now.

**8:22 KJV**

We know that in everything God works for good with those who love him, who are called according to his purpose. For those whom he foreknew he also predestined to be conformed to the image of his Son, in order that he might be the first-born among many brethren. And those whom he predestined he also called; and those whom he called he also justified; and those whom he justified he also glorified.

**8:28–30 RSV**

What then shall we say to this? If God is for us, who is against us? He who did not spare his own Son but gave him up for us all, will he not also give us all things with him? Who shall bring any charge against God's elect? It is God who justifies; who is to condemn? Is it Christ Jesus, who died, yes, who was raised from the dead, who is at the right hand of God, who indeed intercedes for us? Who shall separate us from the love of Christ? Shall tribulation, or distress, or persecution, or famine, or nakedness, or peril, or sword? As it is written, 'For thy sake we are being killed all the day long; we are regarded as sheep to be slaughtered.' No, in all these things we are more than conquerors through him who loved us. For I am sure that neither death, nor life, nor angels, nor principalities, nor things present, nor things to come, nor powers, nor height, nor depth, nor anything else in all creation, will be able to separate us from the love of God in Christ Jesus our Lord.

**8:31–39 RSV**

Brethren, my heart's desire and prayer to God for Israel is, that they might be saved.

**10:1 KJV**

That if thou shalt confess with thy mouth the Lord Jesus, and shalt believe in thine heart that God hath raised him from the dead, thou shalt be saved. For with the heart man believeth unto righteousness; and with the mouth confession is made unto salvation.

**10:9–10 KJV**

For whosoever shall call upon the name of the Lord shall be saved.

**10:13 KJV**

O the depth of the riches both of the wisdom and knowledge of God! how unsearchable are his judgments, and his ways past finding out! For who hath known the mind of the Lord? or who hath been his counsellor?

**11:32–34 KJV**

Source, Guide, and Goal of all that is—to him be glory for ever! Amen.

**11:36 NEB**

I beseech you therefore, brethren, by the mercies of God, that ye present your bodies a living sacrifice, holy, acceptable unto God, which is your reasonable service. And be not conformed to this world: but be ye transformed by the renewing of your mind, that ye may prove what is that good, and acceptable, and perfect, will of God.

**12:1–2 KJV**

Don't let the world around you squeeze you into

its own mould.
12:2 JBP

Never flag in zeal, be aglow with the Spirit, serve the Lord. Rejoice in your hope, be patient in tribulation, be constant in prayer. Contribute to the needs of the saints, practise hospitality.
12:11–13 RSV

Let every soul be subject unto the higher powers. For there is no power but of God: the powers that be are ordained of God.
13:1 KJV

Then let us no more pass judgment on one another, but rather decide never to put a stumbling block or hindrance in the way of a brother.
14:13 RSV

May the God of hope fill you with all joy and peace in believing, so that by the power of the Holy Spirit you may abound in hope.
15:13 RSV

# 1 Corinthians

But we preach Christ crucified, unto the Jews a stumbling block, and unto the Greeks foolishness; but unto them which are called, both Jews and Greeks, Christ the power of God, and the wisdom of God.
1:23–24 KJV

For I decided to know nothing among you except Jesus Christ and him crucified. And I was with you in weakness and in much fear and trembling; and my speech and my message were not in plausible words of wisdom, but in demonstration of the Spirit and of power, that your faith might not rest in the wisdom of men but in the power of God.
2:2–5 RSV

For while there is jealousy and strife among you, are you not of the flesh, and behaving like ordinary men? For when one says, 'I belong to Paul,' and another, 'I belong to Apollos,' are you not merely men? What then is Apollos? What is Paul? Servants through whom you believed, as the Lord assigned to each. I planted, Apollos watered, but God gave the growth.
3:3–6 RSV

Do you not know that your body is a temple of the Holy Spirit within you, which you have from God?

You are not your own; you were bought with a price. So glorify God in your body.
6:19–20 RSV

Only, let every one lead the life which the Lord has assigned to him, and in which God has called him. This is my rule in all the churches.
7:17 RSV

For necessity is laid upon me. Woe to me if I do not preach the gospel!
9:16 RSV

To the weak I became weak, that I might win the weak. I have become all things to all men, that I might by all means save some.
9:22 RSV

Therefore let any one who thinks that he stands take heed lest he fall. No temptation has overtaken you that is not common to man. God is faithful, and he will not let you be tempted beyond your strength, but with the temptation will also provide the way of escape, that you may be able to endure it.
10:12–13 RSV

So, whether you eat or drink, or whatever you do, do all to the glory of God.
10:31 RSV

But I want you to understand that the head of every man is Christ, the head of a woman is her husband, and the head of Christ is God.
11:3 RSV

For I received from the Lord what I also delivered to you, that the Lord Jesus on the night when he was betrayed took bread, and when he had given thanks, he broke it, and said, 'This is my body which is for you. Do this in remembrance of me.' In the same way also the cup, after supper, saying, 'This cup is the new covenant in my blood. Do this, as often as you drink it, in remembrance of me.' For as often as you eat this bread and drink the cup, you proclaim the Lord's death until he comes. Whoever, therefore, eats the bread or drinks the cup of the Lord in an unworthy manner will be guilty of profaning the body and blood of the Lord. Let a man examine himself, and so eat of the bread and drink of the cup. For any one who eats and drinks without discerning the body eats and drinks judgment upon himself. That is why many of you are weak and ill, and some have died.
11:23–30 RSV

Now there are varieties of gifts, but the same Spirit; and there are varieties of service, but the same Lord; and there are varieties of working, but it is the same God who inspires them all in every one. To each is given the manifestation of the Spirit for the common good.
12:4–7 RSV

To one is given through the Spirit the utterance of wisdom, and to another the utterance of knowledge according to the same Spirit, to another faith by the same Spirit, to another gifts of healing by the one Spirit, to another the working of miracles, to another prophecy, to another the ability to distinguish between spirits, to another various kinds of tongues, to another the interpretation of tongues. All these are inspired by one and the same Spirit, who apportions to each one individually as he wills.
12:8–11 RSV

For by one Spirit we were all baptized into one body—Jews or Greeks, slaves or free—and all were made to drink of one Spirit.
12:13 RSV

Now you are the body of Christ and individually members of it. And God has appointed in the church first apostles, second prophets, third teachers, then workers of miracles, then healers, helpers, administrators, speakers in various kinds of tongues. Are all apostles? Are all prophets? Are all teachers? Do all work miracles? Do all possess gifts of healing? Do all speak with tongues? Do all interpret? But earnestly desire the higher gifts.
12:27–31 RSV

If I speak in the tongues of men and of angels, but have not love, I am a noisy gong or a clanging cymbal. And if I have prophetic powers, and understand all mysteries and all knowledge, and if I have all faith, so as to remove mountains, but have not love, I am nothing. If I give away all I have, and if I deliver my body to be burned, but have not love, I gain nothing. Love is patient and kind; love is not jealous or boastful; it is not arrogant or rude. Love does not insist on its own way; it is not irritable or resentful; it does not rejoice at wrong, but rejoices in the right. Love bears all things, believes all things, hopes all things, endures all things. Love never ends; as for prophecies, they will pass away; as for tongues, they will cease; as for knowledge, it will pass away. For our knowledge is imperfect and our prophecy is imperfect; but when the perfect comes, the imperfect will pass away. When I was a child, I spoke like a child, I thought like a child, I reasoned like a child; when I became a man, I gave up childish ways. For now we see in a mirror dimly, but then face to face. Now I know in part; then I shall understand fully, even as I have been fully understood. So faith, hope, love abide, these three; but the greatest of these is love.
13 RSV

Let all things be done decently and in order.
14:40 KJV

For I delivered to you as of first importance what I also received, that Christ died for our sins in accordance with the scriptures, that he was buried, that he was raised on the third day in accordance with the scriptures, and that he appeared to Cephas, then to the twelve.
15:3–5 RSV

Now if Christ is preached as raised from the dead, how can some of you say that there is no resurrection of the dead? But if there is no resurrection of the dead, then Christ has not been raised; if Christ has not been raised, then our preaching is in vain and your faith is in vain. We are even found to be misrepresenting God, because we testified of God that he raised Christ, whom he did not raise if it is true that the dead are not raised. For if the dead are not raised, then Christ has not been raised. If Christ has not been raised, your faith is futile and you are still in your sins. Then those also who have fallen asleep in Christ have perished. If for this life only we have hoped in Christ, we are of all men most to be pitied. But in fact Christ has been raised from the dead, the first fruits of those who have fallen asleep. For as by a man came death, by a man has come also the resurrection of the dead.
15:12–21 RSV

The last enemy that shall be deestroyed is death.
15:26 KJV

So it is with the resurrection of the dead. What is sown is perishable, what is raised is imperishable. It is sown in dishonour, it is raised in glory. It is sown in weakness, it is raised in power. It is sown a physical body, it is raised a spiritual body. If there is a physical body, there is also a spiritual body.
15:42–44 RSV

Behold, I shew you a mystery; we shall not all sleep, but we shall all be changed, in a moment, in the twinkling of an eye, at the last trump: for the trumpet shall sound, and the dead shall be raised incorruptible, and we shall be changed. For this corruptible must put on incorruption, and this mortal must put on immortality. So when this corruptible shall have put on incorruption, and this mortal shall have put on immortality, then shall be brought to pass the saying that is written, death is swallowed up in victory. O death, where is thy sting? O grave, where is thy victory? The sting of death is sin; and the strength of sin is the law. But thanks be to God, which giveth us the victory through our Lord Jesus Christ. Therefore, my beloved brethren, be ye stedfast, unmoveable, always abounding in the work of the Lord, forasmuch as ye know that your labour is not in vain in the Lord.
15:51–58 KJV

# 2 Corinthians

But thanks be to God, who in Christ always leads us in triumph, and through us spreads the fragrance of the knowledge of him everywhere.
2:14 RSV

You yourselves are our letters of recommendation, written on your hearts, to be known and read by all men.
3:2 RSV

Now the Lord is the Spirit, and where the Spirit of the Lord is, there is freedom. And we all, with unveiled face, beholding the glory of the Lord, are being changed into his likeness from one degree of glory to another; for this comes from the Lord who is the Spirit.
3:17–18 RSV

We have renounced disgraceful, underhanded ways; we refuse to practise cunning or to tamper with God's word, but by the open statement of the truth we would commend ourselves to every man's conscience in the sight of God.
4:2 RSV

But we have this treasure in earthen vessels, that the excellency of the power may be of God, and not of us.
4:7 KJV

We are afflicted in every way, but not crushed; perplexed, but not driven to despair; persecuted, but not forsaken; struck down, but not destroyed; always carrying in the body the death of Jesus, so that the life of Jesus may also be manifested in our bodies.
4:8–10 RSV

We may be knocked down but we are never knocked out!
4:9 JBP

So we do not lose heart. Though our outer nature is wasting away, our inner nature is being renewed every day. For this slight momentary affliction is preparing for us an eternal weight of glory beyond all comparison, because we look not to the things that are seen but to the things that are unseen; for the things that are seen are transient, but the things that are unseen are eternal.
4:16–18 RSV

We walk by faith, not by sight.
5:7 RSV

Therefore if any man be in Christ, he is a new creature: old things are passed away; behold, all things are become new.
5:17 KJV

When someone becomes a Christian he becomes a brand new person inside. He is not the same any more. A new life has begun!
5:17 LB

All this is from God, who through Christ reconciled us to himself and gave us the ministry of reconciliation; that is, in Christ God was reconciling the world to himself, not counting their trespasses against them, and entrusting to us the message of reconciliation. So we are ambassadors for Christ, God making his appeal through us. We beseech you on behalf of Christ, be reconciled to God. For our sake he made him to be sin who knew no sin, so that in him we might become the righteousness of God.
5:18–21 RSV

We want you to know, brethren, about the grace of God which has been shown in the churches of Macedonia, for in a severe test of affliction, their abundance of joy and their extreme poverty have overflowed in a wealth of liberality on their part. For they gave according to their means, as I can testify, and beyond their means, of their own free will, begging us earnestly for the favour of taking part in the relief of the saints—and this, not as we expected, but first they gave themselves to the Lord and to us by the will of God.

**8:1–5 RSV**

For ye know the grace of our Lord Jesus Christ, that, though he was rich, yet for your sakes he became poor, that ye through his poverty might be rich.

**8:9 KJV**

Each one must do as he has made up his mind, not reluctantly or under compulsion, for God loves a cheerful giver.

**9:7 RSV**

Thanks be to God for his inexpressible gift!

**9:15 RSV**

Are they Hebrews? So am I. Are they Israelites? So am I. Are they the seed of Abraham? So am I. Are they ministers of Christ? (I speak as a fool) I am more; in labours more abundant, in stripes above measure, in prisons more frequent, in deaths oft. Of the Jews five times received I forty stripes save one. Thrice was I beaten with rods, once was I stoned, thrice I suffered shipwreck, a night and a day I have been in the deep; in journeyings often, in perils of waters, in perils of robbers, in perils by mine own countrymen, in perils by the heathen, in perils in the city, in perils in the wilderness, in perils in the sea, in perils among false brethren; in weariness and painfulness, in watchings often, in hunger and thirst, in fastings often, in cold and nakedness.

**11:22–27 KJV**

And to keep me from being too elated by the abundance of revelations, a thorn was given me in the flesh, a messenger of Satan, to harass me, to keep me from being too elated. Three times I besought the Lord about this, that it should leave me; but he said to me, 'My grace is sufficient for you, for my power is made perfect in weakness.' I will all the more gladly boast of my weaknesses, that the power of Christ may rest upon me. For the sake of Christ, then, I am content with weaknesses, insults, hardships, persecutions, and calamities; for when I am weak, then I am strong.

**12:7–10 RSV**

Examine yourselves to make sure you are in the faith; test yourselves. Do you acknowledge that Jesus Christ is really in you? If not, you have failed the test.

**13:5 JB**

The grace of the Lord Jesus Christ, the love of God, and the fellowship of the Holy Spirit be with you all.

**13:13 GNB**

# Galatians

I am astonished that you are so quickly deserting him who called you in the grace of Christ and turning to a different gospel—not that there is another gospel, but there are some who trouble you and want to pervert the gospel of Christ. But even if we, or an angel from heaven, should preach to you a gospel contrary to that which we preached to you, let him be accursed!

**1:6–8 RSV**

But when Peter came to Antioch, I opposed him in public, because he was clearly wrong. Before some men who had been sent by James arrived there, Peter had been eating with the Gentile brothers. But after these men arrived, he drew back and would not eat with the Gentiles, because he was afraid of those who were in favour of circumcising them. The other Jewish brothers also started acting like cowards along with Peter; and even Barnabas was swept along by their cowardly action. When I saw that they were not walking a straight path in line with the truth of the gospel, I said to Peter in front of them all, 'You are a Jew, yet you have been living like a Gentile, not like a Jew. How, then, can you try to force Gentiles to live like Jews?' Indeed, we are Jews by birth and not 'Gentile sinners,' as they are called. Yet we know that a person is put right with God only through faith in Jesus Christ, never by doing what the Law requires. For no one is put right with God by doing what the Law requires.

**2:11–16 GNB**

For I through the law died to the law, that I might live to God. I have been crucified with Christ; it is no longer I who live, but Christ who lives in me; and the life I now live in the flesh I live by faith in the Son of God, who loved me and gave himself for me.

**2:19–20 RSV**

There is neither Jew nor Greek, there is neither bond nor free, there is neither male nor female: for ye are all one in Christ Jesus.

3:28 KJV

But when the time had fully come, God sent forth his Son, born of woman, born under the law, to redeem those who were under the law, so that we might receive adoption as sons. And because you are sons, God has sent the Spirit of his Son into our hearts, crying, 'Abba! Father!'

4:4–6 RSV

As for you, my brothers, you are called to be free. But do not let this freedom become an excuse for letting your physical desires control you. Instead, let love make you serve one another.

5:13 GNB

So I say, live by the Spirit, and you will not gratify the desires of the sinful nature.

5:16 NIV

Now the works of the flesh are plain: immorality, impurity, licentiousness, idolatry, sorcery, enmity, strife, jealousy, anger, selfishness, dissension, party spirit, envy, drunkenness, carousing, and the like. I warn you, as I warned you before, that those who do such things shall not inherit the kingdom of God.

5:19–21 RSV

But the fruit of the Spirit is love, joy, peace, patience, kindness, goodness, faithfulness, gentleness, self-control; against such there is no law.

5:22–23 RSV

Do not be deceived; God is not mocked, for whatever a man sows, that will he also reap. For he who sows to his own flesh will from the flesh reap corruption; but he who sows to the Spirit will from the Spirit reap eternal life. And let us not grow weary in well-doing, for in due season we shall reap, if we do not lose heart. So then, as we have opportunity, let us do good to all men, and especially to those who are of the household of faith.

6:7–10 RSV

# Ephesians

Blessed be the God and Father of our Lord Jesus Christ, who has blessed us in Christ with every spiritual blessing in the heavenly places, even as he chose us in him before the foundation of the world, that we should be holy and blameless before him. He destined us in love to be his sons through Jesus Christ, according to the purpose of his will, to the praise of his glorious grace which he freely bestowed on us in the Beloved. In him we have redemption through his blood, the forgiveness of our trespasses, according to the riches of his grace which he lavished upon us.

1:3–8 RSV

I do not cease to give thanks for you, remembering you in my prayers, that the God of our Lord Jesus Christ, the Father of glory, may give you a spirit of wisdom and of revelation in the knowledge of him, having the eyes of your hearts enlightened, that you may know what is the hope to which he has called you, what are the riches of his glorious inheritance in the saints, and what is the immeasurable greatness of his power in us who believe.

1:16–19 RSV

As for you, you were dead in your transgressions and sins, in which you used to live when you followed the ways of this world and of the ruler of the kingdom of the air, the spirit who is now at work in those who are disobedient. All of us also lived among them at one time, gratifying the cravings of our sinful nature and following its desires and thoughts. Like the rest, we were by nature objects of wrath. But because of his great love for us, God, who is rich in mercy, made us alive with Christ even when we were dead in transgressions—it is by grace you have been saved.

2:1–5 NIV

For by grace are ye saved through faith; and that not of yourselves: it is the gift of God: not of works, lest any man should boast. For we are his workmanship, created in Christ Jesus unto good works, which God hath before ordained that we should walk in them.

2:8–10 KJV

So then you are no longer strangers and sojourners, but you are fellow citizens with the saints and members of the household of God, built upon the foundation of the apostles and prophets, Christ Jesus himself being the cornerstone.

2:19–20 RSV

Unto me, who am less than the least of all saints, is this grace given, that I should preach among the Gentiles the unsearchable riches of Christ.

3:8 KJV

That Christ may dwell in your hearts through faith; that you, being rooted and grounded in love, may have power to comprehend with all the saints what is the breadth and length and height and depth, and to know the love of Christ which surpasses knowledge, that you may be filled with all the fullness of God.

3:17–19 RSV

Now unto him that is able to do exceeding abundantly above all that we ask or think, according to the power that worketh in us, unto him be glory in the church by Christ Jesus throughout all ages, world without end. Amen.

3:20–21 KJV

Rather, speaking the truth in love, we are to grow up in every way into him who is the head, into Christ.

4:15 RSV

Be ye angry, and sin not: let not the sun go down upon your wrath.

4:26 KJV

And grieve not the holy Spirit of God, whereby ye are sealed unto the day of redemption.

4:30 KJV

And be not drunk with wine, wherein is excess; but be filled with the Spirit; speaking to yourselves in psalms and hymns and spiritual songs, singing and making melody in your heart to the Lord; giving thanks always for all things unto God and the Father in the name of our Lord Jesus Christ; submitting yourselves one to another in the fear of God.

5:18–21 KJV

Finally, my brethren, be strong in the Lord, and in the power of his might. Put on the whole armour of God, that ye may be able to stand against the wiles of the devil. For we wrestle not against flesh and blood, but against principalities, against powers, against the rulers of the darkness of this world, against spiritual wickedness in high places. Wherefore take unto you the whole armour of God, that ye may be able to withstand in the evil day, and having done all, to stand. Stand therefore, having your loins girt about with truth, and having on the breastplate of righteousness; and your feet shod with the preparation of the gospel of peace; above all, taking the shield of faith, wherewith ye shall be able to quench all the fiery darts of the wicked. And take the helmet of salvation, and the sword of the Spirit, which is the word of God: praying always with all prayer and supplication in the Spirit, and watching thereunto with all perseverance and supplication for all saints; And for me, that utterance may be given unto me, that I may open my mouth boldly, to make known the mystery of the gospel, for which I am an ambassador in bonds: that therein I may speak boldly, as I ought to speak.

6:10–20 KJV

# Philippians

I thank my God upon every remembrance of you, always in every prayer of mine for you all making request with joy, for your fellowship in the gospel from the first day until now.

1:3–5 KJV

And it is my prayer that your love may abound more and more, with knowledge and all discernment, so that you may approve what is excellent, and may be pure and blameless for the day of Christ, filled with the fruits of righteousness which come through Jesus Christ, to the glory and praise of God.

1:9–11 RSV

For me to live is Christ, and to die is gain.

1:21 KJV

I am pulled in two directions. I want very much to leave this life and be with Christ, which is a far better thing; but for your sake it is much more important that I remain alive.

1:23–24 GNB

So if there is any encouragement in Christ, any incentive of love, any participation in the spirit, any affection and sympathy, complete my joy by being of the same mind, having the same love, being in full accord and of one mind.

2:1–2 RSV

Have this mind among yourselves, which is yours in Christ Jesus, who, though he was in the form of God, did not count equality with God a thing to be grasped, but emptied himself, taking the form of a servant, being born in the likeness of men. And being found in human form he humbled himself and became obedient unto death, even death on a cross. Therefore God has highly exalted him and bestowed on him the name which is above every name, that at the name of Jesus every knee should bow, in heaven and on earth and under the earth, and every tongue confess that Jesus Christ is Lord, to the glory of God the Father.

2:5–11 RSV

Work out your own salvation with fear and trembling; for God is at work in you, both to will and to work for his good pleasure.

2:12–13 RSV

Holding forth the word of life.

2:16 KJV

If any other man thinks he has reason for confidence in the flesh, I have more.

3:4 RSV

Indeed I count everything as loss because of the surpassing worth of knowing Christ Jesus my Lord.

3:8 RSV

That I may know him and the power of his resurrection, and may share his sufferings, becoming like him in his death, that if possible I may attain the resurrection from the dead.

3:10–11 RSV

Not that I have already obtained all this, or have already been made perfect, but I press on to take hold of that for which Christ Jesus took told of me.

3:12 NIV

But one thing I do, forgetting what lies behind and straining forward to what lies ahead, I press on towards the goal for the prize of the upward call of God in Christ Jesus.

3:13–14 RSV

Rejoice in the Lord always; again I will say, Rejoice. Let all men know your forbearance. The Lord is at hand. Have no anxiety about anything, but in everything by prayer and supplication with thanksgiving let your requests be made known to God. And the peace of God, which passes all understanding, will keep your hearts and your minds in Christ Jesus.

4:4–7 RSV

Finally, brethren, whatsoever things are true, whatsoever things are honest, whatsoever things are just, whatsoever things are pure, whatsoever things are lovely, whatsoever things are of good report; if there be any virtue, and if there be any praise, think on these things. Those things, which you have both learned, and received, and heard, and seen in me, do: and the God of peace shall be with you.

4:8–9 KJV

Not that I complain of want; for I have learned, in whatever state I am, to be content. I know how to be abased, and I know how to abound; in any and all circumstances I have learned the secret of facing plenty and hunger, abundance and want. I can do all things in him who strengthens me.

4:11–13 RSV

Here then, is my receipt for everything you have given me—and it has been more than enough! I have all I need now that Epaphroditus has brought me all your gifts. They are like a sweet-smelling offering to God, a sacrifice which is acceptable and pleasing to him.

4:18 GNB

And my God will supply every need of yours according to his riches in glory in Christ Jesus.

4:19 RSV

# Colossians

He is the image of the invisible God, the first-born of all creation; for in him all things were created, in heaven and on earth, visible and invisible, whether thrones or dominions or principalities or authorities—all things were created through him and for him. He is before all things, and in him all things hold together. He is the head of the body, the church; he is the beginning, the first-born from the dead, that in everything he might be pre-eminent. For in him all the fullness of God was pleased to dwell, and through him to reconcile to himself all things, whether on earth or in heaven, making peace by the blood of his cross.

1:15–20 RSV

To them God chose to make known how great among the Gentiles are the riches of the glory of this mystery, which is Christ in you, the hope of glory.

1:27 RSV

Him we proclaim, warning every man and teaching every man in all wisdom, that we may present every man mature in Christ.

1:28 RSV

See to it that no one makes a prey of you by philosophy and empty deceit, according to human tradition, according to the elemental spirits of the universe, and not according to Christ. For in him the whole fullness of deity dwells bodily, and you have come to fullness of life in him, who is the head of all rule and authority.

2:8–10 RSV

Therefore let no one pass judgment on you in questions of food and drink or with regard to a festival or a new moon or a sabbath. These are only a shadow of what is to come; but the substance belongs to Christ.

2:16–17 RSV

If ye then be risen with Christ, seek those things which are above, where Christ sitteth on the right hand of God. Set your affection on things above, not on things on the earth. For ye are dead, and your life is hid with Christ in God. When Christ, who is our life, shall appear, then shall ye also appear with him in glory.

3:1–4 KJV

And let the peace of God rule in your hearts, to the which also ye are called in one body; and be ye thankful. Let the word of Christ dwell in you richly in all wisdom; teaching and admonishing one another in psalms and hymns and spiritual songs, singing with grace in your hearts to the Lord. And whatsoever ye do in word or deed, do all in the name of the Lord Jesus, giving thanks to God and the Father by him.

3:15–17 KJV

Whatever your task, work heartily, as serving the Lord and not men.

3:23 RSV

Conduct yourselves wisely toward outsiders, making the most of the time. Let your speech always be gracious, seasoned with salt, so that you may know how you ought to answer every one.

4:5–6 RSV

# 1 Thessalonians

We give thanks to God always for you all, constantly mentioning you in our prayers, remembering before our God and Father your work of faith and labour of love and steadfastness of hope in our Lord Jesus Christ. For we know, brethren beloved by God, that he has chosen you; for our gospel came to you not only in word, but also in power and in the Holy Spirit and with full conviction. You know what kind of men we proved to be among you for your sake. And you became imitators of us and of the Lord, for you received the word in much affliction, with joy inspired by the Holy Spirit; so that you became an example to all the believers in Macedonia and in Achaia.

1:2–7 RSV

For we never used either words of flattery, as you know, or a cloak for greed, as God is witness; nor did we seek glory from men, whether from you or from others, though we might have made demands as apostles of Christ. But we were gentle among you, like a nurse taking care of her children. So, being affectionately desirous of you, we were ready to share with you not only the gospel of God but also our own selves, because you had become very dear to us.

2:5–8 RSV

And we also thank God constantly for this, that when you received the word of God which you heard from us, you accepted it not as the word of men but as what it really is, the word of God, which is at work in you believers.

2:13 RSV

For this is the will of God, your sanctification: that you abstain from unchastity.

4:3 RSV

But I would not have you to be ignorant, brethren, concerning them which are asleep, that ye sorrow not, even as others which have no hope. For if we believe that Jesus died and rose again, even so them also which sleep in Jesus will God bring with him. For this we say unto you by the word of the Lord, that we which are alive and remain unto the coming of the Lord shall not prevent them which are asleep. For the Lord himself shall descend from heaven with a shout, with the voice of the archangel, and with the trump of God: and the dead in Christ shall rise first. Then we which are alive and remain shall be caught up together with them in the clouds, to meet the Lord in the air: and so shall we ever be with the Lord. Wherefore comfort one another with these words.

4:13–18 KJV

For you yourselves know perfectly that the day of the Lord so cometh as a thief in the night. For when they shall say, Peace and safety; then sudden destruction cometh upon them, as travail upon a woman with child; and they shall not escape.

5:2–3 KJV

Rejoice evermore. Pray without ceasing. In every thing give thanks: for this is the will of God in Christ Jesus concerning you. Quench not the Spirit. Despise not prophesyings. Prove all things; hold fast that which is good. Abstain from all appearance of evil. And the very God of peace sanctify you wholly; and I pray God your whole spirit and soul and body be preserved blameless unto the coming of our Lord Jesus Christ.

5:16–23 KJV

# 2 Thessalonians

God will do what is right: he will bring suffering on those who make you suffer, and he will give relief to you who suffer and to us as well. He will do this when the Lord Jesus appears from heaven with his mighty angels, with a flaming fire, to punish those who reject God and who do not obey the Good News about our Lord Jesus. They will suffer the punishment of eternal destruction, separated from the presence of the Lord and from his glorious might, when he comes on that day to receive glory from all his people and honour from all who believe. You too will be among them, because you have believed the message that we told you.

1:6–10 GNB

Now concerning the coming of our Lord Jesus Christ and our assembling to meet him, we beg you, brethren, not to be quickly shaken in mind or excited, either by spirit or by word, or by letter purporting to be from us, to the effect that the day of the Lord has come. Let no one deceive you in any way; for that day will not come, unless the rebellion comes first, and the man of lawlessness

is revealed, the son of perdition.

2:1–3 RSV

While we were with you, we used to say to you, 'Whoever refuses to work is not allowed to eat.' We say this because we hear that there are some people among you who live lazy lives and who do nothing except meddle in other people's business. In the name of the Lord Jesus Christ we command these people and warn them to lead orderly lives and work to earn their own living.

3:10–12 GNB

# 1 Timothy

The glorious gospel of the blessed God, which was committed to my trust.

1:11 KJV

This is a faithful saying, and worthy of all acceptation, that Christ Jesus came into the world to save sinners; of whom I am the chief.

1:15 KJV

Now unto the King eternal, immortal, invisible, the only wise God, be honour and glory for ever and ever. Amen.

1:17 KJV

I exhort, therefore, that, first of all, supplications, prayers, intercessions, and giving of thanks, be made for all men; for kings, and for all that are in authority; that we may lead a quiet and peaceable life in all godliness and honesty.

2:1–2 KJV

For there is one God, and one mediator between God and men, the man Christ Jesus.

2:5 KJV

A bishop then must be blameless, the husband of one wife, vigilant, sober, of good behaviour, given to hospitality, apt to teach; not given to wine, no striker, not greedy of filthy lucre; but patient, not a brawler, not covetous; one that ruleth well his own house, having his children in subjection with all gravity.

3:2–4 KJV

Great indeed, we confess, is the mystery of our religion: He was manifested in the flesh, vindicated in the Spirit, seen by angels, preached among the nations, believed on in the world, taken up in glory.

3:16 RSV

Now the Spirit expressly says that in later times some will depart from the faith by giving heed to deceitful spirits and doctrines of demons, through the pretensions of liars whose consciences are seared, who forbid marriage and enjoin abstinence from foods which God created to be received with thanksgiving by those who believe and know the truth. For everything created by God is good, and nothing is to be rejected if it is received with thanksgiving; for then it is consecrated by the word of God and prayer.

4:1–5 RSV

Let no one despise your youth, but set the believers an example in speech and conduct, in love, in faith, in purity. Till I come, attend to the public reading of scripture, to preaching, to teaching. Do not neglect the gift you have, which was given you by prophetic utterance when the council of elders laid their hands upon you.

4:12–14 RSV

If any one does not provide for his relatives, and especially for his own family, he has disowned the faith is worse than an unbeliever.

5:8 RSV

Drink no longer water, but use a little wine for thy stomach's sake and thine often infirmities.

5:23 KJV

There is great gain in godliness with contentment; for we brought nothing into the world, and we cannot take anything out of the world; but if we have food and clothing, with these we shall be content.

6:6–8 RSV

For the love of money is the root of all evil.

6:10 KJV

But thou, O man of God, flee these things; and follow after righteousness, godliness, faith, love, patience, meekness. Fight the good fight of faith, lay hold on eternal life, whereunto thou art also called, and hast professed a good profession before many witnesses.

6:11–12 KJV

God, the blessed and only Ruler, the King of kings and the Lord of lords. He alone is immortal; he lives in the light that no one can approach. No one has ever seen him; no one can ever see him. To him be honour and eternal dominion! Amen.

6:15–16 GNB

# 2 Timothy

For God hath not given us the spirit of fear; but of power, and of love, and of a sound mind.

1:7 KJV

But I am not ashamed, for I know whom I have believed, and I am sure that he is able to guard until that Day what has been entrusted to me. Follow the pattern of the sound words which you have heard from me, in the faith and love which are in Christ Jesus; guard the truth that has been entrusted to you by the Holy Spirit who dwells within us.

1:12–14 RSV

You then, my son, be strong in the grace that is in Christ Jesus, and what you have heard from me before many witnesses entrust to faithful men who will be able to teach others also. Share in suffering as a good soldier of Christ Jesus.

2:1–3 RSV

The saying is sure: If we have died with him, we shall also live with him; if we endure, we shall also reign with him; if we deny him, he also will deny us; if we are faithless, he remains faithful— for he cannot deny himself.

2:11–13 RSV

Do your best to present yourself to God as one approved, a workman who has no need to be ashamed, rightly handling the word of truth. Avoid such godless chatter, for it will lead people into more and more ungodliness.

2:15–16 RSV

But as for you, continue in what you have learned and have firmly believed, knowing from whom you learned it and how from childhood you have been acquainted with the sacred writings which are able to instruct you for salvation through faith in Christ Jesus. All scripture is inspired by God and profitable for teaching, for reproof, for correction, and for training in righteousness, that the man of God may be complete, equipped for every good work.

3:14–17 RSV

Preach the word, be urgent in season and out of season, convince, rebuke, and exhort, be unfailing in patience and in teaching.

4:2 RSV

As for you, always be steady, endure suffering,

do the work of an evangelist, fulfil your ministry.

**4:5 RSV**

For I am now ready to be offered, and the time of my departure is at hand. I have fought a good fight, I have finished my course, I have kept the faith: henceforth there is laid up for me a crown of righteousness, which the Lord, the righteous judge, shall give me at that day: and not to me only, but unto all them also that love his appearing.

**4:6–8 KJV**

# Titus

To the pure, all things are pure, but to the corrupt and unbelieving nothing is pure; their very minds and consciences are corrupted. They profess to know God, but they deny him by their deeds; they are detestable, disobedient, unfit for any good deed.

**1:15–16 RSV**

But as for you, teach what befits sound doctrine.

**2:1 RSV**

For the grace of God has appeared for the salvation of all men, training us to renounce irreligion and worldly passions, and to live sober, upright, and godly lives in this world, awaiting our blessed hope, the appearing of the glory of our great God and Saviour Jesus Christ, who gave himself for us to redeem us from all iniquity and to purify for himself a people of his own who are zealous for good deeds.

**2:11–14 RSV**

But when the goodness and loving kindness of God our Saviour appeared, he saved us, not because of deeds done by us in righteousness, but in virtue of his own mercy, by the washing of regeneration and renewal in the Holy Spirit, which he poured out upon us richly through Jesus Christ our Saviour, so that we might be justified by his grace and become heirs in hope of eternal life. The saying is sure. I desire you to insist on these things, so that those who have believed in God may be careful to apply themselves to good deeds; these are excellent and profitable to men.

**3:4–8 RSV**

# Philemon

For love's sake I prefer to appeal to you—I, Paul, an ambassador and now a prisoner also for Christ Jesus—I appeal to you for my child, Onesimus, whose father I have become in my imprisonment.

**9–10 RSV**

It may be that Onesimus was away from you for a short time so that you might have him back for all time. And now he is not just a slave, but much more than a slave: he is a dear brother in Christ. How much he means to me! And how much more he will mean to you, both as a slave and as a brother in the Lord! So, if you think of me as your partner, welcome him back just as you would welcome me. If he has done you any wrong or owes you anything, charge it to my account. Here, I will write this with my own hand: I, Paul, will pay you back. (I should not have to remind you, of course, that you owe your very self to me.) So, my brother, please do me this favour for the Lord's sake; as a brother in Christ, cheer me up!

**15–20 GNB**

# Hebrews

God, who at sundry times and in divers manners spake in time past unto the fathers by the prophets, hath in these last days spoken unto us by his Son, whom he hath appointed heir of all things, by whom also he made the worlds; who being the brightness of his glory, and the express image of his person, and upholding all things by the word of his power, when he had by himself purged our sins, sat down on the right hand of the Majesty on high; being made so much better than the angels, as he hath by inheritance obtained a more excellent name than they.

**1:1–4 KJV**

For if the message declared by angels was valid and every transgression or disobedience received a just retribution, how shall we escape if we neglect such a great salvation?

**2:2–3 RSV**

Thou [God] hast put all things in subjection under his [Jesus] feet. For in that he put all in subjection under him, he left nothing that is not put under him. But now we see not yet all things put under him. But we see Jesus, who was made a little lower than the angels for the suffering of death, crowned with glory and honour; that he by the grace of God should taste death for every man.

2:8–9 RSV

For the word of God is living and active, sharper than any two-edged sword, piercing to the division of soul and spirit, of joints and marrow, and discerning the thoughts and intentions of the heart. And before him no creature is hidden, but all are open and laid bare to the eyes of him with whom we have to do.

4:12–13 RSV

Since then we have a great high priest who has passed through the heavens, Jesus, the Son of God, let us hold fast our confession. For we have not a high priest who is unable to sympathize with our weaknesses, but one who in every respect has been tempted as we are, yet without sin. Let us then with confidence draw near to the throne of grace, that we may receive mercy and find grace to help in time of need.

4:14–16 RSV

But solid food is for the mature, for those who have had their faculties trained by practice to distinguish good from evil.

5:14 RSV

For how can those who abandon their faith be brought back to repent again? They were once in God's light; they tasted heaven's gift and received their share of the Holy Spirit; they knew from experience that God's word is good, and they had felt the powers of the coming age. And then they abandoned their faith! It is impossible to bring them back to repent again, because they are again crucifying the Son of God and exposing him to public shame.

6:4–6 GNB

Indeed, under the law almost everything is purified with blood, and without the shedding of blood there is no forgiveness of sins.

9:22 RSV

It is appointed unto men once to die, but after this the judgment.

9:27 KJV

And every priest stands daily at his service, offering repeatedly the same sacrifices, which can never take away sins. But when Christ had offered for all time a single sacrifice for sins, he sat down at the right hand of God.

10:11–12 RSV

Therefore, brethren, since we have confidence to enter the sanctuary by the blood of Jesus, by the new and living way which he opened for us through the curtain, that is, through his flesh, and since we have a great priest over the house of God, let us draw near with a true heart in full assurance of faith, with our hearts sprinkled clean from an evil conscience and our bodies washed with pure water. Let us hold fast the confession of our hope without wavering, for he who promised is faithful; and let us consider how to stir up one another to love and good works, not neglecting to meet together, as is the habit of some, but encouraging one another, and all the more as you see the Day drawing near.

10:19–25 RSV

It is a fearful thing to fall into the hands of the living God.

10:31 KJV

Now faith is the substance of things hoped for, the evidence of things not seen.

11:1 KJV

Wherefore seeing we also are compassed about with so great a cloud of witnesses, let us lay aside every weight, and the sin which does so easily best us, and let us run with patience the race that is set before us, looking unto Jesus the author and finisher of our faith; who for the joy that was set before him endured the cross, despising the shame, and is set down at the right hand of the throne of God.

12:1–2 KJV

For the moment all discipline seems painful rather than pleasant; later it yields the peaceful fruit of righteousness to those who have been trained by it. Therefore lift your drooping hands and strengthen your weak knees, and make straight paths for your feet, so that what is lame may not be put out of joint but rather be healed.

12:11–13 RSV

Therefore let us be grateful for receiving a kingdom that cannot be shaken, and thus let us offer to God acceptable worship, with reverence and awe; for our God is a consuming fire.

12:28–29 RSV

Let brotherly love continue. Do not neglect to show hospitality to strangers, for thereby some have entertained angels unawares.

13:1–2 RSV

Jesus Christ is the same yesterday and today and for ever.

13:8 RSV

Now the God of peace, that brought again from the dead our Lord Jesus, that great shepherd of the sheep, through the blood of the everlasting covenant, make you perfect in every good work to do his will, working in you that which is wellpleasing in his sight, through Jesus Christ; to whom be glory for ever and ever. Amen.

13:20–21 KJV

# James

Count it all joy, my brethren, when you meet various trials, for you know that the testing of your faith produces steadfastness.

1:2–3 RSV

If any of you lacks wisdom, let him ask God, who gives to all men generously and without reproaching, and it will be given him. But let him ask in faith, with no doubting, for he who doubts is like a wave of the sea that is driven and tossed by the wind. For that person must not suppose that a double-minded man, unstable in all his ways, will receive anything from the Lord.

1:5–8 RSV

Every good gift and every perfect gift is from above, and cometh down from the Father of lights, with whom is no variableness, neither shadow of turning.

1:17 KJV

But be ye doers of the word, and not hearers only, deceiving your own selves.

1:22 KJV

For if any one is a hearer of the word and not a doer, he is like a man who observes his natural face in a mirror; for he observes himself and goes away and at once forgets what he was like. But he who looks into the perfect law, the law of liberty,

and perseveres, being no hearer that forgets but a doer that acts, he shall be blessed in his doing.

1:23–25 RSV

Religion that is pure and undefiled before God, the Father, is this: to visit orphans and widows in their affliction, and to keep oneself unstained from the world.

1:27 RSV

For if a man keeps the whole law apart from one single point; he is guilty of breaking all of it.

2:10 NEB

Thou believest that there is one God; thou doest well: the devils also believe, and tremble. But wilt thou know, O vain man, that faith without works is dead?

2:19–20 KJV

You see that a man is justified by works and not by faith alone.

2:24 RSV

And the tongue is like a fire. It is a world of wrong, occupying its place in our bodies and spreading evil through our whole being. It sets on fire the entire course of our existence with the fire that comes to it from hell itself. Man is able to tame and has tamed all other creatures—wild animals and birds, reptiles and fish. But no one has ever been able to tame the tongue. It is evil and uncontrollable, full of deadly poison. We use it to give thanks to our Lord and Father and also to curse our fellow-man, who is created in the likeness of God. Words of thanksgiving and cursing pour out from the same mouth. My brothers, this should not happen! No spring of water pours out sweet water and bitter water from the same opening.

3:6–11 GNB

This wisdom is not such as comes down from above, but is earthly, unspiritual, devilish.

3:15 RSV

But the wisdom from above is first pure, then peaceable, gentle, open to reason, full of mercy and good fruits, without uncertainty or insincerity. And the harvest of righteousness is sown in peace by those who make peace.

3:17–18 RSV

You do not get what you want, because you do not pray for it. Or, if you do, your requests are not granted because you pray from wrong motives, to spend what you get on your pleasures.

**4:2–3 NEB**

Submit yourselves therefore to God. Resist the devil and he will flee from you. Draw near to God and he will draw near to you. Cleanse your hands, you sinners, and purify your hearts, you men of double mind. Be wretched and mourn and weep. Let your laughter be turned to mourning and your joy to dejection. Humble yourselves before the Lord and he will exalt you.

**4:7–10 RSV**

Come now, you who say. 'Today or tomorrow we will go into such and such a town and spend a year there and trade and get gain'; whereas you do not know about tomorrow. What is your life? For you are a mist that appears for a little time and then vanishes. Instead you ought to say, 'If the Lord will, we shall live and we shall do this or that.'

**4:13–15 RSV**

Come now, you rich, weep and howl for the miseries that are coming upon you. Your riches have rotted and your garments are moth-eaten. Your gold and silver have rusted, and their rust will be evidence against you and will eat your flesh like fire. You have laid up treasure for the last days. Behold, the wages of the labourers who mowed your fields, which you kept back by fraud, cry out; and the cries of the harvesters have reached the ears of the Lord of hosts. You have lived on the earth in luxury and in pleasure; you have fattened your hearts in a day of slaughter.

**5:1–5 RSV**

Is any sick among you? Let him call for the elders of the church; and let them pray over him, anointing him with oil in the name of the Lord: and the prayer of faith shall save the sick, and the Lord shall raise him up; and if he have committed sins, they shall be forgiven him. Confess your faults one to another, and pray one for another, that ye may be healed. The effectual fervent prayer of a righteous man availeth much.

**5:14–16 KJV**

# 1 Peter

Elect according to the foreknowledge of God the Father, through sanctification of the Spirit, unto obedience and sprinkling of the blood of Jesus Christ: Grace unto you, and peace, be multiplied.

**1:2 KJV**

Blessed be the God and Father of our Lord Jesus Christ! By his great mercy we have been born anew to a living hope through the resurrection of Jesus Christ from the dead, and to an inheritance which is imperishable, undefiled, and unfading, kept in heaven for you, who by God's power are guarded through faith for a salvation ready to be revealed in the last time. In this you rejoice, though now for a little while you may have to suffer various trials, so that the genuineness of your faith, more precious than gold which though perishable is tested by fire, may redound to praise and glory and honour at the revelation of Jesus Christ. Without having seen him you love him; though you do not now see him you believe in him and rejoice with unutterable and exalted joy. As the outcome of your faith you obtain the salvation of your souls.

**1:3–9 RSV**

You know that you were ransomed from the futile ways inherited from your fathers, not with perishable things such as silver or gold, but with the precious blood of Christ, like that of a lamb without blemish or spot.

**1:18–19 RSV**

As newborn babes, desire the sincere milk of the word, that ye may grow thereby.

**2:2 KJV**

Come to him, to that living stone, rejected by men but in God's sight chosen and precious; and like living stones be yourselves built into a spiritual house, to be a holy priesthood, to offer spiritual sacrifices acceptable to God through Jesus Christ.

**2:4–5 RSV**

Unto you therefore which believe he is precious.

**2:7 KJV**

But you are a chosen race, a royal priesthood, a holy nation, God's own people, that you may declare the wonderful deeds of him who called you out of darkness into his marvellous light. Once you were no people but now you are God's people; once you had not received mercy but now you have received mercy.

2:9–10 RSV

He committed no sin; no guile was found on his lips. When he was reviled, he did not revile in return; when he suffered, he did not threaten; but he trusted to him who judges justly. He himself bore our sins in his body on the tree, that we might die to sin and live to righteousness. By his wounds you have been healed. For you were straying like sheep, but have now returned to the Shepherd and Guardian of your souls.

2:22–25 RSV

But in your hearts reverence Christ as Lord. Always be prepared to make a defence to any one who calls you to account for the hope that is in you, yet do it with gentleness and reverence.

3:15 RSV

For Christ also died for sins once for all, the righteous for the unrighteous, that he might bring us to God, being put to death in the flesh but made alive in the spirit.

3:18 RSV

The end of all things is at hand; therefore keep sane and sober for your prayers. Above all hold unfailing your love for one another, since love covers a multitude of sins.

4:7–8 RSV

Beloved, do not be surprised at the fiery ordeal which comes upon you to prove you, as though something strange were happening to you. But rejoice in so far as you share Christ's sufferings, that you may also rejoice and be glad when his glory is revealed.

4:12–13 RSV

For the time has come for judgment to begin with the household of God; and if it begins with us, what will be the end of those who do not obey the gospel of God?

4:17 RSV

Humble yourselves therefore under the mighty hand of God, that in due time he may exalt you. Cast all your anxieties on him, for he cares about you. Be sober, be watchful. Your adversary the devil prowls around like a roaring lion, seeking some one to devour. Resist him, firm in your faith, knowing that the same experience of suffering is required of your brotherhood throughout the world. And after you have

suffered a little while, the God of all grace, who has called you to his eternal glory in Christ, will himself restore, establish, and strengthen you. To him be the dominion for ever and ever. Amen.

5:6–11 RSV

# 2 Peter

Therefore, brethren, be the more zealous to confirm your call and election, for if you do this you will never fall.

1:10 RSV

But false prophets also arose among the people, just as there will be false teachers among you, who will secretly bring in destructive heresies, even denying the Master who bought them, bringing upon themselves swift destruction.

2:1 RSV

First of all you must understand this, that scoffers will come in the last days with scoffing, following their own passions and saying, 'Where is the promise of his coming? For ever since the fathers fell asleep, all things have continued as they were from the beginning of creation.'

3:3–4 RSV

But do not ignore this one fact, beloved, that with the Lord one day is as a thousand years, and a thousand years as one day. The Lord is not slow about his promise as some count slowness, but is forbearing toward you, not wishing that any should perish, but that all should reach repentance. But the day of the Lord will come like a thief, and then the heavens will pass away with a loud noise, and the elements will be dissolved with fire, and the earth and the works that are upon it will be burned up. Since all these things are thus to be dissolved, what sort of persons ought you to be in lives of holiness and godliness, waiting for and hastening the coming of the day of God, because of which the heavens will be kindled and dissolved, and the elements will melt with fire! But according to his promise we wait for new heavens and a new earth in which righteousness dwells.

3:8–13 RSV

But grow in the grace and knowledge of our Lord and Saviour Jesus Christ. To him be the glory . both now and to the day of eternity. Amen.

3:18 RSV

# 1 John

This is the message we have heard from him and proclaim to you, that God is light and in him is no darkness at all.

1:5 RSV

If we say we have fellowship with him while we walk in darkness, we lie and do not live according to the truth; but if we walk in the light, as he is in the light, we have fellowship with one another, and the blood of Jesus his Son cleanses us from all sin. If we say we have no sin, we deceive ourselves, and the truth is not in us. If we confess our sins, he is faithful and just and will forgive our sins and cleanse us from all unrighteousness.

1:6–9 RSV

My little children, these things write I unto you, that ye sin not. And if any man sin, we have an advocate with the Father, Jesus Christ the righteous: and he is the propitiation for our sins: and not for ours only, but also for the sins of the whole world. And hereby we do know that we know him, if we keep his commandments.

2:1–3 KJV

Love not the world, neither the things that are in the world. If any man love the world, the love of the Father is not in him. For all that is in the world, the lust of the flesh, and the lust of the eyes, and the pride of life, is not of the Father, but is of the world. And the world passeth away, and the lust thereof: but he that doeth the will of God abideth for ever.

2:15–17 KJV

Behold, what manner of love the Father hath bestowed upon us, that we should be called the sons of God: therefore the world knoweth us not, because it knew him not. Beloved, now are we the sons of God, and it doeth not yet appear what we shall be; but we know that, when he shall appear, we shall be like him; for we shall see him as he is.

3:1–2 KJV

The reason the Son of God appeared was to destroy the works of the devil.

3:8 RSV

Whoever is a child of God does not continue to sin, for God's very nature is in him; and because God is his Father, he cannot continue to sin.

3:9 GNB

We know that we have passed out of death into life, because we love the brethren.

3:14 RSV

But if any one has the world's goods and see his brother in need, yet closes his heart against him, how does God's love abide in him?

3:17 RSV

By this we shall know that we are of the truth, and reassure our hearts before him whenever our hearts condemn us; for God is greater than our hearts, and he knows everything. Beloved, if our hearts do not condemn us, we have confidence before God; and we receive from him whatever we ask, because we keep his commandments and do what pleases him. And this is his commandment, that we should believe in the name of his Son Jesus Christ and love one another, just as he has commanded us.

3:19–23 RSV

This is how we may recognize the Spirit of God: every spirit which acknowledges that Jesus Christ has come in the flesh is from God.

4:2 NEB

He who is in you is greater than he who is in the world.

4:4 RSV

Beloved, let us love one another: for love is of God; and every one that loveth is born of God, and knoweth God. He that loveth not knoweth not God; for God is love. In this was manifested the love of God toward us, because that God sent his only begotten Son into the world, that we might live through him. Herein is love, not that we loved God, but that he loved us, and sent his Son to be the propitiation for our sins. Beloved, if God so loved us, we ought also to love one another. No man hath seen God at any time. If we love one another, God dwelleth in us, and his love is perfected in us.

4:7–12 KJV

And we have seen and do testify that the Father sent the Son to be the Saviour of the world.

4:14 KJV

There is no fear in love, but perfect love casts out fear. For fear has to do with punishment, and he who fears is not perfected in love.

4:18 RSV

For this is the love of God, that we keep his commandments. And his commandments are not burdensome. For whatever is born of God overcomes the world; and this is the victory that overcomes the world, our faith.

5:3–4 RSV

He that hath the Son hath life; and he that hath not the Son of God hath not life.

5:12 KJV

# 2 John

The elder to the elect lady and her children, whom I love in the truth, and not only I but also all who know the truth.

1 RSV

I rejoiced greatly to find some of your children following the truth, just as we have been commanded by the Father. And now I beg you, lady, not as though I were writing you a new commandment, but the one we have had from the beginning, that we love one another.

4–5 RSV

For many deceivers have gone out into the world, men who will not acknowledge the coming of Jesus Christ in the flesh; such a one is the deceiver and the antichrist.

7 RSV

If any one comes to you and does not bring this doctrine, do not receive him into the house or give him any greeting; for he who greets him shares his wicked work.

10–11 RSV

# 3 John

For I greatly rejoiced when some of the brethren arrived and testified to the truth of your life, as indeed you do follow the truth. No greater joy can I have than this, to hear that my children follow the truth. Beloved, it is a loyal thing you do when you render any service to the brethren, especially to strangers.

3–5 RSV

I have written something to the church; but Diotrephes, who likes to put himself first, does not acknowledge my authority.

9 RSV

Beloved, do not imitate evil but imitate good. He who does good is of God; he who does evil has not seen God.

11 RSV

# Jude

Jude, a servant of Jesus Christ and brother of James, To those who are called, beloved in God the Father and kept for Jesus Christ: May mercy, peace, and love be multiplied to you.

1–2 RSV

Beloved, being very eager to write to you of our common salvation, I found it necessary to write appealing to you to contend for the faith which was once for all delivered to the saints. For admission has been secretly gained by some who long ago were designated for this condemnation, ungodly persons who pervert the grace of our God in licentiousness and deny our only Master and Lord, Jesus Christ.

3–4 RSV

For even though you know all this, I want to remind you of how the Lord once rescued the people of Israel from Egypt, but afterwards destroyed those who did not believe.

5 GNB

These [godless people] are blemishes on your love feasts, as they boldly carouse together, looking after themselves; waterless clouds, carried along by winds; fruitless trees in late autumn, twice dead, uprooted; wild waves of the sea, casting up the foam of their own shame; wandering stars for whom the nether gloom of darkness has been reserved for ever.

12–13 RSV

But ye, beloved, building up yourselves on your most holy faith, praying in the Holy Ghost, keep yourselves in the love of God, looking for the mercy of our Lord Jesus Christ unto eternal life. And of some have compassion, making a difference: and others save with fear, pulling them out of the fire; hating even the garment spotted by the flesh. Now unto him that is able to keep you from falling, and to present you faultless before the presence of his glory with exceeding joy, to the only wise God our Saviour, be glory and majesty, dominion and power, both now and for ever. Amen.

20–25 KJV

# Revelation

John to the seven churches that are in Asia: Grace to you and peace from him who is and who was and who is to come, and from the seven spirits who are before his throne, and from Jesus Christ the faithful witness, the first-born of the dead, and the ruler of kings on earth. To him who loves us and has freed us from our sins by his blood and made us a kingdom, priests to his God and Father, to him be glory and dominion for ever and ever. Amen. Behold, he is coming with the clouds, and every eye will see him, every one who pierced him; and all tribes of the earth will wail on account of him. Even so. Amen. 'I am the Alpha and the Omega,' says the Lord God, who is and who was and who is to come, the Almighty.

1:4–8 RSV

I John, your brother, who share with you in Jesus the tribulation and the kingdom and the patient endurance, was on the island called Patmos on account of the word of God and the testimony of Jesus. I was in the Spirit on the Lord's day, and I heard behind me a loud voice like a trumpet saying, 'Write what you see in a book and send it to the seven churches.'

1:9–11 RSV

I turned to see whose voice it was that spoke to me; and when I turned I saw seven standing lamps of gold, and among the lamps one like a son of man, robed down to his feet, with a golden girdle round his breast. The hair of his head was white as snow- white wool, and his eyes flamed like fire; his feet gleamed like burnished brass refined in a furnace, and his voice was like the sound of rushing waters. In his right hand he held seven stars, and out of his mouth came a sharp two-edged sword; and his face shone like the sun in full strength. When I saw him, I fell at his feet as though dead. But he laid his right hand upon me and said, 'Do not be afraid. I am the first and the last, and I am the living one; for I was dead and now I am alive for evermore, and I hold the keys of Death and Death's domain.'

1:12–18 NEB

[To the church in Ephesus]' ''I know your works, your toil and your patient endurance, and how you cannot bear evil men but have tested those who call themselves apostles but are not, and found them to be false.'' '

2:2 RSV

' ''But I have this against you, that you have abandoned the love you had at first. Remember then from what you have fallen, repent and do the works you did at first. If not, I will come to you and remove your lampstand from its place, unless you repent.'' '

2:4–5 RSV

Behold, the devil shall cast some of you into prison, that ye may be tried; and ye shall have tribulation ten days: be thou faithful unto death, and I will give thee a crown of life. He that hath an ear, let him hear what the Spirit saith unto the churches.

2:10–11 KJV

[To the church in Philadelphia]' ''I know your works. Behold, I have set before you an open door, which no one is able to shut; I know that you have but little power, and yet you have kept my word and have not denied my name.'' '

3:8 RSV

[To the church in Laodicea]' ''I know your works: you are neither cold nor hot. Would that you were cold or hot! So, because you are lukewarm, and neither cold nor hot, I will spew you out of my mouth.'' '

3:15 RSV

Behold, I stand at the door, and knock: if any man hear my voice, and open the door, I will come in to him, and will sup with him and he with me.

3:20 KJV

And the four living creatures, each of them with six wings, are full of eyes all round and within, and day and night they never cease to sing, 'Holy, holy, holy, is the Lord God Almighty, who was and is and is to come!'

4:8 RSV

Thou art worthy, O Lord, to receive glory and honour and power: for thou hast created all things, and for thy pleasure they are and were created.

4:11 KJV

I saw a strong angel proclaiming with a loud voice, 'Who is worthy to open the scroll and

break its seals?' And no one in heaven or on earth or under the earth was able to open the scroll or to look into it, and I wept much that no one was found worthy to open the scroll or to look into it. Then one of the elders said to me, 'Weep not; lo, the Lion of the tribe of Judah, the Root of David, has conquered, so that he can open the scroll and its seven seals. And between the throne and the four living creatures and among the elders, I saw a Lamb standing, as though it had been slain, with seven horns and with seven eyes, which are the seven spirits of God sent out into all the earth; and he went and took the scroll from the right hand of him who was seated on the throne. And when he had taken the scroll, the four living creatures and the twenty-four elders fell down before the Lamb, each holding a harp, and with golden bowls full of incense, which are the prayers of the saints; and they sang a new song, saying, 'Worthy art thou to take the scroll and to open its seals, for thou wast slain and by thy blood didst ransom men for God from every tribe and tongue and people and nation, and hast made them a kingdom and priests to our God, and they shall reign on earth.' Then I looked, and I heard around the throne and the living creatures and the elders the voice of many angels, numbering myriads of myriads and thousands of thousands, saying with a loud voice, 'Worthy is the Lamb who was slain, to receive power and wealth and wisdom and might and honour and glory and blessing!' And I heard every creature in heaven and on earth and under the earth and in the sea, and all therein, saying, 'To him who sits upon the throne and to the Lamb be blessing and honour and glory and might for ever and ever!' And the four living creatures said, 'Amen!' and the elders fell down and worshipped.
5:2–14 RSV

Now I saw when the Lamb opened one of the seven seals, and I heard one of the four living creatures say as with a voice of thunder, 'Come!'
6:1 RSV

[They] said to the mountains and rocks, Fall on us, and hide us from the face of him that sitteth on the throne, and from the wrath of the Lamb. For the great day of his wrath is come; and who shall be able to stand?
6:16–17 KJV

After this I looked, and behold, a great multitude which no man could number, from every nation, from all tribes and peoples and tongues, standing before the throne and before the Lamb, clothed in white robes, with palm branches in their hands, and crying out with a loud voice, 'Salvation belongs to our God who sits upon the throne, and to the Lamb!' And all the angels stood round the throne and round the elders and the four living creatures, and they fell on their faces before the throne and worshipped God, saying, 'Amen! Blessing and glory and wisdom and thanksgiving and honour and power and might be to our God for ever and ever! Amen.'
7:9–12 RSV

Then one of the elders addressed me, saying, 'Who are these, clothed in white robes, and whence have they come?' I said to him, 'Sir, you know.' And he said to me, 'These are they who have come out of the great tribulation; they have washed their robes and made them white in the blood of the Lamb. Therefore are they before the throne of God, and serve him day and night within his temple; and he who sits upon the throne will shelter them with his presence. They shall hunger no more, neither thirst any more; the sun shall not strike them, nor any scorching heat. For the Lamb in the midst of the throne will be their shepherd, and he will guide them to springs of living water; and God will wipe away every tear from their eyes.'
7:13–17 RSV

'The kingdom of the world has become the kingdom of our Lord and of his Christ, and he shall reign for ever and ever.'
11:15 RSV

And the great dragon was thrown down, that ancient serpent, who is called the Devil and Satan, the deceiver of the whole world—he was thrown down to the earth, and his angels were thrown down with him. And I heard a loud voice in heaven, saying, 'Now the salvation and the power and the kingdom of our God and the authority of his Christ have come, for the accuser of our brethren has been thrown down, who accuses them day and night before our God. And they have conquered him by the blood of the Lamb and by the word of their testimony, for they loved not their lives even unto death.'
12:9–11 RSV

And I heard a voice from heaven saying, 'Write this: Blessed are the dead who die in the Lord henceforth.' 'Blessed indeed,' says the Spirit, 'that they may rest from their labours, for their deeds follow them!'

14:13 RSV

'Behold, I come like a thief! Blessed is he who stays awake and keeps his clothes with him, so that he may not go naked and be shamefully exposed.' Then they gathered the kings together to the place that in Hebrew is called Armageddon.

16:15–16 NIV

'They will make war on the Lamb, and the Lamb will conquer them, for he is Lord of lords and King of kings, and those with him are called and chosen and faithful.'

17:14 RSV

Then a mighty angel took up a stone like a great millstone and threw it into the sea, saying 'So shall Babylon the great city be thrown down with violence, and shall be found no more.'

18:21 RSV

And I heard as it were the voice of a great multitude, and as the voice of many waters, and as the voice of mighty thunderings, saying, Alleluia: for the Lord God omnipotent reigneth. Let us be glad and rejoice, and give honour to him: for the marriage of the Lamb is come, and his wife hath made herself ready.

19:6–7 KJV

And I saw heaven opened, and behold a white horse; and he that sat upon him was called Faithful and True, and in righteousness he doth judge and make war.

19:11 KJV

Then I saw an angel coming down from heaven, holding in his hand the key of the abyss and a heavy chain. He seized the dragon, that ancient serpent—that is, the Devil, or Satan—and chained him up for a thousand years. The angel threw him into the abyss, locked it, and sealed it, so that he could not deceive the nations any more until the thousand years were over. After that he must be let loose for a little while. Then I saw thrones, and those who sat on them were given the power to judge. I also saw the souls of those who had been executed because they had proclaimed the truth that Jesus revealed and the word of God. They had not worshipped the beast or its image, nor had they received the mark of the beast on their foreheads or their hands. They came to life and ruled as kings with Christ for a thousand years.

20:1–4 GNB

After the thousand years are over, Satan will be let loose from his prison, and he will go out to deceive the nations scattered over the whole world, that is, Gog and Magog. Satan will bring them all together for battle, as many as the grains of sand on the sea-shore. They spread out over the earth and surrounded the camp of God's people and the city that he loves. But fire came down from heaven and destroyed them. Then the Devil, who deceived them, was thrown into the lake of fire and sulphur, where the beast and the false prophet had already been thrown; and they will be tormented day and night for ever and ever.

20:7–10 GNB

And I saw a great white throne, and him that sat on it, from whose face the earth and the heaven fled away; and there was found no place for them. And I saw the dead, small and great, stand before God; and the books were opened: and another book was opened, which is the book of life: and the dead were judged out of those things which were written in the books, according to their works. And the sea gave up the dead which were in them: and they were judged every man according to their works. And death and hell were cast into the lake of fire. This is the second death. And whosoever was not found written in the book of life was cast into the lake of fire.

20:11–15 KJV

And I saw a new heaven and a new earth: for the first heaven and the first earth were passed away; and there was no more sea. And I John saw the holy city, new Jerusalem, coming down from God out of heaven, prepared as a bride adorned for her husband. And I heard a great voice out of heaven saying, Behold, the tabernacle of God is with men, and he will dwell with them, and they shall be his people, and God himself shall be with them, and be their God. And God shall wipe away all tears from their eyes; and there shall be no more death, neither sorrow, nor crying, neither shall there be any more pain: for the former things are passed away. And he that sat upon the throne said, Behold, I make all things new. And he said unto me, write: for these words are true and faithful.

21:1–5 KJV

Then he showed me the river of the water of life, bright as crystal, flowing from the throne of God and of the Lamb through the middle of the street of the city; also, on either side of the river, the tree of life with its twelve kinds of fruit, yielding its fruit each month; and the leaves of the tree were for the healing of the nations. There shall no more be anything accursed, but the throne of God and of the Lamb shall be in it, and his servants shall worship him; they shall see his face, and his name shall be on their foreheads. And night shall be no more; they need no light of lamp or sun, for the Lord God will be their light, and they shall reign for ever and ever.

22:1–5 RSV

And the Spirit and the bride say, Come. And let him that heareth say, Come. And let him that is athirst come. And whosoever will, let him take of the water of life freely. For I testify unto every man that heareth the words of the prophecy of this book, If any man shall add unto these things, God shall add unto him the plagues that are written in this book: and if any man shall take away from the words of the book of this prophecy, God shall take away his part out of the book of life, and out of the holy city, and from the things which are written in this book. He which testifieth these things said, Surely I come quickly. Amen. Even so, come, Lord Jesus.

22:17–20 KJV

# APPENDIX

## Five portraits of the church

### BODY OF CHRIST

All of you are **Christ's body**, and each one is a part of it.

1 CORINTHIANS 12:27; SEE ALSO ROMANS 12:4–5; 1 CORINTHIANS 12:12–28; EPHESIANS 1:22–23, 4:1–16.

### BRIDE

And I saw the Holy City, the new Jerusalem, coming down out of heaven from God, prepared and ready, like a **bride** dressed to meet her husband.

REVELATION 21:2; SEE ALSO EPHESIANS 5:23–27.

### BUILDING OR TEMPLE

Christ Jesus . . . is the one who holds the whole **building** together and makes it grow into a sacred **temple** dedicated to the Lord.

EPHESIANS 2:21; SEE ALSO 1 CORINTHIANS 3:9–17; 1 PETER 2:4–8.

### FAMILY OR HOUSEHOLD

. . . God's **household**, which is the church of the living God, the pillar and support of the truth.

1 TIMOTHY 3:15; SEE ALSO GALATIANS 6:10; EPHESIANS 2:19.

### PEOPLE OF GOD

You are the chosen race, the King's priests, the holy nation, **God's own people** . . . At one time you were not God's people, but now you are his people . . .

1 PETER 2:9–10

## Christian fellowship: secrets of success

**accept** one another
ROMANS 15:7

**bear** one another's **burdens**
GALATIANS 6:2

be **concerned** for one another
HEBREWS 10:24

**confess your sins** to one another
JAMES 5:16

**encourage** one another
HEBREWS 10:25

**have fellowship** with

one another
1 JOHN 1:7

**honour** one another
ROMANS 12:10

**live in harmony** with one another
ROMANS 15:5

**love** one another
ROMANS 12:10

**offer hospitality** to one another
1 PETER 4:9

**pray for** one another
JAMES 5:16

**serve** one another
GALATIANS 5:13

**stir up** one another to love and good works
HEBREWS 10:24

be **subject to** one another
EPHESIANS 5:21

**teach and admonish** one another
COLOSSIANS 3:16

## Names, titles and descriptions of God

**Creator**
ISAIAH 40:28

**Father**
MALACHI 2:10; MATTHEW 5:45, 6:9; JOHN 14:6, 20:17; ROMANS 8:15

**Father of lights**
JAMES 1:17

**God almighty**
GENESIS 17:1

**God most high**
GENESIS 14:18

**God of all flesh**
JEREMIAH 32:27

**God of heaven**

NEHEMIAH 2:4

**God of hosts**
PSALM 80:7, 14

**God of Israel**
JOSHUA 24:2

**Holy One**
JOB 6:10

## Parables of Jesus

| | MATTHEW | MARK | LUKE |
|---|---|---|---|
| Lamp under a bushel | 5:14–15 | 4:21–22 | 8:16, 11:33 |
| Houses on rock and on sand | 7:24–27 | | 6:47–49 |
| New cloth on an old garment | 9:16 | 2:21 | 5:36 |
| New wine in old wineskins | 9:17 | 2:22 | 5:37–38 |
| Sower and soils | 13:3–8 | 4:3–8 | 8:5–8 |
| Mustard seed | 13:31–32 | 4:30–32 | 13:18–19 |
| Tares | 13:24–30 | | |
| Leaven (yeast) | 13:33 | | 13:20–21 |
| Hidden treasure | 13:44 | | |
| Pearl of great value | 13:45–46 | | |
| Drag-net | 13:47–48 | | |
| Lost sheep | 18:12–13 | | 15:4–6 |
| Two debtors (unforgiving servant) | 18:23–34 | | |
| Workers in the vineyard | 20:1–16 | | |
| Two sons | 21:28–31 | | |
| Wicked tenants | 21:33–41 | 12:1–9 | 20:9–16 |
| Invitation to the wedding feast; man without a wedding-garment | 22:2–14 | | |
| Fig-tree as herald of summer | 24:32–33 | 13:28–29 | 21:29–32 |
| Ten 'bridesmaids' | 25:1–13 | | |
| Talents (Matthew); Pounds (Luke) | 25:14–30 | | 19:12–27 |
| Sheep and goats | 25:31–36 | | |
| Seedtime to harvest | | 4:26–29 | |
| Creditor and the debtors | | | 7:41–43 |
| Good Samaritan | | | 10:30–37 |
| Friend in need | | | 11:5–8 |
| Rich fool | | | 12:16–21 |
| Alert servants | | | 12:35–40 |
| Faithful steward | | | 12:42–48 |
| Fig-tree without figs | | | 13:6–9 |
| Places of honour at the wedding-feast | | | 14:7–14 |
| Great banquet and the reluctant guests | | | 14:16–24 |
| Counting the cost | | | 14:28–33 |
| Lost coin | | | 15:8–10 |
| The prodigal son | | | 15:11–32 |
| Dishonest steward | | | 16:1–8 |
| Rich man and Lazarus | | | 16:19–31 |
| The master and his servant | | | 17:7–10 |
| The persistent widow and the unrighteous judge | | | 18:2–5 |
| The Pharisee and the tax collector | | | 18:10–14 |

# Miracles of Jesus

| | MATTHEW | MARK | LUKE | JOHN |
|---|---|---|---|---|
| **Healing of physical and mental disorders** | | | | |
| Leper | 8:2–3 | 1:40–42 | 5:12–13 | |
| Centurion's servant | 8:5–13 | | 7:1–10 | |
| Peter's mother-in-law | 8:14–15 | 1:30–31 | 4:38–39 | |
| Two Gadarenes | 8:28–34 | 5:1–15 | 8:27–35 | |
| Paralysed man | 9:2–7 | 2:3–12 | 5:18–25 | |
| Woman with a haemorrhage | 9:20–22 | 5:25–29 | 8:43–48 | |
| Two blind men | 9:27–31 | | | |
| Man dumb and possessed | 9:32–33 | | | |
| Man with a withered hand | 12:10–13 | 3:1–5 | 6:6–10 | |
| Man blind, dumb and possessed | 12:22 | | 11:14 | |
| Canaanite woman's daughter | 15:21–28 | 7:24–30 | | |
| Boy with epilepsy | 17:14–18 | 9:17–29 | 9:38–43 | |
| Bartimaeus, and another blind man | 20:29–34 | 10:46–52 | 18:35–43 | |
| Deaf and dumb man | | 7:31–37 | | |
| Man possessed, synagogue | | 1:23–26 | 4:33–35 | |
| Blind man at Bethsaida | | 8:22–26 | | |
| Woman bent double | | | 13:11–13 | |
| Man with dropsy | | | 14:1–4 | |
| Ten lepers | | | 17:11–19 | |
| Malchus' ear | | | 22:50–51 | |
| Official's son at Capernaum | | | | 4:46–54 |
| Sick man, Pool of Bethesda | | | | 5:1–9 |
| Man born blind | | | | 9 |
| **Command over the forces of nature** | | | | |
| Calming of the storm | 8:23–27 | 4:37–41 | 8:22–25 | |
| Walking on the water | 14:25 | 6:48–51 | | 6:19–21 |
| 5,000 people fed | 14:15–21 | 6:35–44 | 9:12–17 | 6:5–13 |
| 4,000 people fed | 15:32–38 | 8:1–9 | | |
| Coin in the fish's mouth | 17:24–27 | | | |
| Fig-tree withered | 21:18–22 | 11:12–14, 20–26 | | |
| Catch of fish | | | 5:1–11 | |
| Water turned into wine | | | | 2:1–11 |
| Another catch of fish | | | | 21:1–11 |
| **Bringing the dead back to life** | | | | |
| Jairus' daughter | 9:18–19, 23–25 | 5:22–24, 38–42 | 8:41–42, 49–56 | |
| Widow's son at Nain | | | 7:11–15 | |
| Lazarus | | | | 11:1–44 |

**Holy One of Israel**
ISAIAH 1:4

**I am**
EXODUS 3:14

**Judge**
GENESIS 18:25

**King**

JEREMIAH 10:7

**King of kings**
1 TIMOTHY 6:15

**Lord (Jehovah)**
EXODUS 6:3; MALACHI 3:6

**Lord of hosts**
JEREMIAH 32:18

**Lord of lords**
1 TIMOTHY 6:15

**Lord will provide (Jehovah jireh)**
GENESIS 22:14

**Saviour**
ISAIAH 43:3

## Titles and portraits of Jesus

**Alpha and Omega**
REVELATION 1:8

**Ancient of Days**
DANIEL 7:22

**Bread of life**
JOHN 6:35

**Christ**
MATTHEW 16:16

**Door**
JOHN 10:9

**Emmanuel**
ISAIAH 7:14; MATTHEW 1:23

**Everlasting Father**
ISAIAH 9:6

**First-born Son**
COLOSSIANS 1:18

**Good Shepherd**
JOHN 10:11

**Holy One of God**
MARK 1:24

**Jesus**
MATTHEW 1:21

**King of kings**
REVELATION 17:14

**Lamb of God**
JOHN 1:29

**Light of the world**
JOHN 8:12

**Lord**
LUKE 1:42–44

**Lord of lords**
REVELATION 17:14

**Messiah**
JOHN 1:41

**Mighty God**
ISAIAH 9:6

**Prince of Peace**
ISAIAH 9:6

**Resurrection and the life**
JOHN 11:25

**Saviour**
TITUS 2:13

**Second Adam**
1 CORINTHIANS 15:45

**Son of God**
MATTHEW 26:63–64

**Son of man**
MATTHEW 8:20

**Vine**
JOHN 15:5

**Way, the truth and the life**
JOHN 14:6

**Wonderful Counsellor**
ISAIAH 9:6

**Word**
JOHN 1:1

# Prayers of the Bible

Abraham's prayer for Sodom
GENESIS 18:22–33

Isaac's blessing
GENESIS 27

Jacob's desperate prayer at Penuel
GENESIS 32

Jacob blesses his sons
GENESIS 48–49

Moses' song of thanksgiving for deliverance from Egypt
EXODUS 15

Moses' plea for Israel when they had worshipped the golden calf
EXODUS 32; DEUTERONOMY 9

Moses asks to see God's glory
EXODUS 33

Aaron's blessing
NUMBERS 6

Moses' song: God and his people
DEUTERONOMY 32

Moses blesses the people of Israel
DEUTERONOMY 33

Deborah's song of thanksgiving for victory
JUDGES 5

Gideon's prayer for signs
JUDGES 6

Hannah's prayer for a son
1 SAMUEL 1

Hannah's thanksgiving
1 SAMUEL 2

Samuel's prayer for the nation
1 SAMUEL 7

David's prayer following God's promise of a lasting succession
2 SAMUEL 7; 1 CHRONICLES 17

David's song of thanksgiving for deliverance
2 SAMUEL 22; PSALM 18

Solomon's prayer for wisdom
1 KINGS 3; 2 CHRONICLES 1

Solomon's prayer at the dedication of the temple
1 KINGS 8; 2 CHRONICLES 6

Elijah's prayer on Mt Carmel
1 KINGS 18

Elijah and the 'still, small voice'
1 KINGS 19

Hezekiah's prayer at the time of Sennacherib's siege
2 KINGS 19, ISAIAH 37

Thanksgiving as the ark is brought to Jerusalem
1 CHRONICLES 16

David's prayer for Solomon
1 CHRONICLES 29

Ezra's confession of the nation's sin
EZRA 9

Nehemiah's prayer for his people
NEHEMIAH 1

The public confession led by Ezra
NEHEMIAH 9

Job seeks the reason for his suffering
JOB 10

Job pleads his case
JOB 13–14

Job's confession
JOB 42

The Psalms include an enormous number of prayers: some are listed here, under themes:

Evening prayer, 4

Morning prayer, 5

The shepherd psalm, 23

Praise and worship, 24; 67; 92; 95–98; 100; 113; 145; 148; 150

Guidance, 25

Trust, 37; 62

Deliverance, 40; 116

Longing for God, 27; 42; 63; 84

Forgiveness, 51; 130

Thanksgiving, 65; 111; 136

Help in trouble, 69; 86; 88; 102; 140; 143

God's constant love and care, 89, 103; 107; 146

God's majesty and glory, 8; 29; 93; 104

God's knowledge and presence, 139

God's word, 19; 119

God's protection, 46; 91; 125

Prayers of Isaiah
ISAIAH 25; 33; 63–64

Hezekiah's prayer in his illness
ISAIAH 38

Jeremiah's prayers
JEREMIAH 11; 14; 20; 32

The king's dream: Daniel's prayer
DANIEL 2

Nebuchadnezzar praises God
DANIEL 4

Daniel's prayer at the end of the exile
DANIEL 9

Jonah's prayer
JONAH 2

Habakkuk questions God
HABAKKUK 1

Habakkuk's prayer
HABAKKUK 3

**PRAYERS OF JESUS:**

The Lord's Prayer
MATTHEW 6:9–13; LUKE 11:2–4

In the Garden of Gethsemane
MATTHEW 26:36–44; MARK 14:32–39; LUKE 22:46

From the cross
MATTHEW 27:46; MARK 15:34; LUKE 23:34, 46

At the raising of Lazarus
JOHN 11:41–42

Facing death
JOHN 12:27–28

For his followers
JOHN 17

Mary's thanksgiving (Magnificat)
LUKE 1:46–55

Zechariah's prayer (Benedictus)
LUKE 1:68–79

Simeon's prayer (Nunc Dimittis)
LUKE 2:29–35

Prayers of the Pharisee and the tax-collector
LUKE 18:10–13

The church's prayer in the face of threats
ACTS 4:24–30

Stephen's prayer at his death
ACTS 7:59–60

**PRAYERS OF PAUL:**

For the Christians at Rome
ROMANS 1:8–10

For Israel,
ROMANS 10:1

For the church at Corinth
1 CORINTHIANS 1:4–9, 2 CORINTHIANS 13:7–9

Thanksgiving for God's comfort in trouble
2 CORINTHIANS 1:3–4

Thanksgiving for spiritual riches in Christ
EPHESIANS 1:3–14

For the Ephesian Christians
EPHESIANS 1:16–23; 3:14–19

For the Philippian Christians
PHILIPPIANS 1:3–11

For the church at Colossae
COLOSSIANS 1:3–14

For the Thessalonian Christians
1 THESSALONIANS 1:2–3; 2:13, 3:9–13; 5:23;
2 THESSALONIANS 1:3; 2:13 , 16–17, 3:16

For Timothy
2 TIMOTHY 1:3–4

For Philemon
PHILEMON 4–6

**DOXOLOGIES—PRAISE TO GOD— AND BENEDICTIONS**
ROMANS 16:25–27; EPHESIANS 3:20–21, PHILIPPIANS 4:20; 1 THESSALONIANS 3:11–13; HEBREWS 13:20–21, 1 PETER 5:10–11; 2 PETER 3:18; JUDE 24–25